A New Agenda in (Critical) Discourse Analysis

Discourse Approaches to Politics, Society and Culture

The series includes contributions that investigate political, social and cultural processes from a linguistic/discourse-analytic point of view. The aim is to publish monographs and edited volumes which combine language-based approaches with disciplines concerned essentially with human interaction — disciplines such as political science, international relations, social psychology, social anthropology, sociology, economics, and gender studies.

The book series complements the *Journal of Language and Politics*, edited by Ruth Wodak and Paul Chilton

General editors

Paul Chilton and Ruth Wodak
University of East Anglia/University of Lancaster

Editorial address: Paul Chilton
School of Language, Linguistics & Translation Studies
University of East Anglia, Norwich NR4 7TJ, UK
P. A.Chilton@uea.ac.uk and r.wodak@lancaster.ac.uk

Advisory board

Volume 13

A New Agenda in (Critical) Discourse Analysis:
Theory, Methodology and Interdisciplinarity
Edited by Ruth Wodak and Paul Chilton

A New Agenda in
(Critical) Discourse Analysis

Theory, Methodology and Interdisciplinarity

Edited by

Ruth Wodak

Lancaster University

Paul Chilton

University of East Anglia

John Benjamins Publishing Company

Amsterdam / Philadelphia

∞ ™ The paper used in this publication meets the minimum requirements
of American National Standard for Information Sciences – Permanence
of Paper for Printed Library Materials, ANSI z39.48-1984.

Learning Resources
Centre

13702580

Library of Congress Cataloging-in-Publication Data

A New Agenda in (Critical) Discourse Analysis : Theory, Methodology and
    Interdisciplinarity / edited by Ruth Wodak and Paul Chilton.
        p.   cm. (Discourse Approaches to Politics, Society and Culture, ISSN
1569-9463 ; v. 13)
        Includes bibliographical references and index.
        1. Social sciences--Methodology. 2. Critical discourse analysis. 3.
    Discourse analysis. I. Wodak, Ruth, 1950- II. Chilton, Paul A. (Paul
    Anthony) III. Series.

    H61.N482 2005
300'.1'4--dc22   2005046008
    ISBN 90 272 2703 9 (Eur.) / 1 58811 637 9 (US) (Hb; alk. paper)

John Benjamins Publishing Co. · P.O. Box 36224 · 1020 ME Amsterdam · The Netherlands
John Benjamins North America · P.O. Box 27519 · Philadelphia PA 19118-0519 · USA

Table of contents

II. Implementing interdisciplinarity

III. Inside and outside traditional disciplines

.

Acknowledgements

I would like to thank the Leverhulme Trust for awarding me a grant for a visiting professorship to UEA, Norwich, from February 2004 to July 2004 which made the work for this book possible. Through generous funding from the *Bank für Arbeit und Wirtschaft*, the City of Vienna, the University of Vienna, the *Kontrollbank, Czernin Publishers* and *Henkel*, it was possible to invite the members of the international advisory board, who had accompanied the research during six years, as well as some other international scholars whose research had become relevant during the project research to the workshop, "New Agenda in CDA", held in Vienna March 2003.

I am also very grateful to Christoph Bärenreuter for his help in editing the manuscripts and the reviewers for their critical and relevant comments on the first drafts of the papers. I would like to thank Paul Chilton specifically for his involvement during the final editing and reviewing of the chapters. I hope that this volume will trigger even more debates which will lead to relevant and innovative research in the Social Sciences.

Preface
Reflecting on CDA

Ruth Wodak

This volume presents interdisciplinary and international contributions to relevant issues debated in the Social Sciences, specifically in the field of Discourse Analysis and Critical Discourse Analysis. It also marks two celebrations: first, the existence of CDA and its forerunner Critical Linguistics for about thirty years, secondly, the end of a six- year research project financed by the Wittgenstein Prize, awarded to the editor of the present volume by the Austrian Science Foundation (FWF).

Critical approaches to the use of language have, of course, long existed in human civilisations. However, in the contemporary global academy, the roots of what is now known as CDA can be said to go back to the Critical Linguistics of the 1970s. It was at this time that linguistics in its late twentieth-century form was taken up by socially and politically aware scholars at the University of East Anglia. Systematic ways of analysing the political and social import of text were proposed and developed (Hodge & Kress 1979/1993; Fowler, Hodge, & Kress 1979; Fowler 1996). In the following years, the critical turn developed and the cross-fertilisation between linguistics and the social sciences was expanded and enriched into a remarkably interdisciplinary and international project. The further development of CDA has been discussed extensively in Anthonissen (2001), Wodak and Meyer (2001), Weiss and Wodak (2003), Reisigl (2004) and Wodak (2004). We refer readers to these publications and to the papers in this volume which present the most recent debates and developments of major approaches, primarily in CDA itself, but also in the wider field of Discourse Analysis on which CDA needs to draw.

In January 1991, a two-day workshop was hosted by Teun van Dijk in Amsterdam. Norman Fairclough, Gunter Kress, Theo van Leeuwen, Teun van Dijk and Ruth Wodak took part. This workshop marked a significant point in the development of CDA, for it was then that a very stimulating and rapidly expanding debate was begun among different scholars, approaches and methodologies (see Wodak & Meyer 2001). Since 1991, the field has expanded widely.

In the present volume the interdisciplinary and multi-methodological character of CDA is visible throughout. Although the choice of topics might seem diverse and disparate at first glance, all the papers are drawn together by several common threads:

– Reflection on the manifold functions, communicative and social practices of communication and the analysis of verbal, written and visual communication;
– Reflection on the impact of CDA in interdisciplinary research;
– Reflection on the future agenda, perspectives and also the limits of the CDA enterprise.

Related to the dimensions sketched out above, Part I of this volume deals with issues, problems and models of interdisciplinary research. The contributions of Theo van Leeuwen, Norman Fairclough, Paul Chilton, Teun van Dijk and Suzie and Ron Scollon present detailed – and indeed critical – discussions of theoretical and methodological attempts at inter/trans/multidisciplinarity. These considerations are illustrated with examples from own research. The possible limitations of CDA are explicitly mentioned and debated.

Part II is dedicated to on-going research in CDA on socially relevant topics such as the European Convention, the construction of European identities and therapeutic discourse (Ruth Wodak, Gilbert Weiss, Florian Oberhuber, Christoph Bärenreuter, Michał Krzyżanowski and Peter Muntigl). These papers present detailed text analyses while applying different grammatical, pragmatic and discourse-analytical means to written and spoken texts.

In Part III, the volume concludes with three papers, two from sociologists (Tom Burns and András Kovács) and one from an anthropologist (Irene Bellier) which all manifest the integration of specific notions and approaches of Discourse Analysis into their disciplinary research and discuss the usefulness and fruitfulness of the 'linguistic and cultural turns' for their traditional paradigms.

References

Anthonissen, C. (2001). "On the Effectivity of Media Censorship: An Analysis of Linguistic, Paralinguistic and other Communicative Devices used to Defy Media Restrictions." Unpublished PhD thesis. University of Vienna.

Fowler, R. (1996). *Linguistic Criticism*. Oxford: Oxford University Press.

Fowler, R., Hodge, G., & Kress, G. (1979). *Language and Control*. Routledge and Kegan Paul.

Hodge, R. & Kress, G. (1993 [1979]). *Language as Ideology*. London: Routledge.

Reisigl, M. (2004). "Diskurs ≠ Diskurs ≠ Diskurs. Ein kritische Bestandsaufnahme". *European Journal for Semiotic Studies* (S-EJSS), *16*(2–3).

Weiss, R. & Wodak, R. (Eds.). (2003). *CDA. Theory and Interdisciplinarity*. London: MacMillan.

Wodak, R. & Meyer, M. (Eds.). (2001). *Methods of Critical Discourse Analysis*. London: Sage.

Wodak, R. (2004). "Critical discourse analysis." In C. Seale, G. Gobo, J. F. Gubrium, & D. Silverman (Eds.), *Qualitative Research Practice* (pp. 197–213). London: Sage.

PART I

Interdisciplinarity and (C)DA

Chapter 1

Three models of interdisciplinarity

Theo van Leeuwen
Cardiff University

In this paper I will sketch three models of interdisciplinarity, the "centralist", "pluralist" and "integrationist" models. They are not presented as a kind of menu of choice from which researchers can choose according to their needs, but as approaches that have historically evolved in the order in which I will discuss them and are now co-present, also in my own practice. I see the third and most recent, "integrationist" model as the way forward for interdisciplinary research, although I will also acknowledge some of its pitfalls.

In discussing the models, I will mostly draw on examples from my own practice, in part because I am not particularly interested in criticising the more "mono-disciplinary" research paradigms that have formed me, and in part because the ideas I will present have primarily emerged from reflection on my own practice in various collaborative research projects. If occasionally I do criticise aspects of the paradigms in which my work continues to be located (specifically, systemic functional linguistics, social semiotics and critical discourse analysis), this is intended as a formulation both of the specific contributions they have to offer in new interdisciplinary contexts, and of the specific interdisciplinary connections they need to fulfil their own promises.

The centralist model

A centralist model of interdisciplinarity is essentially a model of the relation between different autonomous disciplines. Though situating itself among other disciplines, each discipline sees itself as the centre of the universe of knowledge, and, from this centre, charts its relations to other disciplines. The core of each discipline is formed by its theories, methods and central subject matters. Relations to other disciplines primarily concern overlapping subject matter, and, sometimes, for instance in the case of relations between humanities and "hard" sciences, methods that might strengthen the claim to scientific rigour of a particular humanities discipline (e.g. the psychology of perception or neurology, in the case of linguistics).

One realisation of the model are the "maps" of the fields of knowledge, in which disciplines cast themselves in the central role, and define other disciplines in terms of their distance from this centre. The map in Figure 1 is an example. Here the core concerns of 20th century linguistics (phonetics and phonology, grammar and lexis and semantics) are central. A boundary is drawn around the field which acknowledges parts of other disciplines as associated with the discipline – the psychology of (speech) perception, "geography" and "socialization" insofar as it impinges on the question of regional and social dialects, history insofar as it impinges on linguistic change and the history of language and language families and, more marginally still, "language as art". A second boundary is drawn to include two further territories co-occupied with other disciplines, language typology, as related to culture, and language universals as related to human biology. All other fields of knowledge fall outside these boundaries. The map therefore bears some resemblance to those medieval maps of cities in which the city itself is drawn large and in the centre, while the representation of the surrounding countryside diminishes in scale and detail as distance from the city increases. Other disciplines, too, have drawn such maps, whether discursively or in the form of an actual "map".

Policies and practices of editing collections of papers can be another realisation of the model. The further a paper is removed from the discipline's "core" of theories, methods and subject matters, the more it is defined as relatively marginal (e.g. as "application", "extension" etc.), and the further down in the book it will be placed. A collection of critical discourse analysis papers on racism, for instance, placed contributions on "visual racism" in the final section of the volume (Reisigl & Wodak 2000), following sections dealing with linguistically realised racist discourses.

Another realisation of the model is the use of other disciplines in the introductions of papers, to provide "context", or, perhaps, to display erudition. I have often enough done it myself. In a critical discourse analysis of the UK Chancellor's Budget Speech and its reporting in the press (Van Leeuwen 1999) I began with a historical introduction. It was based on reading four books on the history of welfare and welfare policies. Not being a historian, and relying only on secondary sources, my account would probably not have passed the review process of a history journal or collection. But I knew that my review-

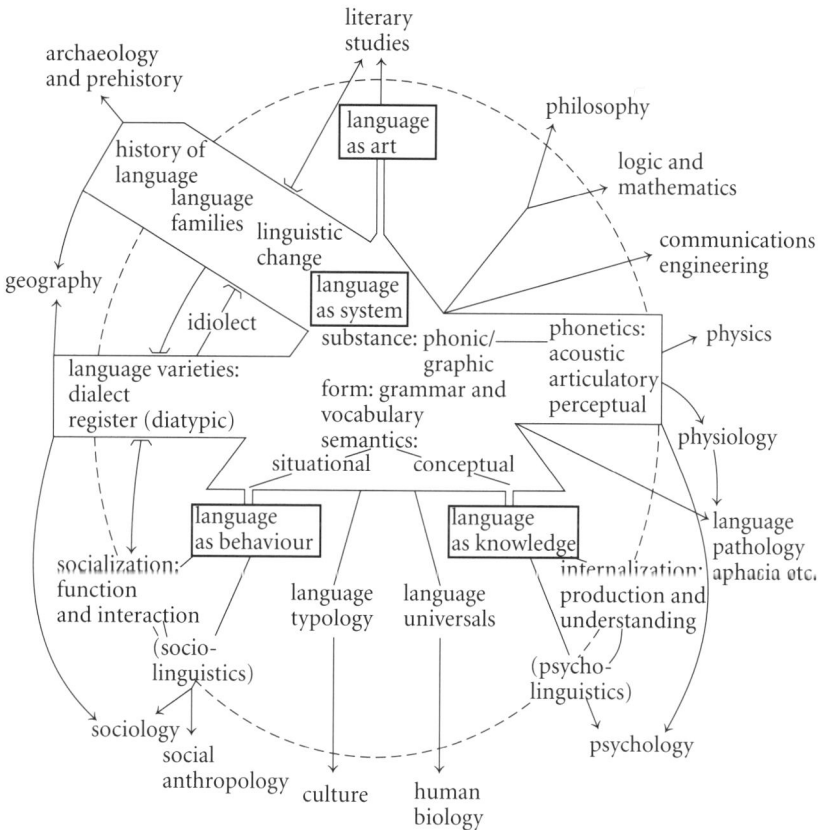

Figure 1. Centralist model of interdisciplinarity (M. A. K. Halliday 1978:11)

ers would judge me on the basis of the fairly detailed and systematic discourse analysis that followed, not on my skills as a historian. In the "integrationist" approach I will discuss below, I would have collaborated with a historian on one and the same paper, as has been done for instance, by Heer et al. (2003), and the resulting paper might have satisfied both linguists and historians.

"Centralist" disciplines have developed powerful methodologies, and this is both their strength and their weakness – their strength because of the disciplined thinking it encourages, and their weakness because important issues are neglected when they cannot be handled by the discipline's methodologies. This is the case, for instance, with the notion of "cultural context" in systemic-functional linguistics. On the one hand this notion, originally drawn from Malinowski, hence from the discipline of anthropology, is used as a key explanatory concept. It is seen as the source of the specific situation types which explain language use and drive language change. On the other hand, while systemic-functional linguistics has developed highly sophisticated methods for analysing language patterns, no such methods have been developed, or adopted, for analysing "context of culture". It either remains undeveloped or is reduced to what *can* be studied with the methodology of systemic-functional linguistics, namely the "semantic system of language" (Halliday 1978:109). And while Halliday has defined "context of culture" as "the ideological and material culture" (ibid.:65), and equated it with "the social system" (ibid.:147), few systemic-functional linguists have attempted to make connections with the extensive literature on "culture" and "ideology". Thus it is on the one hand acknowledged that language is not autonomous, but embedded in society and culture, yet this insight remains peripheral, because it is not fully integrated in the methodologies which form the core of the discipline and the professional expertise of its adherents. A similar argument could be made with respect to its counterpart, the concept of "context of situation".

The pluralist model

While specialist theoretical frameworks and methodologies are at the heart of the epistemological identities and values of centralist models, in pluralist models issues and problems are central, and it is recognised that these may rightfully belong to a number of different disciplines. The pluralist model seeks to bring such disciplines together, as equal partners, rather than that elements of other disciplines are incorporated in a "centralist" discipline. Yet the disciplines themselves remain autonomous and self-sufficient in the way they operate, and their identities and values are not fundamentally affected. Novotny (1997) has called this kind of model "pluridisciplinary" – an approach to research based on cooperation between disciplines treating the same subject from different perspectives.

Frequently the notion of "triangulation" is invoked in this context. Originally a geometrical term for the subdivision of polygons into triangles, it has been adopted in the social sciences for research in which more than one method is used, in principle for purposes of double- (or triple-) checking results. But this latter aspect is often left out and the term is then more vaguely defined, as a "triple viewpoint" or "triangulation of perspectives" (Scollon 2003:172) or as the "more or less systematic inclusion" of a number of different disciplines "in the analysis of a specific discursive occasion" (Weiss &

Wodak 2003:22). Just how these perspectives merge, or what each discipline contributes to the more "holistic" approach is then not necessarily spelled out.

A typical realisation of this model is the research project, or conference, or edited volume, which brings together the perspectives of different disciplines on a given research problem – as "free-standing" contributions in a kind of intellectual "federation". Such projects are therefore interdisciplinary as a whole, but without affecting the modus operandi of the members of the contributing disciplines, or their status and identity as autonomous research professionals.

Much of my own work has taken this approach. One example is the journal *Visual Communication*, which, with three colleagues, I started in 2002. At present, visual communication is not a discipline in its own right. It occupies small, sometimes marginalised, corners of a number of other disciplines – language and communication, anthropology, sociology, cultural and media studies, computing science, to name some of them. The journal publishes papers from all these areas – "text-analytical" approaches based in linguistics and semiotics, quantitative approaches based in the social sciences, studies on classification systems used for searches of visual data, papers from cultural studies scholars, and papers by practitioners of some form of visual communication. So far there is relatively little evidence of these approaches mutually influencing each other or actively collaborating with each other. Nevertheless, they are at least brought together in one place. And our editorial policies and practices do at least attempt to achieve a degree of mutual intelligibility between the disciplines involved. A step forward, we hope, in an area where many journals are still associated with traditional "mono-disciplinary" scientific associations.

There is no doubt that the pluralist model has been gaining influence. The topics of the research programmes and the "thematic priorities" proposed by research councils and other major sponsors of research, for instance, tend to foreground social problems rather than traditional methods and theories, and therefore stimulate pluralist, or even integrationist research. Many universities, similarly, try to break down the institutional barriers between different disciplines by fostering interdisciplinary research centres. Nevertheless, to which degree the pluralist model is able to produce more than the sum of its parts is far from clear.

The integrationist model

Like the pluralist model, the integrationist model focuses on problems rather than methods and brings together researchers from different disciplines. But here it is recognised that no single discipline can satisfactorily address any given problem on its own. As a result disciplines are seen as interdependent, and research projects involve team work with specific divisions of labour and specific integrative principles. This involves a major shift in the way disciplines function, and can at times be seen as threatening the status quo (cf. Weiss & Wodak 2003: 18–19). Disciplines can no longer function as traditional professions, with the autonomy to define what will count as a research problem and how it will be addressed, with their own professional associations and boundary maintenance mechanisms (e.g. through specialist terminologies), and with distinct epistemological perspectives and professional identities. The idea of "discipline" is in effect narrowed down to "skill" – to the analytical and interpretative skills that can contribute in specific ways to integrated projects. In such a context I no longer say, for instance, "I am a linguist", setting myself apart from other researchers, but, "I know how to do certain types of linguistic research and can therefore make a specific and useful contribution to interdisciplinary research projects".

When editing a collection of papers on different approaches to visual analysis (Van Leeuwen & Jewitt 2000), we commissioned an article from two cultural studies scholars, Martin Lister and Liz Wells. In contrast to contributors from fields such as social psychology, anthropology and psychoanalysis, they confessed to a problem with the brief we had given, which assumed that all contributors would outline and exemplify a specific method of visual analysis. They felt that cultural studies is not defined by a method of analysis, but by a particular set of questions, each of which might require different methods. They saw cultural studies as "a compound field rather than a discrete discipline which appropriates and re-purposes elements of theoretical frameworks and methodologies from other disciplines, wherever they seem productive in pursuing its own enquiries" (Lister & Wells 2000: 63).

Most cultural studies scholars work alone, or with other cultural studies scholars, rather than in interdisciplinary research projects, maybe because the field is so interdisciplinary already. From the point of view of "monodisciplinary" researchers, their use of a wide range of sources and methods may result in a more comprehensive view of the phenomena investigated, but can also lead to a lack of depth and methodological rigour, a risk of amateurism and eclecticism (cf. Weiss & Wodak 2003: 19–20). One person cannot do everything well. Nevertheless, Lister and Wells' formulation suggests an important integrative principle for the design of integrationist research projects: the set of questions that defines a comprehensive investigation of a given problem requires a diverse set of methodologies, based in a diversity of disciplines. In the next section I will return to this point by looking at the contributions discourse analysis might make to integrationist projects, and at the particular ways in which it might dovetail with other disciplines, more specifically social theory, ethnography and history.

Another aspect of the practice of cultural studies suggests a second integrative principle for integrationist research projects, and that is its emphasis on theory. There is, in the humanities and social sciences, an increasing tendency for the same theoretical canon to be drawn upon in a range of different disciplines. Even disciplines which do not usually draw explicitly on these theorists can be shown to have undergone their influence in the themes they address and the theoretical assumptions that underpin their methods of work. This is sometimes seen negatively, as a "turn to theory" at the expense of empirical research. But it also opens up the possibility of a common frame of reference for researchers from different disciplines, of what Novotny (1997) has called "transdisciplinarity" and what Weiss and Wodak (2003:20) also refer to as the "integrative" model. Cicourel (1964) has stressed the importance of linking empirical work ("methods and measurements") to social theory, both in the interests of the self-reflexivity that is vital for researchers of social action and its products, and because theory inevitably plays a role in the interpretation of empirical data, whether explicitly or implicitly. I will return to this point in the next section.

An often mentioned problem in interdisciplinary work is the difficulties researchers from different disciplines experience in learning to talk to each other. In part this stems from differences in theoretical assumptions, in part from mutually unintelligible specialist conceptual frameworks and terminologies. To overcome the former it is vital that researchers in integrationist projects take time out for workshop discussions of relevant theoretical issues. To overcome the former, new, interdisciplinary conceptual frameworks and terminologies have to be developed. In my work on multimodality (e.g. Kress & Van Leeuwen 2001), this problem was evident from the start. The disciplines that study the different communicative modes which combine in multimodal texts and events tend to isolate individual modes, and to conceptualise them in terms specific only to that specific mode and incompatible with others. Thus we have linguistics for language, art theory and history for images, musicology for music, and so on, each with its own set of assumptions, its own methods and its own specialist terminologies. Yet it is possible to conceive of a common vocabulary, so long as it centres on the common types of communicative work that are distributed differentially across the different modes and differentially realised in each. The art theorist Shapiro, for instance, has distinguished between "themes of state" and "themes of action" (1972:17–36), while linguists distinguish between stative and dynamic clauses. There is common ground here. Clearly semantic distinctions of this kind belong to the culture as a whole, rather than to specific modes such as language or visual communication. Both these modes have resources for representing a given phenomenon either as a "state of affairs", or as an action, an event or a process. A common terminology is therefore possible at this level. But the common semantic distinction is expressed quite differently in the two modes – in the case of visual communication by different types and configurations of volumes and/or vectors, in the case of language by different types and configurations of nominal and verbal groups. In this respect the different terminologies of the various disciplines can continue to play a role.

The table below recapitulates the main points of the discussion so far:

	Orientation	Dependency	Hierarchy
Centralist model	method-oriented	autonomous disciplines	disciplines not equally valued
Pluralist model	problem-oriented	autonomous disciplines	disciplines equally valued
Integrationist model	problem-oriented	interdependent disciplines	disciplines equally valued

Integrating discourse analysis with other disciplines

In this section I will discuss some of the ways in which discourse analysis can be integrated with other disciplines, more specifically social theory, history and ethnography. Such integration is already practised by many discourse analysts. What I am trying to do here is merely to make explicit what discourse analysis can and cannot do, and at which point it is therefore necessary for other methods to take over.

Discourse analysis and social theory

There are two reasons for integrating discourse analysis and social theory. The first I have already mentioned. Theory can play an integrative role in integrationist research projects.

In a current research programme at Cardiff University, we research a range of issues in the area of language and global communication, using a variety of empirical methodologies. We study the policies and practices of a number of global agencies that affect contemporary language and communication – global media, NGO's and IGO's, tourism, and global grassroots networks. Our methods include sociolinguistic analysis, quantitative surveys, multimodal discourse analysis, ethnographic research, and corpus linguistics.

Theories of globalisation provide a number of broad "positions" relevant to the issues we are investigating. Some see globalisation as a form of economic and cultural imperialism (e.g. Schiller 1971 with respect to global media, Phillipson 1992 with respect to World English). Others argue that globalising tendencies are counteracted by localising tendencies, as global discourses and cultural products are locally taken up and inflected in different ways. Again others take up an intermediate position, arguing for "glocalisation" (Featherstone & Lash 1995). All these theories adopt definite, and to some extent mutually exclusive, "positions". Rather than committing ourselves to one of them as a point of departure, and so, in a sense, biasing the outcome before our research has even started, we see them as providing, together, a set of relevant issues and questions that can give direction and coherence to our research, and that are broad enough to apply to all the fields we are investigating. In ongoing workshops we can then attempt to relate these positions to the picture emerging from our own empirical work, and eventually we may adopt – or modify – one of them, or some combination of them. Provided such theoretical discussion takes place, and provided experienced theorists are involved, this need not lead to the kind of eclecticism Weiss and Wodak have warned against (2003: 20).

A second reason for integrating discourse analysis and social theory is closely related. Contemporary social theorists carry less methodological baggage than researchers who work with intricate and time-consuming empirical methodologies. As a result they tend to "get there" earlier, to discover important new social, political and cultural phenomena ahead of researchers who work within more circumscribed disciplines. As often as not, they will then plant a flag and move on to new territories, leaving the newly discovered territory to be cultivated by more empirically oriented latecomers. The point is, many contemporary social theorists *do* have a special antenna for new social, political and cultural developments, and can alert empirical researchers to issues that are worth exploring in greater depth. Issues such as globalisation and risk have been written about by theorists for many years. Only now are they beginning to spawn large programmes of empirical research. If theorists and empirical researchers worked more closely together, as has happened, for instance in the research groups of Bourdieu and Bernstein, the time lag might be shortened.

Discourse analysis and history

In researching the role of legitimation in discourse (Van Leeuwen & Wodak 1999), we discovered how often legitimation is achieved through the use of expressions with an evaluative dimension, be it a positive, or, in the case of delegitimation, a negative one. Such expressions at once describe the actions that require legitimation *and* legitimate them – through distilling qualities of these actions that can be linked to discourses of value. Studying how Viennese magistrates legitimate their refusal of the applications of immigrant workers who seek to be reunited with their families, we noted, for instance, their use of expressions like *objektive Gesamtbetrachtung* ("objective overview"), *ermessen* ("measure") and *Abwägung* ("balancing") to refer to their own decision making procedures. These expression both refer to the process of decision making and distil from it the qualities that can be seen as legitimating that process – its objectivity, its precision, its impartiality.

However, it has proved impossible to find an explicit, linguistically motivated method for identifying such expressions. As discourse analysts, we can only recognise them on the basis of our common-sense cultural knowledge. The usefulness of linguistic discourse analysis stops at this point, and historical discourse research has to take over. Only the social and cultural historian can *explain* the moral status of these expressions, by tracing them back to the moral discourses that underlie them, thus undoing the "genesis amnesia" (Bourdieu) that allows us to treat such "moral evaluations" as commonsense values that need not to be made explicit – in this case the discourses that have founded the autonomous legal system, according to which formally laid down procedures, based on objective, scientific thinking, can make legal judgement impersonal, rational and predictable.

To give another example, discourse analytical methods allow us to describe in detail how speech and writing are used in the media – to identify, for instance, tendencies such as "marketisation" and "conversationalisation" (Fairclough 1992). But discourse analytical methods cannot tell us how and why they came about. At this point the social and cultural historian has to take over. David Cardiff (1981), for instance, has studied "conversationalisation" historically, by investigating the memorandums which the Head of the BBC Talks Department sent to radio speakers in the early days of radio. These memos explicitly encouraged speakers to "tone down", and to introduce deliberate hesitations and errors (initially all scripted!) to achieve a form of public speech suitable for reception in the living room, and a genre which would retain the logical structure and advance planning of formal public speech, yet also include elements of informal, private conversation. Similar experimentation happened elsewhere, for instance in Franklin Roosevelt's broadcast "fireside chats" and in Nazi Germany, where Goebbels encouraged German radio speakers to use informal, colloquial speech and local dialects so as to "sound like the listener's best friend" (Leitner 1980).

Discourse analysis and ethnography

The texts which discourse analysts analyse form part of social practices – but only part. They realise all or some of the *actions* that constitute the social practices – but they tell us nothing about the agents and patients of the actions, or about their place and time. The may, for instance, allow us to study how journalists report specific kinds of political events, but not the processes of selection and editing that precede such reporting, the division of labour involves in these processes, the rationales their participants may provide, nor the reactions of the public to both the reports themselves and the way in which the media represent events of this kind generally. To discuss these, we have to research the production and reception of the texts ethnographically.

In recent work on the magazine *Cosmopolitan* and its 48 different "localised" versions (Machin & Van Leeuwen 2003, 2004), for instance, we established that the *formats* of the articles are remarkably similar the world over, while the content may differ locally. For instance, many articles use a "hot tips" format which identifies a particular problem and then provides a number of tips for overcoming this problem, from which the reader can choose and pick. Similar problems were presented in all versions of the magazine, but the solutions differed. One recurrent problem, for instance, was people who try to make friends too quickly or eagerly, whether at work or in personal life. In Northern European versions of the magazine, the preferred solution was "communication", "talking it over", and it was represented as almost always leading to positive outcomes. In Asian versions of the magazine, on the other hand, the preferred solution was to radically cut such people off. The point is, such differences can be observed from discourse analysis. And they are interesting in themselves. But discourse analysis cannot explain them, at least not by means of discourse analytical methods. For this we need interviews with the producers of the magazine, both globally and locally, access to style manuals, and so on.

Conversely, ethnographic research also needs discourse analysis. Too often production and reception practices are studied without any form of detailed reference to what it is that is being produced and received. An epistemological division is then installed that reminds of the old theological division between those who hold that the scriptures (the text) reveal the truth and those who hold that the truth is revealed by divine inspiration and resides in the heart of the believer (the receiver). Discourse analysis can provide more precise and specific questions for production and reception research than ethnographic methods can on their own. The two need to work together, and the right order, at least from the point of view of a discourse analyst, is "discourse analysis first, ethnographic analysis second" – discourse analysis to identify the issues, ethnography to explain them and show how they are taken up in society.

One study in which we used this order was a study of baby toys (Van Leeuwen & Caldas-Coulthard 2004). An analysis of baby pram rattles revealed a difference between traditional pram rattles and more recent "postmodern" pram rattles. Traditional pram rattles are made of hard, shiny plastic, use motifs from traditional children's books (e.g. Peter Rabbit-like rabbits with pink and blue jackets), and produce movement, light fluctuations and sound when kicked by babies. Newer pram rattles are made of soft materials, use motifs from the mass media (e.g. Star Wars-like alien monsters) and kicking them does not produce much result as they are soft, velchro-ed together (so that they come apart easily), and produce sounds by squeezing and rubbing (a different sound for each character), something which babies themselves cannot yet do.

The question was, how would these toys, with their different potential for meaning and action, be taken up? Again, this is not a question that can be answered by a semiotic analysis of the artefacts themselves. Another method is needed, and in this case it was a combination of observation and interview research. We filmed 10 mothers using the same 2 pram rattles (the "rabbit" pram rattle, and the postmodern "funny aliens" pram rattle) with their young babies. To make a long story short, they use the traditional pram rattle exactly as it was intended, trying to get their babies to kick it, and providing enthusiastic feedback if the baby responded by moving its limbs and, probably more accidentally than intentionally, kicking the rattle that was placed strategically for that purpose. Initially they tried to use the "funny aliens" rattle the same way, but they soon gave up, and used the individual "aliens" as "characters" in improvised puppet play, or as soft toys. The two toys were thus used, in this case, in distinct ways that clearly related to their design.

The elements of integrated research projects

I will conclude by sketching the elements of an "integrationist" research project. Needless to say, there is more than one way of designing such a project.

The point is to indicate that, in an integrationist model, the component disciplines of an interdisciplinary project can play specific, complementary roles in a larger whole.

Ongoing development of theories and methods

In the project on children's toys mentioned above, we also researched Playmobil (Van Leeuwen 2002). We were interested in Playmobil because it constitutes a microcosm of the social world, with its own inclusions and exclusions, a kind of toy "language" for symbolically representing the social world in the modality of play. It has a specific vocabulary of social actors, through its collection of "characters", and of social actions, through the accessories provided. And it has its own rules of combination, through the design of the toys, which may, for example, make it physically impossible to use specific characters as the riders of a particular motorcycle or the drivers of a particular train, and through the way the toys are marketed, in which only certain characters may be packaged together with a car, or with a particular tool.

The first phase of the project required an interaction between social theory, linguistics/semiotics, social and cultural history and ethnography. Social theory was needed, for instance, to focus the project on the broader issue of the classification of social actors in society, an issue which we saw as part of the relevance of the project. Recently the way in which people are classified has moved away from traditional demographics to "lifestyle" classifications, based on consumption patterns and value systems. Issues of this kind we felt, might be reflected in the types of characters and accessories made available by Playmobil.

Linguistics and semiotics provided methods for the systematic inventory of the elements that make up the Playmobil "system", and for the analysis of their possible combinations. This led to an adaptation of a method of analysis originally developed for linguistics texts, "social actor analysis" (Van Leeuwen 1996), and so also contributed to the ongoing development of methodologies for multimodal discourse analysis.

Out of this analysis then arose questions that could not be explained by discourse analysis alone. Why, for instance, is there an increasing mixture of fictional and historical Playmobil characters, when, traditionally, the system focussed on characters and activities which most children could have observed also in their everyday life – the home, the school the doctor's surgery, the petrol station, and so on? The answer to such questions must lie in the "context of culture" that has given birth to toy systems of this kind, hence in broad social and cultural developments that are less accessible to the microscopic lens which forms the main strength of discourse analysis. But we might also be interested in the answers which the producers of Playmobil give to these questions, and that requires ethnographic production research.

Analysis of discursive practices in specific social settings

In the second phase of the project we looked at the way Playmobil is taken up in specific contexts. This involved both linguistic/semiotic analysis and ethnographic interview research.

One playschool, for instance, had a range of Playmobil toys, but only provided selective access to it. During specific one-hour periods children were placed, in groups of five, at "activity tables", one of which was devoted to Playmobil. But only one kind of Playmobil was provided, for instance only the fire brigade set or only the pirates. This aspect is open to semiotic analysis. We can analyse the set of Playmobil toys acquired by the school, and the multimodal texts formed by our video recordings of the children's play activities. But why this school's use of Playmobil is regimented in this particular way, how much of it, for instance, is based on the broader pedagogic principles the teachers have been trained in (and where these come from) and how much on their own predilections (and how they justify these) can only be ascertained by ethnographic interview research, and background research in the discourses that play a role in the formation of Playschool staff.

Creation of new resources and new uses of existing resources

Finally, integrated research can involve relevant practitioners. It is true that in many fields practitioners have not much need for analytical research of their own practices, as they are secure in their traditional ways of doing things. But where innovation is needed, and where traditional practices are in crisis, researchers can make positive contributions, and open up options that may not have been evident to practitioners.

If the relation is equal, and the practitioners are not used as "subjects" of research, but as partners, and the researchers not as hired hands doing the bidding of their paymasters, but as consultants whose critiques and suggestions it might be prudent to listen to, collaborations between academic researchers and practitioners would give practitioners a chance to benefit from the critical and imaginative stance independent academic researchers can still afford, and academic researchers a chance to make a difference to the world "out there".

References

Cardiff, D. (1981). "The Serious and the Popular: Aspects of the Evolution of Style in the Radio Talk 1928–1939". *Media Culture and Society, 2*, 31.

Cicourel, A. (1964). *Method and Measurement in Sociology.* New York: The Free Press.

Fairclough, N. (1992). *Discourse and Social Change.* Cambridge: Polity.

Featherstone, M. & Lash, S. (1995). "Globalisation, modernity and the spatialisation of social theory". In M. Featherstone, S. Lash, & R. Robertson (Eds.), *Global Modernities* (pp. 1–24). London: Sage.

Halliday, M. A. K. (1978). *Language as Social Semiotic.* London: Arnold.

Heer, H., Manoschek, W., Pollak, A., & Wodak, R. (2003). *Wie Geschichte gemacht wird.* Vienna: Czernin Verlag.

Kress, G. & Van Leeuwen, T. (2001). *Multimodal Discourse – The Modes and Media of Contemporary Communication.* London: Arnold.

Leitner, G. (1980). "BBC English and *Deutsche Rundfunksprache*: A Comparative and Historical Analysis of the Language of the Radio". *International Journal of the Sociology of Language, 26*(1), 75–100.

Lister, M. & Wells, L. (2001). "Seeing beyond belief: Cultural Studies as an approach to analysing the visual". In Van T. Van Leeuwen & C. Jewitt (Eds.), *Handbook of Visual Analysis* (pp. 61–92). London: Sage.

Machin, D. & Van Leeuwen, T. (2003). "Global Schemas and Local Discourses in *Cosmopolitan*". *Journal of Sociolinguistics, 7*(4), 493–512.

Machin, D. & Van Leeuwen, T. (2004). "Global Media: Generic Homogenity and Discursive Diversity". *Continuum, 18*(1), 99–120.

Novotny, H. (1997). "Transdisziplinäre Wissensproduktion – eine Antwort auf die Wissensexplosion?". In Friedrich Stadler (Ed.), *Wissenschaft als Kultur. Österreichs Beitrag zur Moderne* (pp. 188–204). Vienna and New York: Springer.

Phillipson, R. (1992). *Linguistic Imperialism.* Oxford: Oxford University Press.

Reisigl, M. & Wodak, R. (2000). *The Semiotics of Racism – Approaches in Critical Discourse Analysis.* Vienna: Passagen Verlag.

Schiller, H. (1971). *Mass Communication and the American Empire.* Boston: Beacon Press.

Scollon, S. (2003). "Political and Somatic Alignment: Habitus, Ideology and Social Practice". In G. Weiss & R. Wodak (Eds.), *Critical Discourse Analysis – Theory and Interdisciplinarity* (pp. 167–199). London: Palgrave.

Shapiro, M. (1972). *Words and Pictures.* The Hague: Mouton.

Van Leeuwen, T. (1996). "The representation of social actors". In C. R. Caldas-Coulthard & M. Coulthard (Eds.), *Texts and Practices – Readings in Critical Discourse Analysis* (pp. 32–71). London: Routledge.

Van Leeuwen, T. (1999). "Discourses of Unemployment in New Labour Britain". In R. Wodak & C. Ludwig (Eds.), *Challenges in a Changing World – Issues in Critical Discourse Analysis* (pp. 87–101). Vienna: Passagen Verlag.

Van Leeuwen, T. (2002). "The World According to Playmobil". Unpubl. ms.

Van Leeuwen, T. & Caldas-Coulthard, C. R. (2004). "The Semiotics of Kinetic Design". In D. Banks (Ed.), *Text and Texture.* Paris: Harmattan.

Van Leeuwen, T. & Jewitt, C. (2001). *Handbook of Visual Analysis.* London: Sage.

Van Leeuwen, T. & Wodak, R. (1999). "Legitimizing Immigration Control: A Discourse-Historical Analysis". *Discourse Studies, 1*(1), 83–119.

Weiss, G. & Wodak, R. (Eds.). (2003). *Critical Discourse Analysis – Theory and Interdisciplinarity.* London: Palgrave.

CHAPTER 2

Missing links in mainstream CDA

Modules, blends and the critical instinct

Paul Chilton

University of East Anglia

1. The critical stance

Let us first attempt a crude map of the terrain. Critical approaches to text and talk in European scholarship over the past twenty years or so have indeed been interdisciplinary, but this observation has little significance unless one specifies the sources and tributaries. This introductory section is an admittedly partial attempt to sketch the landscape.[1]

'Critical Theory', associated with the Frankfurt School and especially with Jürgen Habermas provides one source in social theory. This source found itself channelled into a sociological variety which did not claim any technical connection with language studies or linguistics (notably, Stuart Hall, Birmingham Contemporary Studies). It was also drawn upon by scholars whose orientation was towards language use, though these scholars were somewhat eclectic in the social theory that they made use of (Fowler et al. 1979; Fairclough 1989; Wodak 1996; Wodak & Meyer 2001). A guiding theme was the notion that language can be used for self-interested ends by power groups.

A further source was the work of Michel Foucault, whose claims were not always viewed as consonant with those of the Habermasian tendency. Foucault's work has given rise to at least two tendencies. One tendency has its context in sociology, political science and to some extent in literary studies, and like Foucault himself, does not analyse language. This tendency has given rise to many studies, too numerous to list here (but cf. for example Shapiro 1984 for examples). Amongst writers in this vein it is common to find the assumption, or claim, that 'discourse' includes the non-linguistic as well as the linguistic. At this point an additional influence needs to be mentioned, namely the post-modernist current that was a confluence of ideas from philosophy, literary studies and sociology (Barthes, Derrida, and others). This kind of work had no contact with formal linguistics but made assertions about the nature of meaning ('free floating signifiers'), epistemology and ontology, attacking alleged essentialism, promoting notions such as 'aporia'. This form of relativism provided for the possibility of indefinitely extended critique that runs the risk of being ethically and politically indiscriminate. It is not possible here to address it directly and will not be referred to again in this chapter.

To return to Foucault, the second Foucauldian influence is to be found among those whose declared preoccupation is, by contrast, with language as such (notably Fairclough 1989, 1992, 1995, 2003; to some extent Wodak 1996). Many of these authors would, however, accept that discourse, understood as language-use, is but one (if perhaps the most salient) manifestation of social action. The insistence that language is a form of social-action is probably the most important tenet amongst this group (see Fairclough & Wodak 1997: 278–279 for a formulation). Those working in this tradition have often had some degree of formation in linguistics and have to a greater or lesser extent proceeded on the assumption that the nature of social action can be elucidated, even unmasked, by various kinds of linguistic analysis.

One can distinguish here several sub-tendencies among the linguistically oriented. Historically the first was Critical Linguistics ('the East Anglia school'), whose early work, drew on George Orwell for inspiration, Bakhtin and to a lesser extent Habermas and to an even lesser extent Foucault for its social theory. For its linguistic theory it drew at first on Chomsky's early versions of transformational grammar (Hodge & Kress 1993 [1979]). This choice was later replaced by Halliday's so-called systemic-functional grammar (Fairclough 1989: 13–14; Fowler 1996: 11).

The second language-oriented trend, chronologically speaking, is Critical Discourse Analysis, most commonly associated with Fairclough, Wodak and van Dijk (cf. van Dijk 1993; Fairclough 1995; Fairclough & Wodak 1997; Caldas-Coulthard & Coulthard 1996). Fairclough, in particular, is influenced by Foucault, especially in his use of the notions of 'order of discourse' and 'discourse formation'. Wodak's approach to the analysis of language in use ('discourse' is understood by all of these authors to be language) comes from various strands of sociolinguistics and ethnography (cf. Reisigl & Wodak 2001: Chapter 2). Van Dijk's work, emerging from relatively formal text linguistics (van Dijk 1977, 1980, 1998; van Dijk & Kintsch 1983), has always had a cognitive orientation, being concerned with mental schemas that represent the social and give rise to stereotypes, that in turn give rise to various ideologies, among which are exclusionary discourses, especially racism.[2] For many in this group of scholars (especially Fowler, Kress, Hodge, Thibault, van Leeuwen, Fairclough and others, but not van Dijk), Halliday's systemic-functional grammar has supposedly provided the toolkit for deconstructing the socially-constructed (thus linguistically constructed) machinery of power.

Yet after twenty years of this form of scholarship, there remain serious problems in the entire endeavour. I will not attempt to deal with the postmod-ernist work that does not address issues of language per se, since this would take us too far afield philosophically. I will focus on CDA understood in a broad sense, occasionally including Fowlerian Critical Linguistics (Fairclough & Wodak 1997; Fowler 1996).

2.   Claims and aims of CDA

Among the serious problems that, to my mind, bedevil CDA, are the following.

1. CDA claims, sometimes implicitly, sometimes explicitly, that its practice provides demystifying and emancipatory effects (see for example, Fowler 1996: 55ff.; Wodak & Meyer 2001: 10; Weiss & Wodak 2003: 14f.). There is of course an argument about whether a supposedly scientific endeavour should allow itself social and political motivation in the first place. One may argue for objectivity here on the grounds that acknowledging one's interests is per se a form of scientific objectivity, an argument that may well be crucial for all social sciences. This is not, however, my main point. Rather, I want to pose the question whether CDA has any credible efficacy, on its own terms, as an instrument of social justice. And if not, or even if the answer to that question is just a bit in doubt, do we need it?

2. This question is connected to its methods and linguistic underpinning. CDA has tended to draw, as we have seen, on social theory of a particu-lar type and on linguistics of a particular type. Despite some limited use of work in psychology and cognitive science (e.g. van Dijk 1991, 1993a, 1993b, 1998, 2004, forthcoming; van Dijk & Kintsch 1983; Wodak 1986; Reisigl & Wodak 2001), it appears to be fair to say that CDA has generally neglected developments in these fields. It has eschewed not only generative linguistics but also cognitive linguistics. (The latter at least does not figure in any seriously comprehended way in CDA literature.)

3. I have just questioned whether CDA has had genuine social effects. It is also questionable whether CDA has any theoretically interesting yield for the

social sciences, and more especially for linguistics. With regard to the latter, apart from the early attempts by serious linguists working around Fowler, Kress and Hodge, CDA in its later manifestation has made, so far as one can see, no contribution to our scientific understanding of the language capacity in homo sapiens. This is strange in view of the CDA insistence that language plays such an enormous role in social and political life.

3.   What is missing from CDA

There is a common element underlying these three criticisms: CDA despite some interest in (mental) representations has by and large not paid any attention to the human mind. There are two consequences of this observation, around which this paper is constructed. They are the following:

1. The lack of attention to mind is an important theoretical lack in its own terms. But there is worse.
2. It is possible that taking stock of recent research in the cognitive sciences leads us to the conclusion that we do not actually need CDA.

If there is anything in this argument, then we need to radically reassess what scholars are doing when they research into the relationship between the socio-political domain and the linguistic domain, and the paper concludes with some conclusions on the matter.

4.   Why CDA needs to consider mind

CDA has since its emergence been interdisciplinary, but selectively so. This aim of this section is to bring to the attention of CD Analysts the existence of a body of empirical research and speculative literature which they have tended to ignore. It is a body of work that has clear implications for a possible cognitive approach to the analysis of discourse in social and political contexts. There is a simple argument underlying the claim that CDA should attend to this cognitive dimension.[3] It starts with the central tenets of CDA itself (cf. Fairclough & Wodak 1997: 258–284). There are three such tenets:

1. discourse is social action (or 'social practice')
2. social action constructs social reality (objects, situations, identities, social relations...)
3. discourse is the use of language.

It follows that discourse constructs social reality. This must imply some sort of causal relation between language use and social action. There are a number of philosophical questions that seem to arise here, which we can only adumbrate. One is the following. It would appear to be the case that CDA is claiming that discourse stands in a causal relationship to social action (by which we might understand social relationships, group membership, the formation of social and political institutions and the like). But discourse is said to be social action, in which cause we seem to have discourse causing itself. Many discourse analysts, particularly those in the post-modernist tradition, would have little problem with this, since they are prepared to adopt the logical conclusion, namely that everything is discourse. CDA authors on the other hand are inclined to resolve the tension by using the term 'constitute' for cause: 'discourse is socially constitutive as well as socially shaped' (Fairclough & Wodak 1997: 258). So far as it goes, this is a useful concept that at least points to a complex dialectally causal relation. However, it is perhaps time to start probing its nature in more detail. To proceed beyond that particular formula, one needs to notice that it is entirely stated with respect to a social domain that appears autonomous: social action *qua* discourse has effects on social discourse that is either (a) also discourse or (b) social action but not (linguistic) discourse.

The way out of the loop is to introduce the cognitive dimension (as van Dijk (e.g. 1980, 1998) has done, and does also in the present volume). The argument is straightforward. Discourse, that is to say language in use, is produced and interpreted by human individuals interacting with one another. Language can only be produced and interpreted by human brains (and vocal apparatus, etc.). If language is produced and interpreted in human brains, then it interacts on any account of language with other cognitive capacities (as well as motor systems). In particular, if language use (discourse) is, as the tenets of CDA assert, connected to the 'construction' of knowledge about social objects, identities, processes, etc., then that construction can only be taking place in the minds of (interacting) individuals.

This argument seems to indicate that if CDA is to be a research enterprise, which I take to mean an enterprise that enhances human understanding and knowledge, then what goes on inside people's heads must become a prime concern. There are many ways in which such a research goal might be pursued. In the present chapter I will merely suggest how some of the existing research in certain areas of contemporary cognitive science and psychology, particularly those varieties that take an evolutionary perspective, might be used to enrich and explore in new ways the sorts of social action and social construction that CDA has classically been preoccupied with.

Let us, then, consider the specific area of racism or xenophobia (not of course necessarily the same thing). CDA is good at showing how particular language users establish exclusionary attitudes and maybe practices by recurrently and selectively asserting certain attributes (i.e. social roles, behavioural characteristics, physical appearance, etc.) of social and ethnic groups (e.g. van Dijk 1991, 1993a, 1993b; Wodak 2000; Reisigl & Wodak 2001). In other words, CDA draws attention to the existence of stereotyped categorisations in daily talk, elite talk and texts. CDA also shows how language users categorise behaviour, actions and attributes – all of which may be observable facts – in ways that express attitudes towards such facts. For example, immigration, which denotationally refers to spatial movements of people in relation to political boundaries, is defined as 'invasion' or 'flood'. It is also good at identifying interactive verbal devices for the implication or presupposition of assertions about social and ethnic groups, and in pin-pointing mitigation devices such as 'apparent denial'. Underlying all these features that are found in text and talk referring to social and ethnic groups is the conceptual process of category formation. On the actual cognitive processes CDA seems to have little new to say, despite the fact that there is an abundant psychological and social psychological literature on the formation of concepts (but cf. summaries in van Dijk 1991, 1993a, 1998 and Reisigl & Wodak 2001). In general, CDA has done a fine descriptive job. Whether the description has altered public awareness significantly enough to achieve emancipatory effects is perhaps not the main point here, though it is obviously not irrelevant. The disturbing fact is that racism, xenophobia and other kinds of exclusionary behaviour continue to appear. This suggests that we may need to delve deeper into *why* this kind of category formation is so persistent a factor in social behaviour, and *why* the language forms associated with it are so potent. These are difficult questions: I am not going to give the answers, but merely propose that anyone seriously interested in these issues needs to address such questions. This means taking an explanatory stance rather than a merely descriptive one and it also means, I am suggesting, taking account of ideas developed in cognitive and evolutionary psychology.

5.   Some aspects of cognitive and evolutionary psychology relevant to CDA

In this section I review some recent ideas emerging from cognitive science and cognitive psychology. Since an evolutionary perspective has proved a fruitful thinking device in these and other areas, and since it can provide an explanatory framework for expanding the discussion of issues that CDA is concerned with, I will bring that too into the picture. But I make no pretence of completeness in regard to this field.

5.1 Modularity of mind

Chomsky postulated back in the 1960s that the human language faculty was an autonomous module of mind. In part, the claim was based on analogy with other human cognitive and perceptual abilities that were regarded on empirical grounds as modular, in particular vision and facial recognition. The notion of modularity was more extensively theorised by Fodor (1983), whose ideas have had a wide impact on psychology, theoretical and applied, on cognitive science and on philosophy. Fodor's theory corresponds roughly to Figure 1. For Fodor, the mind has two tiers: a collection of input modules that are autonomous and have a specific job to do (like the blades of a Swiss army knife) and a central processor that corresponds to what people generally think of as intelligence, creative thinking. The former are hard-wired, localised and provide input to the latter, which is not localised and is characterised by 'its non-encapsulation, its creativity, its holism and its passion for the analogical' (Fodor 1985:4). The last point is worth noting and we shall return to it.

There is much controversy surrounding the two-tier proposal, but the most significant development of the modular concept has been its incorporation

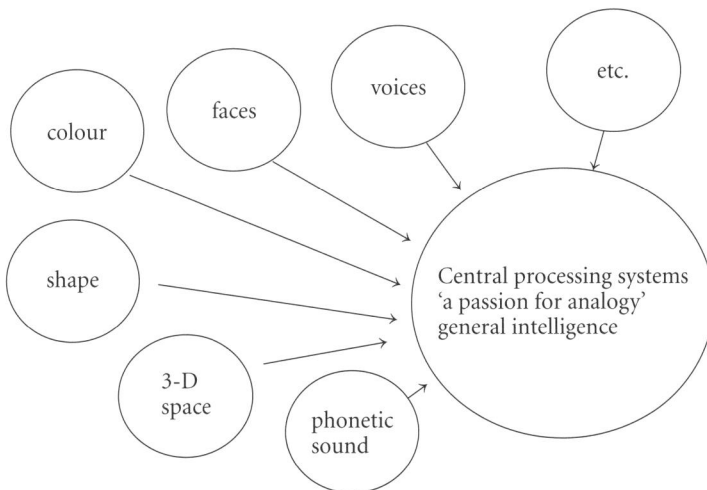

Figure 1. Information from perceptual organs to input systems (modules) (Fodor)

into evolutionary psychology, notably by Cosmides and Tooby (1992), who, in broad terms, argue that the mind of humans as we now know them has emerged not by chance or solely by the impact of particular social and physical environments but by the pressures of evolutionary selection. The mental modules evolved for purposes of survival, just like any other organ of the body. Rather than assuming the existence of some generalised intelligence and learning ability, the tendency is to regard the mind as consisting of many specialised modules, interacting among one another. One type of evidence that is adduced is similar to the familiar Chomskyan argument for the innateness of language: that children develop very many kinds of specific knowledge very rapidly and on the basis of scant input. Cosmides and Tooby think there is a very large number of such modules:

> A face recognition module, a spatial relations module, a rigid objects mechanics module, a tool-use module, a fear module, a social exchange module, an emotion-perception, kin-oriented motivation, an effort allocation and recalibration module, a child care module, a social inference module, a friendship module, a semantic-inference module, a grammar acquisition module, a communication-pragmatics module, a theory of mind module, and so on...
>
> (1992: 113)

Amongst these modules, some of which are empirically attested, some rather more speculative, which should be of interest to researchers interested in the interaction of language and society? Clearly language is one of them, but we will focus on three other possibly modular areas.

5.2   Intuitive psychology ('theory of mind')

Somewhat before Fodor, Humphrey had begun to propose a specific module of social intelligence combined with what is known as a 'theory of mind' module, which refers to what appears to be the innate ability of humans to guess and make pragmatic predictions about the intentions and likely future actions of their fellows (Humphrey 1976). The idea has been picked up and further investigated by Leslie (1991) and Baron-Cohen (2001) in normal and abnormal psychology, and by Whiten (Ed., 1991) in primatology. Essentially, theory of mind implies that humans have an evolved ability to look for the motives and plans of others, an ability that can clearly be used cooperatively or counter-cooperatively. In any event, applied to language behaviour, it suggests that humans naturally and automatically tend to look for interpretations of discourse acts in terms of what speakers are intending to convey and to do.

5.3 Machiavellian intelligence

Similar claims to those outlined in the preceding paragraph have been made also for primates. Byrne and Whiten (1988) and Byrne (1995), for instance, have made empirical studies of chimpanzees that they believe demonstrate clearly that these creatures engage instinctively in social behaviour that display the following:

- the formation and observation of group and subgroup boundaries
- the formation of coalitions in competitive environments, signalled by, inter alia, grooming behaviour
- the formation and observance of dominance hierarchies
- the practice of tactical deception motivated by individual wants.

It is the latter, tactical deception, that has been dubbed 'machiavellian intelligence'. Its workings follow from the ability to read the intentions of others, and to recognise the ability of others to read one's own intentions, leading to the ability to mask one's intentions (Whiten 1991). If a distinct machiavellian module exists in apes, then, so the evolutionary argument goes, it must exist as a distinct ability also in their descendants, homo sapiens. In the case of language-using creatures, the ability to verbally mislead, deceive and to lie is clearly closely related. CDA researchers should not rush to dismiss the argument that humans have an evolved instinctive and specialised ability to exploit one another upon the basis of abilities developed for cooperative social survival purposes. And there is a further very good reason for CDA to look closely at these ideas. It will have been apparent from the preceding arguments that if an individual A has an innate ability to read the minds of B and use deception for his or her own ends, then conversely, B must have the same ability and could in principle use it to read the intention to deceive. This is a highly significant notion for CDA to which we return at the end of this chapter.

5.4 Intuitive biology

We have looked at the claims for innate social and psychological modules. Other modules of mind have been researched that have to do with the human mind's relation to the non-social world. One of these is 'intuitive physics': human understanding of gravity, solidity, orientation, force, and so on appear to be hard-wired, that is, be present at birth as some sort of neurological template that enables the child to deal with the surrounding environment without having to learn it in the way that an empiricist psychology would suggest the human mental tabula rasa has to learn about everything (Spelke 1991). More relevant to the concerns of this paper is 'intuitive biology', which works on the same general principles. What the innate biology module works on is living entities. The research in this field (cf. Atran 1990 and 1994; Kennedy 1992; Keil 1994) indicates that human children automatically make assumptions about the taxonomy of 'natural kinds'. For instance, they seem to take for granted the difference between animate and inanimate entities. Moreover, there is evidence that all human cultures share a basic framework for classifying the natural world (Atran 1990). These folk classifications are highly complex: a reasonable explanation, it is argued, is that there is a common genetic blueprint for it. An analogous argument is often made for the universal innateness of the language instinct. The evolutionary argument would be that human evolution needed to select for the ability to classify the living world because of the survival advantages conferred by such an ability.

One feature of the research on intuitive biology that is of interest to CDA is the claim that this module includes 'essentialism'. That is to say, humans seem intuitively impelled to attribute 'essences' to different kinds of things in their taxonomies of natural kinds. A predisposition to essentialism would provide an important explanatory framework for many social phenomena that interest CDA researchers, and we return to it later in this chapter.

6.   Beyond modules: Cognitive fluidity

As was pointed out above, while the notion of modularity is widely accepted among psychologists and cognitive scientists, the precise form and significance of the modularity is controversial. Karmiloff-Smith (1992), for example, building on her earlier developmental work with Piaget, argues that modules are merely the basis for development that is subject to variable cultural shaping. But the interpretations of modularity that will concern us here are those of Mithen (1996) and those of Sperber (1994) and Cosmides and Tooby (2000).

Mithen, whose background is in archaeology, seeks an explanation for the apparent 'explosion' of human development that occurred between 60,000 and 30,000 years ago. Mithen's hypothesis is that the mind is indeed modular but does not, as in Fodor's account, have an independent general processor. Rather what happened at the critical moment in human evolution was that the autonomous modules began to intercommunicate: Mithen calls this the emergence of 'cognitive fluidity' (Mithen 1996).

Sperber also accepts the modular story, but accounts for human creativity by postulating (with plenty of evidence from language) a further module, the 'module of metarepresentation', an expanded version of the theory of mind module and closely tied to language and communication. What this module must be doing, in Sperber's view, is handling concepts of concepts and representations of representations. It will also be giving space to concepts from several otherwise encapsulated and non-communicating modules, and allowing recombinations and transformations of the concepts formed in the modules.

Mithen seizes on Fodor's comment about general intelligence having a 'passion for the analogical' and proposes that the mechanism by which the modular domains started to interconnect was metaphor. Specifically, he claims that language evolved in the first place for social purposes and was 'metaphorically extended' as it was 'invaded' by concepts coming from the major domains (Mithen 1996: 214). Along with Sperber he retains the metarepresentational module as a key feature of human intelligence, linked to communication, but sees it as an expanded form of social intelligence. This metarepresentational, communicational and social module takes in non-social concepts from other domains and can process them creatively, perhaps using metaphor or some other form of mental transformation.

What Mithen and Sperber do not do is tell us much about is the nature of these processes, particularly where language, which they regard as a key element, is concerned. This is where the work done in cognitive linguistics over the last few decades becomes signally relevant. In particular, there are well developed theories of metaphor and conceptual blending that could be linked with the Mithen-Sperber hypothesis. In Section 8 below we explore the possible application of some recent theorising in cognitive linguistics on conceptual blends (Fauconnier & Turner 2002).

7. The point of all this for CDA

Why should the body of work in cognitive science and evolutionary psychology, of which I have sketched but a small fragment, be of interest to CDA? In brief the reasons are as follows.

i.   Machiavellian intelligence is of course political behaviour, whether conceived as institutionalised politics or informal social movement politics or day-to-day interpersonal manoeuvring and manipulation. The work summarised above proposes that the basic framework for such behaviour is innate in humans, not primarily derived from socialisation, socioeconomic forces and the like, as proposed in the existing heavily socialised accounts of CDA. It is quite likely (as Mithen and Sperber seem to argue) that an innate social intelligence is in some way fundamental and operates in ways that may be innate. But this is very different from CDA's existing assumptions about the primacy of the social and the political. If the field is to take account of all relevant science, then it seems inevitable that it has to confront the question of how the human mind works when engaged in social and political action, which is largely, for humans, verbal action. (For a step forward in this direction, see Teun van Dijk this volume.)

ii. Research on social intelligence has focused inter alia on the formation of social categories, specifically racial categories, and 'essentialism'. This is familiar territory for CDA practitioners. However, the literature outlined above is scarcely if ever drawn on in these studies. In Section 8 below, I introduce some more details that might suggest links of research building on the elements of a cognitive approach already found in CDA work on racism and ideology.

iii. We have seen that when a perspective is adopted that confronts the question of who we are as a species and what we are like, there arises the fundamental question of how we got to be so uniquely creative (often unpleasantly so by our own human values). We have seen the vague but recurrent suggestion in the literature, from Fodor to Mithen, that some metaphorical ability seems to be the explanation of how modular thought is integrated. What is lacking in the evolutionary-cognitive literature is a detailed theory of metaphor. It is also, as it happens, lacking in a lot of CDA work, where it is often simply treated as a 'persusasive' rhetorical device of some sort. However, cognitive linguistics (CL) has two closely related theories of cognitive activity corresponding to Mithen's 'cognitive fluidity'.[4] The CL theories on metaphor are those developed by Lakoff, Johnson and Turner (Lakoff & Johnson 1980; Lakoff 1987; Lakoff & Turner 1989; Lakoff & Johnson 1999) and explored empirically by, for example, Gibbs (1994), Boroditsky (1997) and Glucksberg (2000). The second relevant CL theory I am alluding to is conceptual blending developed by Fauconnier and Turner, which is of importance to CDA because it is specifically a theory of what conceptual activity goes on during discourse processing (Fauconnier & Turner 2002).

iv. CDA as an academic and pedagogical enterprise might not be necessary at all. This startling inference could be drawn from the claim – indeed the evidence – that humans have in any case an innate 'theory of mind' and

a metarepresentational module. If individual humans are innately machiavellian, they are also innately able to counter one another's machinations.
If language is crucial to this ability and associated activity, then they should
have an innate ability not just to use language in machiavellian ways but to
detect and counter one another's machiavellian use of language. I shall return to this argument, which is put forward by Sperber and others, towards
the end of this paper. In the meantime, the question is, given the foregoing
remarks: What is CDA for if people can do it anyway?

Having outlined some of the issues that CDA will have to confront if it is going to be genuinely interdisciplinary, I now move on to what this means for
research into a specific area of social enquiry that that has been the traditional stamping ground of CDA. The area is racism. Section 8 summarises
the work largely ignored by CDA accounts of this area. And Section 9 out-
lines a CL approach that explains how using cognitive linguistics can provide
an account of what the human mind is doing when it does racist discourse.
This approach is not entirely neglected in critical approaches to language
use: see for instance Lakoff (1991, 1996, 2003), Chilton (1996a and 1996b),
Chilton and Lakoff (1999), Rohrer (1995), Dirven (2001), Santa Ana (2002)
and O'Halloran (2003).

8.   A cognitive approach to racism

Most discourse-oriented approaches to racism also make reference to cognitive issues or to the need for an explanatory framework or both. Van Dijk's
approach, for instance, is broadly sociocognitive and is constructed around a
standard psychological model of memory, linking semantic memory to stable
social constructs, episodic memory as a storehouse for previously encountered
narratives, and working memory, in which context and ongoing discourse are
processed (van Dijk 1984, 1991, 1993a, etc.). Reisigl and Wodak (2001:10–
14) review some social-psychological explanations, some psychoanalytic explanations and some cognitive psychology research into categorisation and
stereotyping but do not incorporate them directly into their discourse analysis approach. No CDA work, so far as I am aware, draws on the evolutionary
cognitive science research outlined in Section 5 of the present paper. Essentially, the explanation of racism that has been discussed in the cognitive science
literature draws on the theory of mental modules and on the postulated existence of mechanisms of transfer between autonomous modules. It is worth

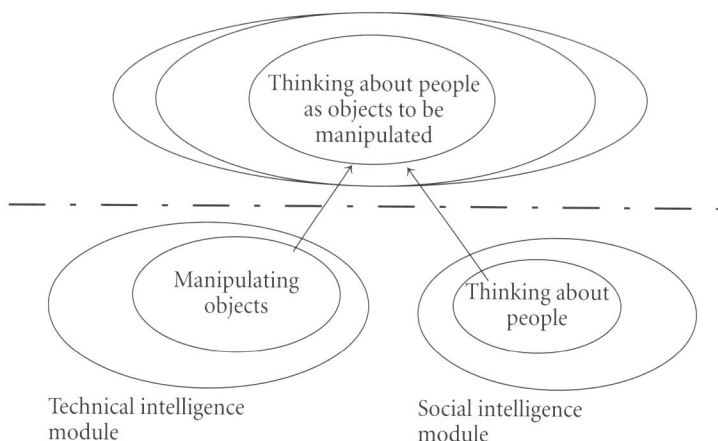

Figure 2. After Mithen (1996:225)

considering it further because of its potential for linking cognition, language and social behaviour in an explanatory framework.

Mithen (1996:224–225) argues that racisms arises from a particular use of 'cognitive fluidity' acting on particular specialised mental modules, namely *technical intelligence* (tool making, manipulation of objects) and *social intelligence* (thinking about people, together with ingredients such as theory of mind that we have mentioned above). The general idea is pictured in Figure 2.

Mithen's notion is that the area above the line represents the modern (i.e. Pleistocene and post-Pleistocene) mind, while the area below the line represents the separate modules of the early human mind. A better interpretation might be to say that the area above the line stands for cognitive effects that can come about in the modern human mind under certain conditions (maybe the ones that CDA is or ought to be able to specify). Another element in Mithen's framework is that intuitive biology (the natural kinds module) accounts for human readiness to accept the existence of different social groups (and label them races, etc.). But it is cognitive fluidity that accounts for our readiness to treat some groups as inferior. This can come about when the thinking-about-people module merges with the thinking-about-tools module. Or when the natural kinds module merges its humans and animals categories for certain groups of the former. What happens is that people can be thought of as either animals (thus inferior) or as objects (tools) or both.

A slightly different, though related account, comes from the work of Atran (1990, 1994), Boyer (1990), Gelman (1994) and Hirshfeld (1994). Gelman's position is that the idea of different human races comes from essentialist beliefs, which are part of the intuitive biology module. As Atran argued, intuitive biology predisposes humans to set up taxonomies of *living kinds* for animals (a schema obviously adaptive for hunter-gatherers in the relevant environment for early humans). Gelman and her colleagues (e.g. Gelman, Coley & Gottfried 1994) have done empirical developmental work with children, producing evidence that children spontaneously attribute 'essences' to living kinds. Their findings show that children consequently also take it for granted that living kinds have their own invisible internal workings, that these internal workings cause certain behaviours, that attributed essential characteristics inevitably develop or grow, and that the attributed identity is permanent, despite changes, because something 'inside' is regarded as fixed. So children and adults develop racial categories, assumed to have fixed essences, by *transfer* from the living kinds module to the people category in the social intelligence module. However, Hirschfeld's (1994) experiments suggest that children have an independent tendency to construct racial categories and thus that it is not a matter of merging elements from the essentialist natural taxonomy module with elements in the people module.

The latter position has serious implications. Does it mean there is a racist module, a domain-specific competence for racial classification? If such a module included the assumption that some races were inferior to others, does this mean racism itself is innate? Sperber (1994) is worried by this implication and proposes an alternative story within the modular framework. In Sperber's view 'proper' domains evolve for survival under specific environmental conditions, but conditions may change, and the module can take on a different role. This would include the case where such a module interacts with components of a later culture (which could of course include linguistically mediated cognitive components). Consequently, for Sperber, a module can *develop* a cultural domain. The example Sperber gives is the following.

Let us assume, as seems plausible, that a zoological domain (i.e. biology module) evolved in early humans whose job was the conceptualisation of animals. Such a module would be adaptive for dealing with local fauna. Then suppose the fauna upon which the original module was based ceased to exist or be not visible (maybe the community moved to another location). It is likely, Sperber argues that the module remained active and could (perhaps, we may interject, in the way Mithen suggests) take input from culture (or as we may say, from discourse). Sperber's speculation is that any module of this kind might be biologically inherited in the modern human mind, but be a rather general *metatemplate*. Further, he speculates, such metatemplates can be 'initialised' by cultural input. To quote Sperber directly:

> A cognitive module stimulates in every culture the production and distribution of a wide array of information that meets its input conditions. This information, being artifactually produced or organized by the people themselves, is from the start conceptualized and therefore belongs to conceptual domains that I propose to call the module's *cultural domain(s)*.
>
> (Sperber 1994: 55; Sperber's italics)

What happens then is that in the process of cultural transmission (one may want to call it 'discourse') causes a mimicking of the module's actual domain based on information coming from another domain. It follows that

> racial classification might result from an ad hoc template derived from the living-kinds metatemplate, through an initialisation triggered by a cultural input.
>
> (ibid.: 58)

As to the precise nature of this cultural trigger:

> the mere encounter with a nominal label used to designate a living thing is enough to tilt the child's categorization of that thing towards an essentialist construal. … It is quite possible that being presented with nominal labels for otherwise unidentified and undescribed humans is enough (given an appropriate context) to activate the initialisation of the ad hoc template.
>
> (Sperber 1994: 59)

This is of course reminiscent of what discourse analysts have long been saying. However, they have been saying it in a theoretical vacuum. What is crucial is that the point being made by Sperber in the last quotation is based on experimental work with children, and is also coherent with the theoretical cognitive evolutionary framework.

So where does this leave the suggestion of a domain-specific racism made by Hirschfeld? What Sperber says on this score, somewhat disturbingly, is this:

> There is, as Hirschfeld suggested, a genetically specified *competence* [my italics] that determines racial classification without importing its models from another concrete domain.
>
> (Sperber 1994: 58)

However, and the point is extremely important, Sperber's approach seems to propose that this competence may itself be derived not from a competence that has racial classification as its proper domain at all but more indirectly from a different genetic modular competence:

> Racial classification may be a mere cultural domain, based on an underlying
> competence that does not have any proper domain.   (ibid.)

His hypothesis (he stresses that it is only a hypothesis) is in fact that there
is a higher level metatemplate whose job is to generate ad hoc templates for
actual zoology and botany domains (living kinds). This metatemplate is 'initialised' for racial classification. The intitialisation of an ad hoc template for
racial classification

> could well be the effect of parasitic, cultural input on the higher-level learning
> module, the function of which is to generate ad hoc templates for genuine
> living-kind domains such as zoology and botany.   (ibid.)

The upshot in relation to the implications of Hirschfeld is that

> no racist disposition has been selected *for* [...] in humans. However, the dis-
> positions that have been selected for make humans all too easily susceptible to
> racism given minimal, innocuous-looking cultural input.
>   (ibid.; Sperber's italics)

Now if we ask what 'cultural input' might be, it is clear that in view of the
genetic endowment for language and the fact that human culture depends critically on linguistic communication, the cultural input initialising racial classification must be talk and text, in other words discourse. We can sum all this up
as in Figure 3.

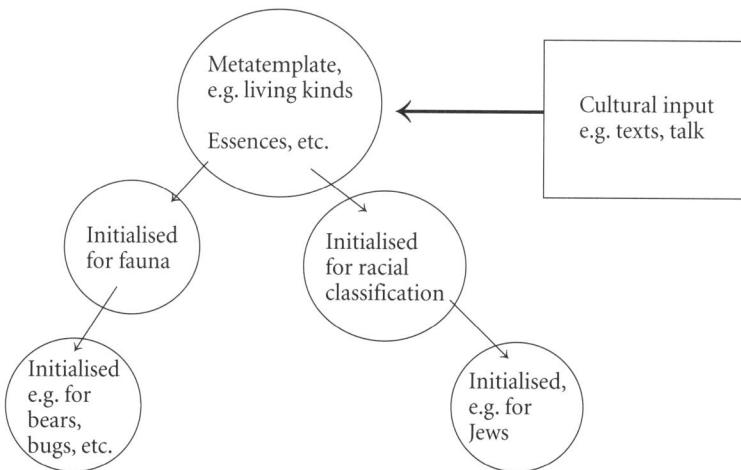

Figure 3. Sperber's initialisation-of-template theory of modules

The value of this kind of approach lies in its potential explanatory power. That is to say, it offers an explanatory account of *how* what Sperber calls 'cultural input' and CDA practitioners may call 'discourse' has any effect in the human mind, *how* it takes hold and has the potential to spread from one mind to another. It also vindicates the work done in CDA, which in effect shows something of how the cultural input is achieved. The gap a Sperberian account fills is the explanation of why the discoursal input should have any effect and be so persistent in human societies. However, there is one area that neither the CDA account nor the Sperberian one tells us about in detail (though Sperber and the other cognitive psychologists and archaeologists certainly come close to it). This area concerns the actual workings of the mind that give rise to what Fodor calls 'passion for the analogical', what Mithen calls 'cognitive fluidity' and what Sperber variously calls 'cultural input', 'initialisation', 'the effect of parasitic information'. In the next section I show how one CL theory, namely blending theory, can give a more detailed account of these processes than is currently available either in the cognitive evolutionary literature we have been surveying or in the standard CDA literature.

9.   Using cognitive models of discourse

There are in fact rather few models of discourse that have a distinct cognitive flavour. The most sophisticated formal theory, which also claims a cognitive element, is DRT (Discourse Representation Theory: see for example Kamp & Reyle 1993 and for developments Asher & Lascarides 2003). Another related type of discourse analysis is Werth's (1999) 'text worlds' approach. However, while CDA cannot seriously claim to make a contribution to discourse analysis without taking account of these highly sophisticated models, I shall leave their further exploration to another occasion. For there is in fact another recent theoretical development which is equally indispensable and which happens to have a direct bearing on the matter of cognitive fluidity, and thus also by hypothesis, on the question of racial categorisation and racism as formulated by the researchers discussed in Section 8.

Fauconnier and Turner (2002) present a theory of cognitive blending developed in a series of earlier papers (e.g. Fauconnier & Turner 1996; Fauconnier 1997). Blending theory is an attempt to explain one of many tricks performed by the human mind, specifically in the processing of discourse. The starting point is the notion of 'mental space', which may be a structure called up from long-term memory or a structure on hold in working memory:

> Mental spaces are small conceptual packets constructed as we think and talk, for purposes of local understanding and action. They are interconnected, and can be modified as thought and discourse unfold. … In blending, structures from two input spaces is projected to a separate space, the 'blend'. The blend inherits partial structure from the input spaces, and has emergent structure of its own.
>
> (Fauconnier & Turner 1996: 113)

> … input spaces under construction recruit structure from more stable, elaborate, and conventional conceptual structures that may have conventional structures of various sorts: shared frame roles, connections of identity or transformation or representation, metaphoric connections. These conventional connections are fully available to the work of blending. Blending may exploit, simultaneously, more than one kind of counterpart connection (e.g. frame-role connection and identity connection). through entrenchment, blending can influence conventional structures and their conventional connections. Blends themselves become conventional.
>
> (Fauconnier & Turner 1996: 116)

These summaries are almost sufficient as a framework for preliminary exposition. In addition, we need to note the characteristic diagrammatic notation developed by Fauconnier and Turner, used below in Figure 4. Its rationale is based in set theory and the mathematical notion of mapping from one domain to another. For present purposes all we need to note is that mappings place elements in different domains in correspondence with one another. An example will illustrate the kind of cognitive phenomenon that is at issue. Consider this kind of discourse, offered by Fauconnier and Turner:

> I claim that reason is a self-developing capacity. Kant disagrees with this on one point. He says it's innate, but I answer that that's begging the question, to which he counters, etc. etc.
>
> (ibid.)

This is a familiar academic genre. How it works is by using two mental spaces, one in which the contemporary speaker is making assertions and another in which Kant is speaking. The two spaces are separate. But they do have something in common (the concepts of thinking, debating, writing) which is connected to both the first two spaces. It is called the 'generic' space. The blend occurs in a fourth mental space which brings together inputs from the modern philosopher space and inputs from the Kant space. The blend space can also draw on other cognitive frames: in this example, it appears to draw on the shared 'debate' frame. Once the blend has emerged, the mind can work in that space, elaborating it, drawing inferences from it, etc. The blended material can feed back into the two input spaces.

It should be already obvious that an explicitly worked out theory along these lines does much to fill in the notion of cognitive fluidity (as suggested also by Turner 2001), the transfer among basic mental modules, postulated by the evolutionary cognitive psychologists and archaeologists. In making that point, I am of course using blending. For I am merging the Fauconnier-Turner model with the modular model. In fact, the suggestion is that it is precisely the modules discussed that can (not always, but can) provide the input spaces in the blending system described above.

Blending crops up in all manner of discourse, however: jokes, poetry, oratory, advertising, ideology, to suggest a few examples. CDA researchers will be interested in ideology. The theory of blending, together with evolutionary cognitive science, could enable us to construct a general cognitive theory of ideology, which has been lacking in CDA.[5] What such a theory would give us, it should be noted, is not a means of combating directly those with whose ideologies we might disagree, but a means of deepening our understanding of what it could mean to give an explanation of how and perhaps why human minds produce such structures. Here we can do no more than sketch out how this task might be broached. Let us take a simple (because extreme) case, which many people in the world today (but not all) would categorically reject: antisemitic nazi propaganda, as found classically in Hitler's *Mein Kampf*.[6]

At the core of nazi antisemitic propaganda was a crucial cognitive blend that spread back into many aspects of discourse. As is well known, *Mein Kampf* uses, inter alia, the following argument:

> X is a parasite (virus, bacillus, etc.) in the body of Y
> bodies can be cured by expelling or destroying parasites
> doctors expel/destroy parasites, etc.
> Therefore, Y can be cured if doctors expel X from Y

What are the cognitive processes involved in an argument of this kind? Following blending theory we can see that we have (i) an input space or source domain, which includes the concept 'parasites'. Now 'parasites' is part of a pre-existing structured cognitive frame, which necessarily includes concepts such as 'host' organism. In fact, it looks uncommonly like what Atran, Sperber, Mithen and others regard as a module of mind that has to with the taxonomy of living kinds, or naive zoology. Recall that this module, according to several accounts, incorporates essentialism: the ascription of inherent and constant properties of 'kinds'. We also have (ii) a second input space, a target domain, which here is a social group that has contingently become distinct in the culture where the discourse (and the formation of concepts in many minds in that culture) is taking place. Clearly, this space is largely formed by many complex inputs from social discourse, including the kinds of linguistic communication ('discourse') studied by van Dijk (1991, 1993a), Reisigl and Wodak (2001) and others, not to mention the large body of explanatory attempts by the Frankfurt School and studies of nazi language by, e.g. Ehlich (1989). In this instance the social group in question is Jews. It could also include other contingent social entities, say nation states, or geographical regions. It is highly relevant that larger groups can contain, or be conceived as containing, smaller groups. In addition, there is a cross domain mapping which establishes analogies between host-parasite and nation-subgroup (Jews).

In terms of mental spaces, we have (iii) a common (or 'generic') conceptual space. In this instance, the relevant one appears to be the image schema container-contained (on image schemas, and specifically, container, see Johnson 1987 and Johnson & Lakoff 1999 and on the importance of this schema in large-scale systems of political belief Chilton 1996a). Finally, we have (iv) the blend space, where the input spaces are merged. Here, and this is the crucial point, is where further inferencing and elaboration is effected. According to Fauconnier and Turner, it is in the blend space that a cognitive phenomenon that they term 'conceptual compression' occurs (Fauconnier & Turner 2002:92–93). At the same time, elaboration is a kind of expansion, which in the case of *Mein Kampf*, and antisemitic discourse in general, recruits further cognitive frames,[7] specifically knowledge frames that structure basic knowledge about disease, healers, healing, and curative methods. Also recruited in ideological discourse of this type are cognitive frames centred on the body which draw on the container image schema. Figure 4 represents a simplified picture of the way the mind's 'cognitive fluidity' operates to creatively produce concepts about social groups.

Such models offer CDA detailed hypotheses about how discourse affects social cognition. Notice that they are dynamic, in the sense that they can enter into inference chains. In the present example, the blend 'nations are hosts, Jews are parasites' engages the cognitive frame of biology and disease. In turn, the disease frame permits inferences of the kind:

(i)   If a is a parasite in b, a causes disease c

(ii)   If c is a disease, b can be cured by d with e and/or by doing f
       Where d is (say) a doctor, e for instance is a medicine that (e) kills a.
       Therefore, to cure b, kill a.

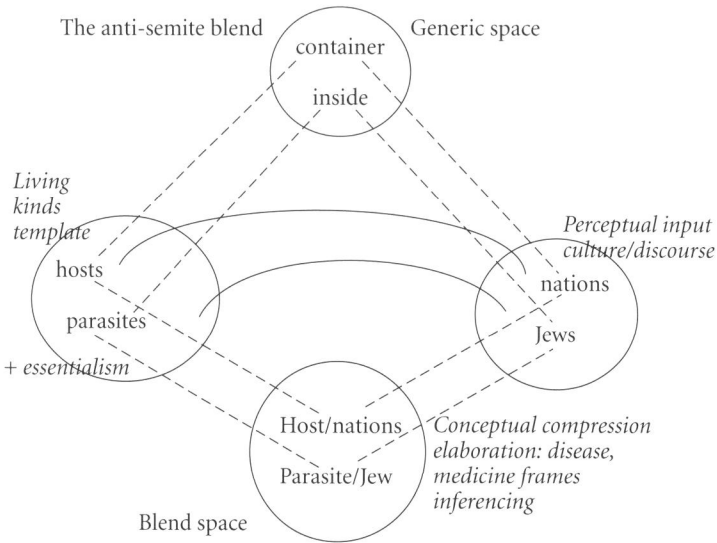

Figure 4. The anti-semite blend

Such inferences are not strictly logical nor empirical, but based on the blend of one domain with another. Simply labelling a group 'parasites' activates a blend, which in turn activates an inferential chain. The conclusion 'kill *a*' may or may not be implanted and result in real exterminations, pogroms and genocides.

This is a hypothesis about how discourse ('cultural input') can affect ('infect', if one wants to use the metaphor) human minds, and lead to acts by humans against other humans. This link is missing from current CDA. The cognitive account tells you the mechanisms. What it does not do is tell you *why* such inferences should lead to certain historical events at a certain time and place. If you want answers to this particular *why*, there are several routes to pursue. One is CDA, which might be able to describe the characteristics of the 'cultural input' (the discourse) that might have activated the blends ('initialised the template' in Sperber's terminology discussed above), facilitated the inferences and promoted the conclusion. It might tell us about the social and political conditions that led to certain kinds of communication network that made such input possible or effective. Typically, with the partial exception of the 'discourse-historical approach' espoused by Wodak and colleagues, CDA does not take this latter step, but sticks at the level of verbal detail. To understand *why* particular cognitive effects arise and *why* they result in action at a certain time or place is not a question cognitive scientists or linguists address.

It is not evident that CDA is equipped to address this question either, without massive collaboration from, at least, the disciplines of political economy and history.

The cognitive account outlined here attempts to fill in some of the missing links that are implicit, or ought to be implicit, in the CDA project – namely, exactly how (i.e. by what mechanisms) can human utterances conceivably lead to appalling human actions?

10. Passive receptors or critical instinct? Do we need CDA?

To sum up the argument so far, to understand discourse requires a cognitive perspective. We have reviewed some of the recent work in evolutionary psychology that appears to have considerable relevance for CDA. We have also reviewed one corner of cognitive linguistics, for the same reason. In Section 9, we have shown two things: one, how blending theory can add detail to some key claims in cognitive psychology and two, how a blend of blending theory and cognitive evolutionary psychology can add detail ('depth') to our understanding of ideology, a classic topic in CDA. In this final section we attempt to draw out some of the implications for CDA of taking this route. To accomplish this we can make further use of recent work in cognitive science. Two kinds of question will guide the discussion. First, does the evolutionary and cognitive perspective imply that the human mind is easily manipulated because of the effects due to innate modules and mechanisms like blending? Second, if CDA took into account the cognitive perspective we have outlined, what sort of research would CDA become and could it still claim emancipatory benefits?

The question of how easily or not the human mind can be tricked, deceived or manipulated through the use of language is a core empirical and theoretical question that CDA has never addressed as such. There are well-known psychological studies on such phenomena as 'groupthink' and on the framing of narratives but little detailed discussion of the very possibility of verbal manipulation or how or to what extent it might work in detail (but cf. Allott forthcoming; Chilton 2002; and Saussure forthcoming). Indeed, from Fowler and others on, in the wake of Orwell's newspeak nightmare, there has simply tended to be an assumption that people are easily hoodwinked by powerful verbalisers. What follows is an attempt to open up this question to closer scrutiny.

We return to recent work in cognitive evolutionary psychology for clues and cues. As was noted earlier, Sperber has postulated a genetically evolved metarepresentation module which he regards as central to a number of characteristically human mental and other behaviours, including creativity and consciousness. Metarepresentation, according to this hypothesis is a second-order module with the ability to form concepts of concepts and mental representations of mental representations, one's own and those of others.

The evolutionary perspective prompts a form of argumentation that goes as follows. Why would homo sapiens have developed such an ability? Because, we may speculate, humans need to know what others are thinking (cf. 'theory of mind', 'machiavellian intelligence'). That is to say, such knowledge has survival value, because it is important to know what others inside and outside one's group are wanting, believing, intending, etc. Further, metarepresentation must be integral to human language/communication, for in processing a speaker's (S's) vocalisation the hearer (H) forms a mental representation of what S is (probably) representing in their own mind. Indeed, communication occurs when H recognises S's intention that H construct some mental representation corresponding with some representation in the mind of S. Comprehension is metarepresentation.

This line of argument has some possible implications for CDA, at least for that part of it that is concerned with strategic deception through language use. Humans may have innate mechanisms for communication and comprehension, but these precisely facilitate tactical deception, that is, machiavellian behaviour. It would make no sense to assume that some had a machiavellian module and some didn't (which doesn't mean that some do not use it and cultivate it more than others, as would be argued for any of the other postulated modules). But if everyone has it, it is also necessary to assume that all individuals have the ability to counter it in others.

The hypothesis is, then, that humans need to be able to detect intentions to engage in deceptive action. Since language use is also a form of action, we must ask whether humans are not also naturally endowed with the ability to detect deceptive language use. Cosmides (1989), on whom Sperber is drawing, regards some such ability as a specialised mental module which she calls the 'cheater detector'. Sperber elaborates on this in a fashion that should attract the attention of CDA:

> The human reliance on communication is so great, the risks of deception and manipulation so ubiquitous, that it is reasonable to speculate that all available cost-effective modes of defense are likely to have evolved. (Sperber 2000:135)

Building on Cosmides, Sperber goes further than Cosmides in grouping together possible component modules of this innate ability. First, there is an in-built facility for checking the reliability of the source of information, in line with the idea of 'source tagging' (Cosmides & Tooby 2000). The recursive syntax of human languages permits embedding of propositions as complements of reportative verbs, evidential and attitudinal verbs, facilitating the metarepresentation of sources (amongst other things).

Second, theory of mind supplies the ability to 'be sensitive to subtle signs of deceptive intent [and] read the relevant attitudinal and emotional signs' (Sperber 2000:135). Third, Sperber proposes that there exists a 'consistency filter', by means of which the human mind is innately inclined to check the logical consistency of language input, on the one hand with respect to the internal logical consistency of a stretch of talk (or text), and on the other hand with respect to external consistency with what the receiver believes to be true and with alternative informational input.

Because a speaker S will recognise a hearer's intention to counter S's deceptive intents, Sperber argues that S will try to penetrate H's defences, resulting in 'a persuasion counter-persuasion arms race' (Sperber 2000:136). This point is in one sense obvious, but it is important to stress the claim that the modular mental basis of such a spiral is an innate ability. Even more specifically, Sperber proposes that this ability will have evolved in such a say as to give rise to a further innate module, a 'logico-rhetorical' module. This is a 'persuader' module that seeks to penetrate H's cheater detector and source tagger. It can display authority and simulate consistency. Again, one must assume that this module too works both ways: that is, it works for S's goals but also for H's defences as a counter-persuader ability. This last point is rather interesting for CDA, since it postulates.

> ...the development of the ability to scrutinise these argumentative displays
> and to find fault with them.   (Sperber 2000:136)

In other words, humans may already have a critical instinct, even perhaps something like a module for CDA. Naturally, people may not use it. But, firstly, to say that people do not use it, makes a claim that needs substantiating. Do they not? The question is not simple, because recognising failure to deploy critical ability requires criteria that would certainly be highly disputable. Secondly, if people do not, or do not all, or do not all of the time, this would not demonstrate an innate critical potential does not exist. Thirdly, if the claim is that people have the critical potential but do not use it, then what we need to know is under which conditions is this the case? Historians, political scientists and other disciplines can do this job as well as, or better than CD analysts. One of CDA's claims seems to be that it is primarily something about the *discourse* (utterances) that hampers the use of the human critical potential and promotes nefarious notions. This claim has not been substantiated. Nor has CDA developed any detailed theory of how cognitive influence might occur as result of discourse input to a human brain. The cognitive theory outlined in this section is a very modest step in addressing this deficit in CDA.

11.   Implications for CDA

Whether the proposals of Sperber, Cosmides and others are valid can of course only rest on further empirical and theoretical work. But sufficient work already exists for the claims to be worthy of consideration.

In this paper we have (a) argued that CDA cannot neglect the cognitive aspect of communication, (b) rapidly summarised some recent work in the field of evolutionary cognitive psychology, (c) rapidly summarised one recent approach in cognitive linguistics, and (d) applied a blend of (b) and (c) to one aspect of an extreme form of racist discourse. This review and application yields two main points. First, the combined cognitive framework can go beyond description and put forward suggestive explanatory stories. Second, the combined cognitive framework raises questions about the status and direction of CDA itself.

What then are the issues for the status and direction of CDA?

i.   The combined framework of cognitive evolutionary psychology and CL yields insights into human nature and human societies that CDA itself has not provided. It may be that CDA, given its adopted methods and goals and the linguistic theories it has predominantly drawn on, may be incapable of going beyond description. I am thinking here primarily of the kinds of CDA which take their theoretical frames predominantly from social theory, without the incorporation of cognitive perspectives, and which also draw in rather limited ways on heavily socialised linguistic models. I exclude those less prominent currents that place cognition at the core and which do draw, to varying degrees, on psychology and on cognitive linguistics.

ii.   Even if we accept only very tentatively the modular model of mind, and the particular modules for which there is evidence or at least plausible deductive arguments, the consequences for CDA as a socially oriented, possibly emancipatory enterprise, have to be re-examined. Put bluntly, if people have a natural ability to treat verbal input critically, in what sense can CDA either reveal in discourse what people can (by the hypothesis) already detect for themselves or educate them to detect it for themselves? There are obvious responses to this question. One might be that, granted a 'critical discourse' module, such a module still needs to be activated and developed. There are problems with such a move, however. One is that it places CDA in a position of responsibility and perhaps power, if an educating or developing role is granted to CDA practitioners. Another is the problem of knowing what sort of technical analysis CDA could conceivably provide that could give what is required for someone to develop their critical discourse module. Stock responses to CDA include the charge that it is stating the obvious and that no technical apparatus is needed anyway to point out what is not perhaps obvious. Such responses might be taken to suggest that people are indeed aware of the existence of their own critical faculties. Moreover, taking the point that technical apparatus is not needed, this means (a) that CDA has no core scientific programme of discovery or elaboration and then (b) also that its ability to bring strategic and tactical language use to awareness may be no greater than that possessed by the non-expert and that it is merely engaging in ordinary political language use.

iii. The last set of points could be taken to imply that the focal research question might be formulated as the question: What prevents people using their innate cheater-detecting logico-rhetorical modules to protect their own interests? I am suggesting that the answer is not that they cannot analyse the verbal input and need help in spotting, for example, nominalisations or agent-less passives, or intertextual cross-overs. Next to nothing is known about whether such things do really have any cognitive effects and thus social action effects. What is clear, however, is that under certain social, economic and political conditions people may not be able, or may not be willing, to respond critically. One can imagine many such conditions, but it is doubtful that any of them can be elucidated by purely linguistic or discourse-analytical means. For they would seem to have to do with economic forces or socio-political institutions that restrict freedom of expression and freedom of access to information, without which you cannot use your source-tagging abilities, your cheat detector, your consistency checker, etc. This is not to deny the central importance of linguistic communication, but it does cast doubt on whether technical or theoretical research or description in CDA has any special social role. In fact, if the preceding argument is correct – that it is institutional or economic restrictions on communicative freedom that is crucial, then what is needed is historical, social, economic and political analysis not the analysis of language itself. And, interestingly enough, it is Chomsky, whose linguistic models have no social or political critique, who has provided an analysis of the restrictions on expression and access in modern capitalist societies ('A propaganda model' in Herman & Chomsky 1988: 1–35).[8]

iv. The last paragraph argues that CDA's would-be theoretical and technical analyses of text and talk may have no direct bearing on social and political conditions. It may be that it could carry a pedagogical role, but in that case it may be doing no more than any politically aware person. If it does set research goals, within the normal understanding of research in the western scholarly and scientific tradition, then it may necessarily separate itself from social and political goals. The route that has been indicated in the bulk of the present paper goes in the direction of deductively elaborating empirical and theoretical research, and also exploring phenomena like racism from within that paradigm. What I have suggested about racism in Section 9 is of no obvious use in combating racism. If it has any value it is of a scientific kind, in so far as it sketches a hypothesis as to how certain conceptual structures take hold in the mind and spread.[9] There remain questions about the socio-economic and political conditions under which certain cognitive effects take hold of whole populations by way of verbal communications (and perhaps other systems), but these are not specifically linguistic matters on which language experts can pronounce. There remain, too, profound philosophical questions about volition, agency and ethical responsibility.

The upshot of these ruminations is that CDA may not be the field within which the most perplexing questions can be pursued that concern the nature of the human mind, of human language, of human language use and of human society.

Notes

1. I am most grateful to Patricia Chilton, Bill Downes, Ron Scollon and Ruth Wodak for critical discussion to do with ideas in this paper. This does not mean that they would agree with anything I say in it.

2. See below on cognitive science and cognitive linguistics in a socio-critical context. It is important also to mention the important work inspired by pragmatics produced by Verschueren, Blommaert, Bulcaen (Blommaert & Verschueren 1998; Blommaert & Bulcaen 1997), who have tended to keep their distance both from mainstream CDA and from Hallidayan linguistics (see Verschueren 2001). Downes (2002) points out that Hallidayan

systemic-functional grammar fails to take account of inferencing and world knowledge in human language understanding. He also argues that CDA fails to resolve the tension between CDA's claim to reveal social functions of discourse and speakers' conscious intentions and rationalisations. These points are somewhat related to O'Halloran's (2003) arguments that the presence of items and structures in text is not necessarily related to the cognitions established by the reader/hearer on the basis of such text features, as well as to his general application of the distinction between low-effort shallow reading and high-effort interest-oriented reading of texts.

3. The more cognitively oriented linguists concerned with social issues do, I think, assume something like this argument; but these are not the authors typically associated with the central tendency of CDA.

4. The theories in cognitive linguistics referred to have developed quite independently of the theories of modularity discussed earlier.

5. Interestingly, such an approach takes us back to the origins of the term *idéologie* as used by Destutt de Tracy, *Eléments d'idéologie* (1817–1818).

6. Cf. Chilton, 'Manipulation, memes and metaphors: The case of *Mein Kampf*' in L. de Saussure, ed. (forthcoming).

7. The mechanisms by which 'recruiting' occurs are not specified by Fauconnier and Turner, but it seems likely that there is overlap between modular knowledge frames. For example, there is at least a culture-based naive medicine frame that intersects with the naive zoology module. Relevance principles may also apply.

8. It has been pointed out to me by Ruth Wodak that in certain highly structured social spheres, e.g. doctor-patient communication, educational institutions; discourse behaviour has been changed as a result of CDA-type activity. This may be correct. However, there is a risk in such claims of drawing CDA's own charge of the 'technologisation of discourse' (cf. Fairclough 1989, 1995, 2003).

9. 'Epidemiologically', Sperber would say (Sperber 1994); cf. also Dawkins on 'memes' (1999) and Chilton (forthcoming).

References

Allott, N. (forthcoming). "The role of misused concepts". In L. de Saussure (Ed.), *New Perspectives on Manipulation and Ideologies: Theoretical Aspects*. Amsterdam: John Benjamins.

Asher, N. & Lascarides, A. (2003). *Logics of Conversation*. Cambridge: Cabridge University Press.

Atran, S. (1990). *Cognitive Foundations of Natural History*. Cambridge: Cambridge University Press.

Atran, S. (1994). "Core domains versus scientific theories: Evidence from systematics and Itza-Maya folklbiology". In L. A. Hirschfeld & S. A. Gelman (Eds.), *Mapping the Mind*. Cambridge: Cambridge University Press.

Barkow, J. H., Cosmides, L., & Tooby, J. (1992). *The Adapted Mind*. New York: Oxford University Press.

Baron-Cohen, S. (2001). *Mindblindness: An Essay on Autism and Theory of Mind*. Cambridge, MA: MIT Press.

Blommaert, J. & Bulcaen, C. (Eds.). (1997). *Political Linguistics*. Amsterdam: John Benjamins.

Blommaert, J. & Verschueren, J. (1998). *Debating Diversity*. London: Routledge.

Boroditsky, L. (1997). "Evidence for Metaphoric representation: perspective in space and time". In M. G. Shafto & P. Langley (Eds.), *Proceedings of the Nineteenth Annual Conference of the Cognitive Science Society*. Mahwah, NJ: Erlbaum.

Boyer, P. (1990). *Tradition as Truth and Communication*. Cambridge: Cambridge University Press.

Byrne, R. (1995). *Thinking Ape. Evolutionary Origins of Intelligence*. Oxford: Oxford University Press.

Byrne, R. & Whiten, A. (Eds.). (1988). *Machiavellian Intelligence. Social Expertise and the Evolution of Intellect in Monkeys, Apes and Humans*. Oxford: Clarendon Press.

Caldas-Coulthard, C.-R. & Coulthard, M. (1996). *Texts and Practices: Readings in Critical Discourse Analysis*. London: Routledge.

Chomsky, N. (1988). *Knowledge of Language: Its Nature, Origin and Use*. Cambridge, MA: MIT Press.

Chilton, P. (1996a). *Security Metaphors*. New York: Peter Lang.

Chilton, P. (1996b). "The meaning of security". In F. A. Beer & R. Hariman (Eds.), *Post-Realism: The Rhetorical Turn in International Relations*. East Lansing: Michigan State University Press.

Chilton, P. (2002). "Manipulation". In J. Verschueren, J.-O. Östman, J. Blommaert, & C. Bulcaen (Eds.), *Handbook of Pragmatics*. Amsterdam/Philadelphia: John Benjamins.

Chilton, P. (forthcoming). "Manipulation, memes and metaphors: The case of *Mein Kampf*". In L. de Saussure (Ed.), *New Perspectives on Manipulation and Ideologies: Theoretical Aspects*. Amsterdam: John Benjamins.

Chilton, P. & Lakoff, G. (1999 [1995]). "Foreign policy by metaphor". In C. Schäffner & A. Wenden (Eds.), *Language and Peace*. Hawood: Academic Publishers.

Cosmides, L. (1989). "The logic of social exchange: Has natural selection shaped how humans reason? Studies with the Wason Selection Task". *Cognition, 31*, 187–276.

Cosmides, L. & Tooby, J. (1992). "Cognitive adaptations for social exchange." In J. Barkow, L. Cosmides, & J. Tooby (Eds.), *The Adapted Mind*. New York: Oxford University Press.

Cosmides, L. & Tooby, J. (2000). "Consider the source: The evolution of adaptations for decoupling and metarepresentations". In D. Sperber (Ed.), *Metarepresentations*. Oxford: Oxford University Press.

Dawkins, R. (1999 [1976]). *The Selfish Gene*. Oxford: Oxford University Press.

Dirven, R., Frank, R., & Ilie, C. (Eds.). (2001). *Language and Ideology. Volume II: Descriptive Cognitive Approaches*. Amsterdam: John Benjamins.

Discourse and Society (2000). Volume 11, number 1, ed. R. Wodak, special issue on discourse and racism.

Downes, W. (2002). "Linguistic criticism and functional explanation". [unpublished ms]

Ehlich, K. (Ed.). (1989). *Sprache im Faschismus*. Frankfurt: Suhrkamp.

Fairclough, N. (1989). *Language and Power.* London: Longman.

Fairclough, N. (Ed.). (1992). *Critical Language Awareness.* London: Longman.

Fairclough, N. (1995). *Critical Discourse analysis: The Critical Study of Language.* London: Longman.

Fairclough, N. (2003). *Analyzing Discourse: Textual Analysis for Social Research.* London: Routledge.

Fairclough, N. & Wodak, R. (1997). "Critical discourse analysis". In T. van Dijk (Ed.), *Discourse as Social Interaction* (pp. 258–284). London: Sage.

Fauconnier, G. (1997). *Mappings in Thought and Language.* Cambridge: Cambridge University Press.

Fauconnier, G. & Turner, M. (1996). "Blending as a central process of grammar". In A. E. Goldberg (Ed.), *Conceptual Structure, Discourse and Language.* Stanford, CA: CSLI Publications.

Fauconnier, G. & Turner, M. (2002). *The Way We Think: Conceptual Blending and the Mind's Hidden Complexities.* New York: Basic Books.

Fodor, J. (1983). *The Modularity of Mind.* Cambridge, MA: MIT Press.

Fodor, J. (1985). "Précis of 'The Modularity of Mind'". *Behavioral and Brain Sciences, 8,* 1–42.

Fowler, R. (1996). *Linguistic Criticism.* Oxford: Oxford University Press.

Fowler, R. (1996). "On critical linguistics". In C. R. Caldas-Coulthard & M. Coulthard (Eds.), *Texts and Practices. Readings in Critical Discourse Analysis* (pp. 3–14). London: Routledge.

Fowler, R., Hodge, G., & Kress, G. (1979). *Language and Control.* London: Routledge and Kegan Paul.

Gelman, S. A., Coley, J. D., & Gottfried, G. M. (1994). "Essentialist beliefs in children: the acquisition of beliefs and theories". In L. A. Hirschfeld & S. A. Gelman (Eds.), *Mapping the Mind.* Cambridge: Cambridge University Press.

Gibbs, R. (1994). *The Poetics of Mind: Figurative thought, Language and Understanding.* Cambridge: Cambridge University Press.

Herman, E. S. & Chomsky, N. (1988). *Manufacturing Consent: the Political Economy of the Mass Media.* London: Vintage Books.

Hirschfeld, L. A. & Gelman, S. A. (Eds.). (1994). *Mapping the Mind: Domain Specificity in Cognition and Culture.* Cambridge: Cambridge University Press.

Hirschfeld, L. A. (1994). "Is the acquisition of social categories based on domain-specific competence or on knowledge transfer?" In L. A. Hirschfeld & S. A. Gelman (Eds.), *Mapping the Mind.* Cambridge: Cambridge University Press.

Hodge, R. & Kress, G. (1993 [1979]). *Language as Ideology.* London: Routledge.

Humphrey, N. (1976). "The social function of intellect". In P. P. G. Bateson & R. A. Hinde (Eds.), *Growing Points in Ethology.* Cambridge: Cambridge University Press.

Johnson, M. (1987). *The Body in the Mind.* Chicago: Chicago University Press.

Kamp, H. & Reyle, U. (1993). *From Discourse to Logic.* Dordrecht: Kluwer.

Karmiloff-Smith, A. (1992). *Beyond Modularity.* Cambridge, MA: MIT Press.

Keil, F. (1994). "The birth and nurturance of concepts by domains: the origins of concepts of living things". In L. A. Hirschfeld & S. A. Gelman (Eds.), *Mapping the Mind.* Cambridge: Cambridge University Press.

Kennedy, J. S. (1992). *The New Anthropomorphism*. Cambridge: Cambridge University Press.

Keysar, B., Yeshayahu, S., Glucksberg, S., & Horton, W. S. (2000). "Conventional language: how metaphorical is it?". *Journal of Memory and Language, 43*, 576–593.

Lakoff, G. (1987). *Women, Fire and Dangerous Things*. Chicago: Chicago University Press.

Lakoff, G. (1991). "Metaphor in Politics". An open letter to the Internet from George Lakoff, http://philosophy.uoregon.edu/metaphor/lakoff-l.htm, accessed 29.03.04.

Lakoff, G. (1996). *Moral Politics. What Conservatives Know that Liberals Don't*. Chicago: Chicago University Press.

Lakoff, G. (1999). *Philosophy in the Flesh*. London: Basic Books.

Lakoff, G. (2003). "Metaphor and war, again", http://www.alternet.org/story.html?StoryID=15414, accessed 29.03.04.

Lakoff, G. & Johnson, M. (1980). *Metaphors We Live By*. Chicago: Chicago University Press.

Lakoff, G. & Johnson, M. (1999). *Philosophy in the Flesh*.

Lakoff, G. & Turner, M. (1989). *More than Cool Reason: A Field Guide to Poetic Metaphors*. Chicago: University of Chicago Press.

Leslie, A. (1991). "The theory of mind impairment in autism: evidence for a modular mechanism of development". In A. Whiten (Ed.), *Natural Theories of Mind: Evolution and Development and Simulation of Everyday Mindreading*. Oxford: Blackwell.

Mithen, S. (1996). *The Prehistory of the Mind: A Search for the Origins of Art, Religion and Science*. London: Thames and Hudson.

O'Halloran, K. (2003). *Critical Discourse Analysis and Language Cognition*. Edinburgh: Edinburgh University Press.

Reisigl, M. & Wodak, R. (2001). *Discourse and Discrimination*. London: Routledge.

Rohrer, T. (1995). "The metaphorical logic of (political) rape: The new wor(l)d order". *Metaphor and Symbolic Activity, 10*(2), Spring 1995.

Santa Ana, O. (2002). *Brown tide Rising: Metaphors of Latinos in Contemporary American Public Discourse*. Austin, TX: University of Texas press.

Saussure, L. de (forthcoming). *New Perspectives on Manipulation and Ideologies: Theoretical Aspects*. Amsterdam: John Benjamins.

Shapiro, M. (Ed.). (1984). *Language and Politics*. Oxford: Blackwell.

Spelke (1991). "Physical knowledge in infancy: reflections on Piaget's theory". In S. Carey & R. Gelman (Eds.), *Epigenesis of Mind: Studies in Biology and Culture*. Hilldale, NJ: Erlbaum.

Sperber, D. (1994). "The modularity of thought and the epidemiology of representation". In L. A. Hirschfeld & S. A. Gelman (Eds.), *Mapping the Mind* (pp. 39–67). Cambridge: Cambridge University Press.

Sperber, D. (2000). "Metarepresentation in an evolutionary perspective". In D. Sperber (Ed.), *Metarepresentations, A multidisciplinary perspective*. Oxford: Oxford University Press.

Sperber, D. (Ed.). (2000). *Metarepresentations. A Multidisciplinary Perspective*. Oxford: Oxford University Press.

Thibault, P. (1986). "Text, discourse and context: towards a social semiotic perspective". *Toronto Semiotic Circle Monographs, 3*.

Turner, M. (2001). *Cognitive Dimensions of Social Science*. Oxford: Oxford University Press.

van Dijk, T. (1977). *Text and Context: Explorations in the Semantics and Pragmatics of Discourse*. New York: Longman.

van Dijk, T. (1980). *Macrostructures: An Interdisciplinary Study of Global Structures in Discourse, Interaction, and Cognition.* Mahwah, NJ: Erlbaum.

van Dijk, T. (1984). *Prejudice in Discourse.* Amsterdam: Benjamins.

van Dijk, T. (1991). *Racism and the Press: Critical Studies in Racism and Migration.* London: Routledge.

van Dijk, T. (1993a). *Elite Discourse and Racism.* Newbury Park, CA: Sage.

van Dijk, T. (Ed.). (1993b). *Critical Discourse Analysis,* Special Issue. *Discourse and Society, 4*(2).

van Dijk, T. (1998). *Ideology. A Multidisciplinary Approach.* London: Sage.

van Dijk, T. (1998). "Context models in discourse processing". In H. Oostendorp & S. Goldman (Eds.), *The Construction of Mental Models during Reading* (pp. 123–148). Hilsdale, NJ: Erlbaum.

van Dijk, T. (2004). "Text and context of parliamentary debates". In P. Bayley (Ed.), *Cross-Cultural Perspectives on Parliamentary Discourse.* Amsterdam: Benjamins.

van Dijk, T. (forthcoming). "Contextual knowledge management in discourse production: A CDA perspective". In R. Wodak & P. Chilton (Eds.), *A New Research Agenda in CDA: Theory and Multidisciplinarity.* Amsterdam: Benjamins.

van Dijk, T. & Kintsch, W. (1983). *Strategies of Discourse Comprehension.* New York: Academic Press.

van Leeuwen, T. (1996). "The representation of social actors". In C. R. Caldas-Coulthard (Ed.), *Texts and Practices.* London: Routledge.

Verschueren, J. (2001). "Predicaments of criticism". *Critique of Anthropology, 21*(1), 59–81.

Waal, F. de (1982). *Chimpanzee Politics.* London: Jonathan Cape.

Weiss, G. & Wodak, R. (Eds.). (2003). *Critical Discourse Analysis: Theory and Interdisciplinarity.* Basingstocke: Palgrave Macmillan.

Werth, P. (1999). *Text Worlds: Representing Conceptual Space in Discourse.* London: Longman.

Whiten, A. (Ed.). (1991). *Natural Theories of Mind: Evolution, Development and Simulation of Everyday Mindreading.* Oxford: Blackwell.

Wodak, R. (1986). "Normal and deviant texts. The sociopsychological theory of textplanning." In Y. Tobin (Ed.), *From Sign to Text.* Amsterdam: Benjamins.

Wodak, R. (Ed.). (1989). *Language, Power and Ideology.* Amsterdam: Benjamins.

Wodak, R. (1996). *Disorders of Discourse.* London: Longman.

Wodak, R. (2000). "The rise of racism: An Austrian or a European problem". *Discourse and Society, 11*(1), 5–6.

Wodak, R. & Meyer, M. (Eds.). (2001). *Methods of Critical Discourse Analysis.* London: Sage.

CHAPTER 3

Critical discourse analysis in transdisciplinary research

Norman Fairclough
Lancaster University

In this paper I shall be advancing a particular view of interdisciplinary research as "transdisciplinary" (Dubiel 1985; Halliday 1993; Kellner 1989). A transdisciplinary approach is distinguished on the one hand from forms of interdisciplinary research which assemble diverse disciplinary resources (theories, methods) for particular research projects without expecting or seeking any substantive change in these resources or in the relationship between them as a result, and on the other hand from aspirations towards "post-disciplinarity" which do not confront the thorny theoretical and methodological problems involved in transcending disciplinary boundaries. A transdisciplinary approach asks "how a dialogue between two disciplines or frameworks may lead to a development of both through a process of each internally appropriating the logic of the other as a resource for its own development" (Chiapello & Fairclough 2002).

The paper which this quotation comes from was an attempt at such a transdisciplinary dialogue between critical discourse analysis (CDA) and "the new sociology of capitalism", represented by an influential book on the "new spirit of capitalism" by Boltanski and Chiapello (1999). One objective of the paper was to explore how such a dialogue might help the latter to enrich its analysis of the processes and change it is concerned with in the textual materials in its research base (bodies of management texts from the 1960s and 1990s). We approached this by conceptualizing the "new spirit of capitalism" in CDA terms as an "order of discourse", a distinctive articulation of discourses, genres and styles.

In this paper I shall pursue a transdisciplinary dialogue in another though not unrelated direction, that of recent sociological theory and research on governance (Jessop 2002; Robertson 2002) which is already working with CDA. The aim is to continue a dialogue which is already in process. I shall begin summarizing certain aspects of this research, and then discuss some ways in which the existing presence of CDA within the political economic and state/governance theories these scholars are using might be further developed and enhanced. I shall then discuss how the theoretical framework and analytical categories of CDA can be developed through such dialogue, referring in particular to the category of "genre" and genre analysis. I shall conclude by arguing that a transdisciplinary approach accords with the dialectical view of discourse in its relation with other (non-discoursal) elements of social life which is a feature of the version of CDA I work with.

Some recent research on governance

The aim of Jessop's book (2002) is to "elaborate the theoretical foundations of a research agenda on the capitalist type of state in contemporary capitalism", not to analyse particular cases in detail. Its concern is with the relationship between economic and non-economic preconditions for capital accumulation, on the premise of "the inherent improbability of stable capital accumulation based solely on market forces". It considers "the main contributions of the capitalist type of state in conjunction with other non-market mechanisms in securing crucial preconditions for accumulation". Its focus is on "the structural coupling and co-evolution of accumulation regimes and political regimes". The book is based upon a critical realist philosophy of science. What makes it of particular interest to discourse analysts is that one of the four main theoretical perspectives which it draws upon, and which are seen as consistent with or open to appropriation within critical realist analysis, is critical discourse analysis. The others are: the regulation approach to the political economy of capitalism, a theory of the state and politics in the tradition of Gramsci and Poulantzas, and Luhmann's autopoietic systems theory.

This is a significant book for critical discourse analysts, because here we have a major social theorist who offers a distinctive vision of the relationship between discoursal and non-discoursal moments of social processes in contemporary social transformations, in particular, of "the contribution of discourse to the construction of the capitalist economy as an object of regulation and of the national state as an imagined institutional ensemble". It is a different vision from that of, for instance Laclau (Laclau & Mouffe 1985) in that it accommodates the discoursal moment of social processes, relations and transformations while avoiding a reduction of them to discourse. The book does not offer models for critical discourse analysis, no concrete texts or interactions are analysed, it addresses the political economy of capitalism at a relatively high level of abstraction from concrete events. But it speaks to theoretical assumptions about the relationship between discourse and other moments of the social which underpin critical discourse analysis, and more concretely it points to how critical discourse analysts might fruitfully contribute to critical research on aspects of "new capitalism" (see the Language in New Capitalism website, http://www.cddc.vt.edu/host/lnc/).

I cannot do full justice to the theoretical framework which is developed in the book, nor is that my intention. I shall focus on Jessop's treatment of discourse. A way into how discourse is viewed in this theory is through its perspective on crises, its view of discourse in the transformation of accumulation regimes and state forms, of the discursive mediation of crisis (see especially pages 92–94).

A crisis emerges when existing structural forms and their ways of containing contradictions no longer work as expected, and a crisis becomes acute when crisis tendencies accumulate across structures. Such moments create the space for strategic interventions to significantly redirect the course of events (or to protect the existing "fix"). The dialectic between structures and strategies (i.e. between structure and agency) is fundamental in this theory – structures constrain but do not determine strategies, structures are produced and reproduced through strategies, structures can be transformed through strategies. Moments of crisis open up struggles for hegemony between competing strategies. But strategies "are always elaborated in and through discourses", different "narratives that seek to give meaning to current problems by construing them in terms of past failures and future possibilities". (Narratives are discourse-relative i.e. narratives are the "stories" of crisis associated with particular discourses.)

Discourses (and narratives) "simplify" ("translate" and "condense" in the terms of Harvey 1996; see Fairclough & Thomas forthcoming) economic and political relations – the latter are so complex that any action oriented towards them requires "discursive simplification", a selectivity in terms of what is included and excluded, hence the constitution of discourses as "imaginaries". Which competing discourses (narratives, imaginaries), which strategies, succeed in establishing themselves depends upon a number of factors. First, "structural selectivities": structures are more open to some strategies than to others. Second, the scope and "reach" of the discourse (narrative) – for instance, the discourses of "globalization" or "knowledge-based economy" might be seen as "nodal discourses" which articulate many other discourses (e.g. those we can sum up with the labels "lifelong learning", "social exclusion", "flexibility"). Third, the differential capacities and power of the social agents whose strategy it is "to get their messages across", e.g. their access to and control over mass media and other channels and networks for diffusion. Fourth, the "resonance" of discourses, their capacity to mobilize people, not only in the institutions but also in the lifeworld.

Discourses (and narratives) have non-discursive effects. Thus "the economy as an object of regulation is viewed as an imaginatively narrated system", and "the state system is treated as an imagined political entity", and discourses "have a key role in the always tendential constitution and consolidation of the economic, political and other systems, shaping the forms of their institutional separation and subsequent articulation". This does not imply that either economies or states are "just discourse", for discourses "help modify their institutional materiality". On the other hand, it does imply that regimes of accumulation and types of state are "co-constituted" (alongside other non-discursive constitutive factors) by discourses (narratives, imaginaries). Discourses also work as rhetoric – for instance, neo-liberal narratives of globalization whose imaginaries are used to legitimize unpopular policies such as cuts in the "social wage".

Let me turn more briefly to Robertson, who also draws upon CDA in her work on governance of education at a European Union level (Robertson 2002). Robertson and her collaborators argue that

> categories such as 'the European economy' and 'European competitiveness' are not self-evident entities. Rather, they are social constructions that are worked at discursively and materially to embed a set of social relations at a new scale – the supranational. … as we have argued elsewhere in relation to the World Trade Organisation – a powerful agent engaged in the construction of a 'global' scale of governance – spaces and their territories, like the 'global' or the 'national' are not neutral containers; they are themselves constructed and reconstructed, spaces that are mapped as places which are, on the one hand, governed and, on the other, lived in and through social relationships and social relations.   (Robertson, Bonal, & Dale 2002)

Similarly, Rosamond (2002), in an analysis of the construction of a competitive Europe, argues that "imagining the European economy" is a rhetorical strategy as part of a more complex process of constructing a regime of economic governance being developed around the European Union.

According to Robertson (2002),

we can see how the constant narration of ideas like a 'European education space', a 'competitive and knowledge based economy' and 'public private partnerships', as well as the institutions engaged with their narration, come to be viewed as commonsense ideas at a scale that sits beyond the national and the local. We can also see the way these ideas are scaffolded into existence and sedimented into institutions and operative networks as material practices through additional policy manoeuvres such as benchmarking. Finally we can see how these strategies privilege particular kinds of interests and institutional arrangements (as in the eLearning Summit Taskforce and the subsequent development of *Career Space*) and embed a particular kind of framework for action, a particular type of commonsense.

Both Jessop and Robertson – though Jessop more explicitly than Robertson – envisage a "dialectics of discourse" (Harvey 1996), a dialectical relationship between discourse and non-discursive elements of social life which has the following cyclical character, with a process of political struggle mediating the "internalisation" of non-discursive in discursive elements, and discursive in non-discursive elements.

A. Emergence of discourses/narratives as "translations/condensations" (Harvey 1996) or "simplifications" of complex realities (including non-discursive elements) in association with strategies to redirect (including "re-scale") those realities.
B. A political process of gaining "plausibility" for discourses/narratives, diffusion, hegemonic struggle.
C. Discursive reconstruction of (non-discursive elements of) realities, materialization, institutionalization, enactment ("scaffolding", "framework for action") and inculcation ("common sense").

Enhancing research on governance through developing the dialogue with CDA

I want now to indicate some ways in which the existing uptake and incorporation of CDA within this research on governance can be developed – how CDA can further enhance this work in its discourse aspect, both theoretically (I shall discuss in particular the category of "genre") and methodologically (through interdiscursive and linguistic analysis of text).

Genre

Jessop and Robertson, like many social scientists, see "discourse" in the abstract sense (discourse as an element of the social, in particular relations with non-discursive elements) solely in terms of "discourses" in the sense of particular ways of representing aspects of the world. We might say that discourse is reduced to discourses. This is such a common reduction, and in many cases confusion, that it makes sense to find a different term for discourse in the abstract sense ("semiosis" is used in this way in Fairclough, Jessop, & Sayer 2004). In my more recent work (e.g. Fairclough 2003) I have argued that semiosis (discourse in the abstract sense) figures in three main ways in social events and practices: in representing the world, as a modality of acting and interacting (and the associated social relations), and in identifying, i.e. constructing social and personal identities. Correspondingly, there are more or less durable ways of representing ("discourses"), ways of (inter)acting semiotically ("genres"), and ways of being or identities in their semiotic aspect ("styles"). I want to comment in particular on the importance of attending to genres as well as discourses in research on governance.

The semiotic resources for strategic success in Jessop's account of crisis already covertly include resources with respect to genres, as well as explicitly resources with respect to discourses (which need to have properties of nodality, resonance etc.), though this is not immediately obvious. The factors conditioning strategic success include the differential capacities and power of the social agents whose strategy it is "to get their messages across", e.g. their access to and control over mass media and other channels and networks for diffusion. If one considers this in semiotic terms, the capacity and power of social agents to "get their message across" includes their capacity with respect to genres, their "generic power", their capacity to access and control for instance news genres and genres of publicity and advertising. Strategic success entails capacities with respect to mediation, "acting at a distance", which in turn entail capacities with respect to ways of acting and interacting, i.e. in semiotic terms, genres.

Similarly Robertson's account of strategies for opening up a space of governance of education at a European Union level (i.e. creating a level at which the EU can directly intervene in regulating education within the Union) includes "ideas" such as the "knowledge-based economy" being "scaffolded into existence and sedimented into institutions and operative networks as material practices through additional policy manoeuvres such as benchmarking". In semiotic terms, this points to the dialectical process whereby discourses ("ideas") such as the discourse of the "knowledge-based economy" are operationalized ("scaffolded", "sedimented") as ways of acting and interacting, practices, procedures, whose semiotic element is again genres. "Imagining" a European economy, a "knowledge-based economy", is in dialectical terms a semiotic "moment" (i.e. an element which is dialectically related to other elements, Fairclough, Jessop, & Sayer 2004) in constructing a new "regime of governance". But the moment of semiosis is not limited to imaginaries: a "regime of governance" has itself a partly semiotic character, for it includes new genres, and can indeed be conceptualized semiotically as a distinctive network of genres (interconnected ways of acting and interacting).

Robertson's data show that discourses which construct imaginary spaces of/for governance tend in so doing to construct/imagine "frameworks for action", procedures which network social practices (activities) in particular ways. Here for instance is a Recommendation from the Summit Declaration of the European eLearning Summit (2001):

> Expand eLearning communities and forums
> Best practice has been identified and knowledge networks are starting to appear but what is now needed is an easily accessible inventory (possibly in the form of a portal) that would allow systematic and comprehensive tracking of current developments. Such an information source needs to be put in place quickly and should be promoted by a widespread information campaign. As a next step, an evaluation instrument should be developed to help codify and benchmark best practice and provide indicators on pedagogical innovation.
> (Summit Declaration, European eLearning Summit 2001)

From a semiotic perspective the "framework for action" that is being imagined and envisaged here is a complex set of network relationships between genres. A "knowledge network" is itself a network of ways of acting and interacting, i.e. semiotically a genre network, and what is being imagined is the networking of this genre network with others (identified here as an inventory/portal, an information campaign, and an evaluation instrument).

What I am arguing is that as soon as one gets beneath such abstract descriptors to the practices they signify, the imagined new regime of governance (and any actual regime of governance) shows itself semiotically to be a new set of relations (articulations and intersections) between genres and networks of genres. From this perspective, the possibilities of a semiotic approach to the construction of new regimes of governance are currently underdeveloped in both Robertson's work and Jessop's (though in more recent work Jessop has begun to address questions of genre).

Jessop differentiates three primary modes of governance: hierarchies (e.g. bureaucracies, "imperative coordinated by the state"), markets ("the anarchy of exchange"), and "the heterarchy of self-organization" (e.g. "horizontal networks"). These different modes of governance are from a semiotic perspective different networks of genres – the forms of (inter)action between participants in hierarchies are different from those in markets and in networks (see for instance Sarangi & Slembrouck 1996 on hierarchies). New regimes of governance are increasingly the object of reflexive processes of design within "metagovernance", which states and inter-state institutions like the European Union are increasingly involved in, and they are characteristically "judicious mixtures" of hierarchies, markets and networks. It is a measure of the uneven deployment of a discourse perspective in Jessop's book that the discussion of metagovernance (see especially pages 240–243) takes place without any reference to discourse. Yet from a semiotic perspective metagovernance can be seen as what I have referred to elsewhere as the "technologization of discourse" (Fairclough 1992a) at the highest level – the reflexive redesign of highly complex networks of genres.

Summing up, genres and networks of genres are a crucial semiotic condition of existence for any "action at a distance" and any form of governance, and changes in networks of genres are a crucial part of changes in regimes of governance. Correspondingly, analysis of changes in governance needs to include analysis of genres – limiting the semiotic moment to discourses is missing these crucial semiotic characteristics of regimes of governance. A transdisciplinary perspective does not however simply entail political economists or state theorists borrowing the category of genre from discourse analysts, it involves applying a process analogous to the process Jessop has gone through with the category of "strategy" (reworking it to incorporate a discoursal moment in terms of "discourses" and "narratives") to categories such as "regime" (reworking it to incorporate "genre" and "genre network"). That is, using categories and concepts from other theories in one's own process of theoretical development and elaboration.

Linguistic analysis of texts

Perhaps the greatest divide within discourse studies is between those who see detailed analysis of texts as a sine qua non, and those who do not. A significant part of the dialogue between CDA and various areas of social theory and research is arguments from CDA that a variety of aims and objectives in social research could be further advanced through forms of detailed textual analysis (see Fairclough 1992b, 2003). These include arguments for interdiscursive analysis of texts, for linguistic analysis, and for analysis of other (non-linguistic) semiotic modalities such as visual images. I shall comment on just the first two in this case.

Interdiscursive analysis of texts is analysis of the specific articulations[1] of different discourses, genres and styles (assuming that texts are normally complex – or hybrid, or mixed – with respect to each of these categories) that characterizes a particular text. Interdiscursive analysis contributes to social analysis a mediating level between various forms of social analysis on the one hand, and detailed linguistic analysis of text on the other – mixtures of discourses, genres and styles in a text can for instance on the one hand be mapped onto boundary shifts between different social fields (and so impinge on social issues such as the commodification of arts or education), and on the other hand be seen as realized in lexical, semantic and grammatical heterogeneities. It also takes a profoundly relational view of change – changes in discourses for instance are characteristically not simply the substitution of one discourse for another, but changes in relations between discourses, a new articulation of discourses which includes prior discourses (as we showed in Chiapello & Fairclough 2002). Extracts from one of the texts which Robertson analyses (the Summit Declaration from the EU Lisbon Council) will serve as a brief example:

> the most competitive and dynamic *knowledge-based economy* in the world capable of *sustainable economic growth* with *more and better jobs* and greater *social cohesion.*
>
> To meet these goals, Europe rapidly needs to expand educational *opportunity.* We need to ensure the entire population achieves high educational *standards,* and to embed a *culture* of lifelong learning to respond to evolving *skill* requirements.

The emergent discourse brings together into a particular articulation the italicized elements which can be seen to emanate from a variety of prior discourses, which are found separately from each other elsewhere, but brought together in a distinctive way in the body of texts represented here.

With respect to linguistic analysis,[2] CDA can for instance give greater specificity to the "narratives" which Jessop (like many other social researchers) refers to by pinpointing features of their characteristic modes of textual organisation, or "texturing" (Fairclough 2003). A case in point is contemporary policy narratives of the following sort, which have contributed significantly to the emergence and diffusion of neo-liberal strategies for a new "fix":

The modern world is swept by change. New technologies emerge constantly, new markets are opening up. There are new competitors but also great new opportunities.

Our success depends on how well we exploit our most valuable assets: our knowledge, skills and creativity. These are the key to designing high-value goods and services and advanced business practices. They are at the heart of a modern, knowledge driven economy.

This new world challenges business to be innovative and creative, to improve performance continuously, to build new alliances and ventures. But it also challenges Government: to create and execute a new approach to industrial policy.

That is the purpose of this White Paper. Old-fashioned state intervention did not and cannot work. But neither does naïve reliance on markets.

The Government must promote competition, stimulating enterprise, flexibility and innovation by opening markets. But we must also invest in British capabilities when companies alone cannot: in education, in science and in the creation of a culture of enterprise. And we must promote creative partnerships which help companies: to collaborate for competitive advantage; to promote a long term vision in a world of short term pressures; to benchmark their performance against the best in the world; and to forge alliances with other businesses and employees. All this is the DTI's role.

We will not meet our objectives overnight. The White Paper creates a policy framework for the next ten years. We must compete more effectively in today's tough markets if we are to prosper in the markets of tomorrow.

In Government, in business, in our universities and throughout society we must do much more to foster a new entrepreneurial spirit: equipping ourselves for the long term, prepared to seize opportunities, committed to constant innovation and enhanced performance. That is the route to commercial success and prosperity for all. We must put the future on Britain's side.

Tony Blair (signature)

The Rt Hon Tony Blair MP, Prime Minister

(Foreword to Department of Trade and Industry White Paper 1998)

This text is typical of such narratives in texturing a relation between the "global economy" as fact, and policy prescriptions, between what "is" and what consequently "must" be done. The opening paragraph represents the "global economy" as fact, and characteristic features of such representations include: the representation of "change" as devoid of social agents (so technologies "emerge" and markets are "opening up", there are no social agents – corporations, governments – acting to bring these changes about), of "change" itself as an agent ("the modern world is swept by change"); in terms of modality, categorical assertions of fact, and more specifically of banal truisms ("the world *is swept* by change", "new technologies *emerge*" etc.); the representation of change without temporal or spatial specification or limit – change as taking place in some unlimited ("timeless") present, and spatially universal, indifferent to place; and change represented through a logic of appearances (as a list of evidences) rather than through an explanatory logic which makes causal connections (between, for instance, the pace of technological change and intensified competitiveness). In short, the "change" which constitutes the new "global economy" is simply a given, not attributable to (contingent and therefore changeable) actions or decisions on the part of specific social agents, a mere fact of life, to which we "must" respond in certain ways. Social researchers (including Bourdieu & Wacquant 2001) have commented on the spurious impression in neo-liberal discourse that contemporary economic changes are inevitable and irreversible, but we need such more detailed analyses of narratives of the "global economy" to appreciate how this impression is created.

Jessop points out that any strategy for acting upon highly complex economic and political realities requires "discursive simplification", selectivity in terms of what is included and excluded, and hence the construction of discourses as "imaginaries". Again, the resources of detailed linguistic analysis of texts are called for to give specific accounts of how such simplification and selectivity is achieved. A particularly relevant descriptive framework is available in van Leeuwen's work on representation (1993, 1995, 1996), which has been widely used within CDA, and which can provide precise descriptive accounts of selectivity (inclusion/exclusion, degrees of salience and backgrounding), relative concreteness and abstraction/generalization, as well as such options as generic and specific reference. Van Leeuwen's work is of particular relevance in the context of this paper, because it already constitutes an attempt to develop resources for textual analysis on a transdisciplinary basis, seeking to operationalize in textual analysis, for instance, approaches to legitimation in social theory and research (van Leeuwen & Wodak 1999). Jessop's account of crisis and "discursive simplification" (together with for instance the concepts of "condensation" and "translation" in Harvey's account of the dialectics of discourse, Harvey 1996) constitutes a further transdisciplinary framing and principle of relevance for this approach to the analysis of representation.

Enhancing CDA through transdisciplinary dialogue

The aim in transdisciplinary research is development and enrichment through dialogue of all the disciplines and theories involved. So in this case it is not just a matter of what research on governance can gain from engagement with CDA, but also of what CDA can gain from research on governance. I will illustrate this again with respect to the CDA category of genre. If the category of genre can enhance theorisation of, and research on governance in respect of its discourse moment, the category of genre and the analysis of genres can conversely be enriched by theoretical work on governance and on political economy exemplified by the contributions I have discussed (as well as for instance Pickles & Smith 1998). Such enrichment of genre as a theoretical category and of genre analysis through transdisciplinary dialogue has already been taking place recently within CDA. I shall summarize some salient features of the treatment of genre in the version of CDA I am currently working with (Chouliaraki & Fairclough 1999; Fairclough 2000; Fairclough 2003), noting how this has developed through transdisciplinary dialogue.

As I noted above, genres are seen (e.g. in Fairclough 2000) as ways of (inter)acting in their semiotic aspect. Genres, discourses (ways of representing) and styles (ways of being, identities) are interconnected categories at the level of social practices. Chouliaraki's doctoral research (see Chouliaraki 1995) set up a dialogue between CDA and Bernstein's sociology of pedagogy (Bernstein 1990) which resulted in genres being seen as "framing" devices (with respect to Bernstein's distinction between "framing" and "classification"), institutionalized ways of regulating interaction. A connection was also established between genres and "recontextualization" in Bernstein's sense, the selective appropriation of elements of one social practice within another in accordance with distinctive "recontextualization principles" associated with social practices (for instance, the science of Physics is differently recontextualized as "school Physics" in different pedagogies which have different recontextualizing principles). Relations of recontextualization between social practices can be reconceptualized semiotically as relations of recontextualization between genres in these different social practices (e.g. between political speeches in politics, and news reports in the media), and recontextualizing principles can be seen as attaching to genres. These developments are reflected in Chouliaraki and Fairclough (1999).

Focusing upon recontextualization relations between genres also leads to a view of genres as organised in "chains" or "networks", a perspective which is strengthened through dialogue with organizational studies (Iedema 1999, 2003). Genres in chains or networks are regularly brought into contact through being articulated together in intra-organisational or cross-organisational procedures, routines and practices, and there are regular "movements" between such genres which are regulated by recontextualizing principles which result in predictable transformations, exclusions and additions of "material" moved from one to another. Iedema (1999) has for instance investigated the relationship between stakeholder meetings and official reports emanating from those meetings in such terms. One aspect of these recontextualizing relations is that genre chains or networks operate as "filtering devices" with respect to discourses (see also Fairclough, Jessop, & Sayer 2004), selectively including or excluding discourses in the shift from one genre to another in intra-organisational or cross-organisational processes (thus there are discourses which can figure within stakeholder meetings which are filtered out in official reports). For Bernstein, recontextualization relations are relations of appropriation – the principles according to which one social practice selectively appropriates others. In Chouliaraki and Fairclough (1999), Habermas's views of the colonisation of the lifeworld by systems are brought into the account, and recontextualization is reconceived as a colonisation/appropriation dialectic. Is for instance the recontextualizing relation between political speeches and news reports a relation of colonization of the latter by the former, a relation of appropriation of the former by the latter, or rather – as we suggest – a relation which sets up a dialectic between colonization and appropriation which may be played out in different ways according to a range of contextual factors?

In Fairclough (2003), regimes of governance and metagovernance are seen semiotically as genre networks, and relations of governance and metagovernance as a particular class of relations of recontextualization.

Genres can be classified as governing or governed genres, with the proviso that some genres are both. For example, policy genres such as government White Papers and Green Papers in the UK are genres of government which govern practices and genres (e.g. interviews between welfare officials and claimants) in such domains as welfare provision (Fairclough 2000), though such policy genres themselves may be "meta-governed" in processes of "modernizing government". The way in which the colonization/appropriation dialectic is played out for a particular genre depends upon its position in a regime of (meta)governance – where genres are in a governing/governed relation, appropriation by the former and colonisation of the latter have primacy. Recontextualization "cycles" can be identified wherein governing genres appropriate (and in so doing transform) "material" from governed genres which are then colonized by this transformed "material" – though there is no colonization without potential for appropriation. This corresponds for instance to a common view of the recontextualization relation between (the genres of) management science and (the genres of) practical management.

Developing the category of genre and genre analysis through such transdisciplinary dialogue enhances their capacity to be productively integrated into social research. Let me stress that it is not just a matter of adding categories from other theories and disciplines to CDA, it is a matter of an internal elaboration of categories and relations within CDA which allows such categories to be translated into, operationalized within, new theorisations and methods of analysis which are specifically those of CDA. In the case of recontextualization for instance, it is partly a matter of refocusing genre analysis on relations between genres in chains and networks, the filtering effects of such relations with respect to discourses, and the sort of specific linguistic changes (in forms of argumentation, semantic relations between clauses and sentences, modality, nominalisation of processes, and so forth) which take place when organizational processes involve for instance the "translation" of stakeholder meetings into an official report.

Transdisciplinarity and the dialectics of discourse

The version of CDA which I am currently working with takes a dialectical view of the relationship between semiosis and other (non semiotic) elements of social life, and I want to argue that there is an affinity between such a view of the dialectics of discourse and a transdisciplinary way of conducting interdisciplinary research. Let me first give one summary formulation of the dialectics of discourse – compare my summary with the view of the dialectics of discourse assumed in especially Jessop's work above (see also Fairclough 2000, 2003; Fairclough, Jessop, & Sayer 2004).

1. Semiosis is one element of social life, along with other, non-semiotic, elements.
2. While these elements are different, they are not discrete: they are dialectically related, i.e. non-semiotic elements are "internalised" (Harvey) in semiosis, and vice-versa. (Or, alternatively, there is a relationship of "overdetermination" in the Althusserian sense between them, see Fairclough, Jessop, & Sayer 2004; Fairclough forthcoming.)
3. Social life is reflexive, subject to ongoing processes of discursive representation. Representation of social life in discourses is a selective "translation" and "condensation" (Harvey) and "simplification" (Jessop).

4. Contestation and struggle between strategies for action and change are in part contestation and struggle over discourses, whose outcome is dependent on discoursal (scale, scope and articulatory complexity of discourses; access of social agents to genres, genre chains, styles; resonance of discourses) as well as non-discoursal conditions.

5. ("Successful") discourses may be enacted in new ways of acting and interacting (including new genres), inculcated in ways of being or identities (including new styles), materialized in new technologies, physical environments etc. Wider social change may originate in the imaginaries projected in discourses.

The implications of such a view of the dialectics of discourse for distinctions and relations between academic disciplines in the social and human sciences are twofold. First, since elements of social life are diverse and different, knowledge and understanding of these elements has gained from the development of separate specialist disciplines such as Sociology and Linguistics. Second, since elements of social life are not discrete, since they internalize each other, since they are not "pure" with respect to each other, disciplinary boundaries can also limit and impede knowledge and understanding.

The consequences for interdisciplinary research are that it should be oriented to developing relations between disciplines which enhance their capacity, separately and in collaboration, to address the dialectical nature of the relations between the elements and areas and aspects of social life, while not foregoing the gains associated with specialisation. This is what I have presented as a transdisciplinary approach to interdisciplinary research. One can distinguish the implications of a transdisciplinary approach with respect to theory, to methodology, and to the object of research – all with the object of facilitating elucidation and research of dialectical relations.

> Theory: developing categories within one discipline (e.g. "discourse", "genre") through thinking with categories in other disciplines (e.g. "ideology", "recontextualization", "governance"). A category such as "genre" is primarily discourse-analytical but is overdetermined by categories in other theories/disciplines (framing, recontextualization, regime). Conversely, a category such as "regime" in political economy is discursively overdetermined, i.e. a "regime" is "also" an "order of discourse".

> Methodology: for instance, developing new resources for textual analysis (e.g. van Leeuwen's work on representation; analysis of relations of equiv-

alence and difference, or of time and space, in Fairclough 2003) which help to "operationalize" categories in other disciplines.

Object of research: so designing the objects of research and research agendas of particular disciplines as to facilitate transdisciplinary research – for instance, approaching problems of change in governance through asking how new scales of governance are constituted facilitates transdisciplinary dialogue between discourse analysis, policy studies, and institutional analysis.

A transdisciplinary approach stands in opposition on the one hand to forms of interdisciplinarity which assemble different disciplines around particular themes and projects without any commitment to change the boundaries and relations between them, and on the other hand to declarations of "postdisciplinarity" which do not address the theoretical and methodological work entailed in, for instance, the sort of developments around the concept of genre which I have referred to.

Conclusion: View of CDA

Through focusing on discourse, CDA aims to elucidate the discoursal moment of social processes, practices, and change in its dialectical relations with other moments. It develops its theory, method, and agenda (objects of research) through transdisciplinary dialogue aimed at (a) coherent integration of discourse and discourse analysis (including detailed textual analysis) within social theories and methods of research, (b) development of its own theory of discourse and methods of discourse and text analysis in ways which are consistent with a dialectical view of social reality.

Notes

1. The category of "articulation" is used both in CDA and in Jessop's work, and the source in both cases is Laclau and Mouffe (1985). It is a category within a dialectical-relational view of the social and of social change which sees relations as having primacy over entities – entities are constituted through networks of relations which articulate them together in particular ways. Social change is seen as processes of disarticulating existing articulations of entities, and rearticulating them, i.e. positioning them in new networks of relations. Entities (e.g. discourses) are transformed through these processes of disarticulation and rearticulation –

an entity within one network of relations is different from "the same" entity in another network of relations.

2. In principle any framework for linguistic analysis may be drawn upon in doing CDA. Some researchers in CDA have favoured Systemic Functional Linguistics (see for instance Halliday 1994), but this is a choice based upon their particular academic backgrounds. My purpose here is simply to point to a few aspects of linguistic analysis of texts which might be productively incorporated into research on governance, without assuming any particular framework for linguistic analysis. See Fairclough (2003) for one approach to linguistic analysis of texts, specifically designed for social researchers.

References

Bernstein, B. (1990). *The Structuring of Pedagogic Discourse*. London: Routledge.

Boltanski, L. & Chiapello, E. (1999). *Le nouvel esprit du capitalisme*. Paris: Gallimard.

Bourdieu, P. & Wacquant, L. (2001). "New-Liberal Speak: notes on the new planetary vulgate". *Radical Philosophy, 105*, 2–5.

Chiapello, E. & Fairclough, N. (2002). "Understanding the new management ideology: a transdisciplinary contribution from critical discourse analysis and new sociology of capitalism". *Discourse & Society, 13*(2), 185–208.

Chouliaraki, L. (1995). "Regulation in 'progressivist' pedagogic discourse: individualized teacher-pupil talk". *Discourse & Society, 9*(1), 5–32.

Chouliaraki, L. & Fairclough, N. (1999). *Discourse in Late Modernity*. Edinburgh: Edinburgh University Press.

Dubiel, H. (1985). *Theory and Politics: Studies in the Development of Critical Theory*. Cambridge, MA: MIT Press.

Fairclough, N. (1992a). *Discourse and Social Change*. Cambridge: Polity Press.

Fairclough, N. (1992b). "Discourse and text: linguistic and intertextual analysis within discourse analysis". *Discourse and Society, 3*(2), 193–217.

Fairclough, N. (2000). "Discourse, social theory and social research: the case of welfare reform". *Journal of Sociolinguistics, 4*(2), 163–195.

Fairclough, N. (2003). *Analyzing Discourse: Textual Analysis for Social Research*. London: Routledge.

Fairclough, N. (2004). "Critical discourse analysis in researching language in the New Capitalism: overdetermination, transdisciplinarity and textual analysis". In L. Young & C. Harrison (Eds.), *Systemic Functional Linguistics and Critical Discourse Analysis*. London: Continuum.

Fairclough, N., Jessop, B., & Sayer, A. (2004). "Critical realism and semiosis". In J. Joseph & J. M. Roberts (Eds.), *Realism Discourse and Deconstruction* (pp. 23–42). London: Routledge.

Fairclough, N. & Thomas, P. (forthcoming). "The globalization of discourse and the discourse of globalization". In C. Hardy et al. (Eds.), *Handbook of Organizational Discourse*. Thousand Oaks, CA et al.: Sage.

Halliday, M. (1993). *Language in a Changing World*. Occasional Paper no 13. Applied Linguistics Association of Australia.

Halliday, M. (1994). *An Introduction to Functional Grammar* (2nd edition). London: Edward Arnold.

Harvey, D. (1996). *Justice, Nature and the Geography of Difference*. Cambridge, MA: Blackwell.

Iedema, R. (1999). "Formalising organisational meaning". *Discourse & Society, 10*(1), 49–66.

Iedema, R. (2003). *Discourses of Post-Bureaucratic Organization*. Amsterdam/Philadelphia: John Benjamins.

Jessop, B. (2002). *The Future of the Capitalist State*. Cambridge: Polity.

Kellner, D. (1989). *Critical Theory, Marxism and Modernity*. Cambridge: Polity Press.

Laclau, E. & Mouffe, C. (1985). *Hegemony and Socialist Strategy*. London: Verso.

Muntigl, P., Weiss, G., & Wodak, R. (2000). *European Union Discourses on Un/employment*. Amsterdam/Philadelphia: John Benjamins.

Pickles, J. & Smith, A. (1998). *Theorising Transition: the Political Economy of Post-Communist Transformations*. London: Routledge.

Robertson, S. (2002). *Changing governance/changing equality? Understanding the politics of public-private-partnerships in education in Europe*. Department of Education, University of Bristol.

Robertson S., Bonal, X., & Dale, R. (2002). "GATS and the Education Service Industry: The Politics of Scale and Global Re-territorialisation". *Comparative Education Review, 46*(4), 472–496.

Rosamond, B. (2002). "Imagining the European Economy: 'Competitiveness' and the Social Construction of 'Europe' as an Economic Space". *New Political Economy, 7*(2), 157–177.

Sarangi, S. & Slembrouck, S. (1996). *Language, Bureaucracy and Social Control*. London et al.: Longman.

van Leeuwen, T. (1993). "Genre and field in critical discourse analysis". *Discourse & Society, 4*(2), 193–223.

van Leeuwen, T. (1995). "Representing social action". *Discourse & Society, 6*(1), 81–106.

van Leeuwen, T. (1996). "The representation of social actors". In C. Caldas-Coulthard & M. Coulthard (Eds.), *Texts and Practices: readings in Critical Discourse Analysis* (pp. 32–70). London et al.: Routledge.

van Leeuwen, T. & Wodak, R. (1999). "Legitimizing immigration control: a discourse historical analysis". *Discourse Studies, 1*(1), 83–118.

CHAPTER 4

Contextual knowledge management in discourse production*
A CDA perspective

Teun A. van Dijk
Universitat Pompeu Fabra

Introduction

One of the major contributions of psychology and AI to the theory of discourse has been the fundamental insight that discourse production and comprehension require vast amounts of shared knowledge of the participants. Against the background of various theories about the nature of knowledge representation, it has been proposed that relevant portions of knowledge are being activated and applied in the understanding of words and sentences, the establishment of local coherence, the formation of overall topics or semantic macrostructures, and more generally the generation of any kind of inference, among many other aspects of discourse understanding. Since the production and comprehension of discourse about events and actions, such as stories and news reports, basically involves mental models in episodic memory, and the construction of these models also requires the application of (more or less) knowledge, we may conclude that knowledge in discourse processing is pervasive. This insight has become so obvious that it is sometimes forgotten that until the 1970s this was not a standard part of the theory language processing at all (for details, and among many other studies in the last decades, see, e.g., Britton & Graesser 1996; Clark 1996; Graesser & Bower 1990; Johnson-Laird 1983; Markman 1999; Schank & Abelson 1977; Van Dijk & Kintsch 1983; Van Oostendorp & Zwaan 1994; Wilkes 1997).

Another well-known insight in the theory of discourse is that discourse production and comprehension is context-dependent. Although in many areas of discourse studies this is nearly as trivial an observation as emphasizing the role of knowledge, cognitive psychology has largely ignored this aspect of discourse processing. In linguistics, discourse analysis and the social sciences, the role of context is extensively discussed, but without much explicit theorizing, and thus far without a single monograph on the theory of context (see however Duranti & Goodwin 1992; Leckie-Tarry 1995). In an earlier paper (Van Dijk 1999) I proposed that the role of context in discourse processing should be accounted for in terms of mental models of the relevant dimensions of the communicative event or situation, mental models I called "context models" or simply "contexts".

In the present paper, I shall examine the interface of these two fundamental aspects of discourse processing, namely the way knowledge in discourse production and comprehension is managed as a function of context. It will be argued that contexts, defined as mental models, need a special knowledge component that represents the relevant beliefs of speakers or hearers about the knowledge of their interlocutors. In other words, language users not only need to have general "knowledge of the world", and not only knowledge about the current communicative situation, but of course also mutual knowledge about each others' knowledge. These assumptions are relevant dimensions of the current communicative situation, and hence must be accounted for in a theory of context models. In other words, how do language users actually manage the common ground of knowledge they need in order to be able to be mutually comprehensible. This question of "common knowledge" or "common ground" is hardly new in the theory of language and discourse processing (see, e.g., Clark 1996; Keysar, Barr, Balin, & Paek 1998; Planalp & Garvin-Doxas 1994), but so far has not been explicitly related to a theory of context models. In this respect this paper is intended as a contribution to a new theory of the role of knowledge in discourse processing as well as a contribution to a new theory of context.

A theory of the way knowledge is managed in discourse and interaction is also relevant for critical discourse analysis. Indeed, many of the ways power abuse operates in communication, as is the case for manipulation, involve specific knowledge strategies in discourse. In this sense this theoretical paper is also intended as a contribution to CDA.

The definition of knowledge

The theory of knowledge has been the object for thousands of years of epistemology in various cultures, and of psychology and the social sciences for many decades, and it is therefore impossible to summarize the most important results of so much reflection, theory and research (of the thousands of books on knowledge, I shall cite only the recent reader of Bernecker & Dretske 2000).

I shall therefore merely state my own position in a very long and complex debate, and basically define knowledge in terms of shared beliefs satisfying the specific (epistemic) criteria of an (epistemic) community. This very succinct definition is rather pragmatic and socio-cognitive than philosophical and abstract, and does not feature, for instance, the notion of "truth", as it is used in the traditional definition of knowledge in epistemology as "justified true beliefs". I take truth as a notion that only applies to language use, discourse or speech acts, and not to beliefs. Each community, or historical moment of a community, has its own criteria that allow members to establish that some beliefs are treated and shared as knowledge, whereas others are not. Obviously, these criteria are different in for instance scientific communities and in the "common sense" community of the public at large. One of the empirical criteria is surprisingly simple, and directly relevant in the study of discourse: A belief is treated as knowledge in a community if it is presupposed in the public discourses of that community, for instance in storytelling, songs, or news reports.

Types of knowledge

Both in discourse studies and in the psychology of text processing, we usually deal with one type of more or less abstract and general "knowledge of the world", e.g., the kind of knowledge represented in scripts or similar knowledge structures, and usually assumed to be stored in "semantic" memory. Apart from speculations about the neurological or formal aspects of knowledge representations in memory (or in the brain), there is surprisingly little explicit theorizing about the various types of knowledge. And since it is likely that different kinds of knowledge also may affect discourse processing in different ways, it is crucial to devise an explicit theory of knowledge types. Summarizing a long discussion, I therefore propose that knowledge may be typologically variable along the following criteria, for instance:

–   Scope: personal, interpersonal, group, organization, nation, culture.
–   Specificity: more or less general or specific knowledge.
–   Concreteness: more or less abstract or concrete knowledge.
–   "Reality": More or less "fictional" or knowledge about the "real" world.
–   Objects: The objects of knowledge: people, animals, things, nature, etc.
–   Firmness: More or less "sure" knowledge.

These and other types mix in complex ways, such that we may have, for instance, knowledge shared by the members of an organization about specific, concrete events that actually might have happened, but that might also be a company myth, but which all members nevertheless treat as "real." Much "knowledge of the world" is general, abstract and shared by members of a whole culture. It is this knowledge that is presupposed in the public discourses of that culture.

It will also be assumed that such knowledge is represented in semantic or social memory, and that personal knowledge about specific (autobiographical) events – one's personal memories or experiences – are stored in mental models in episodic memory, and that these different kinds of memories mutually influence each other (Tulving 1983). Thus, our interpersonal knowledge about specific events (such as about the dinner we had last night) may be instances of general, abstract knowledge about dinners, and vice versa, we learn about general properties of eating and dinners by generalizing and abstracting from these more detailed, ad hoc and varied instances. Beyond these elementary notions, we have little idea about the representation formats of all these different kinds of knowledge, and about where and how they are stored in the brain. In fact, we have surprisingly little solid knowledge about knowledge in general!

Context as mental model

It is fairly generally agreed upon that a sound theory of discourse should comprise not only a theory of the structures of text and talk, but also a theory of context, of the relations between text/talk and context and of (re)contextualization processes in general (Auer 1992; Duranti & Goodwin 1992; Gumperz 1982). The notion of context used in most of these approaches in the humanities and social sciences is however quite vague and intuitive, and based on the concept of a social "environment" or "situation" of language use. Such situations would involve categories such as Setting (Time, Place, etc.), Participants in various roles, Actions, and Cognitions (aims, knowledge, opinions, etc.). A context would in that case more specifically be the structure consisting of the *relevant* categories of such a situation, that is, those categories that make a difference (in the production and comprehension) of discourse structures. In other words, contexts have to do with relevance (see also Sperber & Wilson 1995).

There is one major problem with this concept of context. It lacks the cognitive interface that is able to account for subjective "relevance" in the first place: Settings, participant roles or aims of communicative events are not relevant *as such*, but are *defined* as such by the participant themselves. That is, both the definition of the communicative situation as well as the relevance of its properties for discourse production and understanding is not only interactionally but also mentally accomplished. What may be obvious for psychologists is less so for many discourse analysts interested in context, namely that such a social context cannot possibly be "causally" related to text or talk: Social structures, participant roles, actions, time or place, etc. simply have no way to influence discourse directly, and cannot be influenced directly by discourse either. Hence we need a cognitive interface between social situations and discourse. Mental models fit that role perfectly. I therefore define a context as the mental representation of the participants about the relevant properties of the social situation in which participants interact, and produce and comprehend text or talk. This mental representation is called a "context model". Such models are stored in episodic memory, just like any kind of mental model of ongoing events and actions (for details, see Van Dijk 1999). Indeed, context models are just a special case of the kind of mental models that define all our personal experiences and that control all the situations and interactions in which we participate.

Interpreting communicative situations (and "contexts" in the traditional sense) in terms of context models has many advantages. They account for the fact that the different participants may have different interpretations and hence different models of the current situation, and these different context models will also have different effects on what they say or write or on what they understand, possibly also leading to misunderstanding and conflict. Thus context models may be seen as the crucial interface between actual discourse and the surrounding communicative situation, including the way participants represent themselves and the others as speakers and hearers.

Just like more general experience context models are not static but *dynamic,* ongoing, interpretations and representations of the current situation, That is, context models change constantly – if only because of the ongoing discourse, which dynamically changes at least what the participants know (such as the things talked about), as well as the relations between participants in interaction, as a result of what is being said. Thus, context categories influence all structures of discourse that may vary, including speech acts, rhetoric, lexical and syntactic style, and so on.

The K-device

One important category of these context models is *knowledge.* That is, it is crucial for participants that they mutually represent the knowledge of the other participants, because many aspects of discourse depend on what the speaker assumes the hearer to know or not to know. Indeed, whenever the speaker assumes that the hearer knows something, the speaker no longer needs to assert such knowledge, but may tacitly or explicitly presuppose it, or perhaps remind it when it might have been forgotten or when it is not easily accessible, such as information about recent events. It is this knowledge component of context models that will be dealt with in the rest of this paper.

Because knowledge is such a crucial component of context models, I shall assume it has a specific status as a cognitive device, which I shall call the *K-device.* This device is permanently active "calculating" what the recipients know at each moment of a communication or interaction. This device adapts the structure of talk or text to the dynamically changing common ground of knowledge, for instance by selecting the appropriate speech act (assertions or questions), definite or indefinite articles, presupposed that-clauses, conversational markers such as "You know", reminding markers such as "as I told you yesterday" or "as we reported last week", providing explanatory details, giving accounts, and so on. In other words, if we assume, in line with current theorizing in cognitive psychology, that what participants know about an event is represented in a subjective mental model of that event (Van Dijk & Kintsch 1983; Van Oostendorp & Goldman 1999), the K-device of their context model tells participants which of such event knowledge must be asserted, which knowledge should be reminded and which knowledge can be presupposed because it is irrelevant or can be inferred by the recipients themselves.

Of course, these and other features of discourse also depend on other characteristics of the context model, such as one's intentions, the kind of people one is addressing, the nature of the interaction, the institutional setting and so on. That is, one presupposes and expresses different kinds of knowledge when speaking to children, students, one's colleagues on the job or one's spouse or friends. Indeed, expressing or presupposing knowledge not only depends on what we know that the recipients already know, but also on what we know they may *want* to know, e.g., because it is *interesting* or *relevant* for them.

That is, the K-device is related to the other characteristics of the context model. It does so reflexively in the sense that the other categories of the context model are themselves produced by the K-device. For instance, if we have a conversation with a friend, we have an ongoing context model with a participant in the social role of a friend, that is, a person we know. In order to be able to represent such information in the context model, the very K-device needs to activate and make available the now relevant knowledge about that person. Thus, what information is included in the current context model necessarily means that participants now *know* in which setting, with whom and why they are communicating or interacting. Whereas context models are the controller of all interaction and discourse, the K-device is itself the controller of the context model. Indeed, it should even represent our knowledge of self – who we are, and as what we are now participating in the current ongoing interaction.

Since the K-device must manage a vast amount of permanently changing contextualized knowledge, it is plausible that it operates strategically, that is, by fast but imperfect operations, as we know from the strategic processing of discourse more generally (Van Dijk & Kintsch 1983). For instance, if speakers or writers must take into account what (they think) recipients know already, it would be impossible to feed all such knowledge to the K-device. Rather, there must be a fast decision strategy that says something like: *Recipient knows all I know, except X and Y,* in which case we would have one of the contextual conditions of asserting *X* and *Y*. Of course, several other contextual conditions must be satisfied before *X* or *Y* can be appropriately asserted, such as our beliefs about whether such information is relevant for the recipients or meets social conditions of politeness, but these conditions will not further be detailed here. It only needs to be emphasized that also these other conditions are of course controlled by the K-device, as argued above.

Since knowledge is generally defined as the shared beliefs of an epistemic community, such a strategy also has an empirical basis: If two people are members of the same epistemic community, they share, by definition, all the general knowledge of that community. On the other hand, this is not the case for all personal knowledge, much of which is not shared by others and hence must be asserted first before it can be presupposed later in the same communicative event or in next communicative events with the same recipients. Now, let us examine these and other strategies more systematically, assuming that each type of knowledge, as defined above, may need its own management strategies.

K-strategies

Let us examine some hypothetical strategies for different kinds of knowledge.

Personal knowledge

Personal knowledge is autobiographical knowledge about personal experiences (Neisser & Fivush 1994). The K-device assumption for all personal knowledge is that it is "private" and hence not shared by others who did not participate in the relevant experiences, unless communicated. This means that if personal knowledge is presupposed, speakers need to remember that they told their interlocutor about the experience before. This means that speakers must activate a previous context model, featuring the relevant information. If they have access to such a context model, that is, if they remember they told the recipient before, then this personal knowledge need not be expressed and asserted, but it may be reminded if the corresponding context model of the recipient is probably difficult to access. It would be anomalous if the speaker were to repeat the same assertions or remind the interlocutors several times in the same communication event, unless repetition is necessary for didactic, rhetorical or other reasons. On the other hand, if the communicative event took place years ago, and the information communicated is not very relevant for the recipient, it is likely that it has been forgotten, in which case a reminder will be necessary.

Interpersonal knowledge

Interpersonal knowledge is personal knowledge that is shared by two or more individuals on the basis of previous interpersonal communication or common experiences. The strategy here is already explained above for personal knowledge: If speakers have access to an experience model or a context model of a communicative event in which the relevant information was shared, they may presuppose that the recipients know such information. In that case an assertion would be anomalous and a reminder necessary if the context model is old and the event model not very relevant for the recipient. The relevant context model would typically be one of storytelling in which personal experiences are told.

Group knowledge

Group knowledge is socially shared knowledge, either of group experiences, or of general, abstract knowledge acquired by the members of a group, such as a professional group, a social movement or a sect. In the first case, such experiences may be told to new members of the group (children, apprentices, novices, rookies, etc.) in various forms of "collective" stories, which may be oral or told in various kinds of literature (legends, histories, etc.) or movies reproduced by the group. In the second case, the socially shared knowledge of the group is being taught as general, abstract knowledge, for instance the kind of knowledge shared by linguists or physicians. Intragroup communication presupposes group knowledge, as is the case in scholarly articles or technical conversations. Note that our concept of knowledge is by definition relative: What is called "knowledge" within a group, may well be called mere "beliefs" or "superstition" by members of other groups.

Institutional or organizational knowledge

Institutional knowledge is social knowledge shared by the members of an institution or organization, and in general satisfies the strategic criteria of group knowledge and discourse. Competent members of institutions or organizations may presuppose all knowledge acquired as members in the process of socialization, for instance during training or "telling the code" to newcomers. Shared organizational or institutional knowledge may itself vary between more or less official or unofficial knowledge, where the official knowledge is not only partially known to competent members but typically also recorded in institutional documents of various kinds, ranging from the minutes of a meeting to the trade secrets of a company or the "morgue" of a newspaper.

National knowledge

National knowledge is knowledge shared by the citizens of a country. It is typically acquired at school and through the mass media, and presupposed by all public discourse in the country. Since most everyday communication for most people is with members of the same country, most national knowledge will be presupposed in most conversations as well as in most public discourse. Indeed, in such communicative events it is not necessary to recall the name of the country, the capital, the current president or the great historical heroes of a country, or a host of other national knowledge we learn as citizens of a country. Little of the shared national knowledge will be personal or interpersonal. The same is true for smaller political units, such as villages and cities, although then the shared social knowledge may also feature (inter)personal knowledge, for instance about leaders or specific events.

Cultural knowledge

Cultural knowledge is the general knowledge shared by the members of the same "culture". Although the notion of "culture" is fuzzy, we shall nevertheless assume that people may identify with a culture, for instance on the (possibly combined) basis of language, religion, history, habits, origin or appearance. All discourse of competent cultural members presupposes cultural knowledge, which is in turn acquired by all discourses of the culture, first in the family, then through schools and the media and in interaction with friends.

Cultural knowledge is the fundamental Common Ground for all other discourses and for all other kinds of knowledge, and hence presupposed by all discourses – except the didactic ones – of the culture. Most of what is traditionally called "knowledge of the world" is cultural knowledge. Cultural knowledge is usually general and abstract, and hence not about concrete social or historical events, as is the case for much national knowledge.

The general strategy for cultural knowledge is that for the large majority of intra-cultural interactions, such knowledge is supposed to be shared by the recipients. In other words, in most situations the K-device assumes that what I know is also known by the recipients, and vice versa. All other types of knowledge are supposed to include cultural knowledge.

We see that although the amount and diversity of knowledge presupposed in interaction and discourse is huge, the K-strategies of context models are fairly simple. They may be summarized as follows:

- If the recipients are believed to be members of my own epistemic community (culture, country, group, etc.), presuppose all socially shared knowledge of this epistemic community to be known by the recipient(s).
- If the recipients are believed to be members of another epistemic community, then activate knowledge about that other community. If such knowledge fails, assume that knowledge may be the same or similar to that of your own community. When in doubt, ask or otherwise show ignorance.
- If I have just acquired new knowledge, e.g., about specific events, it is probably not socially shared throughout the community, and hence not to be presupposed to be known to the recipients unless these recipients are known to have used the same source of information (e.g. the media).
- Interpersonal knowledge by definition may be presupposed to be known by the recipients with whom it was shared. In doubt, it should be reminded.
- Personal knowledge is not assumed to be shared by recipients, and should hence not be presupposed.

We see that there is a gradual transition between general cultural knowledge and specific personal knowledge, the first being virtually always presupposed to be known, the latter virtually always presupposed to be unknown to the recipients.

This means that language users may focus on a relatively simple set of alternative condition for special cases.

For personal information this means activation of previous contexts in which some personal experience may have been talked about. If such a context can be retrieved, the knowledge should be presupposed if the context was of a recent date and/or the knowledge item was interesting or relevant for the recipients; otherwise it should be reminded. Since searches in episodic memory are difficult, it will frequently happen that speakers "tell the same story twice". Such repeated partial contexts are recalled better, so that repeating the same story many times becomes less and less likely, also because recipients will comment on such repetition, and such a comment will become part of the (recalled) context model.

For new social information, i.e., any general knowledge that is not part of the common ground, or any specific knowledge about recent events, speakers or writers will not presuppose such knowledge to be known to the recipients, unless these are believed to share the same sources of information as the speaker (such as reading the newspaper, watching TV, reading the same books, etc.).

For recipients who are known to the speaker, this is rather easy, because in that case also much of their information sources may be known. In any case, when in doubt, speakers in conversation will preface any assertions with questions such as "Did you read (hear, see…) this about….?". In written communication, such doubts may be expressed in reminders, such as "as we previously reported" or "as was reported in the press last week".

Although, as we see in many communicative events, the K-strategies are rather straightforward, in the sense that the speakers or writers know what knowledge to presuppose or not, we see that the most difficult situation is one of written communication about unknown general social knowledge or unknown specific social knowledge about events.

The first is typical for all situations of learning, that is, in educational contexts, in schools and universities, or when communicating science through the mass media or other popularization situations. In both cases, if speakers (and their K-device) assume ignorance of the recipients, it needs to figure out how much the recipients (already) do know, and build the new knowledge from there by various strategies of explanation (definitions, descriptions, metaphors, comparisons, etc.) (Calsamiglia & Van Dijk 2003). Similar strategies are applied in communicative situations in which recipients are from another epistemic community (culture, country, etc.).

The second situation, however, is also quite typical of communicative events within the same epistemic community, for instance for all forms of public information, such as that of the mass media, books, and so on.

Indeed, how do, for instance, journalists or writers know what knowledge to presuppose in their writings? We have seen that for all general cultural and national knowledge, also in this situation, such knowledge will be presupposed, and that new social knowledge (e.g., about the human genome) may be partly explained. For new specific knowledge, for instance about recent news events, writers only need to know whether the recipients are likely to have used information sources that may have communicated the same knowledge. If such information is very recent (typically of the same day) and not yet reported in the media, journalists may assume that recipients do not yet know. If the information has been reported by the mass media, the journalists may assume that many people already know, but probably not all, in which case the knowledge will typically be reminded.

If we want to summarize these various conditions in one general meta-strategy, we may formulate them as follows:

> In communication with members of the same epistemic community, presuppose all shared general knowledge, as well as all specific new knowledge that has recently been communicated before.

There are other ways to formulate the same or similar general (meta-) strategies for the K-Device, such as:

> Presuppose all I knew for a long time and do not presuppose what I have just learned.

Of course, the latter strategy does not apply to didactic contexts, e.g., in education or science communication, but it will apply to most everyday situations, conversations as well as the mass media.

The point is that with the vast amounts of knowledge that must be managed, language users need to have fairly simple but efficient strategies when calculating what their recipients know already or do not yet know. This is easy for general cultural common ground, which is more or less stable and only changes gradually. It is also relatively easy for everyday interaction and personal knowledge, which only requires reactivating context models, and where various forms of checking knowledge are possible. For written communication about new public events, usually by the mass media, the easiest strategy is:

> What the media have not reported before, the recipients don't know.

Now we have a first informal idea about plausible knowledge strategies in discourse and communication, we need to be more specific about their more precise cognitive basis. How does all this work in actual discourse processing? How does the K-device actually work in context models?

Processing assumptions

We have argued that in each communicative event participants construct and ongoingly update a mental model of the communicative situation, that is, a context model. We have also assumed that such context model construction does not occur from scratch, since context models are specific cases of ongoing experience models. This means that significant parts of the categories and contents of context models are already in place: Setting (place, time, etc.), Self (who we are, what current social identity is relevant, etc.), other participants and their roles, ongoing social actions, and so on. The same is true for the knowledge that is relevant in such experience models, from general cultural knowledge to personal knowledge shared with the other participants. In other words, the K-device of a context model is often overlapping with the K-device of the experience model(s) that precede it.

We only have rather general insights into the strategic construction of experience models in episodic memory, but it may be assumed that they are ongoingly built from combinations of (a) new perception data, (b) previous experience models, and (c) various types of socially shared knowledge. Thus, we now "know" that we are having breakfast with our partner on the basis of previous similar events, as represented in previous experience models in autobiographical (episodic) memory, on the basis of instantiated general, cultural knowledge about breakfast, on the basis of generalized personal knowledge about our partner, and finally the now relevant (self) perceptions such as the time of day (typically morning), place (say the kitchen) and other setting characteristics (table, food, etc.), the perception of my partner being present, and so on. These and other properties of the ongoing event will both trigger similar previous events in episodic memory, that is, previous experience models, as well as general cultural knowledge about breakfasts, all of which will result in the current definition of the situation as "We are having breakfast". Similar processes are at work for the definition of all social events in which we participate.

Since context models are specific forms of experience models, they basically are constructed in the same strategic way. Thus, in the breakfast example, the context model for the conversation we may have with our partner will be construed by the same general processes and constraints, that is, of ongoing perceptions of the social situation (settings, props, participants, etc.), previous context models (earlier conversations with our partner) and general cultural knowledge about breakfast, interaction and conversation – as well as about the topics of conversation.

Note that experience models are not some kind of mental representation of all properties of a physical setting, participants or a social interaction, *but a construction of what is relevant in the ongoing situation for the (inter) actions of the participants.* Thus, in the breakfast scene it will most likely be relevant that we are in a specific place where one can have breakfast (e.g., the kitchen), that there is something to eat, and so on, but not for instance the color of the table or the precise size of a package of cereals, among a host of other "objective" properties of a breakfast scene. That is, in order to be able to successfully "do" breakfast, we only need a much reduced construct of the – for us – relevant aspects of a social situation. Since experience models are by definition personal and subjective, also these definitions of what counts as such an event (what having breakfast means for us) may be largely subjective. However, strong cultural constraints exercise control over such definitions, such that having a walk or a steak at night is not usually interpreted and described as having breakfast. In other words, experience models are subjective, but culturally speaking not arbitrary, and hence formed also by instantiations of cultural knowledge.

All this also is true for context models. Thus, a conversation at breakfast needs the construction of context models of the participants in which a large part of the experience model is already present, such as setting, participants and ongoing social action. The same is true for the relevant K-device of the context model: we already know who our recipient is, and have a pretty good idea what he or she already knows about. In other words, context models are seldom built from scratch, especially not when they are part of a more comprehensive experience model, such as a conversation during breakfast, a testimony in court or a question in a classroom. Only when major changes in ongoing events and interaction occur, context models may overlap very little with ongoing or previous experience models, as when reporters, professors or politicians engage in public discourses (a TV report, a lecture or a speech in parliament) following informal conversational or other interactions with friends, colleagues or family members. In such a case we need to construct a new setting, new participants and their relevant properties, including their relevant knowledge, and a host of other relevant social dimensions. It is also likely that such context models are already partly constructed during anticipation: public speeches, lectures or TV shows are typically engaged in by professional participants who also mentally plan and prepare such events, that is, design future context models. In a sense, this is probably also true for more mundane situations, such as going to a shop to buy something, to ask a colleague on the job for help, or to phone our parents or children: we usually already "plan" many of these events before, that is, we already construct part of the context model before: where we go, with whom (or with what kind of person) we will speak, and so on.

In sum, context models are seldom built from scratch at the moment the communicative event begins, especially in situations in which we initiate such events. And when initiated by others, and when unexpected, then it will need fast strategic comprehension to construct the relevant model of the situation, as when a stranger asks us directions in the street. In other words, most context models are parts, or further developments of, ongoing experience models, very similar to previous context models in similar social situations, partly previously planned, or instantiations of well-known cultural knowledge, such as scripts for buying things in shops or asking a question in class. Strategically this means that at the beginning of the communicative event and ongoingly during the communicative event, a large part of the context model is already in place and only needs to be attended to or changed marginally. Thus, most of the mental resources can be dedicated to modeling the properties of the communicative situation that are changing constantly: what has (not) been said before, what recipients (now) know, how the social relationship with the recipients is developing, and so on.

One of the crucial differences between experience models and context models, and one of the reasons to distinguish them theoretically even if they have many properties in common, is that in communicative events participants not only need to monitor each others' knowledge about the current situation and the ongoing interaction, but also about (a) discourse and discourse structures, and (b) about what the discourse is *about*. We shall not further deal with the first kind of knowledge, which is (a very specific) part of more general national or cultural knowledge, and hence presupposed by the speech participants, and a general condition on verbal communication in the first place.

It is the second kind of knowledge that is the object of this paper, and that was traditionally called "knowledge of the world", and which we proposed to subject to further analysis, typology and processing assumptions. Thus, we have assumed a difference between, e.g., personal, interpersonal group, institutional, national and cultural knowledges, of which the first tend to be represented as specific, autobiographical event knowledge, that is, as mental models, in episodic memory, and the latter as more general knowledge in "social" memory. If the K-device in the context model needs to manage the regulation of these kinds of knowledge, we must assume that together with the rest of the context model, it controls the verbal expression of event models and general knowledge and their formulation in discourse. For instance, if we want to tell an everyday story about a personal experience to our partner or a friend, as part of a conversation, the context model and the K-device will regulate which information of our mental model of that event will be selected for inclusion as propositions in the semantic representation of the story. Hypothetically, this process may be thought of as featuring the following strategic mental operations in the K-device of the context model for telling a conversational story about event E:

- Assume that the recipient has more or less the same social and cultural knowledge as I have.
- Hence assume that the recipient has more or less the same general knowledge about events such as E.
- Assume that the recipient is interested in knowing things like E.
- I have not told the same recipient about E before.

In these hypothetical conditions we recognize, not surprisingly, some of the usual appropriateness conditions of the speech act of assertions. When these conditions apply, that is, when the speaker or writer makes these assumptions, then only the relevant new information of the mental model of the event will be selected for inclusion in the semantic representation.

We see that in the process of discourse production the context model will always be constructed first, as may be expected from the theory that takes context models as special cases of ongoing experience models. It is the context model that is the result of the analysis of the communicative and interactional situation, including the conclusion that it is now possible or necessary to tell a story about E. This involves the previous or current activation of M(E), the model of E, and then a process of context-dependent selection of information in M(E) that satisfies the contextual criteria represented in the context model, including the previous knowledge assumed to be known by the recipients.

The knowledge of the recipients about E is, however, not the same during the whole communicative event: by interpreting and understanding the story about E, the recipients construct their own mental model of E, implying gradually increasing knowledge about E. The context model of the speaker, including a model of the text, strategically keeps track of what has been asserted, so that the K-device may be constantly updated with the assumed new knowledge of the recipients about E. Although these K-strategies of the speakers are fast, they are not perfect, and speakers therefore may occasionally forget what they have told already, and hence repeat what they already have said, especially in long discourses. The theoretical ideal-case strategy is, though, that each proposition asserted by the speaker is added to the model the speaker has about the knowledge of the recipient.

Knowledge management in CDA

Let me finally sketch some of the possible application of the theoretical proposals made above in the area of the critical study of discourse. These suggestions are made within the general framework of an approach to CDA that does not only analyze the social conditions and consequences of discourse, but also the sociocognitive ones. The main arguments for this orientation are, firstly, that cognition is a necessary interface between society and discourse, and secondly that the cognitive structures we deal with are *at the same time* social, as is the case for knowledge, attitudes, ideologies, norms and values. Indeed, these social cognitions are primarily defined in terms of the beliefs shared by members of groups and communities. It is also within this perspective that we defined knowledge not as personal beliefs, but as social beliefs certified, shared and hence discursively presupposed by the members of epistemic communities. The conditions formulated above for the management of knowledge of discourse are in that sense social in a double sense, namely as beliefs that are socially shared, on the one hand, and because they are managed by context models that are representations of communicative situations, on the other hand. We have seen at the same time, however, that these mental models are at the same time personal, even when also socially based, because they must of course integrate the individual personal experiences, aims and interests of language users. It is also in this sense that language is inherently social, but of course used with individual variation in concrete social situation. Only in this way can we *both* explain the social, cultural and political dimensions of discourse, *and* the unique, individual variation of each specific instance of text and talk. That is, a sociocognitive approach to discourse offers a unique and necessary interface between the macro aspects of society, and the micro aspects of discourse and interaction.

Such a theoretical framework is also crucial for a more critical perspective. CDA specifically deals with the study of the discursive reproduction of power abuse, with forms of domination and social inequality. This also means that CDA needs to make explicit the way socially shared beliefs are discursively reproduced and how such beliefs are abused in the maintenance and legitimation of domination. This is not only true for ideologies, as I have shown elsewhere (Van Dijk 1998), but also needs to be examined for knowledge. If knowledge is defined as socially certified, shared beliefs of a community, it is obvious that those groups or institutions who have preferential access to public discourse, such as that of the media, or other forms of power and authority, such as politicians, professors or priests, are in an excellent position to influence people's knowledge formation. The contextual strategies of knowledge management discussed above need therefore also to be examined in such a more critical social perspective. Indeed, it is quite common in CDA to talk about the discursive manipulation of the audience, but as is the case for many of such critical notions, they are hardly defined and analyzed in a rigorous way. Manipulation, thus, means manipulation of the mind, and hence needs to be examined (also) in sociocognitive terms.

CDA is specifically interested in the power and dominance of the symbolic elites, those who have special access to public discourse. Let us therefore limit this brief discussion to the contextual knowledge strategies for such discourse, and ignore personal and interpersonal knowledge management and control.

We have seen that the K-strategies for public discourse are based on the assumption that knowledge may also be defined as the beliefs that are presupposed by such public knowledge. Indeed, politicians, journalists and professors assume to be known by their audience what they do not assert. Such an assumption, however, has important social conditions, consequences and biases. First of all, it is based on ideas about the knowledge of "average", more or less well-educated citizens, and ignores vast segments of the audience that do not have such knowledge, thus excluding them from adequate comprehension of public discourse. Secondly, the symbolic elites may presuppose as knowledge beliefs that are not – certified, accepted – knowledge at all, but opinions or prejudices. By not explicitly asserting such beliefs, but just pretending that such beliefs are generally accepted, they may manipulate many readers into accepting such biased, ideologically based beliefs as certified knowledge of the community. We might call *presumptions* such presupposed beliefs that are in fact ideological assumptions and not knowledge. Typical examples, in much current elite discourse, is the association of immigration and delinquency, and that terrorism is the major problem of today's world. Since people learn by the acquisition of new knowledge through public discourse, they may thus be manipulated into believing that such presumptions of authoritative sources are in fact forms of knowledge that no longer need to be certified (demonstrated, proved, etc.).

Also the opposite happens: Elite speakers may presuppose that their audience does *not* share in general knowledge, and thus in fact treat them as being ignorant. This may not only be generally a feature of many TV programs, but more specifically when white male elites (politicians, journalists, professors, etc.) address women or specific minorities. Indeed, infravaloration is a well-known form of sexism and racism, consistent with the general polarized pattern of positive self-images and negative other-images between ingroups and outgroups. In other words, discourse that is *too* explicit, may in some cases be a manifestation of class, gender or race domination. It is therefore crucial in all forms of communication that the contextual K-strategies are finely tuned to the actual knowledge shared by the audience.

Third, another form of what could be called the abuse of the contextual K-device is the assumption in much elite discourse that knowledge is *only* conveyed by elite discourse. We have seen that the media generally use the overall strategy that what they have reported is assumed to be true, and what has not been reported is not shared knowledge. Due to the vast influence of the media in contemporary society, such a presumption may not be entirely false in actual fact, but obviously people also learn from everyday interaction, experiences, and forms of alternative discourse and communication that are not controlled by the media – such as the internet today. In this case presuming ignorance of the audience is not just a question of infravaloration, but rather an example of the corresponding process of supravaloration of the self as the only instance of "truth". A characteristic example is that if the media do not widely report about racism in European society, including of course in the media itself, then racism does not exist. If mentioned at all, it will then typically appear between quotes, that is, as a mere belief, as an accusation of an outgroup (NGO, antiracists, minorities, an international institution, etc.). Indeed, it is in this way that certain kinds of facts are *not* routinely presupposed in public discourse, typically those that have to do with the power abuse of the elites themselves. We see that in this way, all the details of the strategies of the K-device discussed above may be examined further for specific social and critical implications. The same is true for the manifold complications in the way knowledge is managed in multicultural communication, interaction and discourse – where "western" beliefs are not only taken to be knowledge in the speaker's own cultural community, but in fact as universal knowledge. Much more work along these lines, combining sociocognitive strategies of knowledge management in discourse, and critical analyses of the social and cultural conditions of such strategies, is still on the agenda.

An example

To illustrate these contextual K-strategies, let us examine a few examples. Consider for instance the following beginning of a routine news report in the *New York Times* (June 16, 2003; see the Appendix for the full text):

> **Deal Seems Near on Israeli Pullout From North Gaza**
> **By Greg Myre**
>
> JERUSALEM, June 15 – Israel and the Palestinians appeared today to be edging toward an agreement that would remove Israeli troops from the northern Gaza Strip, the scene of repeated confrontations, and replace them with Palestinian security forces.
>
> Visiting American and Egyptian delegations were trying to broker the deal with the larger goal of moving ahead on an international peace plan. However, violence persisted today, with Israeli troops shooting one Palestinian militant to death in northern Gaza, and Palestinians firing several rockets at Israeli towns.

In order to write this news article, the reporter Greg Myre in Jerusalem first constructs a context model for his writing a news report for the NYT, featuring the following schema categories, among others:

Macro-context:

  – Global Domain: Media
  – Global Action: Informing the public
  – Global Participants: NYT, NYT readers

Micro-context

  – Setting

    – Date: June 16
    – Location: Jerusalem, Israel

  – Participants

    – Writer: Greg Myre: Role: Foreign Correspondent NYT in Jerusalem
    – Reader of NYT

Note that several of the context categories are explicitly, and deictically, expressed at the beginning of the report, such as the correspondent's name, as well as his location, whereas the date is presupposed to be known by the readers of today's newspapers (and printed on top of the page). In other words, a relevant part of the context model for news reports (the current date) is already assumed to be part of the recipients' context model, but for instance not the identity and location of the current speaker/writer. We shall not further pursue these other contextual properties of news report production and reading, and focus on the management of knowledge. However, we see that knowledge is not only presupposed or expressed about the events talked about in the news, such as the Israeli pull-out from Gaza, but also about the communicative situation and hence about context models themselves. The correspondent knows that the readers of his article know that they are reading (a report in) in the NYT and that this is a newspaper. And he supplies the contextual information that most readers do not know: the name and the location of the NYT correspondent in Jerusalem. Note that such understandings also presuppose the activation of relevant general (geographical) knowledge, namely that Jerusalem is a city and that it is located in Israel. Readers are also assumed to know of course that news reports are usually written by journalists, and that journalists located in foreign cities are usually the newspaper's foreign correspondents in that city or country.

Now, when writing this fragment, what knowledge does the NYT correspondent presuppose, remind or assert? The headline ("Deal seems near on Israeli pullout from North Gaza"), presupposes the following general (geographical) knowledge propositions, among others:

> Israel is a country
> Gaza is part of Palestine
>
> – Gaza is a region.

Similarly, the headline presupposes part of a mental model of a historical event or situation, namely that Israel has occupied (North) Gaza. Presupposed but reminded for those who have forgotten or obliquely asserted for those who did not know is the fact that there have been plans for a pullout. That is, in that case the only new information is that the pullout is imminent. All other information that enable the correspondent to write this headline is presupposed general (geographical) and specific historical knowledge (the Israeli occupation), and perhaps recent specific event information (there have been plans for a pullout).

Let us now examine the first lines of the body of the news report, and list first the various kinds of knowledge presupposed by the K-device of the correspondent:

General, sociocultural knowledge

- Israel is a country in the Middle East.
- Palestinians are the people of Palestine.
- Gaza is a region that is part of Palestine.
- Northern Gaza borders with Israel.
- Most countries have military troops.
- Countries or peoples can make agreements or a deal.
- Difficult agreements or deals between countries may be witnessed or brokered by (delegations of) other countries.
- Egypt is a country in the Middle East, bordering with Gaza and Israel.
- (The United States of) America is a country.

Specific sociopolitical, historical knowledge

- Parts of Palestine are occupied by Israeli troops.
- Gaza is occupied by Israeli troops.
- Palestinians have been resisting the occupation (Intifada).
- Egypt and the US have been involved in early attempt to mediate between Israel and Palestine.
- There is an international peace plan.
- There is violence in the relationship between Israel and Palestine.

Explicitly reminded specific sociopolitical knowledge

- The Gaza strip is the scene of repeated confrontations.

New information/knowledge

- Israel and Palestinians appeared today to be edging toward an agreement.
- The agreement would remove Israeli troops from the northern Gaza strip.
- The Israeli troops would be substituted by Palestinian security forces.
- Visiting delegations…broker the deal.
- They share the goal to move ahead with the international peace plan.
- Violence persisted today.
- Israeli troops shot one Palestinian militant in Northern Gaza.
- Palestinians were firing several rockets at an Israeli town.

We see that the actual "news" consists of only a few propositions, and that much of the news report consists of expressions whose understanding presupposes various kinds of general (geographical, historical, sociopolitical) knowledge, as well as more specific knowledge about recent events. It is interesting that the news article also features a "reminded" piece of recent event knowledge, namely a description of Gaza as the scene of repeated confrontations (between Israelis and Palestinians). Note that even the new events are not totally new in the sense that they appear as referring to events that are instantiations of a fairly general script, of the following kind:

- Country A occupies country B.
- B resists
  - A reacts to B's resistance, etc.
- A and B want to make peace
  - Countries C and D are mediators.
- A and B stop hostilities
- A withdraws from B.

This general script may of course feature various sub-scripts. Thus, resisting occupation may be executed by various kinds of military or militant actions (such as firing rockets), and reactions to resistance may consist of killing militants.

The contextual knowledge management of the reporter thus consists in assuming that the readers of the NYT of course have very general, sociocultural information (for instance that countries have troops), specific political-historical knowledge (about the occupation of Palestine by Israel and about Palestinian resistance) as well as knowledge about "recent developments" of such historical events, such as the current peace plan. The correspondent is able to make these assumptions because he knows that the NYT has been regularly reporting on these events before, so that the writer may assume that readers have updated their (complex) mental model of the Israel-Palestinian conflict accordingly. On the other hand, more detailed knowledge about the conflict, namely that Gaza was the scene of earlier confrontations may not be known to the readers, and must hence be reminded, by an oblique assertion in a relative clause. Finally, the correspondent may assume that the readers cannot know about the most recent developments (e.g. of today), such as the contents of a new plan, and recent fighting, since such information has not be supplied by the newspaper, and hence is to be dealt with as "new", and hence to be asserted. We see that also the general metastrategy applies here: the reporter treats as new what he could not know himself a day earlier, or about which he had not reported before.

Apart from the different kinds of knowledge being expressed and presupposed by the reporter, note that also the "modality" of the knowledge may thus be managed. Indeed, the correspondent does not plainly assert that there is an agreement on withdrawal, but rather, quite cautiously, that Israel and the Palestinians "appear to be edging toward an agreement". As suggested before, one of the modalities of knowledge is that it may be more or less sure, and such a modality is typically expressed in various kinds of hedgings ("appear", "edging toward").

The rest of the article basically follows the same pattern of mixing presupposed knowledge of various kinds, with new information. The latter largely concerns the following information:

– Details of the preparation of the agreement, and actors involved.
– Details of the attacks mentioned (time, place, kind of attack, victims, etc.).
– Declarations of several people, from president Bush to local leaders.

There are also some typical forms or reminding of "old" knowledge, such as the recent summit meeting on June 4, and the year (2000) that the current violence started, that is, the beginning of the Intifada, and finally a brief summary of the most recent events (recent violence). Note that these various kinds of knowledge also are related to different schematic categories of news discourse, such as Current Events, Previous Events, Historical Background, Context, Verbal Reactions, and Expectations (Van Dijk 1988). Of the vast amounts of old knowledge presupposed by the news report, also observe the pragmatic criterion of the *relevance* for the readers in the US, such as the death of the cousin of the US ambassador to Israel, as an added detail about the previous violence (such as a Palestinian suicide attack on an Israeli bus). That much of the current news events are themselves communicative events (declarations of politicians involved) shows also how the news is routinely gathered, namely by seeking comments from various important people on current events.

Finally, as suggested in the theoretical section above, such analyses of news may take a more critical perspective. We already have seen that some K-assumptions of this article are not only biased towards the knowledge shared by US citizens – which would of course be normal for a US newspaper – but also by citizens who have a minimum of political and geographical knowledge. There are however some other, more interesting critical dimensions to the analysis. Thus when in the first paragraph the NYT describes the Gaza strip as "the scene of repeated confrontations", it presupposes or obliquely asserts (reminds) that it is true that what happened in the Gaza strip is "confrontations", namely between Israeli troops and Palestinians. However, from another perspective the description of the events in terms of the nominalized expression "confrontation" might be seen as a euphemism in which especially the active role of the occupying Israeli troops – killing Palestinian citizens – is underemphasized, if not hidden. In other words, presupposed knowledge may not only take the form of (false) presumptions, as shown above, but also as presumptive forms of denying or hiding facts by euphemistic descriptions. Similarly, the new knowledge reported about "violence persisted today", in the second paragraph, mentions violence by both sides of the conflict, and is thus balanced. However, note that the events are described by one general category of "violence", whereas others may want to described the same "facts" as killings by occupying troops, on the one hand, and in terms of acts of resistance by those who are occupied, on the other hand. In other words, as we have seen, knowledge is essentially relative, and what is "known" by one (national) community, such as the USA or Israel on the one hand, may be a form of biased representation of the "facts" from the perspective of Palestinians or Arabs, on the other hand. In other words, an analysis of the contextual K-device strategies used by journalists, such as this one, should carefully and critically examine not only what beliefs are taken for granted as knowledge, but also how this is done. The "same" facts may be described as different "truths" from different perspectives, and by different communities. This again shows that knowledge and other forms of social cognition, such as attitudes and ideologies, are closely related.

Conclusions

A sound theory of text processing needs both a powerful knowledge component as well as a theory of context processing. Thus, standard theories of the role of "world knowledge" in discourse processing should be further refined for different kinds of knowledge. Unlike the definition of knowledge in epistemology as "justified true beliefs", I use a more pragmatic, socio-cognitive definition: the shared beliefs of a knowledge community that are based on the knowledge criteria of that community. Secondly, many aspects of discourse processing, such as speech acts, politeness phenomena, style, rhetoric, deictic expressions and many more, are controlled by context. However, there is no direct link between social context and text, and hence we need a cognitive interface in the form of subjective mental models ongoingly constructed by the participants of the current communicative events: context models.

One of the central properties of such context models is the knowledge of language users about the knowledge of the recipient. This K-device is crucial for the control of many important aspects of discourse, such as what information is explicitly expressed and asserted, which information is reminded, and what information is presupposed. Since however it is impossible that such a K-device includes all the assumed knowledge of the recipients, speakers need to make use of fast and flexible strategies.

In this paper we discuss a number of these strategies, and show how for various kinds of knowledge (personal, interpersonal, group, institutional, national or cultural) different kinds of presuppositions are managed in discourse production and comprehension. Although the various strategies allow speakers to make more specific assumptions about what recipients know, the overall (meta) strategies are surprisingly simple, such as: When the recipients are members of my community, assume that they know all that I know, except the information about recent personal experiences or sources not (yet) used by the recipients. This will account both for everyday storytelling as well as for news in the press. For special cases, e.g. of new knowledge acquisition in learning and science communication, there are more specific strategies, which, however, also presuppose a common ground of shared general, sociocultural knowledge.

All these K-device strategies may also be critically examined from a CDA perspective, for instance in order to study various forms of manipulation. Thus, symbolic elites may impose their own beliefs as generally accepted knowledge, marginalize large audience segments by presupposing knowledge that is not generally known, or conversely by infravalorating non-dominant groups as ignorant.

These general theoretical assumptions about the role of the K-device in context models were finally illustrated by a partial analysis of a routine news report in *The New York Times* about a recent event in the Middle-East conflict. In that example we see how the structure of the discourse, and hence its production and comprehension is controlled by a context model in which the correspondent of the NYT in Jerusalem makes assumptions about what the readers of the NYT do know, could know, could have forgotten and do not yet know. These different ways of presupposing and asserting knowledge also relate to the standard categories of news reports, such as Headlines, Current Events, Previous Events, Historical Background, Context and Expectations. Thus, the information expressed in the Previous Events category is information earlier reported by the press, and hence in principle part of the event models of the readers, but possibly forgotten, and hence in need of a reminder. Besides this specific knowledge about specific historical events, most of the knowledge presupposed in the news report is general geographical knowledge (about the

Middle-East), and specific historical-political knowledge (about the Middle-East conflict). New knowledge that provides the very basis of news pertains to current events, occurring today or yesterday, about which the newspaper has not yet reported, and which the readers are not likely to know, unless from earlier reports on the radio or TV.

A CDA perspective on such a K-analysis of news also shows that what are presupposed truths for one epistemic community, nation or newspaper, may be at best a euphemistic, incomplete or otherwise biased "version" of the facts from another perspective.

We thus see that our theory of contextual knowledge management not only accounts for many aspects of text processing, but also explains several structures of important genres such as news reports.

Note

¹ This is a new version of a paper read at the conference of the Society for Text and Discourse, Madrid, 26–28 July, 2003.

References

Auer, P. (Ed.). (1992). *The contextualization of language*. Amsterdam et al.: John Benjamins.

Bernecker, S. & Dretske, F. I. (Eds.). (2000). *Knowledge: Readings in contemporary epistemology*. Oxford: Oxford University Press.

Britton, B. K. & Graesser, A. C. (Eds.). (1996). *Models of understanding text*. Mahwah, NJ: Erlbaum.

Calsamiglia, H. & Van Dijk, T. A. (2004). "Popularization discourse and knowledge about the genome". *Discourse & Society, 15*(4), 369–389.

Clark, H. H. (1996). *Using Language*. Cambridge, UK: Cambridge University Press.

Duranti, A. & Goodwin, C. (Eds.). (1992). *Rethinking Context: Language as an Interactive Phenomenon*. Cambridge: Cambridge University Press.

Graesser, A. C. & Bower, G. H. (Eds.). (1990). *Inferences and text comprehension. The psychology of learning and motivation*, Vol. 25. New York: Academic Press.

Gumperz, J. J. (1982). *Language and social identity*. Cambridge, UK and New York: Cambridge University Press.

Johnson-Laird, P. N. (1983). *Mental models: Towards a cognitive science of language, inference and consciousness*. Cambridge: Cambridge University Press.

Keysar, B., Barr, D. J., Balin, J. A., & Paek, T. S. (1998). "Definite reference and mutual knowledge: Process models of common ground in comprehension". *Journal of Memory & Language, 39*(1), 1–20.

Leckie-Tarry, H. (1995). *Language & Context. A functional linguistic theory of register.* Edited by David Birch. London: Pinter.

Markman, A. B. (1999). *Knowledge representation.* Mahwah, NJ: Erlbaum.

Neisser, U. & Fivush, R. (Eds.). (1994). *The Remembering self. Construction and accuracy in the self-narrative.* Cambridge: Cambridge University Press.

Planalp, S. & Garvin-Doxas, K. (1994). "Using mutual knowledge in conversation: Friends as experts on each other". In S. Duck (Ed.), *Understanding relationship processes IV: The dynamics of relationships* (pp. 1–26). Newbury Park, CA: Sage.

Schank, R. C. & Abelson, R. P. (1977). *Scripts, plans, goals, and understanding: An inquiry into human knowledge structures.* Hillsdale, NJ: Lawrence Erlbaum Associates.

Sperber, D. & Wilson, D. (1995). *Relevance: Communication and cognition.* Cambridge, MA: Blackwell Publishers.

Tulving, E. (1983). *Elements of episodic memory.* Oxford: Oxford University Press.

Van Dijk, T. A. (1988). *News as discourse.* Hillsdale, NJ: Erlbaum.

Van Dijk, T. A. (1998). *Ideology: A multidisciplinary approach.* London, UK: Sage Publications.

Van Dijk, T. A. (1999). "Context models in discourse processing" In H. van Oostendorp & S. R. Goldman (Eds.), *The construction of mental representations during reading* (pp. 123–148). Mahwah, NJ: Lawrence Erlbaum Associates.

Van Dijk, T. A. & Kintsch, W. (1983). *Strategies of discourse comprehension.* New York: Academic Press.

Van Oostendorp, H. & Goldman, S. R. (Eds.). (1999). *The construction of mental representations during reading.* Mahwah, NJ: Lawrence Erlbaum.

Van Oostendorp, H. & Zwaan, R. A. (1994). *Naturalistic text comprehension.* Norwood, NJ: Ablex.

Wilkes, A. L. (1997). *Knowledge in minds. Individual and collective processes in cognition.* Hove: Psychology Press.

Appendix

New York Times, June 16, 2003
Deal Seems Near on Israeli Pullout From North Gaza
By Greg Myre

JERUSALEM, June 15 – Israel and the Palestinians appeared today to be edging toward an agreement that would remove Israeli troops from the northern Gaza Strip, the scene of repeated confrontations, and replace them with Palestinian security forces.

Visiting American and Egyptian delegations were trying to broker the deal with the larger goal of moving ahead on an international peace plan. However, violence persisted today, with Israeli troops shooting one Palestinian militant to death in northern Gaza, and Palestinians firing several rockets at Israeli towns.

"I'm taking this as a serious proposal from the United States," said Ghassan Khatib, a Palestinian cabinet minister, refering to the Gaza security plan. "We believe the American administration can deliver when it wants to."

On June 4, the Israelis and Palestinians held a summit meeting, their most ambitious peace effort since the current period of attacks and counterattacks began in September 2000.

But last week brought a surge of violence that left more than 50 people dead, and was accompanied by angry promises from both sides of still greater violence to come. In the past two days, pressure from the United States and others has induced the warring parties to restart talks.

Earlier today, the Israeli and Palestinian cabinets held separate sessions in which they endorsed the basic principle of having the Palestinians police part of the Gaza Strip, while setting several conditions. Israeli news reports said the Palestinian security chief, Muhammad Dahlan, met for the second straight night with senior Israeli security officials about details of the plan.

The Israeli prime minister, Ariel Sharon, said his government would continue to pursue members of the Islamic group Hamas and other Palestinian militants if they were planning to strike Israel.

President Bush, speaking in Kennebunkport, Me., said, "The free world and those who love freedom and peace must deal harshly with Hamas and the killers."

Senator Richard G. Lugar, Republican of Indiana and chairman of the Senate Foreign Relations Committee, suggested that American forces might be needed to fight Hamas.

In a television interview on Sunday, he said, "Clearly, if force is required, ultimately to rout out terrorism, it is possible that there will be an American participation."

Hamas, which has always opposed peace talks with Israel, has rejected the Mideast peace plan.

The group carried out a suicide bombing on Wednesday that killed 17 people on a Jerusalem bus, including Anna Orgal, 55, identified as the cousin of Daniel C. Kurtzer, the American ambassador to Israel.

Hamas is facing pressure to suspend attacks, and group leaders today joined other Palestinian factions in discussions with an Egyptian delegation seeking to negotiate a truce.

Mr. Sharon said if the Palestinian leadership could persuade Hamas and other militant groups to agree to a truce, it would be welcomed.

"We will hold our fire, except in cases of self-defense against ticking bombs," Mr. Sharon was quoted as saying by a cabinet official.

The Palestinians said that they were prepared to take over security in northern Gaza, and that they wanted the Israeli forces to leave other areas in the coastal strip, as well as the West Bank town of Bethlehem. They also want American guarantees that Israel will not reoccupy areas it vacates, and that it will stop the targeted killings of militants.

"We don't want a random Israeli withdrawal," said Nabil Amr, the Palestinian information minister. "It should be based on a political vision."

The head of the visiting American delegation, Assistant Secretary of State John S. Wolf, met with Israeli officials today and planned to see Mr. Sharon on Monday.

After that, he will meet with Palestinian leaders. The Palestinian prime minister, Mahmoud Abbas, was expected to travel Monday from his West Bank headquarters in Ramallah to Gaza, to renew the dialogue on a cease-fire.

Before dawn today, Israeli forces entered the northern Gaza town of Beit Hanun, the site of frequent Palestinian rocket launchings at Israel.

The troops came under heavy fire and shot back, the military said. Palestinians said a militant was killed, identifying him as a member of Al Aksa Martyrs Brigades, a group with ties to the Fatah movement of Yasir Arafat, the Palestinian leader.

Later in the day, Palestinians fired several rockets from northern and southern Gaza at Israeli towns, but caused no damage or injuries.

The Israeli Army also said it arrested three wanted Palestinian militants in a cave outside the West Bank town of Bethlehem. One of the men, Essa Batat, was the local leader of Islamic Jihad and was linked to attacks that killed six Israelis, according to the army.

In another development, Peace Now, an Israeli group that monitors settlements, said Jewish settlers had established five outposts in the West Bank over the past week, though the peace plan calls for recently erected settlements to be dismantled.

"The settlers are nervous, and things are much more tense," said Dror Etkes, a Peace Now official. "But it's the same old story. The construction is still going on."

The Israeli military demolished 10 uninhabited settlements last week, and planned to remove five that had a small number of residents. The settlers have challenged the plan in court, and no action has been taken.

The army took down one additional outpost today, removing a bus that had been fashioned into living quarters on a hill south of Hebron, in the West Bank, witnesses said. No one was living there.

CHAPTER 5

Lighting the stove

Why habitus isn't enough
for Critical Discourse Analysis

Ron Scollon and Suzie Wong Scollon
Georgetown University

Two examples

For those of us who have chosen to focus our research and life energies on the study of language, there may be no problem more urgent than coming to understand the complex linkages among discourse and action in the world. Each day we are assaulted with new discursive moves which seem designed to prefigure or to legitimate courses of disastrous action. In a world in which international political leaders hurl insults at one another, urging each other to war and seeking to cow whole populations of citizens into grudging submission, it cannot be doubted that our work is a central work of both intellectual and social consequence. We take Critical Discourse Analysis (CDA) to be at the forefront of this potentially catalytic movement to bring the study of language into an engagement with the powers of social action in the real world in which we live.

Unfortunately, the study of discourse and its engagement with the world of action is often more a potential for catalytic involvement than a transforming action in itself. In this paper we put forward the argument that for CDA the weak link in this chain of discourse and action, of action and discourse is the psychological one. We argue that it is an urgent task of CDA and likewise of action-activity theories of psychology to more closely theorize just how discourse becomes action and action becomes discourse. We will argue that the weakness lies principally in the current conceptualization of habitus. We will briefly propose that Nishida's (1958) dual concepts of the "historical body" and of "action-intuition" more usefully capture the psychological entity upon which we need to focus than the rather vague concept of habitus. Then we will sketch out the idea, hardly original with us, of the discursive or semiotic cycle – a recursive cycle of re-semiotizations, to use Iedema's (2003) apt phrase – by which we can bring into interdisciplinary engagement both sociological work in practice theory and psychological work in action-activity theory. For convenience we will conclude by giving a name to this theoretical and methodological linkage – nexus analysis.

In the spirit of a research agenda that is predicated on the study of concrete actions, objects, and discourses we will use two examples which we have elaborated more fully elsewhere in our research (R. Scollon 2002, 2003; R. Scollon & S. Scollon 2002, 2003, 2004) to ground our argument. Both examples are rather mundane and apparently insignificant, but because of their simplicity we believe the theoretical principles upon which we would like to focus are all the more apparent. Our purpose, of course, is to use the example of lighting a small camp stove to make breakfast as well as the later example of a child learning to read the word "trilogy" as prototypical cases which, we believe, follow principles that would be found in the most complex forms of human action and discourse.

The ontogenesis of practice: Internalization

We must begin with a simplification and argue not that all practice originates in discourse but that only some practice does, but this case should be sufficient to develop our argument. On the morning of July 8, 2001 we made a breakfast of tea and bannocks – a kind of flat bread made widely throughout the Canadian and Alaskan north which originated with Scottish traders throughout the region. We can begin the sketch of this action (we might also say these actions or this activity) by saying that making breakfast is doubly constituted in two sub-sets of action (or activity), making tea and making bannocks. Each of these, in turn, are constituted in multiple sequences of action. For example, in making tea there are the actions of unpacking the stove, lighting the stove, filling a pot with water, boiling the water, putting tea leaves in a teapot, steeping the tea, and the rest. Even these action-activities form a complex array that we could not easily sort out within the scope of our argument here. Some of these other issues we have taken up in other places as we have noted above.

From the point of view of an interest in discourse and action, the mediated discourse approach we are taking requires us as well to look at the mediational means by which these mediated actions (making tea, making bannocks, etc.)

are taken. For this we have at least three broad classes of mediational means, the food (tea, water, oat flour, etc.), the utensils (the camp stove, matches, water pot, etc.), and language. And so the first point that we believe is crucial is that in this case as in very many, perhaps all cases, language does not occur as the sole mediational means by which an action is taken. Actions tend to be inherently multimodal, to use a currently popular term for what should be apparent in any event (Kress & van Leeuwen 2001; Norris 2004).

If we then continue our simplification of this very complex action-activity sequence to narrow the focus just to the discourse which is relevant to lighting the stove, we will need to set aside such conversational sequences as:

> What shall we have for breakfast?
> Bannocks?
> Good, I'll make tea?

There is nothing in this sequence or in anything else actually recorded on the scene that makes reference to the lighting of the stove. That action is carried out, as Filliettaz (2004) following Habermas notes, as a case in which the discourse and the moment-by-moment actions are not linked in the moment of action. That piece of discourse is what de Saint-Georges (2004) analyzes as anticipatory discourse; that is, it is discourse which occurs prior to the action which pre-figures that action in significant ways, but which is not concurrent with it as part of the action itself.

None of this is to say that there are not other abundant discourses present at the moment and within this action. The "discourses in place" (Scollon & Scollon 2003) include not only these conversational snippets about the breakfast or about the hike we were planning to take that day. They include what we might call enabling discourses. These include the background discussions we have had with friends about the use of this piece of property upon which we were camped. We would also want to include the discourse of academic research which is present in the form of videotape and notebook records of this hour or so of making a breakfast of tea and bannocks.

But, as we have said, those are still not directly relevant to the question of lighting the stove. For that we need to look at the abundant commercial discourses circulating through this moment in the form of things written on the box in which the camp stove was stored as well as on the stove itself. There we find the following:

– Product labels (the "Exponent" model of stove)
– Company labels (Coleman company)

- Parts of the stove (the pump)
- Labels on the labels (part numbers on each of the labels)
- Lighting instructions
- Warning to read the lighting instructions

These constitute at least six different types (genres or categories) of discourses present on the surface of this object, this mediational means by which we are trying to boil water for tea. There is also a certain degree of intertextuality and intermodality among these bits of discourse. For example, in the instructions for lighting the stove the first instruction is:

RED FUEL LEVER must be "OFF"

Capitalization represents three different types of intertextuality as we can see in Photo 1.

"FUEL LEVER" is a label, red letters in a white box background which identifies the lever. Unlike the other labels, however, this is not placed *on* the mechanical lever itself, it is placed at the top (ideal position; Kress & van Leeuwen 1998) of a graphic which includes pictures of the three positions this lever can

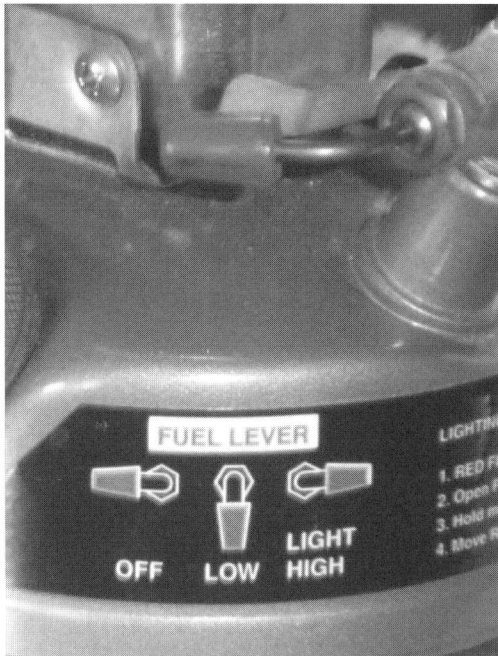

Photo 1. The fuel lever

take ("OFF", "LOW", and "LIGHT/HIGH"). Thus the capital letters index both the word in the graphic and the mechanical lever at the top of Photo 1.

"OFF" in the instructions indexes both one of the positions of the mechanical lever and the word in the graphic. "RED" indexes not a word but the color of the tip of the mechanical lever. Thus, capital letters index these three different kinds of things in the world: a graphic, a word within the graphic which is also a position of a mechanical lever, and a color of a portion of the lever. Letters which are not capitalized in these instructions are to be read as the non-indexical grammar of the actual instructions, "must be".

Although we might want to develop these interesting and complex relations among texts and objects and the use of color, placement, and typography to cue these relations of indexicality, it is the instructions for lighting the stove on which we want to focus our attention now with the reminder that in order to make our point we have intentionally had to set aside the rest of these multiple discourses and intertextualities which also remain present in this action of making tea and bannocks for breakfast.

In May of 2001 this was a new stove. We had bought it to replace an older, different type of stove, and so we had to learn how to use it. We took the new stove out onto the back deck of our house and tried it out. To do this, Ron went through the instructions which are printed on the stove in careful detail:

> 1. RED FUEL LEVER must be "OFF".
> 2. Open PUMP one turn (with a curved right arrow).
>   Pump 25 full strokes. Close PUMP (with a curved left arrow).
> 3. Hold match at burner.
> 4. Move RED FUEL LEVER to LIGHT/HIGH.

There are also a few subsequent instructions about how to maintain the pressure once it is lit which are not relevant here.

On July 8th, the day we're thinking about now, Ron did not read these instructions to light the stove. He paid no attention to the intertextuality, nor did he give a thought to these complex indexicalities; he just lit the stove. That is, he checked to see that it was full of fuel; he opened the pump and pumped it up; he closed the pump and lit a match; and then he opened the fuel lever. The stove lit and he then pumped it up a bit more and put the tea water on to boil.

In the months from May to early July we went from using the printed instructions on the stove to simply lighting the stove; we went from a little, but nevertheless complex discourse to an action. This was done by an incremental process of reading and acting in conjunction, one stove lighting at a time, each time paying less attention to the instructions and more attention to the working of the stove until the instructions were no longer anywhere in conscious access. To use the Vygotskian term, we had internalized this external discourse and then externalized it as action in the practice of lighting the stove.

But of course we should bear in mind that the text was still on the surface of the stove. This allows us to point out that often enough at the moment of an action, discourses may be present either as overt and explicit texts (such as writing or speech, but also as images and graphics) or as internalized discourses which have become practice in the unreflecting actions of a person just doing something. In many cases they are present in both forms as well, of course.

The interdisciplinary linking of activity theory and practice theory

We have begun with this rather mundane example to make our first point: Discourse may be present at any moment of human action in at least these two forms: As overt, explicit spoken or written language (or images and graphics or other semiotic codes) or as internalized discourse through a process much like what we have just seen. Through a sequence of actions over time a discourse may be "sunk" into habitus and "appear" in the world only in the form of human action. This is a point which lies at the center of what many would call activity theory or in some cases sociocultural psychology (Cole 1995; Cole & Wertsch 1996; Lantolf 1999; Lantolf & Genung 2002; Leontiev 1978; Vygotsky 1978; Wertsch 1985, 1991, 1998). This is also the line of argument made by Bakhtin (1981) and his alter ego Vološinov (1986 [1929]), that the language we use always originates in the social languages of the world in which we conduct our social lives.

In this sense we would argue that activity theory (sociocultural psychology) provides a workable answer to the perennial problem with the concept of "habitus" as used within practice-theory based conceptions of the social world. On the whole the notion of habitus has been used as a way of avoiding being very specific about just how text is produced or interpreted by readers/social actors. CDA, as one of the practice-theory approaches to language has let itself rest in the idea of habitus a bit too easily. We are content to say that discourse in general is sedimented as habitus, but how has remained to be dealt with later.

To put this another way, social theory or practice views of social action have quite rightly focused attention on the role of discourse in social formation – both in the sense of the production and legitimation of hegemonic discourses and in the sense of the production of the legitimating social institutions of society. In these views, however, habitus has largely remained as an unexamined residual category which really only locates the point at which psychological processes must take over in the analysis but largely leaves those processes unexamined. We have put forward this example to argue that sociocultural psychology/activity theory is a viable approach to opening up the problem of habitus for examination.

At the same time sociocultural psychology has, on the whole set itself up under a different spotlight. In the work following on Vygotsky, Luria, or Leontiev, particularly in the West, the focus has been on psychological formation and relatively little interest has been given over to building theoretical linkages between the processes of psychological formation and social formation. From this point of view and holding in mind an interest in discourse, we feel that CDA offers an important theoretical position to which we can make a theoretical bridge from the more psychological theories of sociocultural psychology.

Again the concept of habitus lies at the heart of the matter. As it is now mainly formulated such as in the most often cited work of Bourdieu (1977, 1990) habitus remains an unexamined category. From the point of view of Western work in sociocultural psychology there are few studies of the ways in which major social issues and major sociopolitical discourses become sedimented in habitus. This is, in part, because habitus, as it is mostly used, blurs the crucial distinction between the collective and the biological individual. By blurring this distinction, the notion of habitus obscures the methodology by which an interdisciplinary engagement may be made. When one is at once talking about the psychological – action process of a particular social actor *and* the social reservoir of habituated practice of a group, there is no principled means by which we can examine how the social becomes the psychological or how the psychological becomes the social. These crucial processes have mostly become background considerations both for activity theory and practice theory.

We believe that we can, however, now begin to construct this theoretical and methodological engagement of practice and activity theories and that one of the building blocks has been provided by the now rather forgotten work of Nishida Kitaro (1958). The term Nishida used for this point at which the social and the psychological become engaged is the much more concrete term, the "historical body" (*rekishi-teki-shintai*). We realize that putting forward a Japanese term has considerably lower theoretical cachet than a French or Latinate one, but it is precisely because the term habitus tends to have a blinding effect on its users that we feel a departure might be salubrious at this point in the development of practice-activity theory.

Because of space limitations here we propose simply that we adopt Nishida's wording in place of habitus because of its insistence on the continuity of the human life experience as an independent (though obviously ecologically interdependent) organism. To put it simply, by adopting the term "historical body" we return both social theory and activity theory to their materialist sources by disallowing any slippage of the term into super-organic categories such as frequently occurs with habitus.

A second term Nishida uses which is of importance to us is "action-intuition" (*koi-teki-chokkan*). Here the emphasis is on deflecting any theoretical requirement to attach conscious intention to the actions of the social actor. In Nishida's view, human action arises out of the historical body, that is, out of the social actor's full life-history of existential experience (formed, of course, within his or her social world) through a merged and simultaneous action of unaware and unreflective continuation of the self in a real present and through a process of reflection more accurately perceived as an intuition than an intention. In this his view strikes us as being much like that of the discursive psychologists (e.g. Edwards & Potter 1992; Harré 1994, 1998; Harré & Gillett 1994) than is normally recognized.

To summarize, then, we believe that an engagement of practice theory and activity theory perspectives is now in need of development and that to do this it is crucial to re-examine the concept of habitus. This re-examination seems best supported by a return to the concrete material reality of the human lived experience, and we suggest Nishida's terms "historical body" and "action-intuition" if not his whole philosophy will be useful in this re-examination.

We began, then, by giving a rather mundane example of one case in which a discourse which began as a discourse printed on a camp stove became internalized in the historical body of a person and then re-externalized as the action-intuition of simply lighting a camp stove. One common criticism of discourse-to-action theories of action is to argue that surely not every action a person takes originates in language external to the person in the social world. A strong Vygotskian position would argue that, in fact, this is exactly what happens. We do not take this strong position because we believe we can argue that some, perhaps many, psychological formations are internalized first as actions and only subsequently externalized as discourse. In order to illustrate what we mean, we would like to turn to a few examples from the life of a four to five-year-old child.

RUN TRILOGY: From historical body to text via action: Externalization

When our son Tommy was four he could not read or write. He was interested in the use of our new Apple II+ computer and had many times watched us as we used it to write programs, to play games, and to do word processing. While we gave him no specific instructions other than to answer his questions, he learned to create and to save text files and to print them out. He could not read any of the words – that is, he could not put down letters in any spelling order for words he knew nor could he pronounce any of the characters which he made appear on the screen as words. As an example we can look at the following file which he "wrote":

```
            #5
    sgff#5
    #5
    #4
    #3
    #2
    #1



    frr gsfvcdgcc


    i


    dxs
```

This text file is nonsense as a message. Tommy made no attempt to "read" it, that is, to pronounce it. He claimed it was a program – instructions to run the computer. We should also mention that at this time he could edit and run a simple music synthesizer program as well as the well-known program LOGO. More complex than these and more interesting from the point of view of discourse are the two programs he particularly liked to run called "TRILOGY" and "KALEIDOSCOPE".

He did what he did with the computer as an action sequence that was guided by such things as the physical design of the machine – he knew where to insert the floppy disk, knew how to switch the power on and off – and by the correspondence in the form of letters on the screen and on the keyboard. That is he could "read" a "C" on the screen and find the same "C" on the bottom row on the keyboard and push that key.

With these action skills he would run through the following sequence:

- Insert a disk in the external disk drive
- Switch on the power to the computer
- Push the keys "C", "A", "T", "A", "L", "O", "G" in correspondence with those same letters written on a crib sheet stuck on the front of the monitor
- Select the list of programs from the catalog on the screen
- At the prompt (]), type the sequence RUN (which he could do without consulting another source)
- After "RUN" push the space bar and then in sequence the letters TRILOGY copying them one at a time from the catalog list.

He could do the same for the program KALEIDOSCOPE. If he encountered any error, he simply turned the computer off, turned it back on, and repeated the sequence of actions until the program he wanted was running.

In all of this it is important to remember that he could not answer the request to "spell TRILOGY" nor could he answer "How do you type TRILOGY?" What he could do was to act to the request, "Let's play TRILOGY." In other words, Tommy could run the programs TRILOGY and KALEIDOSCOPE (and quite a few others) through this sequence of actions without in any way externalizing these operations as language or discourse. His ability to run these programs was very much like our ability to light the camp stove as a sequence of actions arising out of the historical body under the action-intuition conditions of wanting to play the game (or our wanting to boil water). In Tommy's case, however, there was no prior time in which these actions were pre-figured as a discourse; the action sequence was internalized a step at a time from the observation of the actions of other social actors (ourselves).

We believe this is an important point to make because of the easy reductionism that occurs in some forms of activity and practice theory that assumes that all action (as action-intuition of the historical body) derives from discourse in the prior experience of that same historical body. Of course we must recognize that on the social level this is a different issue altogether. These actions of Tommy's arose in his historical body as observations of actions in our historical bodies. Our own action-intuitions on this early computer were themselves derived from discourse very much like our actions in lighting the stove were. We read the computer manuals carefully before beginning to do things. We were, like all good adults, terrified of turning off the computer in the middle of an operation for fear we might damage an expensive piece of technology. When there was an error we stopped in our tracks, read the manual carefully, and tried to retrace our steps carefully to the point of the error, guided all the while by the printed manual. Our point here is that in the life experience of the historical body, actions may be sedimented as practice either directly through observation of action and objects in the world or through discourse, and it is counter-productive for any theoretical position to dogmatically insist on one or the other of these options.

But Tommy did not always remain in the dark about how these action sequences of his might be represented as discourse. He learned to read. Some time after he had become very practiced at running these programs on the computer, Tommy and his father were in a bookstore. There was a novel on a shelf in a row of books with the title "*TRILOGY*". Tommy went up to his father and said, "Daddy, what's that?" His father said, "Maybe you know?" and Tommy whispered, but with emphasis, "Trilogy!"

In this moment Tommy had made that enormous leap from action to discourse, he had made the connection between a complex set of actions and thoughts he was able to organize into an activity and a semiotic object in the world. In this way, we argue, discourse may also be an outcome of action in the often theorized moment of representation.

This is a sequence which has occurred at some time for every child or adult who has learned to read. It has happened at every other occasion in which a social actor has made this leap of representation from the action-intuitions of the historical body to the externalized utterances of discourse. We believe that these two examples, the sedimentation of discourse in the historical body through action as practice and the externalization of the historical body through action as discourse form a semiotic cycle that is the proper unit of analysis alike for studies of discourse, for studies of social action, and for studies of human psychological formation. It is this cyclical linkage among the historical body of social actors, the action-intuitions of social actors, and discourse as representational objects in the world that are the minimal necessary units for our interdisciplinary development of what have largely been independent academic disciplines.

The discourse cycle: Semiotic cycles as the theoretical linkage of action and discourse

Our thinking about discourse cycles or what is better really thought of as semi-otic cycles derives not just from our own research as suggested by the two examples we have given here. We have found work in the Vygotskian tradi-tion (cited above) very important in guiding this thinking, particularly the interest in internalization and externalization of social meanings. Others, how-ever, such as Silverstein and Urban (1996) and the other scholars published in that volume, have written cogently about these processes from the point of view primarily of text as "entextualizations" as has Blommaert (2005). Also, of course, Bernstein's (1990) concept of "recontextualization" is a very impor-tant contribution to this body of thinking. More recently Iedema's (2003) term "resemiotization" has, we think, captured the fuller, multiply moded nature of semiotic cycles in which discourses are transformed into objects and the his-torical body through actions and, reciprocally, the historical body and objects are transformed through actions into discourse and other semiotic codes.

It might be useful to imagine these processes as operating in a kind of cycle much like the water cycle (indicated in Figure 1).

Discourse cycles or cycles of resemiotization, to use Iedema's term again, could be seen to have two relatively stable states: On the one hand there are the "solid" forms of objects and the historical bodies of social actors and on the other hand there are the actional processes of speaking and writing (or, of course, also drawing, gesturing and any other semiotic signalling). Among the "precipitative actions" we might want to think of writing or other forms of im-age making – the actions that Kress and van Leeuwen (2001) would group as production in their four-tier analysis (discourse, design, production, distribu-tion) of the hierarchy from discourse to the material placement of discourse(s) in the world. Of course to remain consistent with their model we would want to emphasize the difference between "discourse" as action in the world in the upper regions of our diagram and "discourse" as code, system, or design in the historical body or the objects of this world.

Among the "anticipatory" actions would be those which arise as physical, material, or social constraints on what may be said. A conversation is pre-figured in the intimate seating and table arrangments of a cafe, for example. Here we would want to include everything from Foucault's "archive" (1976) of possible utterance to de Saint-Georges' (2004) interest in the role of fu-ture tenses and other future-oriented linguistic forms in shaping the course of future actions. This cycle is sketched out programmatically in Figure 2.

WATER
VAPOR
(CLOUDS)

EVAPORATION

PRECIPITATION
(RAIN, SNOW)

LAKES, RIVERS
GROUND WATER

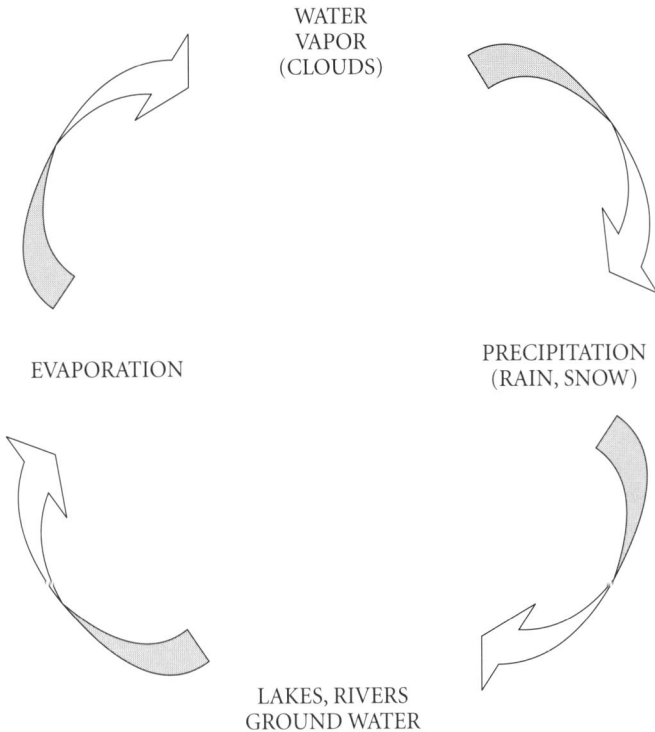

Figure 1. The water cycle

And as long as we are drawing pictures, we feel it is important to emphasize that even though the model we are presenting of the semiotic or discourse cycle is considerably more complex and interdisciplinary than models largely being used at the present, it is hardly sufficient in itself. We have suggested that a psychology that accounts for both the internalization of the social semiotic world and the externalization from the historical body through its action-intuitions into the social semiotic has been insufficient in that it does not include a carefully theorized account of that social semiotic world itself. CDA, in its turn, like other practice-based theories of social life has provided important insights and analysis of the social semiosis of the social world which must be that which is internalized, but has not integrated that analysis with a theorization of the processes of internalization and externalization except to assert the concept of the habitus as the location of those processes.

We believe that an engagement of these two lines of analysis is absolutely crucial to the development of our understanding of just how the social world is

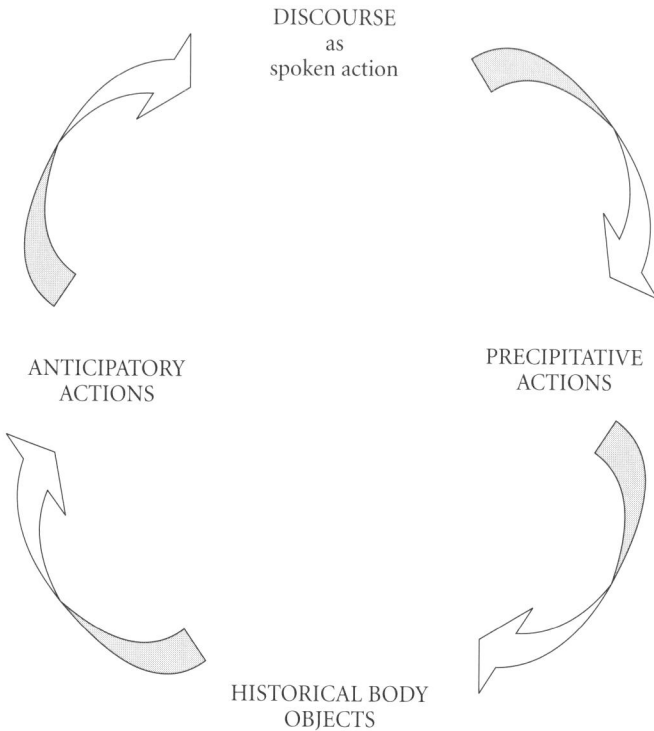

DISCOURSE
as
spoken action

ANTICIPATORY
ACTIONS

PRECIPITATIVE
ACTIONS

HISTORICAL BODY
OBJECTS

Figure 2. A discourse cycle

internalized and just how the historical body of a social actor externalizes itself through action-intuition. But even if we become much clearer about how these cycles of resemiotization work in concrete cases, as we have hoped to suggest in the two examples we have just given, we remain at some crucial distance from understanding, in fact, how either the social or the psychological world work. Now we would like to remind the reader that at the outset of our first and very simple example we set aside "for the moment" a fairly wide range of discourses from the multiplicity of commercial and other discourses present on the camp stove to the enabling discourses and objects of our presence at that particular camp site. As a very simple example of what we mean, we have set aside the discursive/semiotic cycle that produced the fuel in that camp stove which enabled the action of lighting the stove upon which we have focused our narrow attention. No fuel, no lighting the stove. By airbrushing out the fuel so that we could focus on the cycle of internalization of the instructions for lighting the stove, we have airbrushed out our very deep involvement in world

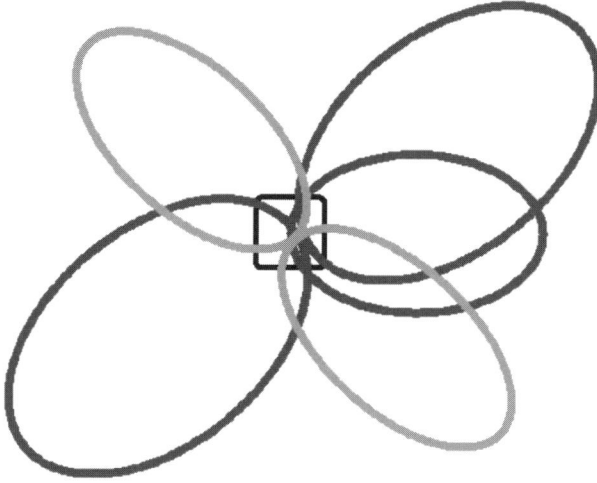

Figure 3. Nexus analysis

discursive cycles of the production and distribution of crude oil resources from talk of war to stock market values or OPEC price setting.

From this point of view, then, what we argue is needed is a much broader conceptualization of moments of social action which are rich enough to encompass not only cycles of discourse and resemiotization along the arcs of the specific discourses upon which we are focused, but also the ecological interactions among the multiple cycles of discourse which circulate through each particular moment of action. A rough and intimidating sketch of the kind of interdisciplinary vision we are suggesting is given in Figure 3.

We have begun to call a research strategy which seeks to map out the multiple semiotic cycles which circulate through a moment of social action a *nexus analysis*. We make no claim that a nexus analysis is in any way an easy thing to do; we do claim, however, that it is urgent that we begin.

References

Bakhtin, Michail M. (1981 [1934–1935]). *The dialogic imagination.* Austin: University of Texas Press.
Bernstein, Basil (1990). *The structuring of pedagogic discourse.* London: Routledge.
Blommaert, Jan (2005). *Discourse: A critical introduction.* Cambridge: Cambridge University Press.

Bourdieu, Pierre (1977). *Outline of a theory of practice*. Richard Nice, trans. Cambridge: Cambridge University Press.

Bourdieu, Pierre (1990). *The logic of practice*. Stanford: Stanford University Press.

Cole, Michael (1995). "The supra-individual envelope of development: Activity and practice, situation and context". *New Directions for Child Development, 67*, Spring 1995, 105–118.

Cole, Michael & Wertsch, James V. (1996). *Contemporary Implications of Vygotsky and Luria*. Worcester, MA: Clark University Press.

de Saint-Georges, Ingrid (2004). "Materiality in discourse: the influence of space and layout in making meaning". In P. LeVine & R. Scollon (Eds.), *Georgetown University Round Table on Languages and Linguistics: Discourse and technology: Multimodal discourse analysis*. Washington, DC: Georgetown University Press.

Edwards, Derek & Potter, Jonathan (1992). *Discursive psychology*. London: Sage.

Filliettaz, Laurent (2004). "The multimodal negotiation of service encounters". In P. LeVine & R. Scollon (Eds.), *Georgetown University Round Table on Languages and Linguistics: Discourse and technology: Multimodal discourse analysis*. Washington, DC: Georgetown University Press.

Foucault, Michel (1976). *The archeology of knowledge*. New York: Harper and Row.

Harré, Rom (1994). "Is there still a problem about the self?". *Communication Yearbook, 17*, 55–73.

Harré, Rom (1998). *The singular self: An introduction to the psychology of personhood*. London: Sage.

Harré, Rom & Gillett, Grant (1994). *The discursive mind*. Thousand Oaks, CA: Sage.

Iedema, Rick (2003). "Multimodality, Resemiotisation: Extending the Analysis of Discourse as Multi-Semiotic Practice". *Visual Communication, 2*(1), 29–57.

Kress, Gunther & Van Leeuwen, Theo (1998). *Reading images: The grammar of visual design*. London: Routledge.

Kress, Gunther & Van Leeuwen, Theo (2001). *Multimodal discourse: The modes and media of contemporary communication*. London: Arnold.

Lantolf, James P. (1999). "Second culture acquisition: Cognitive considerations". In E. Hinkel (Ed.), *Culture in second language teaching and learning* (pp. 28–46). Cambridge: Cambridge University Press.

Lantolf, James P. & Genung, Patricia B. (2002). "'I'd rather switch than fight:' An activity theoretic study of power, success, and failure in a foreign language classroom". In C. Kramsch (Ed.), *Language acquisition and language socialization: Ecological perspectives* (pp. 175–196). London: Continuum.

Leontiev, A. N. (1978). *Activity, consciousness, and personality*. Englewood Cliffs, NJ: Prentice Hall.

Nishida, Kitaro (1958). *Intelligibility and the philosophy of nothingness*. Tokyo: Maruzen Co. Ltd.

Norris, Sigrid (2004). *Analyzing multimodal interaction: A methodological framework*. London: Routledge.

Scollon, Ron (2002). *Nexus analysis: Toward an ethnography of motives*. Martin Spector Lecture in Applied Linguistics, Center for Language Acquisition, Pennsylvania State University, October 10, 2002.

Scollon, Ron (2003). "Intercultural communication as nexus analysis". *Logos and Language: Journal of General Linguistics and Language Theory, III*(2), 1–17.

Scollon, Ron & Scollon, Suzie Wong (2002). *Nexus analysis: Expanding the circumference of discourse analysis.* PARC Forum, December 12, 2002, Palo Alto, California: Palo Alto Research Center.

Scollon, Ron & Scollon, Suzie Wong (2003). *Discourses in place: Language in the material world.* London: Routledge.

Scollon, Ron & Scollon, Suzie Wong (2004). *Nexus analysis: Discourse and the emerging internet.* London: Routledge.

Silverstein, Michael & Urban, Greg (1996). *Natural histories of discourse.* Chicago: University of Chicago Press.

Vološinov, Valentin N. (1986 [1929]). *Marxism and the philosophy of language.* Cambridge, MA: Harvard University Press.

Vygotsky, L. S. (1978). *Mind in society: The development of higher psychological processes.* Cambridge: Harvard University Press.

Wertsch, James V. (1985). *Culture, communication and cognition: Vygotskian perspectives.* Cambridge: Cambridge University Press.

Wertsch, James V. (1991). *Voices of the mind: A sociocultural approach to mediated action.* Cambridge, MA: Harvard University Press.

Wertsch, James V. (1998). *Mind as action.* New York: Oxford University Press.

PART II

Implementing interdisciplinarity

CHAPTER 6

Analyzing European Union discourses

Theories and applications

Ruth Wodak and Gilbert Weiss

Lancaster University / University of Salzburg

1. Introduction

> Let us remember that Europe is a civilization, that is at one and the same time
> a territory, a shared history, a unified economy, a human society and a variety
> of cultures which together form one culture.   (Lionel Jospin, 28th May 2001)

In his speech of 28th May 2001, Lionel Jospin, then French Prime Minister, listed some important elements that are involved in the construction of a national or supranational identity. Unlike concepts of "national identities", which are similarly based on a shared history, present and future, what is emphasized here is the fact that there are multiple cultures that nonetheless belong to Europe as "civilization" (cf. Wodak et al. 1998, 1999; Weiss 2002). In this way Europe is no longer defined only as a "cultural nation" and, by implication, it is also distinguished from the concepts presented in Huntington (1996). Instead there is one "culture" that is determined by many cultures. According to this view, Europe is unified by common goals and values, by a particular model of society, and by economic and legal agreements.

At the same time, Europe uses this idea to distinguish itself from other "global players", such as the USA or Japan – a topos that permeates many different genres of EU texts (cf. Wodak & Weiss 2001; Muntigl, Weiss, & Wodak 2000). For identity is always determined by *idem* and *ipse* (Ricoeur 1992) as well as by those elements or processes from which one differs. Identity always implies difference as well (Benhabib 1996).

The Danish historian and sociologist Jan Ifversen considers the move from a cultural definition to a sociological and political construction of a European identity to be one of the decisive conceptual changes of recent years, before and after the millennium (Ifversen 2002: 3ff.). Using a semantic history of the term "Europe" in the sense of Kosselleck (1972), Ifversen traces precisely a development over the last few centuries from a cultural meaning to one of civilization, and ultimately to a political construct. More particularly, the Swedish historian Bo Strâth (2000a, b, c) stresses, on the one hand, the multiplicity of historical meanings and traditions in Europe, and on the other, he finds a range of different meanings and aspects in European identities: *"Europe is a discourse", "a normative center", "a political program"* (Strâth 2000b: 14). Accordingly we find contradictions juxtaposed and a variety of opinions about the meanings of Europe and *"European citizens"* (cf. also Shahin & Wintle 2000; Tassin 1992; Weiler 1997).

"The challenge is to radically rethink the way we do Europe. To re-shape Europe", as Romani Prodi said to the European Parliament in January 2000. *"Doing Europe"* stresses in particular the constructive aspect as well as the radical way (in the metaphorical sense). This kind of definition, using concrete material verbs, places the action, the "doing", the conscious discursive construction in the foreground. This is in contrast to many texts that are characterized by cognitive processes, i.e., by "thinking, discussing, considering, suggesting, believing", and so on, which we analyzed in our projects on EU decision making processes as well as on attitudes towards EU enlargement. Right now, therefore, we see an integration of linguistic-semantic and historical-sociological categories. Because of the enlargement of the EU, Europe will have to be changed: on this all the politicians agree. An institutional reform, a precisely defined community of values and a greater degree of democratization, because of growing discontent among citizens, have all been promised. One way out of the democratization dilemma proposed by the commission in the White Paper on Governance, July 2001, are the creation of new public spaces and new communication channels, comprehensible genres and dialogic means with European citizens. This implies new challenges for linguists, both on the level of practical applications of our results and insights, as well as on the theoretical levels of analysis and methodologies.

It is difficult, of course, to present all details of our theoretical framework to analyze European Union Discourses in one paper. We have thus decided to focus on a few aspects, which illustrate some open questions in interdisciplinary research, which we have come across during our teamwork in recent years. In contrast to other scholars in the field, we have tried to work in an *inter- and transdisciplinary way*, both concerning the contents, theories and methodologies in our research, as well as debating all this between the two of us: between the discourse analyst and socio-linguist, on the one hand, and the sociologist and political theorist, on the other. Many *problems of integrating* and not just adding different approaches, terminologies and research strategies have thus touched and occupied us on several levels: on the level of research, on the level of our joint work, and on the level of possible applications of our insights in various fields.

All of the research in the Research Center "DPI" (http://www.univie.ac.at/discourse-politics-identity) was designed in an interdisciplinary way from the outset. Our focus in this paper on the discursive construction of European Identities serves as one example for some of the theoretical approaches, methods and research strategies developed together in multiple team settings and long debates in the course of six years (always encouraged and critically supported by our advisory board to whom we are extremely grateful).[1]

At the end of these six years, we have come to see some shortcomings, many open questions, interesting results, and stimulating perspectives for future research. Every end also marks a new beginning, and this is where we would like to start a new theoretical debate by discussing recent theory formation in some approaches of Critical Discourse Analysis and by elaborating some thoughts on the "mediation between the social and discourse". All of these issues are not new, but they need to be newly discussed. We believe that the interdisciplinary approach allows for some innovative and creative proposals, which the perspective from inside one traditional field might restrict.

2.   Theory formation

Epistemologically, CDA has its roots in a combination of critical-dialectical and phenomenologic-hermeneutic approaches. But apart from that, it is quite difficult to make consistent statements about the theoretical foundations of CDA. There is no such thing as a uniform, common theory formation determining CDA; in fact, there are several approaches. Michael Meyer came to the conclusion: "There is no guiding theoretical viewpoint that is used consistently within CDA, nor do the CDA protagonists proceed consistently from the area of theory to the field of discourse and then back to theory" (2001: 18; see also Wodak & Ludwig 1999: 11). Meyer also points out that epistemological theories but also general social theories, middle-range theories, micro-sociological theories, socio-psychological theories, discourse theories and linguistic theories can be found in CDA. (Cf. Weiss & Wodak 2003 for more details; also Wodak 2000; Wodak & Meyer 2001; Lemke 1995; Chouliaraki & Fairclough 1999.) Attention should however be drawn to the fact that it is essential to be aware of the different levels of theory types proposed by Meyer.

This is of particular importance since in the discourses of applied sciences the concept "theory" refers to all levels without any further qualification. Let us take two philosophers as an example who undoubtedly had a strong influence on the development of CDA, i.e. Michel Foucault on the one hand, and Jürgen Habermas on the other (cf. Foucault 1972; Habermas 1981; and Wodak 1996: 24f.). The different levels of theory are often mixed up in the CDA reception both of Foucault and Habermas. Foucault's tools are, for example, used both on the epistemological level and on the level of discourse theory (Lemke 1995: 29; Fairclough 1992; Wodak 1996: 26). The approach developed by Habermas is applied as a general social theory, a micro-sociological interaction theory and a discourse theory (Chouliaraki & Fairclough 1999: 88f.). Of course, this indiscriminatory mixing leads to inconsistencies in terms of concepts and categories, which in turn have an adverse effect on any systematic theory formation.

Under the – often trendy – influence of other so-called "grand theories", e.g. those developed by Pierre Bourdieu, Anthony Giddens, and Niklas Luhmann (Bourdieu 1980; Giddens 1984; Luhmann 1997), this problem has become even more acute. On the whole, the theoretical framework of CDA seems eclectic and unsystematic for many observers and critics. However, this can also be viewed as a positive phenomenon. The plurality of theories and methodologies can be highlighted as a specific strength of CDA, to which this paradigm ultimately owes its creative dynamics (Wodak 2002). However, we would like to emphasize that researchers need to be conscious of such eclecticism and justify it for each distinctive issue. Only constant reflection of the research processes avoids epistemological contradictions.

What is of particular relevance for the theory formation process in CDA in general, and in our project on EU discourses in particular, is the often quoted but never sufficiently elaborated "*mediation between the social and the linguistic*". Major difficulties of operationalization in the research process are usually related to this mediation problem (Wodak 2001: 12; Fairclough & Wodak 1997). Discourse analysts agree to a large extent that the complex interrelations between discourse and society cannot be analyzed adequately unless linguistic and sociological approaches are combined; already Basil Bernstein and William Labov, as two founders of Sociolinguistics, were aware of this challenge almost thirty years ago. Sociological and linguistic categories, however, are basically not compatible as they tend to have diverging *Horizontgebundenheit*, as Husserl called the fact that they were dependent on "different horizons". Thus, in sociological contexts the term "representation" usually denotes something different (or has a wider meaning) than in specific linguistic analyses. The term "institution" is used in discourse-analytical concepts and sociological theories with a completely different meaning. A theoretical foundation capable of reconciling sociological and linguistic categories (mediation) is therefore required.

No such uniform theoretical framework of mediation has been proposed in CDA to date. Nevertheless, one can speak of a theoretical synthesis of conceptual tools developed in different theoretical schools, as illustrated to a certain extent by Chouliaraki and Fairclough (1999). Foucault's *discursive formations*, Bourdieu's *habitus*, or *register and code* as defined by Halliday and Bernstein (Lemke 1995:19f.) could be considered as such tools. This synthesis of theories is by no means a monistic theory model, and it does not claim to be "more true" than the individual theories, from which singular conceptual ideas are drawn. It is primarily committed to a "conceptual pragmatism" (Mouzelis), focusing on "criteria of utility rather than truth" (Mouzelis 1995:9). Such a pragmatic approach would not seek to provide a catalogue of context-less propositions and generalizations, but rather to relate questions of theory formation and conceptualization closely to the specific problems that are to be investigated. In this sense, the first question we have to address as researchers is not, "Do we need a grand theory?" but rather, "What conceptual tools are relevant for this or that problem and for this and that context?" With this question, the fact that the context of discursive practices needs to be addressed adequately should be emphasized. Hence, some CDA representatives have concentrated on the issue of the "context" and the development of a "context model" in recent years (van Dijk 2001; Wodak 2000).

To summarize our introductory remarks, we propose the following steps for developing an integrated theoretical framework capable of reconciling different (sociological and linguistic) perspectives without reducing them to one another, and this is where we get to the heart of the problems with interdisciplinarity:

1. **Clarifying the basic theoretical assumptions** regarding *text, discourse, language, action, social structure, institution, society*. This is done on a level preceding the actual analysis. It constitutes the framework for developing conceptual tools, for establishing categories and for analytical operationalization. This step is vital for sociology and linguistics to arrive at "mutual understanding".

2. **Developing conceptual tools** capable of connecting the level of text or discourse analysis with sociological positions on institutions, actions and

social structures. Conceptual tools are elements of theory allowing a connection in both directions (linguistics and sociology). As analytical interfaces (e.g. the above-mentioned concepts of discursive formation, order of discourse, habitus, register and code) they guarantee a socio-linguistically integrated model in the strict sense. Their plausibility determines whether further categorization will be successful. In other words, if these tools do not work, it will not be possible to reconcile the respective positions in the research strategies at a later date.

3.   After clarifying the theoretical assumptions and identifying the conceptual tools the third basic step consists in defining categories, i.e. of analytical concepts to denote the content of specific phenomena. Categories are based on disciplinary or methodological borders only to a minor extent; they depend primarily on the object of investigation. Categories of this kind are for example *public space, identity, legitimacy, prejudice, discrimination, power, racism*, etc. It is important to identify both parallels and differences between the process of analytical category formation on the one hand, and categorization in everyday discourses on the other. Category formation is not the exclusive privilege of scientific theorists but it is also an important and pervasive part of people's common sense knowledge and discourses. Quoting Eric Voegelin (1987: 27), one could also say: "…man does not wait for science to have his life explained to him, and when the theorist approaches social reality he finds the field pre-empted by what may be called the self-interpretation of society."

The question how categories are constituted in everyday discourse and what functions they satisfy is therefore – in the strictest sense of the word – also a fundamental question regarding the categorization of theories. But even though analytical categories are very closely linked to categories constructed by players in conversations, e.g. to include or exclude specific social groups, they differ in one important aspect: they are instruments of an observer "relieved of action". In this respect they are, to put it in the words of Alfred Schutz, *second-grade constructions*, as opposed to the *first-grade constructions*, i.e. the categories of "everyday discourse" (see Schutz 1962: 3f.).

Let us now move on to our example and to the difficulties when fitting these proposals into our research practices.

3.   EU discourses: The complexity of "text in context"

In approaching EU institutional discourse and policy-making practices, we were confronted with a high degree of intertextual and interdiscursive complexity. Discursive acts/symbolic practices are embedded in other discursive acts/symbolic practices and so forth. As a result of this, an analytical balance between **text** and **context must be** aimed at. In very simplified terms, we understand "discourse" as "text in context", and this suggests an interdisciplinary approach:[2] the **structural and cognitively perceived context** is investigated by experts from neighboring disciplines; for example, our teams are made up of political scientists, sociologists, historians, and linguists. At particular times, we also involve consultants (such as economists or lawyers). The results from the contextual research and the text analysis are then brought together in an **integrative approach.**

Texts and discourses are, of course, not isolated in space. It is rather the case that individual texts always relate to past or even present texts. This may be characterized as "**intertextuality**".[3] Discourses behave in a similar way: they also overlap and are interconnected. This is known as "**interdiscursivity**". These two concepts are central to our work. On one hand, in the investigation of large quantities of data from historical phases that refer to each other in a wide range of grammatical forms and genres, but also on the other hand, where comparable texts from different cultures relate to each other. Individual discourses (for example, on employment policy) likewise relate to others (such as social policy).

In addition, we have substantially refined the concept of **recontextualization**.[4] This concept incorporates the discursive dynamics and modification of arguments, themes, topoi, and speech acts in the transformation from one genre to another or from one public space to another. The study of recontextualization, therefore, permits a systematic comprehension and reconstruction of media reports, for example, and the (separate) development of "**discursive strands**" in a variety of other settings and genres.

In investigating processes of decision-making and the textual production of policy documents in EU organizations, we were, for example, able to record, describe, and explain the most important recontextualization strategies and their functions for organizational structures and discourses.

All in all, in the recent six years (1997–2003), we investigated policy papers, interviews, spontaneous conversations, multi-modal and printed media texts, web-sites, speeches, legal texts, focus groups, opinion polls, etc. These different genres create different public spaces, which are connected in complex ways with each other, which we were able to grasp systematically through the concepts mentioned above. Moreover, we were able to distinguish major recurring topics and topoi in these texts, which are realized in systematically different grammatical ways. Thus we uncovered the whole range of possible meanings/choices and linguistic modes for discourses on "un/employment", on "European identities", on "attitudes towards EU Enlargement" and on "multilingualism" or "language policies", to name a few. The nature of context-dependency also played a major role in our research findings. We proposed a heuristic model to study the mediation between "discourse" and "society" in EU-discourses, which is published elsewhere (Wodak 2000; Weiss & Wodak 2003).

4.   EU discourses and European identities: Our theoretical framework

Let us now return to the beginning of our paper: to the political rhetoric about the "Construction of European Identities". In the following, we first present four theoretical claims which grew out of our research findings during the past six years; finally, we would like to propose a theoretical framework which draws these claims together and conclude with some open questions:

–   We claim, – and this is our first major theoretical point – that the plural form "identities" is deliberately chosen, since something like a single unified identity for Europe should not and can not be hypostasized in advance. On the contrary, our primary concern has been to investigate the formation of different constructions and images of Europe and also the possible meanings and interpretations of Europe in the particular political, historical and cultural contexts. We will have to accept and live with many different regional, local, national and European identities, which are constantly re-negotiated and co-constructed by different elites and social groups.

–   There is therefore a context-dependent negotiation of identities, and these are discursively co-constructed in interactions. This is our second claim. This aspect was very clearly shown, for example, in our analysis of focus group discussions in three projects (cf. Kovács & Wodak 2003). But identities are also attributed and allocated on the basis of hierarchical and institutional power. The freedom of strategic and need-oriented choice is strongly dependent on position and context. To this extent, membership is only partially elective. In this context, shifting borders, new/old ideologies, languages and language conflicts, and new laws determine and restrict the possibilities of participation of citizens in the EU.

–   Thirdly, we claim that the relationship between discourse, politics, and identity is characterized today by new and frequently hybrid forms such as, for instance, the "visionary speeches on Europe" analyzed elsewhere (Wodak & Weiss 2004). The processes of (economic) globalization on the one hand, and (social) fragmentation, on the other, are calling into question the established identities or identity constructions of groups, institutions, and states. New public spaces, media, and communication technologies have changed the basic rules for discourses by shaping the space-time-structures. Political, economic, and media discourses frequently constitute a field of tensions and antinomies that does not permit simple or traditional classifications. The analysis of internet forums and discussion websites which the European Commission has established for better communication for European citizens (see Paper on European Governance) manifests such new hybrid forms which have to be investigated more thoroughly to be able to understand possible developments in the future. (Who uses these public spaces, who is included, who is excluded?)

–   We also observe in the same line – this is our fourth claim – the standardization of scripts, pictograms and forms, of curricula and medical protocols, as well as of literature ("Euro-literature") on the one hand. On the other hand, there is a growing awareness and appreciation within Europe of local cultures, languages, and products. The focus on "diversity" is an expression of a new ideology, of a "multicultural society". On the basis of the "subsidiarity principle", many political activities are decentralized, i.e. they remain situated and controlled at local, regional and national levels; nevertheless policy-making processes in Europe as such are increasingly dependent on the "central" institutions in Brussels and Strasbourg. Furthermore, the more the EU de-regulates in certain areas (e.g., free market policies), the more requirement for regulation is given in other areas (e.g., financial, monetary policies), not to speak of the fact, that even de-regulation processes have to be regulated.

A heuristic model, which summarises the basic tensions and antinomies serves as a general frame for the claims we have just enumerated (Figure 1).

These four claims inspired our more general interdisciplinary framework, which we can only briefly characterise in this paper:

> The present Europe-discourses consist, as a rule, of the interplay of three dimensions and respective goals:
>
> (a) *Making meaning of Europe* (ideational dimension),

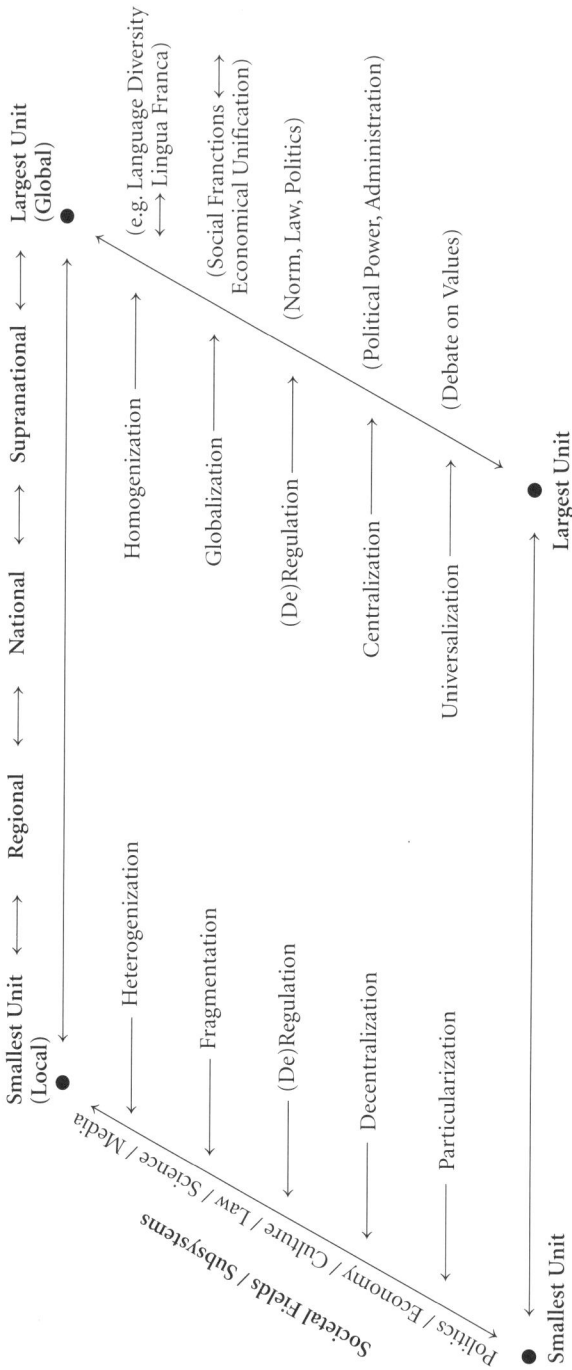

Figure 1. Antinomies

    (b) *Organising Europe* (organisational dimension),
    (c) *Drawing borders* (geographical dimension).

It is the interplay of these three dimensions that constitutes the specific form of the speculative talk on European identities as well as of other policy processes in many areas. The first dimension refers to the *idea* of Europe, the essence, substance or meaning. The second dimension reflects the question of how Europe shall be organised, which *institutional forms of decision-making and political framework* are appropriate for the future. The third dimension concerns the question of *border-construction*: who is inside, who stays outside? With these three dimensions and goals three forms of legitimizing the political construction of the EU (and its enlargement) are connected:

a. *legitimization through idea* (identity, history, culture),
b. *legitimization through procedure*[5] (participation, democracy, efficiency) and
c. *legitimization through "standardization"* (of humanitarism, of social standards, economic standards).

These legitimization strategies touch essential problems of political representation.

The dimension of *inclusion and exclusion* touches another perspective, which is relevant on all three dimensions and for all three legitimization strategies. The general concept of *insiders and outsiders* is salient in all societies and between societies. Niklas Luhmann (1997) claims that the social sciences do not have a precise description and analysis of the processes of social inclusion and social exclusion. He defines inclusion and exclusion as the two vital *meta-distinctions of our times*: certain social groups lead *"parallel lives"*; the social problems thereby transcend the traditional values of justice and democracy. Only those who feel themselves to be included still adhere to democratic values:

> [t]he variable of inclusion/exclusion in many parts of the globe is on the point of assuming the role of a meta-difference and mediating the codes of the systems of functions. Whether the difference between right and wrong will have a chance and whether it will be dealt with according to programmes proper to legal systems will depend in the first instance on a prior filtering by inclusion/exclusion...
> (ibid.:533)

At this point we must emphasize that inclusion and exclusion are not to be considered as static categories: the person who is excluded today may belong tomorrow, and *vice versa*. Although membership can always be redefined, important gate-keepers decide who will have access: new laws, new ideologies, and new borders. Mostly it is not up to individuals to define or redefine their membership: this depends on structural phenomena of exclusion. The desired "opening-up" of the European Union", the greater participation and democratisation, therefore, still has to overcome some essential obstacles if it is to reunite the so-called "parallel lives".

5. Perspectives and open questions

Three complexes of questions for future research in our framework may thus be distinguished:

– Elaborating the *historical perspective*: What historical Europe-concepts underlie the national discourses? And how are the concepts and images that have been handed down reproduced in modern fields of discourse (political speeches, media discourses, everyday discourses)? What effect do the historical traditions have on present-day politics and programmes? What patterns of argumentation and types of rhetoric may be distinguished in this? How, in this context, should we look at the newly arising "flag-words"(such as "community of values" or "civil and civic society" or "convention") which seem to ubiquitously usable, i.e. "beyond left and right" (Giddens 1995)?
– Elaborating the *communication perspective:* How are the respective images of Europe transmitted or communicated inter-culturally and multi-modally? How are they "dealt with" in international committees? What roles are played by the new media and publics (e.g. television, internet, email) in the formation of new/old European identities? How and which new public spaces are created by these new media?
– Elaborating the *participation and representation perspectives:* What are the implications of the images of Europe of the respective national discourse traditions for questions of political legitimization at the supra-national level? How is the discursive relationship "identity-legitimization-representation" to be understood beyond the nation-state, i.e. adequately represented theoretically? These questions mark the work of the European Convention at this point, which Michal Krzyzanowski and Florian Oberhuber have started to investigate (see the papers by Krzyzanowski & Oberhuber in this volume).

As was – hopefully – demonstrated at the beginning of this paper, the analytical tools for such a project have been developed in six years of interdisciplinary research in DPI. We believe that our theoretical framework, which most certainly will have to be differentiated and elaborated, allows for the explanation of many phenomena mentioned above and also to formulate new hypotheses for the new contexts to be investigated (see Bauböck, Mokre, & Weiss 2003; Wodak & Puntscher-Riekmann 2003). We are optimistic that we will be able to pursue our new agenda in one institutional way or another. In any case, the intellectual resources that we have gained in the course of these years will find new challenges for application.

Notes

1. Major stimulating comments on the EU-research came from Aaron Cicourel, Theo van Leeuwen, Irene Bellier, Anton Pelinka, Helga Nowotny, Norman Fairclough, Rick Iedema, Jim Martin and András Kovács. We are particularly grateful to the "Forward Studies Unit" in Brussels which supported our fieldwork. Moreover, we would like to thank Caspar Einem, Rudolf Scholten and Raoul Kneucker for making our fieldwork possible from the official Austrian side involved.

2. In our definition of inter/trans/multidisciplinarity, we relate primarily to the ideas of Nowotny (1997). (See also Wodak & Weiss 2002; Weiss & Wodak 2003.)

3. See Chouliaraki and Fairclough (1999) for an extensive discussion of these concepts.

4. See van Leeuwen and Wodak (1999) for an extensive discussion.

5. The formula "legitimization through procedure" is taken from the sociologist Niklas Luhmann: "*Legitimation durch Verfahren*"; cf. Luhmann (1969).

References

Bauböck, R., Mokre, M., & Weiss, G. (Eds.). (2003). *Europas Identitäten. Mythen, Konflikte, Konstruktionen.* Frankfurt a. M./New York: Campus.

Benhabib, S. (1996). *Democracy and Difference.* Princeton, NJ: Princeton University Press.

Bourdieu, P. (1980). *Le sens pratique.* Paris: Les éditions de Minuit.

Chouliaraki, L. & Fairclough, N. (1999). *Discourse in Late Modernity: Rethinking Critical Discourse Analysis.* Edinburgh: Edinburgh University Press.

Fairclough, N. (1992). *Discourse and Social Change.* Oxford, UK and Cambridge, MA: Polity Press and Blackwell.

Fairclough, N. & Wodak, R. (1997). "Critical discourse analysis". In T. van Dijk (Ed.), *Discourse Studies: A Multidisciplinary Introduction. Volume 2* (pp. 258–284). London: Sage.

Foucault, M. (1972). *L'ordre du discours.* Paris: Gallimard.

Giddens, A. (1984). *The Constitution of Society. Outline of the Theory of Structuration.* Cambridge: Polity Press.

Giddens, A. (1995). *Beyond left and right. The future of radical politics.* Stanford: Stanford University Press.

Habermas, J. (1981). *Theorie des kommunikativen Handelns.* 2 Volumes. Frankfurt a. M.: Suhrkamp.

Huntington, S. P. (1996). *The Clash of Civilizations and the Remaking of World Order.* New York: Simon & Schuster.

Ifversen, J. (2002). "Europe and European Culture – a conceptional analysis". *European Societies, 4*(1), 1–26.

Kosselleck, R. (1972). "Einleitung". In C. Brunner & R. Kosselleck (Eds.), *Geschichtliche Grundbegriffe, Band 1* (pp. xiii–xxvii). Stuttgart: Ernst Klett Verlag.

Kovács, A. & Wodak, R. (Eds.). (2003). *NATO, Neutrality and National Identity: the Case of Austria and Hungary.* Vienna: Böhlau.

Lemke, J. (1995). *Textual Politics. Discourse and Social Dynamics.* London: Taylor and Francis.

Luhmann, N. (1969). *Legitimation durch Verfahren.* Neuwied/Berlin: Luchterhand.

Luhmann, N. (1997). *Die Gesellschaft der Gesellschaft.* 2 Volumes. Frankfurt a. M.: Suhrkamp.

Meyer, M. (2001). "Between theory, method, and politics: positioning of the approaches to CDA". In R. Wodak & M. Meyer (Eds.), *Methods of Critical Discourse Analysis* (pp. 14–31). London: Sage.

Mouzelis, N. (1995). *Sociological theory: What went wrong? Diagnoses and remedies.* London: Routledge.

Muntigl, P., Weiss, G., & Wodak, R. (2000). *European Union Discourses on Un/Employment. An interdisciplinary approach on employment policy-making and organizational change.* Amsterdam: Benjamins.

Nowotny, H. (1997). "Transdisziplinäre Wissensproduktion – eine Antwort auf die Wissensexplosion?". In F. Stadler (Ed.), *Wissenschaft als Kultur* (pp. 180–210). Vienna/ New York: Springer.

Ricoeur, P. (1992). *Oneself as Another.* Chicago, IL: University of Chicago Press.

Schutz, A. (1962). *The Problem of Social Reality. Collected Papers. Volume 1.* The Hague: Martinus Nijhoff.

Shahin, J. & Wintle, M. (Ed.). (2000). *The Idea of a United Europe: Political, Economic, and Cultural Integration since the Fall of the Berlin Wall.* New York: St. Martin Press.

Stråth, B. (Ed.). (2000a). *Europe and the Other and Europe as the Other.* Brussels: Peter Lang.

Stråth, B. (2000b). "Introduction: Europe as a discourse". In B. Stråth (Ed.), *Europe and the Other and Europe as the Other* (pp. 8–18). Brussels: Peter Lang.

Stråth, B. (2000c). "Multiple Europes: integration, identity and demarcation to the other". In B. Stråth (Ed.), *Europe and the Other and Europe as the Other* (pp. 385–420). Brussels: Peter Lang.

Tassin, E. (1992). "Europe: a political community". In C. Mouffe (Ed.), *Dimensions of Radical Democracy* (pp. 67–89). London: Verso.

Van Dijk, T. A. (2001). "Multidisciplinary CDA: a plea for diversity". In R. Wodak & M. Meyer (Eds.), *Methods of Critical Discourse Analysis* (pp. 95–120). London: Sage.

Van Leeuwen, T. & Wodak, R. (1999). "Legitimizing immigration control. A discourse-historical analysis". *Discourse Studies, 1*(1), 83–118.

Voegelin, E. (1987). *The New Science of Politics. An Introduction.* Chicago: Chicago University Press.

Weiler, J. (1997). "To be a European citizen – Eros and civilization". *Journal of European Public Policy, 4*(4), 495–519.

Weiss, G. (2002). "A.E.I.O.U. – Austria Europae Imago, Onus, Unio?". In M. af Malmborg & B. Stråth (Eds.), *The Meaning of Europe* (pp. 563–284). Oxford/New York: Berg.

Weiss, G. & Wodak R. (Ed.). (2003). *Critical Discourse Analysis. Theory and Interdisciplinarity.* London: Palgrave/MacMillan.

Wodak, R. (1996). *Disorders of Discourse.* London: Longman.

Wodak, R. (2000). "Does sociolinguistics need social theory? New perspectives on critical discourse analysis". *Discurso & Sociedad, 2*(3), 123–147.

Wodak, R. (2001). "What CDA is about – a summary of its history, important concepts and its developments." In R. Wodak & M. Meyer (Eds.), *Methods of Critical Discourse Analysis* (pp. 1–14). London: Sage.

Wodak, R. (2002). "Aspects of Critical Discourse Analysis." *Zeitschrift für Angewandte Linguistik, 36*, 5–31.

Wodak, R. (2004). "National and transnational Identities. European and other identities constructed in interviews with EU-officials". In R. K. Herrmann, T. Risse, & M. B. Brewer (Eds.), *Transnational Identities. Becoming European in the EU* (pp. 97–128). Lanham et al.: Rowman & Littlefield.

Wodak, R., de Cillia, R., Reisigl, M., Liebhart, K., Hofstätter, K., & Kargl, M. (1998). *Zur diskursiven Konstruktion nationaler Identität.* Frankfurt/Main: Suhrkamp.

Wodak, R., de Cillia, R., Reisigl, M., & Liebhart, K. (1999). *The Discursive Construction of National Identity.* Edinburgh: Edinburgh University Press. (Revised and shortenend translation of Wodak, R., de Cillia, R., Reisigl, M., Liebhart, K., Hofstätter, K., & Kargl, M. 1998.)

Wodak, R. & Ludwig, C. (1999). "Introduction". In R. Wodak & C. Ludwig (Eds.), *Challenges in a Changing World. Issues in Critical Discourse Analysis* (pp. 11–20). Vienna: Passagen.

Wodak, R. & Meyer, M. (Eds.). (2001). *Methods of Critical Discourse Analysis.* London: Sage.

Wodak, R. & Weiss, G. (2001). "'We are different than the Americans and the Japanese!' A critical discourse analysis of decision-making in European Union meetings about employment policies". In E. Weigand & M. Dascal (Eds.), *Negotiation and Power in Dialogic Interaction* (pp. 39–63). Amsterdam: Benjamins.

Wodak, R. & Weiss, G. (2002). Organizing, Legitimizing and Negotiating European Identities. Plenary lecture LAUD 2002, Landau, March 25–28, 2002.

Wodak, R. & Weiss, G. (2004). "Möglichkeiten und Grenzen der Diskursanalyse: Konstruktionen europäischer Identitäten". In O. Panagl & R. Wodak (Eds.), *Text und Kontext. Theoriemodelle und methodische Verfahren im transdisziplinären Vergleich* (pp. 67–86). Würzburg: Königshausen & Neumann.

Wodak, R. & Puntscher-Riekmann, S. (2003). "'Europe for all' – diskursive Konstruktionen europäischer Identitäten". In R. Bauböck, M. Mokre, & G. Weiss (Eds.), *Europas Identitäten. Mythen, Konflikte, Konstruktionen* (pp. 283–304). Frankfurt a. M./New York: Campus.

CHAPTER 7

'European identity wanted!'
On discursive and communicative dimensions of the European Convention

Michał Krzyżanowski
Lancaster University

1.   Introduction: European Convention and EU's political identity

This article[1] analyses the European Union's most recent attempt at improving its political and institutional structure, viz. the European Convention. The central argument of this article is that the works, effects and achievements of the recently-completed European Convention have a profound influence on not only the "institutional architecture" of the Union, but, much more, on "the European identity", i.e. the institutional identity of the transnational EUropean polity. Willing to closely and systematically examine how the constructions and reformulations of EU's institutional "self-definition" actually took place within the European Convention, the interdisciplinary approach proposed here must be taken in order to (a) cope with the multitude of highly-complex and multifarious processes that give rise to renegotiations of European (institutional) identity within the Convention, and, (b) approach the latter in a way closely corresponding to the complexity of the multilayered context (viz. EU-institutions) of those renegotiations. Through the perspective presented here, an interdisciplinary approach to researching European Union institutions is taken, combining theories from various strands of social sciences and humanities as well as proposing a methodological approach linking linguistic, discourse-based research to other methods from widely understood social sciences (e.g. ethnographic observations widely established in social anthropology, etc.). Additionally, this article also aims at contributing to the ongoing academic debates concerning the "meaning" and "future" of Europe and of the European Union within such disciplines as, *inter alia*, European studies, political science, and social-scientific research on collective identities (including Critical Discourse Analysis).

The European Convention, which convened for sixteen months between February 2002 and July 2003, was installed following the decisions of the 2001 EU summit in Laeken, Belgium. Among the main tasks of the Convention were: fulfilling the expectations of EU citizens, improving and reforming the functioning of EU institutions, and delineating further ways of tackling challenges arising from the EU's changing intra-institutional structure (i.e. Enlargement), as well as the altering EU-external environment. Surprisingly enough, the European Constitution, or, as it was defined in the Laeken mandate, "a Constitution for European Citizens" (cf. Laeken Declaration 2001:23) was just one of the very many points on the agenda of the European Convention. However, as it soon turned out, the "constitutional task" of writing a draft of a new European Constitution, and thus earning a place in European history, soon pushed aside many other questions that the Convention might have deliberated on in detail.[2]

It is assumed here that one of the main tasks of the European Convention was, apart from sketching out improvements and reforms of the European Union, to strengthen the EU's democratic legitimacy, or, actually, to diminish its apparent and widely-discussed "democratic deficit", primarily through changing its collective image to the one of a representative polity. If political legitimacy is defined as "a generalised degree of trust of the addressees of the EU's institutional and policy outcomes towards the emerging political system" (Maurer 2003:168), it could be suggested that it is exactly within such "search for social trust" that declarations and reformulations concerning the political or other (collective) identity of such a system would become very prominent. Therefore, the search for the EU's political legitimacy entails a search for a redefinition of a European (institutional) identity.

As a very prolific academic discussion in humanities and social sciences has shown, the search for European identities is anything but an easy task (cf. Delanty 2003; Krzyżanowski 2003; Niethammer 2000; Stråth 2000 and 2000a; Wodak & Puntscher-Riekmann 2003). This task seems to be particularly difficult if it concerns Europe's political identity, born in a long-term process of re-foundations and re-considerations of the social and political role of EU institutions.

It needs to be stated right from the outset that, out of various meanings of European identity, the focus here is on political and institutional identity of the EU. Hence, following Sobrina Edwards' distinction, the European identity in this case should be interpreted as the "institutional European identity"

(Edwards 2003: 1). Secondly, as Bo Stråth suggests, "European identity is not a phenomenon in an essentialist sense (...). Rather, European identity is discursively shaped in a historical situation, and our task is to investigate under which circumstances this formation took place" (Stråth 2000: 14). Consequently, the aim of this article is to look at particular, historical and political circumstances (EU in general, the European Convention in particular) under which the discursive shaping of a European identity has been taking place. Therefore, following some key, constructive approaches, the European identity is seen here as a multitude of various discursive negotiations and reformulations, which altogether combine to build a social or political discourse in particular realms and settings (such as, e.g., the European political identity constructed within the realm of EU politics and institutions). As Gerard Delanty suggests, a collective identity "is not simply the aggregation of individual identities, but the self understanding of a particular group" (Delanty 2003: 3) achieved within its "collective voices" (i.e. discourses). Thus, through the analyses presented here, I would like to present how the eventual construction of "collective voices" in the Convention actually proceeded, leaving its mark on the process of the European identity formation within the EU institutions.

2.   Analytical standpoint

While most of the academic literature in legal studies (cf. Haltern 2003; Somek forthcoming), and social and political sciences (cf. Closa 2003; Habermas 2001; Menéndez 2003; Slominski 2003) has focused on the Convention as a display of what is often called "the Constitutional process of the EU", only very few studies have investigated the Convention as a political and institutional process that has significant impact on the process of creation and development of a European identity. The aim of this article is to bridge this gap, and to present an in-depth, discourse-based analysis of the Convention as (a) an arena of institutional communication, and (b) as an arena of discursive negotiations (cf. below, for further details), all of which are to be analysed from the point of view of their (potential and eventual) impact on the process of formation and renegotiation of Europe's political identity.

This article constitutes an attempt to analyse the European Convention as a communicative and discursive process. The analyses which are presented here can be understood as "in-depth" in two ways. First, by means of analysing the empirical material provided in this study (the interviews with members of the European Convention and ethnographic observations of the proceedings of the Convention), I offer a practice-oriented effort at qualitative and systematic analysis of discursive phenomena taking place in the works of the Convention. Secondly, the "inside" look into the works of the Convention (on-site observations of the Convention's works, interviews with the ones directly and indirectly involved in its works) presents an attempt to analyse the Convention as an arena of institutional communication, rather than analysing it from a strictly political- or institutional-theoretical point of view. It is hoped that the in-depth perspective on the functioning of the Convention presented here may shed a somewhat different light on how the Convention succeeded in achieving its overall political goals, and how it might have affected the process of developing the EU's political identity.

3.   Empirical data

The discourse-based data presented here were gathered within the pilot field-work of our case study "The European Convention".[3] The fieldwork took place in early December of 2002, at the premises of the European Parliament in Brussels, where all plenary meetings of the European Convention along with some Working Group meetings take place. The fieldwork took five, full working days, throughout which we performed nine, previously-scheduled interviews along with detailed, ethnographic observation of the plenary session. It needs to be mentioned that while the on-site observations and interviews are limited to our Brussels fieldwork, further information about the Convention, gathered from various sources during later stages of Convention's works, are also used in order to support some of the claims presented here.

Within the fieldwork, two closely interconnected and inter-supporting methods of data collection were used. First, we applied the method of ethnographic observations of the Plenary Session of the European Convention, during which we tried to follow the physical arrangement of the Convention meetings (room design, distribution of seats among the members, etc.) in order to get acquainted with the impact that those features might have on the flow of communication during the plenary meetings (cf. below, for details). The observations allowed us to precisely define the context of verbal interactions taking place in the plenary sessions. Such an approach to 'context' was also indispensable for our thorough analysis of discourse data which we examined, following some basic methodological assumptions of the Viennese discourse-historical method of Critical Discourse Analysis (cf. Wodak & Meyer 2001). Furthermore, the direct, on-site observations turned out to be the only source for getting any impression about what was actually taking place in the plenary sessions of the European Convention.

Our second method of data collection comprised semi-structured interviews, carried out with the previously contacted officials involved in the works of the European Convention. Among the interviewed officials were those directly involved in the works of the Convention (i.e. full and alternate members of the Convention) as well as officials (in a way) involved indirectly, i.e. supporting selected groups of members of the Convention. Among the latter group were the officials working in special tasks forces, of both the European Commission (EC), and the European Parliament (EP), responsible for supporting those EC and EP members who were selected to represent their institutions in the Convention. Like our colleagues who performed similar interviews within the institutions of the European Union earlier (cf. Muntigl, Weiss, & Wodak 2000, for further details) we need to stress that some of our interviews took place in conditions which were far from ideal (e.g. in a crowded cafeteria of the EP building, etc.)

As is usually the case with semi-structured interviews, we did not use any "strict" set of questions posed to the interviewees, but, instead, we used "topical frames" which only helped us structure some general themes of "conversations". This allowed us to gain more feedback, as, while uttering their opinions and views on particular topics, the interviewees were able to present their opinions without the feeling of being directly "interrogated" or "questioned". Of course, this also left room for some officials' invoking and applying some already "well trained" statements on particular topics or using some standard elements of the "EU-jargon". In order to make our questions more concrete, we supported some of them by quotations from well known speeches and documents concerning some conceptions of the construction and future of Europe and the EU. The following topical frames were used:

1. *Interviewee's definition of Europe* (as a geographical, territorial, political or other entity).
2. *Interviewee's vision of future development and finality of the "European Project"* (expectations on the final outcome of political processes taking place within the EU).
3. *Interviewee's vision of EU and its relation to citizens of the Union* (accuracy of statements about "bringing the Union closer to the people", definition of the European Citizenship and its complementariness/contradiction to national citizenships).

4. *Interviewee's vision of EU as a democratic system* (future of democracy within the EU, preferred models of EU's democratic system).

5. *Interviewee's conception of EU's relation with the World (Others)* (global challenges of the EU, new conceptions of political polarization of the world into Europe, USA and Japan, defining "immediate" and "far" environment of Europe).

6. *Interviewee's opinions on EU-Enlargement* (general assessment of the Enlargement process, historical, political and other dimensions of the enlargement).

7. *Interviewee's conceptions of Unity, Diversity and Identity within Europe and the EU* (diversity of cultures and traditions of Europe; presence/absence of the European Identity; EU's political impact on issues of identity and diversity).

8. *Interviewee's account of the history of the "European Project"* (Europe and its political developments since 1945; impact of those developments on interviewee's country of origin).

9. *Interviewee's images/symbols/metaphors of Europe* ("one big family" or other metaphors; personal expectations of EU's further development).

The thematic frames were constructed in a way which would allow us to cover, in either implicit or explicit manner, all aspects of what we defined as the "EU discourse about the future of Europe" (cf. below), ranging from very concrete, political issues of the current EU agenda (viz. Enlargement, Common Foreign and Security Policy, development of EU institutions), through issues of democracy and legitimacy in the Union, to the most abstract aspects of visions, images and metaphors of Europe. The very broad structuring of the thematic frames of our interviews helped us elicit a very differentiated set of interviewees' opinions.

4.   Analytical methodology

The multi-method approach of Critical Discourse Analysis, particularly of its Viennese tradition (the so-called "Discourse-Historical-School") developed by Ruth Wodak and her collaborators in recent years, is largely followed within the analytical methodology deployed below. As has been proved in numerous studies, the discourse-historical approach has become one of the major tools for systematic and in depth-analysis of collective identities (cf. Wodak et al. 1999), communicative aspects of EU institutions (cf. Muntigl, Weiss, & Wodak

2000), and, most recently, the issues of European identity constructions (cf. Weiss 2002; Wodak 2004; Wodak & Weiss 2004).

Within the analysis of discourse presented below, the main discursive categories developed and summarized by Martin Reisigl and Ruth Wodak (2001) and originally deconstructing various discursive strategies of (collective and individual) self- and other-presentation are largely followed. Within those strategies (cf. Reisigl & Wodak 2001: 31–90, for further details) the main distinction is made between (a) reference and nomination, (b) predication, (c) perspectivation and involvement, (d) intensification and mitigation, and (e) argumentation. The analysis of the latter is further supplemented by the examination of constructive strategies (strategies of creation of "groups" in discourse) proposed by Ruth Wodak and her collaborators somewhat earlier (cf. Wodak et al. 1999: 37–39, for further details).

5. The European Convention as an arena of institutional communication

The analysis of Communicative space created by the European Convention needs to be divided into two areas. First, the flow of communication, along with the variety of genres functioning within that flow, will be looked at. Secondly, the actual, "physical" set up of the plenary sessions of the Convention and the functioning of verbal and other interactions within that space will be analysed.

5.1 Examining communication flows in the European Convention

The flow of communication within the European Convention took place within a set of genres and through communication channels which were selected and accepted by the Presidium at the very beginning of the operations of the Convention.[4] Figure 1 below illustrates, in a general way,[5] the flow of communication (through genres within the Convention, cf. below).

The basic communication channel of the European Convention was constituted by the Plenary Sessions. Within those sessions, members of the Convention (or their alternates) were entitled to give two to three minute speeches. However, in order to make a speech, a member was obliged to apply to the Secretariat of the Convention (directly linked to the Presidium) before a session. During plenary sessions, members were also entitled to make one-minute-long interventions, within the so-called "blue-card period" initiated by one of the members of the presidium chairing a particular session. Interventions served

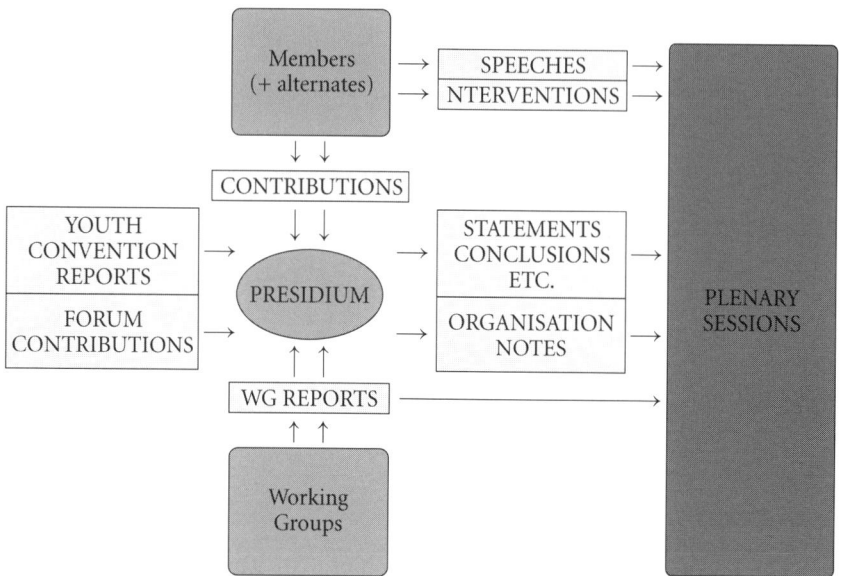

Figure 1. Communication channels and genres within the European Convention

as immediate reactions and comments to issues and reports currently discussed within a given session. The reports of the working groups as well as contributions of the "quasi-external" parties, such as the Youth Convention or the Civic Forum, also needed to be "filtered" by the secretariat and presidium prior to reaching the Convention members and publicly-open plenary sessions.

The communicative flow of the Convention, which, just to remind, supposed to be a truly deliberative-democratic body, displays a surprisingly high level of control of the presidium over contents of contributions and over the length of interventions and speeches. Only contributions and speeches were translated into official languages and considered as official proceedings.[6] The latter were also the only documents which were eventually made public, either during plenary sessions, or, by being placed on the Convention's web-page (speeches and contributions). By the same token, not all of the interventions, which were often vivid reactions to what was taking place during plenary sessions, were translated and made public. Despite the fact that plenary sessions were being videotaped, the tapes were made public with significant delay. Moreover, even if one was able to access official recordings, those were inadequate, as they did not show what was taking place in the plenary room apart from presenting the speaker currently taking the floor.

	EU	C	CZ	ESI	HU	LAT	LIT	M	PL	SK	SI	BG	TU	RO
■ Contributions	206	0	5	0	1	1	0	0	4	1	1	0	0	4
■ Speeches	81	0	4	9	1	0	4	0	19	10	6	6	16	7
□ Total	287	0	9	9	2	0	4	0	23	11	7	6	16	11

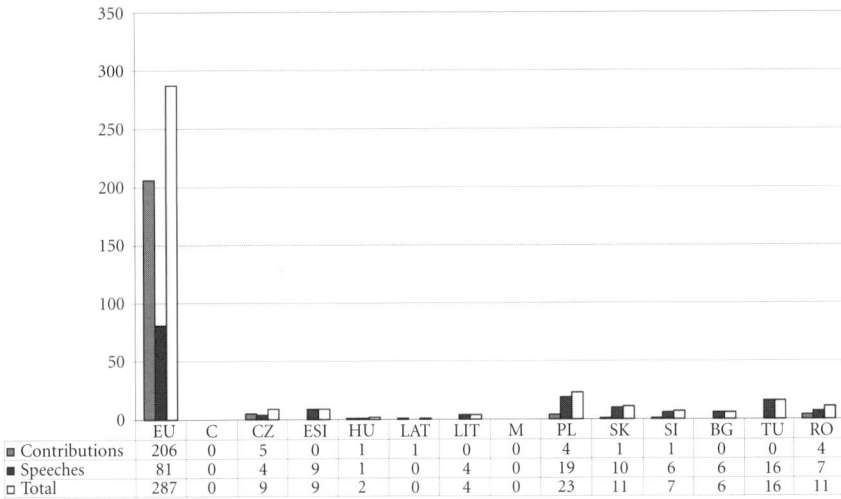

Table 1. Contributions and speeches (EU vs. candidate countries) published on the Convention's web-page http://european-convention.eu.int between February 2002 and January 2003

The statistical analysis of the number of speeches and contributions which have been made public through the Convention's web-page displays immense discrepancy in the number of contributions and speeches made by members of the Convention according to their national origin. During the first period of the Convention's activity (February 2002 till January 2003, cf. Table 1) there were 287 contributions and speeches by the Convention members from EU states which were put onto the web-page. During the same period, the Convention members from "immediate" or "further" EU-Candidate countries produced only 99 contributions (little more than one third of the current EU members) and speeches which were made public through the internet. This discrepancy may show that, on the one hand, the set-up of the communication flow of the Convention might have had some very strict effects (giving voice to some, silencing others), and, on the other hand, that the hypothesis of "mainstreaming of voices" in the Convention (cf. below) seems very plausible.

5.2 Observing plenary sessions of the European Convention

The ethnographic observations of the plenary sessions seem to display a set of interesting processes, which, as in case of the aforementioned communication flows, seem to depict certain important aspects which have influenced the operation of the Convention.

The analysis of the physical set-up was based on the observation of a plenary session taking place in one of the plenary rooms of the European Parliament Building in Brussels (PHS Building, Part C). The Convention gathered in the analysed room until spring 2003, when it moved to a larger room in part A of the building. The fact of moving to a "more representative" room (with bigger and much larger observers' balcony as well as more space for assistants and auxiliary staff) might also be prompted by the fact that, in later stages of the Convention's activity (i.e. in spring and summer 2003), the media and public interest in the Convention rose significantly and giving the Convention the main plenary room of the EP might have seemed to enhance its public image.

While in the plenary sessions held in the "smaller" room, the members of the Convention were seated in rather strict alphabetical order (cf. Figure 2 for a detailed sketch), this was not as clear anymore in the later stages. The seating of the members started with the second row of seats (counting the room upwards from the presidium table) in which, first, the members of the presidium not currently seated behind the presidium table took their seats,[7] and then, the other members of the Convention were seated alphabetically (from the left to the right side of the room). The alphabetical seating of the members continued in further rows, while in the last three to four rows assistants and auxiliary staff were seated.

The fact of the first row being left empty during the observed session could not be clarified. As it seemed, however, it could function as a sort of 'buffer' dividing the presidium from the rest of the Convention members (there were numerous members of the auxiliary staff who could not be seated in far too few, last rows – those members of staff were seated in the larger room, though). Secondly, in the first phases of the Convention, no differentiation between the types of members (full, alternate) and their origin (EC, EP, national parliaments, government representatives) was made in the arrangement of seats. While in the second phase (larger room), the members of the representatives of the European Commission along with their alternates were seated in front of the room, opposite the members of the presidium not seated behind the presidium table (along with members of the Convention's secretariat), and then followed by full representatives (alphabetically) and alternates (again, alphabetically) followed by a far larger group of assistants and members of the auxiliary staff than before. This could be explained in a claim, that, perhaps, as the Convention approached its final stage, the "voices" of members according to institutions they represented (EC, governments, parliaments) started to be more important than in the first phase, i.e. in the so called listening phase

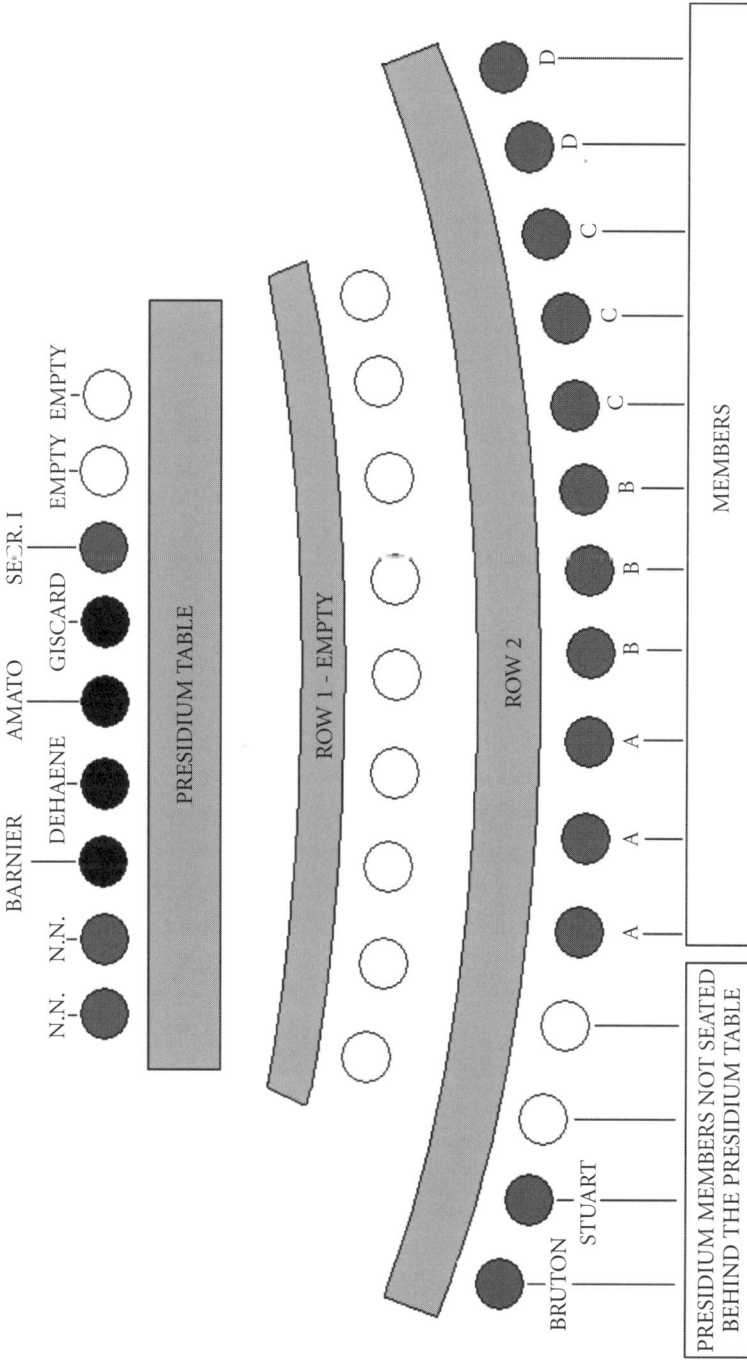

Figure 2. Room-design and distribution of seats in the plenary session of the European Convention of December 5th, 2002

(*phase d'écoute*). The arrangement of the later phase also gave room for the presidium and "crucial members" (EC, presidium members) to influence the debate, and extend the "buffer" from just one empty row to a set of rows filled by some "trusted members". The controlling mood could also be observed, once some of the member states decided to replace their government representatives with foreign ministers, i.e. government members, as was the case with Germany's placing Joschka Fischer and France's placing Dominique De Villepin as the members of the Convention. What came out as controversial, however, was that in order to have the French foreign minister "closer" to the presidium (led by the former French president), his name was interpreted as starting with the letter "D", while the Dutch government representative Gijs de Vries was "alphabetically" seated among those, whose names started with the letter "V"! Thus, as it may be interpreted, even when the arrangement of seats in the Plenary Sessions was still fairly "equal for all" of the members of the Convention, some possibilities for manoeuvre could still be found to make some of the members seemingly "more equal" than others.

6.   Exploring characteristics of the 'EU discourse about the future of Europe'

6.1   The "mainstream voice"

Judging by the preliminary, discourse-analytic examination of our interviews, it can be stated that the textual material from the interviews with Convention Members display many of the features similar to those enumerated by Weiss (2002) with respect to the so-called "speculative talks on Europe" (cf. also Wodak & Weiss 2004; Wodak 2004).

According to Weiss, the speculative talks on Europe, recently very prevalent in various political settings of the EU,[8] are predominantly characterised by two discursive dimensions, viz. "(a) *Making meaning of Europe* (ideational dimension), [and] (b) *Organising Europe* (organisational dimension)" (Weiss 2002:62, Weiss' emphases). The first dimension, as Weiss suggests, "refers to the *idea* of Europe, the essence, substance, meaning, so to speak. The second dimension reflects the question of how Europe shall be organised, which institutional forms of decision-making and political framework are appropriate for the future" (ibid.). Both of the discursive dimensions of the speculative talks on Europe can be further related to two, basic modes of legitimation, i.e. "(a) *legitimation through idea* (identity, history, culture), (b) *legitimation through procedure* (participation, democracy, efficiency)" (ibid.). As has also been suggested (cf. Wodak & Weiss 2004), the speculative talks on Europe are also being very often supported by the third, discursive dimension, i.e. drawing borders (geographical dimension) as well as by yet another mode of legitimation, i.e. legitimation through standardisation, supported by common references to humanism, social and economic standards, etc. On the level of discursive (textual) realisations (cf. Weiss 2002:63), the speculative talks on Europe are most commonly characterised by such elements as: (a) the dualism between political actors ("we") and the people, (b) the topos of "cultural diversity" and "cultural plurality", (c) the globalisation rhetoric, and, (d) the reference to EU Enlargement as *'nécessite historique'*.

In a similar vein, it is argued here that many of the aforementioned dimensions and characteristics of the "speculative talks on Europe" (cf. below) are not genre-specific and limited to speeches/talks only. As the analysis of our interviews shows, the elements enumerated as typical for the speculative talks on Europe are easily traceable in visions and ideas of Europe put forth by many of the members of the European Convention. Furthermore, as the dimensions and characteristics have become prevalent elements in a variety of genres, from concrete policy papers and official EU documents, up to, and including, the most recent draft of the Constitutional treaty,[9] it can be assumed that those features are elements of a larger discourse which semantically frames the discursive constructions of the European space. Hence, the aforementioned dimensions and characteristics become immanent features of what can be defined here as the "EU discourse about the future of Europe".

From the perspective advocated here, the "EU discourse about the future of Europe" has one, overriding purpose (irrespective of its exact, textual realisations): it serves the legitimisation of political actions of the EU, and, by achieving that, this discourse also serves the constructing and re-constructing of the political and institutional identity of the EU. Through discursive re-contextualisation of various discourse topics, as well as through multiplied application of discourse dimensions and argumentation strategies, the "EU discourse about the future of Europe" serves, in an implicit way, the construction and reproduction of a set of visions of Europe which may be defined as "the mainstream voice". The "mainstream voice" is to be understood as a certain form of a collective voice, which stems from a way of self-understanding (cf. Delanty 2003, and above) of the political group of those directly involved in EU-politics and EU-institutions. However, the mentioned self-understanding is in a way imposed by those who, through their political position, are able to control and design such issues as communication flows or public images of EU institutions and politics. Therefore, the "mainstream voice" may be seen as a form of overriding ideology, which legitimises EU politics and its broad, social and political influence.

The discursive displays of the "mainstream voice" seemed to be most visible among representatives of current EU member states involved in ("denationalised") EU institutions, such as, in this case, in the European Convention (cf. below, for details). However, the discourse about the future of Europe among the representatives of the EU-Candidate countries also exhibits some features of the "mainstream voice". Thus, the tracing of such elements may reveal some aspects of EU-Candidate representatives' adjustment to EU (mainstream) visions of the future of Europe. Moreover, as is presented below, the visions of the future of Europe shared by (some) EU-candidate representatives are additionally fostered by very strong expectations for the future. Those "on the other side of the spectrum", i.e. the Convention members who do not adjust to the "mainstream", display modified or other discourse characteristics.

Analytically speaking, the "mainstream voice" is an interdiscursive construction, which can be traced in a variety of textual realisations and genres. The construction of the mainstream demonstrates, to a large extent, a set of features typical for the aforementioned speculative talks on Europe. Hence, one can observe that: (a) similar discourse topics, (b) similar discourse dimensions, and, (c) argumentation strategies supported by "smaller" linguistic elements (such as, e.g., pronouns "we" supporting constructive strategy of group creation), are to be found in most of the textual realisations of the EU discourse about the future of Europe.

6.2 Mainstream vs. non-mainstream and the dissolution of national standpoints in the European Convention

The discursive realisations of the "mainstream voice" display a considerable interconnectedness between various discursive elements. The quotes from one of our interviews (cf. MM 1, below[10]) serve as a very good example of frequent characteristics of the construction of "mainstream voice" in discourse. Those realisations displayed frequent use of the discourse topic of "positive evaluation of the EU and the Convention" and is strongly supported by "globalisation rhetoric":

> MM 1: *we* create a such a successful experiment in integration that others wish to join *us* to and *we* are the example for the world *we* can teach

something about reordering the global relationships that are at present so fragile

The frequent use of the personal pronoun "we" (a form of nomination) shows little perspectivation (and interviewee's deep involvement in collective "action") while, by the same token, it also serves as an element of the strategy of group-construction (we ≈ the EU). The "globalisation rhetoric" (serving legitimation "through idea") portrays the EU as a significant player (metaphors of "example for the world" or "successful experiment" who "can teach...")). The "mainstream voice" is amplified by the definition of Europe:

> MM 1: Europe (...) I see it as a *civilisation* I see it a lot more in philosophical terms than in mechanical design (...) but *it is also a piece of art* so let us be proud of *our* artistic talent

Within the definition of Europe, two different, highly-abstract metaphors ("civilisation", "piece of art") are evoked. The mentioned "mechanical design" of Europe (cf. Abélès 2000) is also further amplified by the presentation of a vision of the ongoing integration of Europe:

> MM 1: well that is up to our successes to decide but no as far as I am concerned that is the process of the integration- integration in lots of different ways *obviously market integration* but increasingly in other ways too *political integration* and it will not have a stop there is no sense that we will ever achieve status quo that we would be complacent with I hope I would be very surprised if that would be the case.

Moreover, the EU-Enlargement as a "historical necessity" or a "moral duty" of "profound importance" is referred to very frequently:

> MM 1: I think that we *have the moral duty to enlarge* I am I think that it is a profound importance that we understand but it is also true that it is very problematical – for us and for the accession countries it will not be concluded on the first of whatever it is 2004 that is not the end of the process *and the enlargement it will transform our geopolitical position* it will be it is as we see in the Convention having a dramatic impact on our work upon ourselves our political construction is being transformed.

The description of enlargement is mostly portrayed as important to "us" (again, nomination and a group-constructive strategy), and far less as important to those (viz. accession countries) whom the process directly affects. Additionally, similar to the EU-integration (above) the Enlargement, as a part of constructing Europe, is also a "process" with no foreseen vision of its finality.

Analysing interviews with those who display typical characteristics of the previously-defined "mainstream voice", one may claim that such views are common for a certain type of collective identity (a "self-understanding") of those, who being involved in EU politics, and who share certain visions of Europe and the EU. However, not all of the representatives of the current EU-Member states (as in the quoted MM 1) demonstrate the characteristics of mainstream voice. As was observed, those members of the Convention who may be classified (due to the characteristics of their discourse) as "non-mainstream" (or "counter-mainstream") display opposite characteristics to those enumerated before within the "mainstream". Thus, the ones representing non-mainstream would assess the Convention in a negative way (as a sort of reply to positive, mainstream topics), e.g.:

> MM 2: but my *disappointment* is this I hope that at least to start with it would the Convention would deal with ideas it would be free-thinking would be creative but instead *it has degenerated rather quickly into a process of institutional bargaining* and I notice that each of the existing institutions and groups of interest are each bidding for more influence and the good example of that is the Commission's paper today which is really arguing for more powers for the Commission simply as simple as that and the European parliament also defends its interest the only group which does not do it very well is the national parliamentarians because we are very varied we do not know each other we come from many different countries we are not an institution so we are in danger of losing out (…) and *one of the criticisms I have of the Convention is that we are very erm inward looking we have had no witnesses or comments from outside.*

The 'non-mainstream' topics are thus developed with use of very "negative" verbs and nouns ("degenerated", "disappointment", "danger"), while the "positive" aspects are negated (the Convention is neither "free thinking" nor "creative"). Furthermore, the non-mainstream is characterised by a definition of Europe which is very different from the quoted mainstream one:

> MM 2: we have that expression in English that strong fences make good neighbours in other words I can put it like this I see Europe as a housing estate where I have good neighbours very friendly neighbours and with whom we exchange presents with and and we we go out together and we we have common holidays together even but we don't live in the same house *and if we did live in the same house we would fall particularly if we sare shared the same bank account.*

Within the non-mainstream definition of Europe, a complex metaphor (of a "housing estate") is deployed. Similarly, the vision of the future construction of Europe is also different from the mainstream one. The non-mainstream vision gives much more importance to the national arenas, while it also questions the hegemonic attempts of the EU governance system:

> MM 2: it would be a Europe of democracies it would ah bring Europe together but *not under a single hegemonic structure* it is a myth to suppose that ah to reunite Europe we need a single power [...] in fact free free countries inhabited by free people find many ways to co-operate it it is natural for for people to trade together to exchange their goods services to travel and to co-operate with good neighbours in common endeavours that is the Europe I want instead *we are forcing Europe into a single mode overriding national consideration* and indeed creating a new gap between people and rulers and so under my model we could more quickly unite Europe but it would be a different sort of structure but one closer to the people.

As is visible, the "non-mainstream" representative also uses numerous "we" pronouns (as nominations), which, however, unlike in the case of "mainstream" representatives, emphasise lack of his identification with the collective "we" of the Convention (a "mainstream-we") and rather deconstructs the Convention's positive vision of its collective stance. Finally, a "global rhetoric" used by the non-mainstream members is quite different from that represented by the mainstream:

> MM2: *the Commission imposes a form of globalisation on member states* if you ask some of the smaller countries candidate countries they will say that *the Commission and the European Union are behaving like a a a globalising power* in making people conform to a regulatory regime erm em which is inappropriate.

Within the non-mainstream "global rhetoric" the negative metaphor (of a "globalising power") is used and further strengthened by negative actions ("imposing globalisation", "making people conform"). Typically for the members of "EU opposition", "the people" (viz. European demos) are nominated as those directly undergoing the negative actions of the EU and being forced to subsume to "globalising conformity" of the EU.

Judging by the fact that both of the previously quoted Convention Members are of the same national origin, and such differences were also frequently observable in case of other, national groups, the hypothesis of national standpoints' dissolving in the inter-institutional bargaining of the Convention may also be put forth. Of the above-quoted examples, MM 1 is a Member of the European Parliament, while MM 2 represents his country's national parliament. Hence, it needs to be tested whether the institutional affiliation (a "national" or a "European" one) may have impact on the national standpoints dissolving within the Convention (cf. also Wodak 2004, for the impact of such a situation on identity construction). In this light, the mainstreaming of voices serves as a demobilising and dissolving factor for national standpoints. However, such an effect of the "mainstream voice" is only visible among the representatives from current EU-member states, while, in the case of representatives from the EU-Candidate countries it would much rather serve as a mobilising and voice-unifying factor. As an example of the voice-unifying effect of mainstreaming we may take, the following examples (MM 3 and FM 2, below) of positive evaluation of the Convention, along with its social and political importance, by members of one national origin:

> MM 3: No one objected the personal set-up of the Convention so *that was accurate* and it gave representation to representatives of particular societies to governments of those societies as well as to European institutions

> FM 2: well my answer here is *very positive* because well since the very beginning I have been among those who assessed *the Convention as a very important process* because it is practically *for the first time its unprecedented* because the previous Convention was very limited and had a slightly different structure and procedure but here practically for the first time in the history of the European Union we have this debate which is almost completely open to the public the debate about the future of the European Union in which the- re take part in which we take part practically on an equal rights basis

Here, the number of positive predications of "the Convention" (as either having "accurate set-up" or, again, as "important process") becomes most apparent. Apart from displaying mainstream-like, very clear visions of the future, political and institutional construction of the EU, as well as invoking strictly mainstream global rhetoric, the Convention Members from the Enlargement countries also possess very clear definitions of the European identity (a rather unique feature of discourse, less frequently and less strongly displayed in the case of current EU-members). Those definitions are based on such ideas as, either, the concrete project of European Citizenship:

> MM 3: Well I think that *something as a European identity or mentality of a European* will come into existence in some time there will be an interim period during *which people will identify themselves as I the European from Poland* because because the dynamics of those processes will weaken this identity *if we introduce European citizenship beside the national one* so that will already determine

or, on abstract issues of shared, collective self-understanding of the Europeans

> FM 2: *the European identity* cannot be built on the basis of making conspicuous how different we are but on the contrary *on displaying what is there in Europe that we really have in common.*

Summing up, the "mainstream voice" of a denationalised, "European elite" shows general discursive elements (further supported by some more detailed, discourse-features) such as: (a) the positive evaluation of the Convention and EU institutions, (b) the positive invocation to the idea of Europe ("ideational" definition of Europe), (c) the future vision of the construction of Europe ("organisational" dimension), (d) the rhetoric of Enlargement as a "historical necessity" or "moral duty", and, finally, (e) the use of global rhetoric (of "global importance", "global challenge"). On the other hand, the non-mainstream discourse is characterised by: (a) the negative evaluation of the Convention and sceptical view of EU institutions, (b) the "realistic" vision of both the future construction of Europe and of the Enlargement, (c) the unusual employment of global rhetoric (interpreting EU institutions as, e.g., a "globalising regime").

6.3 "Adjusting" to the mainstream? On the characteristicsof discourse of Convention members from the EU-Candidate countries

It is noteworthy that the discourse of Convention members from EU-Candidate countries is very polarised and differentiated. However, the opposition of voices among EU Candidate Countries seems to be differently constructed as is the case with current members, i.e., not necessarily along the "mainstream" and "non-mainstream" lines.

Most of the representatives from Enlargement countries (cf. MM 3 and FM 2 above, for respective examples of some clear tendencies observed in a larger number of interviews with "new EU-members") display the features of "mainstream discourse", which is very often supported by references to the future, or as can be analytically determined, to a common "horizon of expectations" (cf. Koselleck 1989). This is also one of the most common aspects of individual and collective identity formation by means of the reference to a common, "future orientation" of a particular group (cf. Kołakowski 1995).

However, as can be observed in the case of some of the Convention members from the Enlargement countries, a very strong reference to the past (in Koselleck's terms "space of experience") characterises their discourses about Europe and the EU. As an example one may cite the interview with one of the Candidate-Country Convention members, who, even when discussing issues relating to the future (her country joining the EU), immediately refers to "past" issues:

> FM 1: I am very very very strong for the European Union because without that it's not possible to give answer to our people who *are in the 1989 we changed the system*

Within the construction of the "past", a very interesting use of nomination/group-construction (through personal pronoun "we") can be observed. Namely, "we", in this case, refers to the national realm, much more clearly than the aforementioned "we" of the Convention. Additionally, those Candidate-Country Convention members who strongly refer to the past, also show a very strong identification with their national origin (which was claimed to be typical for "non-mainstream" voices, cf. above), rather than, as is the case with the "mainstream" ones, strongly identifying with EU politics and with the "supranational level" of the European polity:

> FM 1: if we follow the steps like Mr. Bonde [Jens Peter Bonde, MEP, Denmark, generally perceived as rather sceptical about Enlargement] I am not sure for me it's not possible to be on his side because because he is the member of the European Union so he does not know the feeling of the people *we changed the system before* (...) and next one I know that if we the I can say elderly people and the people with the experience not prepare our countries for European Union we lose all our generation because they go there (...) *if its not that the revolution in 1989 was not necessary not only for the east part but also for the west part of that.*

From their frequent references to the past and their strong identification with national origin, it might be inferred that, like frequent voices from the "EU elite", some of the Convention members from the Enlargement countries are still in the process of "learning how to do EU politics". As there existed strong differentiation in the way various Convention members from the Enlargement countries were treated by the members of current EU member states, those Candidate-country members who adjusted to mainstream voices and visions

sooner than others (i.e. learned EU-politics faster) could gain much more attention of the experienced EU politicians, such as, e.g., of the Members of the
European Parliament, etc.

7. Conclusions and final remarks

Judging by the analyses of the empirical material presented here,[11] it seems
that some, not officially expressed, yet very prevalent, expectations of the European Convention as a "legitimacy-", "democracy-", and "identity-forging"
body have been slightly exaggerated. Instead of delineating the new social
and political order of the EU, the European Convention has rather, both in
explicit and in latent ways, contributed to re-introducing some well known
"mainstream" visions of the future construction of Europe. By doing so, the
attempt at creating a new mode of self-understanding of EU politics and institutions, viz. creating, in a discursive way, the foundations for a constructive
and negotiation-based European political identity, was, in a way, surpassed by
the Convention in its overall drive to create the first European Constitution
according to "mainstream" concepts. Evidently, the drive towards the final effect took place without consideration of the possibilities for gathering various
national and institutional voices and combining them into one EU discourse
on the future of Europe. As has been shown, the mainstreaming of voices (i.e.
adjusting them to well-established, EU-based visions), dissolution of national
standpoints supporting inter-institutional bargaining, and marginalisation of
non-mainstreamed Convention members, all supported by the very specific
and well-controlled communication set-up of the Convention, served the protection of the existing political status quo of the Union, rather than looking for
new ways of self-definition of the European polity.

As mentioned above, most of the academic discussions concerning the
Convention have, so far, focused on the Convention as a display of "the constitutional process of the EU", with the issues of the Convention as a political
and institutional process gaining somewhat less attention. Such a division reveals a difficulty that seems to be inextricably bound to any (critical) attempt
to examine the European Convention. On the one hand, for many months the
Convention had been involved in a process during which actions were taken by
various national and institutional representatives in order to put forward the
issues which were of prime interest to the parties they represented. On the other
hand, however, the final stage was directed exclusively towards writing the draft
of the European Constitution, the existence of which would clearly emphasise

the accuracy of installing the Convention and prove the effects of its long and often questioned procedures. Obviously, examining the final result of the Convention, i.e. a Constitution for Europe, is much easier to do, as the final draft seems to perfectly display what were the reasons for installing the Convention, and what impact the consensus at the end of the Convention's deliberations might have on defining the European Union's self-image for the future. However, if, as has been done here, one looks at the Convention as a process, i.e. if one analyses earlier stages of its work when negotiations, bargaining, political "mainstreaming" and dissemination of voices were still on the daily agenda, one may see that the Convention was anything but a deliberative-democratic process. Therefore, the draft of a Constitution, may only be an attempt to compensate for something that actually did not take place in the Convention, viz. the so much sought after consensus.[12]

In the light of the above-presented empirical material, it is not surprising that the form of the European Convention has been widely discussed and questioned. The Convention method was taken over following the achievements of the "first Convention" responsible for drafting the EU's Charter of Fundamental Rights. As the result of the first Convention remains legally non-binding and highly questionable as to its concrete effect on improving democratic legitimacy of the Union, so might be the fate of the effects of the second (viz. European) Convention, the actual assignment of which was to make up for the democratic failure of the Treaty of Nice, or to just "pave the way for the next IGC" (cf. Laeken Declaration 2001:24) and not to "address the real problem of how to democratise the European governance system" (Höreth 2003:1). As obvious, the Convention method, which was selected as a miraculous alternative to other methods allowing for strict bargaining between national and institutional standpoints, has been equipped by nation states with "several mechanisms that, next to the autonomy of the Convention, preserved their room for manoeuvre of control" (Closa 2003:3). Thus, the form of the Convention, despite being an improvement as to its composition (representatives of governments and parliaments from present and future member states, MEPs, etc.), plainly displayed the fact that "a priori, the democratic profile of the Convention was not the driving force in its design" (ibid.) and a lot of room was still left for national and, predominantly, institutional bargaining. This might also be caused by the fact that, as has been shown here, "everyone in the Convention has certain institutional or institutionalised interests (and) behind the façade of deliberative discourse lies the true struggle of conflicting interests" (Höreth 2003:3).

Secondly, the final result of the European Convention, i.e. the Constitutional treaty, needs to be discussed. The form of a constitution (or, actually, its outline or draft) was seemingly selected to give more significance to the workings of the European Convention (viz. common references to other, historically significant Conventions and their results, i.e. constitutions), as the term "constitution" confers much more far-reaching and fundamental significance than any other sort of text or proposal that the Convention could have proposed to the next IGC. Some argue that the fact of the Convention's drafting of the Constitution for the European Union was the evidence for the actual constitutional process, or as Ulrich Haltern (2003) puts it "constitutionalisation" (cf. also Weiler 1999), which had been taking place in the EU for a long period of time. In this interpretation, the development of EU laws from a set of "legal arrangements binding upon several states into a vertically integrated legal regime" (Haltern 2003: 15) has already been characteristic of the EU's constitutional efforts. However, if it is assumed that the term "constitution" may, or actually has to, mean something completely different than a "treaty" or any similar expression, then it becomes clear that "constitution" may not be used only as an ideological term which would only support the political legitimacy for such and such institution or assembly, e.g., a Convention. "Constitution" needs therefore to refer to the legal structure of a governance system, a "higher law" (Somek forthcoming: 5) regulating relations between the polity and the demos, and hence regulating the "overall system" of the EU's entire political order.

Both of the aforementioned crucial aspects of the European Convention, viz., its form and result (the Convention method and the expected European Constitution), seem to have an ambivalent influence on the process of European Union's redefinition of its political and institutional identity. On the one hand, the actual form of the Convention, i.e. an assembly of very different political voices, seemed to make it impossible for the Convention to achieve any far-reaching consensus along the prescribed methods, while it also makes it difficult for the Convention to become an identity-forging body. Despite the fact that the Convention was supposed to clear the ground for the new "collective project" of the reformed and democratic Union, the examination of the actual working and composition of the Convention show that this has been achieved to a very small degree. In such a situation, one may claim that the EU has perhaps not yet reached a stage where it could construct its definitive self-image, not to mention forge a collective identity for all those affected by the institutional impact of the European Union's regulations and policies, viz. "the European demos". As was shown in the analysis, the intra-institutional communication set up by the Convention actually impaired its democratic character. Assuming that "communication could play a significant role for European identity and the democratisation of the EU at various levels" (Wodak & Puntscher-Riekmann 2003:296), it seems that the flows of communication in the European Convention have not been properly set up and used in order to yield its eventual success, which could also play a significant role in building a European identity.

As far as constitutional conventions are concerned, many references to the issue of identity formation come to mind. As Wodak and Puntscher-Riekmann advocate, the (historically known) constitution-writing Conventions were "powerful symbols of new beginning" (ibid.:293). This, however, has not necessarily been the case as regards the European Convention. It seems that the Convention, rather than defining a new beginning for the Union, has contributed to defending the existing institutional status quo, instead of bringing a new order to the European Union's political system. Furthermore, out of many conceptions of social and political roles of constitutions (cf. Menéndez 2003; or Somek forthcoming, for an overview), the actual role that the Constitution for Europe, submitted by the Convention at the end of its proceedings, may play in democratising the EU, bringing it "closer to the people" or defining its self-image, is rather vague. Somek puts among one of the four basic conceptions of modern constitutions a "conception [which] views a constitution as an act of political self-definition and self-expression" (Somek forthcoming:6). It would be perhaps unfair to say that the final draft of a "Constitution for Europe"[13] displays no elements at all that might serve as an act of the Union's self-expression and self-definition, e.g. declarations in the Preamble, or, references to the Union's values, objectives and fundamental freedoms in Part I. However, the end-effect should not overshadow the process that gave birth to the draft of the EU's constitutional treaty. Thus, staying with Somek's line of thinking regarding the conception of a constitution, it should be stated that the act of self-expression and self-definition, so much looked for as far as the collective identity of the EU as a transnational polity is concerned, should be preceded by a conscious process leading to such an act. As we have seen, such a process found numerous obstacles in the European Convention.

Notes

1. Many thanks to Ruth Wodak, Florian Oberhuber and Michał Remiszewski for their comments on the early draft of this chapter.

2. Cf. Florian Oberhuber's article in this volume for a more detailed description of the origins and functions of the European Convention.

3. The fieldwork, conducted by Florian Oberhuber and myself, constituted a pilot study which further evolved into the Research Project '*The Discursive Re- Construction of European Identities*', carried out at the Department of Applied Linguistics, University of Vienna and financed by the Austrian National Bank's 'Jubilee Foundation' (ÖNB Jubiläumsfonds).

4. This was regulated by the set of Presidium notes on the functioning of the European Convention. The most crucial one is CONV 9/02, Secretariat of the European Convention, Brussels, March 14th, 2002.

5. Cf. Oberhuber (2004) for a more detailed outline of the communication channels within the European Convention.

6. As was agreed right from the beginning of Convention's works, the members from candidate countries were using English in the proceedings of the Convention, due to 'deficiencies' in the level of preparation of the EP Translation Service.

7. Surprisingly, the representative of Enlargement countries to the presidium, i.e. Alojz Peterle of Slovenia, very rarely took his seat among presidium members.

8. Particularly, Joschka Fischer's Speech given at the Humboldt University in Berlin in May 2000 marks the milestone in establishing the form of 'speculative talks on Europe'. Speeches of other renowned politicians, such as Jacques Chirac, Vaclav Havel or Gerhard Schröder, soon followed a similar path of argumentation.

9. "Draft Treaty Establishing a Constitution for Europe", Secretariat of the European Convention, Brussels, July 18th, 2003, No. CONV 850/03.

10. As the quotes are taken from linguistic transcripts of the interviews they may include grammatical mistakes (according to the 'recorded speech') and not use the punctuation in its usual, grammatical functions.

11. The article presents only selected examples of discursive realisations and constructions of various aspects of 'EU Discourse about the Future of Europe' outlined earlier. The limitations of space force the reduction of number of examples and analysed elements.

12. Mentioned on the front page of the very final version of the draft constitution, cf. "*Draft Treaty Establishing a Constitution for Europe*", Secretariat of the European Convention, Brussels, July 18th, 2003, No. CONV 850/03, p. ii.

13. Cf. "*Draft Treaty Establishing a Constitution for Europe*", Secretariat of the European Convention, Brussels, July 18th, 2003, No. CONV 850/03.

References

Abélès, Marc (2000). "Virtual Europe". In I. Bellier & T. M. Wilson (Eds.), *An Anthropology of the European Union: Building, Imaging and Experiencing the New Europe* (pp. 31–50). Oxford: Berg.

Closa, Carlos (2003). *The Convention Method: A Model for Democratising the European Union?* CONV-EU Conference Paper, Centre for International Relations, Warsaw, April 26th, 2003.

Delanty, Gerard (2003). "Is there a European Identity?" Paper presented at the Conference *Institutional Dynamics and Democracy in the EU*, ARENA, Oslo, October 3rd, 2003.

Edwards, Sobrina (2003). "Creating a European Identity: Prospects and Implications." Paper presented at the *BMW Centre for German and European Studies* (CGES Conference), Georgetown, March 21st–22nd, 2003.

Fossum, John-Erik (2001). *Identity Politics in the European Union.* ARENA Working Paper No. 01/17.

Habermas, Jürgen (2001). "Why Europe Needs a Constitution". *New Left Review, 11* (September/October 2001), 5–26.

Haltern, Ulrich (2003). "Pathos and Patina: The Failure and Promise of Constitutionalism in the European Imagination". *European Law Journal, 9*(1), 14–44.

Höreth, Marcus (2003). "From Deliberation to Bargaining Again – the Limits of the Convention Method". Paper presented at the *Meeting of the European Policy Institutes Network* (EPIN) of March, 2003.

Kołakowski, Leszek (1995). "O tożsamości zbiorowej". In Krzysztof Michalski (Ed.), *Tożsamość w Czasach Zmiany: Rozmowy w Castelgandolfo* (pp. 44–56). Cracow: Znak.

Koselleck, Reinhart (1989). *Vergangene Zukunft.* Frankfurt a.M.: Suhrkamp.

Krzyżanowski, Michał (2003). "'My European feelings are not only based on the fact that I live in Europe': On the new mechanisms in European and national identification patterns emerging under the influence of EU Enlargement." *Journal of Language and Politics, 2*(1), 175–204.

Laeken Declaration (2001). *The Laeken Declaration on the Future of the European Union.* Annex 1 to the Presidency Conclusions of the European Council Meeting in Laeken, 14–15 December 2001. Brussels, No. SN 300/1/01 REV 1, 19–27.

Maurer, Andreas (2003). "Less Bargaining – More Deliberation: The Convention Method for Enhancing EU Democracy". *International Politics and Society,* I/2003, 167–190.

Menéndez, Augustín-José (2003). *Three Conceptions of the European Constitution.* ARENA Working Paper 03/12.

Muntigl, Peter, Weiss, Gilbert, & Wodak, Ruth (2000). *European Union Discourses on Unemployment. An Interdisciplinary Approach to employment Policy-Making and Organisational Change.* Amsterdam/Philadelphia: John Benjamins.

Niethammer, Lutz (2000). "A European identity?" In Bo Stråth (Ed.), *Europe and the Other and Europe as the Other* (pp. 87–113). Brussels: PIE-Peter Lang.

Oberhuber, Florian (2004). "Elite Integration in an Enlarging EU: The Case of the European Convention". In S. Antohi, M. Bach, & C. Lahusen (Eds.), *Social Dynamics and Political Institutions in an Enlarging Europe* Budapest: CEU Press (In press).

Reisigl, Martin & Wodak, Ruth (2001). *Discourse and Discrimination.* London: Routledge.

Slominski, Peter (2003). *Legitimacy of the European Convention and its Impact on the IGC.* CONV-EU Conference Paper, Centre for International Relations, Warsaw, April 26th, 2003.

Somek, Alexander (forthcoming). "Constitutional Treaty: A Comment on the Legal Language of the European Union". To appear in *Annual of German and International Law*.

Stråth, Bo (2000). "Introduction: Europe as a discourse". In Bo Stråth (Ed.), *Europe and the Other and Europe as the Other* (pp. 13–44). Brussels: PIE-Peter Lang.

Stråth, Bo (2000a). *EU efforts at creating a European Identity: 1973 and beyond*. Florence: RSCAS-EUI IDNET Conference Paper EUR/72.

Stråth, Bo (2002). "A European identity: To the historical limits of the concept". *European Journal of Social Theory*, 5(4), 387–401.

Weiler, Joseph H. H. (1999). *The Constitution of Europe*. Cambridge: Cambridge University Press.

Weiss, Gilbert (2002). "Searching for Europe: The problem of legitimisation and representation in recent political speeches on Europe". *Journal of Language and Politics*, 1(1), 59–83.

Wodak, Ruth, de Cillia, Rudolf, Reisigl, Martin, & Liebhart, Karin (1999). *The Discursive Construction of National Identity*. Edinburgh: EUP.

Wodak, Ruth & Meyer, Michael (Eds.). (2001). *Methods of Critical Discourse Analysis*. London: Sage.

Wodak, Ruth (2004) "National and transnational Identities: European and Other Identities Oriented to in Interviews with EU Officials". In R. K. Hermann, T. Risse, & M. Brewer (Eds.), *Transnational identities: Becoming European in the EU* (pp. 97–129). Lanham, MD: Rowman and Littlefield.

Wodak, Ruth & Weiss, Gilbert (2004). "Visions, Ideologies and Utopias in the Discursive Construction of European Identities: Organising, Representing and Legitimising Europe". In M. Pütz, J. A. Neff-van Aertselaer, & T. A. van Dijk (Eds.), *Communicating ideologies: Language, Discourse and Social Practice* (pp. 225–252). Frankfurt am Main: Peter Lang.

Wodak, Ruth & Puntscher-Riekmann, Sonja (2003). "Europe for All: Diskursive Konstruktionen europäischer Identitäten". In M. Mokre, G. Weiss, & R. Bauböck (Eds.), *Europas Identitäten: Mythen, Konflikte, Konstruktionen* (pp. 283–304). Frankfurt am Main: Campus.

CHAPTER 8

Deliberation or 'mainstreaming'?
Empirically researching the European Convention*

Florian Oberhuber
University of Vienna

1. Introduction

There is a new animal in the zoology of European institutions, namely the "Convention on the Future of Europe", or we could also ask: What is this new animal that is called the European Convention?

In this chapter, I will present work-in-progress on this question, which we are pursuing in the context of a research project entitled "The discursive (re-) construction of European identities" that is carried out at the Research Center "Discourse, Politics, Identity" (University of Vienna) and funded by the Österreichische Nationalbank's Anniversary Fund for the Promotion of Scientific Research and Teaching (*Jubiläumsfonds der Österreichischen Nationalbank*, project no. 10222). Originally, the project was designed by Gilbert Weiss, but was subsequently carried out by Michał Krzyżanowski and Florian Oberhuber, and coordinated by Ruth Wodak. Based on previous research on collective identities (national, supranational, cultural, and other), as well as on the EU as an institutional and political system (cf. Muntigl, Weiss, & Wodak 2000; Weiss & Wodak 2000; Wodak & Weiss 2001; Weiss 2002; Wodak 2004), the project is specifically focussing on the European Convention in the context of the on-going constitutional debates in Europe. Three main research objectives are set: firstly, our aim is to conduct a thorough analysis of the (institutional, political, legal, etc.) *context* of Convention discourse. Such an analysis of context has proven indispensable for understanding the way in which the members act and talk in the Convention. Among various other aspects, this entails providing a description of the genesis, establishment, structure and functioning of the Convention, as well as of parallel discussions in academia, political speeches, legal texts, mass media coverage and so on. The further fate of the Convention's result, the "Draft Treaty Establishing A Constitution for Europe", also needs to be included in the investigation. Secondly, we will look at the Convention as a key institutional arena for the complex process of articulating, (re-)negotiating, (re-)contextualizing of various conceptions of Europe and of the underlying forms of (political, cultural, religious, linguistic, etc.) identities that this debate is based upon. A special focus will be placed on the concrete way that enlargement was debated in the Convention. Lastly, on a theoretical level, we intend to probe the possible contribution of such empirical research to the so-called "democratic deficit" of the European Union.

Concerning the interdisciplinary character of this research agenda, we build on previous experiences of the investigation of language use in institutional settings developed within the framework of the Vienna School of Discourse Analysis (cf. Wodak 2001). The *discourse-historical approach* developed by Ruth Wodak links historical analysis, sociological and political analysis and theories with precise linguistic methods of textual analysis (e.g. systemic-functional linguistics, rhetoric, and theories of argumentation). It is shifting the focus of traditional political science research from structural aspects of policy-making to include the communicative frames within which the policy-making actually takes place. Thus, in contrast to most of the literature on constitutional and fundamental problems of the EU written by legal experts or political scientists, we seek to gain direct access to the field in order to present a dense and complete picture of the concrete communicative and linguistic processes of (re-)constructing 'Europe'. Then, in a second step and based upon the empirical research, questions from legal and political science are reintroduced (see Section 3 below).

In Section 2, some results of a first phase of our research project will be presented and the Convention's mandate, composition, organization and communicative setup will be described. While this part of the project was mainly carried out by the political sociologist in our team, in a second phase the discourse-analytic investigation of interviews with Convention members will be carried out. Thus, in what follows interviews are mainly used as sources of factual information and no in-depth linguistic analyses are performed. However, the information gathered on the Convention process will be used as relevant context for interpreting interviews in the second phase of the project (cf. Leinfellner 2004; Wodak & Weiss 2004:75–76). With regard to this objective, interdisciplinary cooperation manifests itself in a threefold way: firstly, the sociological study of the Convention allows to select interviewees and to design interview guidelines in a well-informed way; secondly, the interpretation of texts and interviews (e.g. with regard to various meanings of Europe) needs to take into account the institutional setting of Convention discourse and the various roles of actors; thirdly, Convention discourse needs to be analyzed in a diachronic dimension, that is as a process of over 16 months where social, cultural and linguistic aspects are intertwined. This third element implies the need to achieve a true integration of perspectives and methods from linguistics and political sociology on a problem-oriented basis (cf. Weiss & Wodak 2003). The main concept put forward in this article, namely "mainstreaming", can be taken as an example. As will be showed in Section 2 below, it involves both, a sociological (issues of power, organization, socialization, etc.) and a linguistic dimension (the narrowing of a discursive space in terms of topics, language, and positions/opinions), or, in other words, "mainstreaming" is conceived as both a social and a discursive process. At this stage of the project, we are still focussing on the first, sociological dimension. However, in the chapter by Michał Krzyżanowski in this volume, first results of a pilot study on discursive realizations of mainstreaming are presented, and the methodology of semi-structured interviews and ethnographic observation are discussed.

1.1 Fieldwork at the European Convention

As summarized in Figure 1, four periods of fieldwork have been administered thus far. The first one, in September 2002, mainly served explorative purposes, as well as the testing of our guidelines for semi-structured interviews (see the paper by Michał Krzyżanowski in this volume). On this basis, all in all 27 interviews with Convention members and staff from the three main EU institutions

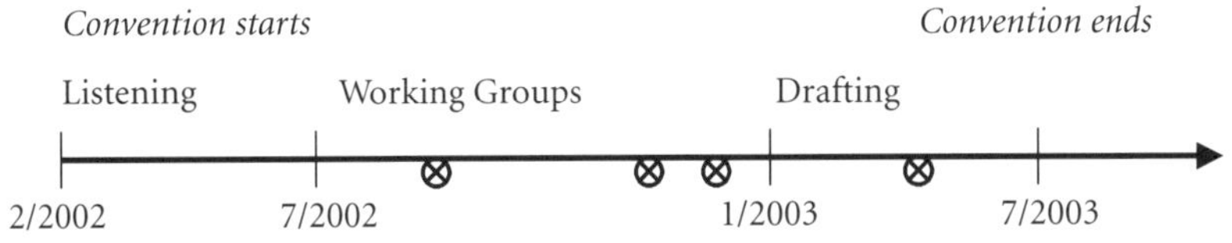

Fieldwork dates
12–13 September 2002: Observations of plenary meetings and interviews
14 November 2002: Observations of Working Group meetings and interviews
2–7 December 2002: Observations of plenary meetings and interviews
25–31 May 2003: Observations of plenary meetings and interviews

Figure 1. Fieldwork periods during the Convention's works

have been conducted at the site of the European Convention in December 2002 and May 2003. Furthermore, we observed several plenary meetings, as well as one Working Group session that was closed to the public, which took place in the Justus Lipsius building of the EU Council of Ministers.

Two limitations of our empirical approach should be noted at the outset. Firstly, as Figure 1 shows, not all of the "phases" of the Convention's works have been covered. Partly, this could be salvaged by drawing on documents that are easily accessible on the Convention's website, verbatim records of Convention proceedings, as well as videotapes of plenary sessions available from the Audio-visual Division of the European Parliament. Secondly, our empirical research may be considered to lack continuity and involvement in the field, particularly when judged by the standards of "participant observation" as a key method in anthropology. While the research team could freely move throughout the buildings of the European Parliament hosting the Convention, utilize the office rooms of one of the Austrian Convention members, and also draw on frequent personal communication with the staff of some Conventioneers, a considerable social distance between the 'observers' and the 'observed' remained. Not being 'one of them', we did not 'participate' in the plenary sessions and the frequent formal and informal meetings, and we were not able to establish close relations of familiarity with Conventioneers. On the other hand, though, the Convention itself, bringing together people from different national and institutional backgrounds, people who often did not know each other before, lacked the kind of cultural 'thickness' peculiar to the traditional objects of anthropological inquiry. Thus, our experience as researchers still resembled those of Convention members: flying to Brussels for a couple of days, interviewing people, socializing and discussing with staff, returning, reading Convention documents and media coverage in order to prepare for our return to Brussels, and so forth.

1.2   Empirical research and theoretical interpretation: A critique of "deliberation"

In the following section, an overview of the collected data will be provided. Our focus will mainly be on presenting a comprehensive contextualization of Convention discourse and thus a general description of the genesis, establishment, structure and functioning of the Convention. As will be shown, this approach implies painting a quite different picture of the Convention than has been revealed prior by the majority of observers and commentators who have described the Convention in terms of deliberation and the normative model of "deliberative democracy". Based upon our empirical research, a critique of the above mentioned accounts will be developed which seem to be missing the very reality of Convention discourse, and, an alternative hypothesis will be put forward. In a third and final section, theoretical reflections on the preconditions and possibilities of empirically researching European 'constitutional politics', and prospects for further research will be discussed.

Three important characteristics of this approach should be highlighted at the outset: Firstly, we began our project with a modest objective, which was to *describe* what happens in the Convention without presupposing any sophisticated model of European integration or politics. The complexity of empirical reality was to be comprehensively accounted for while interpretations were to be left for later phases of the research. Thus, while many commentators of the Convention were starting from the (counterfactual) model of deliberative democracy, we intentionally confined ourselves to a 'phenomenological' approach.

Secondly, when pursuing the said objective, it became clear that the 'object-field' involved an overwhelming complexity in terms of the communication flows, actors involved, relevant context, interrelations with institutions and discourse external to the Convention, and so forth. In our research design, we dealt with this complexity, on the one hand, by using multiple sources of information and attempting to gather as much context information as possible, both in a diachronic and a synchronic dimension. On the other hand, owing to limited resources, we needed to allow departures from a strictly phenomenological approach and find ways to narrow down the data considered relevant. Thus, in what makes up a third characteristic of our research, we ended up applying a standard procedure in qualitative research, namely to go back and forth between data and hypotheses in a hermeneutic 'spiral': First, empirical information was used for formulating our working hypotheses, then, these hypotheses were used as guidelines for further empirical research.

2. The European Convention: Context, structure, functioning

2.1 Pre-history and context

The European Union's long-standing discussion on a reform of its 'constitutional' foundations has yet again gained momentum in the 1990s owing to the prospect of enlargement to the east. In the year 2000, when an effort in transforming this debate into a pragmatic compromise at the Nice European

Council did not produce a comprehensive solution, the idea of a "Convention", which for the first time had been used for drafting the new Charter of Fundamental Rights, was taken up. Soon it became clear that this proposal would find the support of all 15 member states. Then, at the summit meeting during the Belgian presidency (December 2001), the "Declaration of Laeken" set up a Convention composed of representatives of governments, the European Commission, and, mainly, national and European parliamentarians. From February 2002 until July 2003, this new body convened in Brussels, mainly using the meeting rooms and facilities of the European Parliament (cf. Fischer 2003:15–20; Magnette 2002:3–9 for more details).

The mandate of the Convention, as defined by the "Laeken Declaration", was to "consider key issues arising for the Union's future development and try to identify the various possible responses" in order to "pave the way for the next Intergovernmental Conference as broadly and openly as possible" (Laeken Declaration:25). Thus, the 'masters of the treaties', that is the heads of state, would reserve the final power of decision, a procedure known from the negotiation of multilateral treaties in the practice of international law: (1) negotiation of a text, (2) solemn adoption of this text, (3) ratification "in accordance with their [the member states'] respective constitutional requirements" (Treaty on European Union, Art. 48).

While such an account of the Convention's establishment provides a first idea of this body's *raison d'être*, answering the question of why there is a Convention calls for a closer look at its context. As a heuristic scheme, we propose to distinguish between (1) a functional, and, (2) a political context, which shall be briefly sketched out here:

1. To be sure, the "Convention on the Future of Europe" was mainly established to address a number of problems and tensions in the 'operating system' of the Union and between the EU and the national and regional levels, problems which had long been discussed and which would be exacerbated in the aftermath of the EU enlargement in May 2004 (cf. Weiler 1999b). To emphasize this well-established fact, it suffices to note that the Laeken Declaration identified about fifty very concrete questions that the Convention would have to address, ranging from institutional affairs to the dimensions of defense and external relations, and finally the issue of "bringing the Union closer to its citizens". Concerning many of these (functional) questions, the Convention could draw on extensive previous work performed by, for example, think tanks (e.g. the European University Institute, Florence), the European Parliament's Institutional Affairs

Committee or earlier EU Summits. The *road map* agreed upon at the Nice Summit already contained a number of key points of the Convention's future mandate and proceedings. Thus, once again, it can be emphasized that the heads of states were the ones who both initiated the Convention and determined its agenda to a large extent.

2. Concerning the political context of the Convention, in addition to possible strategic considerations of major players within EU politics intending to improve their bargaining position, a key issue in favor of establishing a Convention was a growing preoccupation among politicians and EU officials with the legitimacy crisis of the European project. Here, several events in the immediate past should be noted: the Danish rejection of the Euro (29/09/2000), the mass-protests at the EU Summit of Nice (7–9/12/2000), the first Irish "No" to Nice (8/6/2001), and, at the EU Summit in Gothenburg (14–16/6/2001), again violent protests. In this context, a "Convention" promised to address popular discontent and yield legitimacy in several ways. First, it was composed of elected representatives (most of which are parliamentarians), second, it convened publicly, and third, by establishing a "listening phase" and several other elements (such as an Internet "forum", a Youth Convention, a Civil Society Forum, etc.), the Laeken Summit showed its determination to indeed listen to the citizens' concerns this time.

2.2 Elements of functioning of the Convention: Deliberation or 'mainstreaming'?

In light of the aforementioned context and prehistory of the Convention, soon a prominent interpretation of its *raison d'être* came up and was adopted by a number of Convention members and academic observers alike, namely: The Convention improves the democratic quality of the "constitution-making" process in the EU because – different than Intergovernmental Conferences (IGCs) – it is a more representative institution and it does not follow the logic of bargaining behind closed doors, but the logic of public *deliberation* (cf. for example Magnette 2002; Fossum & Menéndez 2003; Pollak & Slominksi 2003; for a critical discussion Closa 2003a, b; Höreth 2003). To emphasize this thesis, one or more of the following lines of argument were pursued: (1) comparing the Convention with an IGC by using a model of deliberation, (2) exploring the merits of the Convention in terms of tackling the democratic deficit of the Union, (3) asking for the quality of the Convention in terms of making EU constitutional politics more legitimate. – Each of the three strategies of argumentation contains a strong normative dimension. Moreover, the way that they describe the Convention as empirical reality often presupposes an ideal and counterfactual model ("deliberative democracy", cf. Eriksen & Fossum 2000; for a critical discussion Elster 1998; Dryzek 2000), the characteristics of which are used to structure the observations and evaluations. In what follows, I argue that the said approach is prone to miss the very reality of the Convention process, and, in the next section, an alternative account will be put forward. While our main focus will be on the aspect of "deliberation" here, "democracy" will be dealt with in future publications.

Looking at the *mise-en-scène* of the Convention, a stark contrast to the previous practice of treaty revision (by IGCs) can be noted: the Convention convened publicly in assembly halls of the European Parliament and largely adopted its rules of procedure for discussion; it was characterized by a rhetoric of "listening", transparency and responsiveness, and several elements of democratic politics were institutionalized. Specifically, among the many features of the complex communication processes in the Convention, a strong parliamentarian character comes to the fore: firstly, the majority of Convention members came from either the European Parliament or national parliaments; thus, they both had a certain independence from government positions and they represented an independent democratic legitimacy which the heads of states could be expected not to ignore. Secondly, as President Giscard d'Estaing emphasized at numerous occasions since his inaugural speech at the Convention (cf. Magnette 2002:11–12), the structure and proceedings of this body were framed in a way as to impede intergovernmental and other forms of bargaining and alliance-building: thus, publicity of the meetings was aforementioned, another aspect, which nicely illustrates this *will* (effective or not) to avoid coalition-building on an interest-basis, is that Conventioneers were seated in alphabetical order.

It is on these grounds that most commentators argued that the Convention was in fact established because it promised to overcome the weaknesses of the intergovernmental method as they had been identified at the Nice Summit. What the Summit-method could do, it was claimed, is aggregate the various interests and preferences. However, it could not go beyond the lowest common denominator. In other words, it was not able to offer a grand design, to establish a sphere of rationality that was more than just the sum of the individual states' preferences. – Establishing a Convention, from this point of view, could be considered an act of self-binding of the IGC allowing for more efficiency in tackling the well-known functional problems of the EU system as they are, for instance, identified in the Laeken Declaration. In other words, the Convention should come up with results that the IGC itself could not have achieved, while the final power of decision would again rest with the 'masters of the treaties'.

Going beyond this interpretation of the Convention's *raison d'être*, a number of authors have endowed the differences of the Convention vis-à-vis an IGC with additional significance and value by referring to a model of deliberative democracy, as it has for instance been applied to the EU's "comitology system" by Christian Joerges and collaborators (Joerges & Falke 2000; Joerges & Neyer 1997). To characterize the Convention, the following elements of "deliberation" are usually enumerated:

– Preferences are not unilaterally pushed at the cost of others. Discussion, persuasion and compromise prevail over interest-driven bargaining.
– There is fair debate. Participants are free, have equal voice and are prepared to hear all of the arguments of the others.
– Thus, in a reasoned deliberative process, no force is exercised except that of the better argument.

In the Convention, above all the aspects of publicity and relative independence of participants ("room of manoeuvre", cf. Pollak & Slominski 2003) seem to conform to the said model-assumptions. While behind closed doors the various self-interests can be openly raised, the parliamentarian form of the Convention in turn forces speakers to frame particularistic interests in a universalistic way, thus appealing to a common, 'European' good. At the same time, Convention members communicate that their positions are not fixed, but are open to change in the light of information and arguments that are put forward in the course of the discussions (cf. Magnette 2002: 24–25). Thus, as many observers have concluded, the Convention was able to constitute a sphere for *representative deliberative politics*, which endowed the "constitution-building process" of the EU with a far greater degree of democratic legitimacy than an IGC could ever do.

However, looking at the empirical reality of the Convention process, a number of 'departures' from the model can be observed, since bargaining, power politics or aggregation of preferences (instead of arguing) were present in numerous ways (cf. for empirical evidence House of Lords 2002: 12–13; Reh & Wessels 2002; Schönlau 2003; Maurer 2003: 179–186; Closa 2003b):

1. *Institutional barganing*: In those areas of the Convention's work that concerned the so-called "institutional balance" of the EU, not surprisingly, many Conventioneers acted as if they were delegates of their respective institutional backgrounds (that is: EU Council of Ministers, Commission,

European Parliament, national parliaments and governments). In linguistic terms, this can be shown for example by an analysis of the specific use of the pronoun "we" in plenary sessions.[1]

2. *Intergovernmentalism*: Conventioneers (informally) caucused on a national basis and formed international coalitions (e.g. Germany and France, or the 'small' countries versus the 'big', etc.). This intergovernmental aspect especially concerned the crucial institutional questions, for example the establishment of a President of the EU, as well as issues involving the allocation of money to different member states (e.g. the communitarization of border control, cf. the plenary session from 6/12/2003).

3. *Alliance-building and preference aggregation*: "Attempts to caucus are going on at every level: there are regular meetings of each political group, social democrats, conservatives, and the liberals; each set of institutional representatives is trying to co-ordinate its line; and each country has meetings of its own nationals" (House of Lords 2002: 13). – While this quote refers to the early phases of the Convention's works (until July 2002), alliance-building most explicitly took place in its very last phase from May 2003 until the delivery of a "Draft Treaty" to the EU Summit of Thessaloniki (19–20 June 2003), when an increased frequency of meetings and more 'heated' debates could be observed. To put it briefly, the 'hot' questions (Common Foreign and Security Policy, range of issues to be decided upon by Qualified Majority Voting, budget and tax issues, immigration policy, inclusion of the Charter of Fundamental Rights in the Draft Treaty, weighting of votes in the Council of Ministers, etc.) that had already been debated at the Summit of Nice had been postponed by the Presidium until the very last weeks of the Convention's works. Finally, to reach an agreement under these conditions of extreme time pressure, a different working method was introduced: groups were formed on the basis of the Convention's components (that is: government representatives, national parliamentarians, members of the European Parliament), and together with the political families they became the key foci of preference formation, while the Convention Presidents negotiated with each sub-group individually, acted as a mediator, and attempted to strike a compromise everybody could live with.[2]

4. Finally, the *Convention plenary* needs to be looked at since it is here that commentators expected to find the conditions most favorable to deliberation: individuals arguing publicly, unbound by external constraints, enjoying equal rights to speak and to be heard. – However, empirical observations painted a surprisingly different picture. Firstly, though, it has to be noted that the plenary sessions turned out to be an extremely multifaceted

and complex object-field, which can hardly be reduced to one single function or interpretation. In the different phases of the Convention's works and according to the topics on the agenda, different characteristics came to the fore. Nevertheless, as a general observation it can be stated that *discussion* in the sense of arguments exchanged by two or more speakers only rarely took place. Conversely, the process was structured in a very 'centralized' way, that is, the focal point of communications was the Convention Presidium (for an account of the spatial set-up of communications in the plenary sessions, cf. the article by Michał Krzyżanowski in this volume). While most sessions began with a topical introduction by one of the Presidium members, Conventioneers then provided their statements – that is, they often read prewritten texts – which hardly in any way were directly related to previous statements by other speakers. Then, after two or three hours, a Presidium member closed the session by providing a brief summary of the 'debate' and establishing a number of issues on which he or she claimed "consensus" had been reached. Thus, as it seems, the general form, as well as function of plenary sessions significantly departed from a model of deliberation, and therefore alternative accounts need to be thought of. In the following section, an alternative hypothesis will be put forward claiming that plenary sessions mainly served as a device for making the range of voices among Conventioneers visible and at the same time allowing the Presidium to establish what should be the 'mainstream' position on the issues concerned.

In light of the evidence presented above, significant doubts can be raised concerning the application of a model of deliberation for describing and interpreting the Convention process. Moreover, there are fundamental theoretical arguments for questioning as to whether 'deliberation' actually is able to grasp the essence of the Convention's works. Did the necessary conditions for deliberation exist at all, namely a consensual context of values and norms, or at least a shared definition of the state-of-affairs of the Union, a common cognitive framework, in reference to which claims could be evaluated and arguments deliberated, i.e. the 'better solution' identified (cf. Follesdal 2003: 12)? Rather, as Joseph Weiler (1999a: 8) suggested, the EU has "a constitutional legal order the constitutional theory of which has not been worked out, its long-term, transcendent values not sufficiently elaborated, its ontological elements misunderstood, its social rootedness and legitimacy highly contingent." Under these conditions, it can be inferred, there was no 'best solution' to be established in a deliberative process, and the success of the Convention, the composition of which was so heterogeneous in terms of institutional and national background, needs to be explained differently. To put it more pointedly, the Convention's mandate of debating the "future of Europe" "as broadly and openly as possible" apparently implied a paradox: the Convention was asked to establish exactly that kind of consensus which at the same time would have been a prerequisite for its functioning. Like *Baron Münchhausen*, it should pull itself out of trouble on its own shock of hair.

2.3 An alternative hypothesis: Mainstreaming

Only a few commentators were tempted by the French reference to expect from the Convention to overcome this paradox in a truly constitutional act. Those familiar with the culture of European institutions knew that there would be some kind of procedural solution. – Europe, as one of our interviewees put it, is the *process* itself, not the goal, thus never reaching clear solutions, but going "from one complexity to another", always reforming the status quo.

It does not come as a surprise, thus, that the Vice-President of the Convention Giuliano Amato emphasized already in the first session of the Convention that one should not start from scratch or from abstract principles, but build on the existing treaties and draw on previous propositions for reform put forward by think tanks, academia, or the European Parliament's Constitutional Affairs Committee. And indeed, in the Convention's works the crucial as well as contested questions were postponed, and general, more normative issues were deleted from the agenda. If the Convention should work at all, insiders knew, it had to break up its task to a set of manageable and technical problems. Incrementalism was *de rigueur*. A glimpse on the list of working groups (see Figure 2), as well as on the "Skeleton Draft", put forward on October 28, 2002 by Valery Giscard d'Estaing, nicely illustrates this point.

In what follows, we will take a look at the entire process that led from the Convention's unsystematic "listening phase" to the final 'consensual' "Draft Treaty". It has to be noted at the outset though, that this process was of an extremely heterogeneous and complex character, and thus, any hypothesis endeavoring to grasp it as a whole is neglecting the details for a generalizing overall account. However, instead of proposing a counterfactual, normative model such as the one of deliberation, we advocate a descriptive approach staying as close to the data as possible, thus understanding the Convention as a complex *social and communicative process* under specific organizational conditions. – This, as we would like to point out in the following, overcomes the problem that is haunting advocates of deliberation, namely that most of the factual char-

Working Groups		
I	Subsidiarity	(Méndez de Vigo)
II	Charter of Fundamental Rights	(Vitorino)
III	Legal personality	(Amato)
IV	National parliaments	(Stuart)
V	Complementary Competencies	(Christophersen)
VI	Economic Governance	(Hänsch)
VII	External Action	(Dehaene)
VIII	Defence	(Barnier)
IX	Simplification	(Amato)
X	Freedom, Security and Justice	(Bruton)
XI	Social Europe	(Katiforis)

Figure 2. European Convention, list of working groups

acteristics of the Convention have to be accounted for as aberrations from the model.[3]

Using a metaphor of one of our interviewees, we tentatively use the term *mainstreaming* as a title for this alternative working hypothesis. Although the term is used in a different way in the context of public policy, its connotations are very helpful. In the Convention, a 'stream' of communications is inconspicuously but steadily narrowed down, extremes on both sides are discarded, divergent questions and issues are marginalized, deviant positions ignored or ostracized, the stock of taken-for-granted assumptions, which must not be called into question, thus, is accumulated, and a dominant discourse (a 'mainstream') is established (cf. the survey of contributions to plenary sessions in Matl 2003). The "Draft Treaty Establishing a Constitution for Europe" marks the end-point of this process. This is, one might argue, an extremely unlikely result given the initial heterogeneity of opinions, interests and cultural, linguistic or national differences present in the Convention. Below, several factors and conditions facilitating this 'unlikely process' shall be identified (for first hypotheses on discursive realizations of mainstreaming, cf. the chapter by Michał Krzyżanowski in this volume). Of course, this is not to be read as a final word on the issue, but rather as an outline of a research agenda. Ample reference to empirical examples and a discussion of the details is left for further publications (for empirical evidence cf. Maurer 2003: 179–186; Closa 2003b, for a comparison with the 'first' Convention cf. de Búrca 2001; Deloche 2002).

1. *Pre-selection of Convention members*: The question of who is or is not present is among the first to be looked at when analyzing how the production of "consensus" was achieved in the Convention. A two-step procedure

```
Composition of the Convention
15     representatives of Heads of State or Government
30     representatives of national parliaments
16     Members of the European Parliament
2      representatives of the Commission

Candidate Countries:
13     representatives of Heads of State or Government
26     representatives of national parliaments

13     Observers (Economic and Social Committee; Committee of
           Regions; Social Partners; European Ombudsman)
```

Figure 3. Composition of the European Convention

of selection can be observed. In a first step, the Laeken Summit determined the number of Conventioneers per institution according to a rather contingent institutional and geographical scheme (see Figure 3). In a second step, national parliaments, the European Commission, governments of member states and so on nominated their representatives according to their own rules and procedures.

Evaluating the consequences of this two-step-process of nomination would necessitate a thorough analysis of its very details. However, for the purpose of this overview, two aspects shall be emphasized. Firstly, the informal character of the nomination process and especially the absence of voting led to a selection of 'insiders', that is persons who had already been involved in European policy networks or even worked for European institutions. This was especially true for the Presidium, the composition of which, being largely determined by the Laeken Summit in advance, actually represented an important third step in the process of selecting Convention members. Secondly, the fact that the Convention was composed of members coming from very different institutions needs to be thoroughly reflected upon. To name only one consequence, this fact, combined with the absence of voting in the Convention, implied an extremely uneven distribution of power: While member states still had to ratify a future constitution and government representatives were thus in a very strong position, members of national parliaments often had nothing more than their individual opinion to bring to bear.

2. *The "consensus" procedure*: The very essence of the Convention, it might be argued, was defined by the "consensus" procedure as it was frequently

invoked by President Giscard d'Estaing: Reaching a final result everyone could live with, and thus avoiding the formation of antagonistic factions favoring different texts. – The term "consensus" itself comes from the practice of international law. In the United Nations, for instance, decisions are sometimes made by "consensus". In this case, the chair of an assembly declares, without voting, that a particular issue or text has been agreed upon. As long as there is no formal protest, the resolution is considered accepted. The Convention has both adopted and radicalized this procedure. Firstly, as mentioned above, Convention members were only partly delegates of member states' governments involved in a posterior ratification process. The absence of formal voting, thus, implied a fundamental inequality of Convention members: the voice of some could easily be ignored, the voice of others – the government representative of the United Kingdom, for instance – could not. Secondly, even formal protest by at least five Convention members who did not endorse the final text[4] was not considered an obstacle to declaring "consensus". Since the meaning of the term had not been defined at all, the Convention President enjoyed considerable room for interpretation.

3. *Time pressure and workload*: The Convention was working under conditions of a combination of shortage of time and an enormous workload. Moreover, there was a general perception of being doomed to success: The reference to catastrophic consequences of an eventual failure of the Convention clearly was a pervasive *topos* in the Convention's everyday discourse. – Given the logic of the "consensus" procedure, these elements definitely set the most favorable conditions for *mainstreaming*. Complex matters were to be dealt with that could hardly be rationally deliberated in the time given, and obstructing the swift progress of the Convention was deemed unacceptable. Would any group of Conventioneers risk being the 'bad guys' who jeopardize the whole project, particularly when they were not representing powerful member states? Under these conditions, the Presidium enjoyed a generous leeway for steering the process since effective opposition from the 'floor' would hardly crystallize, a phenomenon that does not exactly emphasize the deliberative character of the process, notwithstanding the fact that it is producing "consensus" quite effectively.

4. *The Presidium and its President(s) – central protagonists of* mainstreaming: While it can not be claimed here that there was any powerful subject steering the Convention process as a whole, there was in many ways a privileged position of the Presidium that can hardly be ignored. It was the Presidium that drafted the working procedures of the Convention, de-

termined the order and content of its "phases", chaired working groups, produced the structure ("skeleton") of the draft treaty, had the monopoly for drafting texts, largely set the agenda and framed discourse, for instance with the opening and closing of each session and identifying those points where there was "consensus", as well as those where further reflection was necessary. In the Presidium, the most important lines of communication converged and were transformed (cf. the article by Michał Krzyżanowski in this volume): formal and informal contributions and amendments came in; reports, drafts and organizational notes went out.

From a sociological perspective, of course, the resources of the Presidium – the Secretariat and the structure of the Council of Ministers, where the Presidium's office was set – have to be mentioned. One may think here of Robert Michels' famous "iron law of oligarchy" or analyses of social power which underline the superior organizational capacities of small groups. – In the end, it will be an issue for in-depth studies to determine to what degree the Presidium (and, within the Presidium, the President(s) and also the Secretariat) had been able to influence the Convention process.

5. *Incrementalism*: It has already been noted that the Laeken mandate (in its interpretation by Giscard) triggered an incrementalist dynamics of the Convention as reflected in its agenda and final draft. Very detailed technical questions involving a "consolidation" and restructuring of the existing treaties made up a large part of the Convention's proceedings. Here, consensus could quite easily be achieved (which was not the case, for instance, for the more 'political' issues of "economic governance" or "Social Europe"). By the same token, conflicts leading to an eventual formation of antagonistic groups in the Convention could successfully be avoided.

6. *The plenary sessions*: The absence of debate and the passive character of the Convention plenary – particularly when compared to the Presidium – has already been mentioned. Rather than being the medium for a deliberative process, the plenary sessions' function might be seen in producing a panorama of positions, opinions and sentiments that could easily be overviewed from the Presidium table. Which positions are supported by a broad majority, in which areas is it that vital interests are claimed, which opinions can be seen as minority positions and thus ignored, and so on? – Looked at from the perspective of Conventioneers, the same phenomenon takes on a different character. Here, the plenary can be considered as providing a representation of whether one's own position still conforms to the mainstream or not. Given the logic of the "consensus" procedure, this information alone constitutes a certain social pressure which is further

reinforced by (social) sanctions from the Presidium: whose opinions are honored, and who is ignored or ridiculed, who is included in informal communication networks, and who is not, and so on. By way of an analogy, a similar hypothesis can be proposed concerning the working groups.

7. *Socialization or the gradual formation of an "epistemic community"*: While the model of deliberation emphasizes the "endogenous formation of preferences" vis-à-vis fixed preferences in classical bargaining, the same phenomenon is perceived in a different light according to an empirical approach, namely as a gradual formation of an *esprit de corps*, or, in terms of organizational theory, of an "epistemic community" involving the mutual mimesis of participants over time. Especially the (few) newcomers to EU politics (often national parliamentarians or delegates from candidate countries) have been socialized (or 'integrated') during the Convention process itself. In many of our interviews, this is expressed very clearly. One interviewee, for instance, referred to himself as a "good pupil" of "good teachers"; another proudly claimed to have "learned immensely" in the course of the Convention. Here, positive feedback by the community of the 'experienced' in the Convention (and negative sanctions, such as marginalization, for 'deviant' members) probably played an important role for the process of *mainstreaming*.

To sum up, by *mainstreaming* we would like to propose a research agenda for an empirical account of the Convention process. We do not propose that there was any one powerful subject responsible for mainstreaming. What we describe could rather be called a structural device characterized by a certain inner logic or 'systemic' rationality that cannot be traced back to any individual subject. This rationality is, however, not the same as the 'Reason' invoked by models of deliberation. While the latter is inherent to human communication under particular ideal conditions (cf. above), the rationality of mainstreaming is inherent to the process itself, in a way similar to how Max Weber has described bureaucracy as a rational device.

Not a normative ideal, but the data shall guide this research and the categories it uses. Above, some of the elements we believe to be crucial for understanding the Convention have been laid out. To be sure, this is still a simple and incomplete grid. It is a working hypothesis that has been developed through our observations and now needs to be tested according to a Popperian logic of falsification. Moreover, a description will not be the final objective of this research, but its point of departure. Normative issues as they are dealt with by theories of deliberative democracy are inherent to political reality itself and shall thus not be dismissed, but re-introduced and discussed: Specifically, two key issues will have to be approached, since they constitute important elements of the set-up and self-interpretation of the Convention, namely: the meaning of democracy and the meaning of the term 'constitution' at a European level. Here, the material 'content' of the Convention process that has thus far been put into brackets in favor of the 'process' will be re-introduced, and the fate of the Convention's draft treaty in the larger context of EU politics will be dealt with.

3.   Instead of conclusions: A frame of reference for researching the European Convention

The "Convention on the Future of Europe" has been established to address a number of problems and tensions in the 'operating system' of the Union that had long been discussed. From this perspective, one could compare the Convention with any expert committee that is set-up by an IGC to come up with certain proposals. Consequently, concepts from the sociology of complex organizations seem best suited as tools of analysis, and the Convention could be described as reducing contingency in the context of a self-organizing network characterized by flexible structures of expectation. However, the self-interpretation of the Convention – drafting a "Constitution for Europe" –, its talk of democracy, fundamental values or European identity, and its parliamentarian composition and *mise-en-scène* (to name only a few aspects) present a different picture. The purely instrumental dimension seems to be transcended for the self-definition of a political community in the medium of constitution-making.

The high symbolic value of the term "constitution" needs to emphasized. Being on the one hand the 'highest law' in a legal system, constitutions always have been considered transcending a purely technical, legal-administrative function: symbolizing the *idée directrice* of a polity, setting the basic rules for living together justly, or, as in the classical democratic tradition, instituting a relation of articulation and identification with a demos as *pouvoir constituant*.

For an empirical, discourse-analytical approach, we propose to – in a first step – leave normative and "essentially contested" (W. B. Gallie) concepts such as these (constitution, democracy, etc.) aside and to look at the phenomenological reality of the Convention process itself. From this perspective, the object-field is conceived as a complex process of communications in a particular institutional setting. Both, the setting and the communications can be empirically researched and described. A first observation to be noted is the polyphone and heterogeneous character of the object-field, which escapes any generalizing descriptions.

In a second step, going beyond mere observation and description, the question of the meanings of these communicative acts needs to be reintroduced. This entails looking at the Convention as a *"lieu anthropologique"*, that is a culturally impregnated space whose meanings and practices can be deciphered and reconstructed by the observer. While the specifically *political* dimension of the object-field remains in the background, attention is drawn to its 'cultural' dimension. Among other things, issues of interest include the 'European' way of negotiating and reaching results, the ways of how discourse is ordered in a multilingual and -national setting, what common concepts and images are established in the course of the Convention's works, or how politicians from outside the EU-system, particularly from the accession countries, are 'acculturated' and 'integrated'.[5] In this phase of the project, the discourse-analytic investigation of interviews with Convention members will be performed.

Finally, a third step of interpretation turns to the legal and political dimensions of the Convention. What difference, for instance, does the democratic set-up and *mise-en-scène* of the Convention make? Is it symbolically efficient or merely rhetoric (cf. Haltern 2002 on this point)? Does it constitute a space for democratic politics, or not? – Questions such as these go beyond the concerns of both a sociology of organizations and of an anthropology of institutions, that is, they introduce a perspective from political theory. Concerning this perspective, we propose to neither presuppose theoretical models that are alien to the object-field, nor to naively adopt its own language and interpretations. As part of the political reality of the Convention, its self-interpretations (e.g.: bringing the Union "closer to its citizens", drafting a "constitutional treaty") have to be critically clarified by placing them in the context of a more comprehensive account of this institution's structure, working procedures and history, as well as of EU politics at large. To put it more pointedly: What the Convention tells us may in fact diverge from what it says.

Obviously, the famous issue of the political and legal *form* of the Union is at stake here. In other words, can the Convention serve as key source of information for formulating a political theory of the European Union, as the term *constitutional* Convention suggests? Arguments have been provided both in favor of and against conceiving the EU in terms of "form" (which, after all, presupposes that it constitutes a meaningful whole). To be sure, the Convention is not the only nor a privileged source of information for studying this question of "form".[6] On the other hand, it nevertheless seems to be a case of special interest, since its proceedings and results provide an excellent opportunity to study the relationship between the Union as an 'operating system' on the one hand and its self-interpretation and representation on the other, an issue that seems to be central for understanding the political reality and discourse in today's complex societies.[7]

Notes

* Previous versions of this paper were presented at the symposium "A New Research Agenda in (Critical) Discourse Analysis: Theory and Interdisciplinarity" (Vienna, March 2003) and at the conference "Soziale Dynamiken, politische Institutionen und Identifikationen im Erweiterungsprozess der Europäischen Union" (Passau, June 2003) of the section "Political Sociology" of the German Sociological Association. Insights gathered from those discussions have greatly benefited this article. I also would like to thank the reviewers and editors of the volume for their comments, as well as the participants of an expert workshop for our research project (Vienna, November 2003), Christoph Bärenreuter, Irène Bellier, Ulrich Haltern, Paul Jones, James Kaye, Johannes Pollak, Heinz Schönbauer, Peter Slominski, Alexander Somek, and Gilbert Weiss. The responsibility for what follows, however, lies entirely with the author.

1. As noted above, parliamentarians made up the majority of Conventioneers. In the end, they could be more than satisfied with the Convention's draft treaty. Never before, especially from the perspective of the European Parliament, has a better result been achieved.

2. This account is based, among others, on excellent empirical material collected by Heinz Schönbauer during his research stay at the European Convention from May until July 2003.

3. A similar empirical approach has been pursued by Maurizio Bach (1999) for analyzing the problem-solving strategies practiced by the EU administration. Bach identified elements such as the break-up of complex matters into a number of manageable packages, or the creation of time pressure by defining timetables and deliverables. In a similar way, Martin Heidenreich (2003) has looked at enlargement as a process involving the transformation of major political conflict into a complexity of issues to be dealt with by a network of experts and policy-makers over a longer period of time.

4. On the occasion of the plenary session of May 30th, 2003, five Convention members and four alternate members delivered their "minority report" to President Giscard d'Estaing and called for "another way" for the EU (CONV 773/03). Moreover, a number of Finnish Conventioneers refused to sign the final document. Lastly, it remains unclear, as to whether the third and fourth part of the draft treaty finalized after the solemn adoption of the document presented to the EU Summit of Thessaloniki can be considered to be accepted by the Convention, or not (cf. Fischer 2003:92).

5. Adding a functional analysis to the picture, one might describe the Convention as an attempt to broaden the legitimacy of European institutions by integrating political elites from different levels of the European multilevel system, with integration meaning inclusion

into the European political process and socialization into the political culture of the EU-system.

6. For a long scholarly tradition, the dimensions of the political and the legal converge in the constitution, which might be considered a re-entry of the form in the form. However, the promises of the term *Constitutional* Treaty notwithstanding, it is not clear as to whether the results of the Convention – of normative force or merely pieces of paper? – are an adequate source of information when looking for an answer to the question of the Union's political form. A more comprehensive approach involving among other things the contextualization of legal texts might be more promising.

7. Analyzing the complexity of contemporary politics, Ludwig Jäger (2004) distinguished between *discourses of planning* characterized by the logic of specialization and functional differentiation, and *discourses of public representation* or meaning-making characterized by the logic of modern mass media. Thirdly, he claimed, meaning is also constituted in everyday social interaction and communication, as studies on mass media reception have illustrated.

References

Abélès, Marc (2000). "Virtual Europe". In I. Bellier & T. M. Wilson (Eds.), *An Anthropology of the European Union. Building, Imagining and Experiencing the New Europe* (pp. 31–50). Oxford, New York.

Bach, Maurizio (1999). *Die Bürokratisierung Europas. Verwaltungseliten, Experten und politische Legitimation in Europa.* Frankfurt, New York: Campus.

Closa, Carlos (2003a). *The Convention Method: A Model for Democratising the European Union?* CONV-EU Conference Paper, Center for International Relations, Warsaw, April 2003.

Closa, Carlos (2003b). *Improving EU Constitutional Politics? A Preliminary Assessment of the Convention.* ConWEB: Constitutionalism Web Papers 1/2003.

De Búrca, Gráinne (2001). "The drafting of the European Union Charter of fundamental rights". *European Law Review, 26*(1), 126–138.

Deloche, Florence (2002). "La Convention pour l'élaboration de la charte des droits fondamentaux: une méthode constituante?" In Robert Dehousse (Ed.), *Une constitution pour l'Europe?* (pp. 177–226). Paris: Presses de sciences-po.

Descombes, Vincent (1996). *Les institutions du sens.* Paris: Les Editions de Minuit.

Dryzek, John (2000). *Deliberative Democracy and Beyond. Liberals, Critics, Contestations.* Oxford: Oxford University Press.

Elster, Jon (Ed.) (1998). *Deliberative Democracy.* Cambridge: Cambridge University Press.

Eriksen, Erik Oddvar & Fossum, John Erik (2000). *Democracy in the European Union. Integration through deliberation?* London, New York: Routledge.

Fischer, Klemens H. (2003). *Konvent zur Zukunft Europas. Texte und Kommentar mit einem Geleitwort von Dr. Benita Ferrero-Waldner, enschließlich Begleit-CD-ROM mit Gesamtdokumentation.* Baden-Baden: Nomos Verlagsgesellschaft.

Follesdal, Andreas (2003). *Drafting a European Constitution – Challenges and Opportunities.* ConWEB: Constitutionalism Web Papers, 4/2003.

Fossum, John Erik & Menéndez, Agustín (2003). "The constitution's gift. A deliberative democratic analysis of constitution-making in the European Union". Paper presented at the *CIDEL Zaragoza Workshop*, June 2003.

Haltern, Ulrich (2002). *Pathos and Patina: The Failure and Promise of Constitutionalism in the European Imagination*. ConWEB: Constitutionalism Web Papers, 6/2002.

Heidenreich, Martin (2003). "Die Osterweiterung auf der Zielgeraden: Von rhetorischem Handeln zum Beitritt". In Peter Baum et al. (Eds.), *Die Erweiterung der Europäischen Union. Ein Exkursionsbericht* (Bamberger Beiträge zur Europaforschung und zur internationalen Politik 7/2003) (pp. 5–14). Bamberg: Otto-Friedrich Universität.

Höreth, Marcus (2003). "From Deliberation to Bargaining Again – the Limits of the Convention Method". Paper presented at the *Meeting of the European Policy Institutes Network* (EPIN), March 2003.

House of Lords, Select Committee on the European Union (2002). *The Convention on the Future of Europe. With Evidence*. London: The Stationery Office Limited.

Jäger, Ludwig (2004). "Sprache als Medium der politischen Kommunikation. Anmerkungen zur Transkriptivität kultureller und politischer Semantik". In U. Frevert & W. Braungart (Eds.), *Sprachen des Politischen. Medien und Medialität in der Geschichte* (pp. 332–355). Göttingen: Vandenhoeck & Ruprecht.

Joerges, Christian & Falke, Josef (Eds.). (2000). *Das Ausschußwesen der Europäischen Union. Praxis der Risikoregulierung im Binnenmarkt und ihre rechtliche Verfassung*. Baden-Baden: Nomos.

Joerges, Christian & Neyer, Juergen (1997). "From Intergovernmental Bargaining to Deliberative Political Processes: The Constitutionalisation of Comitology". *European Law Journal*, 3/1997, 273–299.

Laeken Declaration (2001). *The Laeken Declaration on the Future of the European Union*. Annex 1 to the Presidency Conclusions of the European Council Meeting in Laeken, 14–15 December 2001. Brussels, No. SN 300/1/01 REV 1, 19–27.

Leinfellner, Elisabeth (2004). "Vom Bild ohne Rahmen zum Rahmen ohne Bild – und das Jenseits von Rahmen und Bild: Eine Diskussion zu 'Text und Kontext'". In O. Panagl & R. Wodak (Eds.), *Text und Kontext. Theoriemodelle und methodische Verfahren im transdisziplinären Vergleich* (pp. 267–296). Würzburg: Königshausen & Neumann.

Magnette, Paul (2002). "Délibération vs. négociation. Une première analyse de la Convention sur l'avenir de l'Union". Paper presented at the 7th congress of the *French Association for Political Science*, September 2002.

Matl, Saskia (2003). *Die Beiträge des Konvents bis zum 28.10.2002 (Plenardebatte)*. Berlin: Stiftung Wissenschaft und Politik.

Maurer, Andreas (2003). "Less Bargaining – More Deliberation: The Convention Method for Enhancing EU Democracy". *International Politics and Society*, 1/2003, 167–190.

Muntigl, Peter, Weiss, Gilbert, & Wodak, Ruth (2000). *European Union Discourses on Unemployment. An interdisciplinary approach to employment policy-making and organizational change*. Amsterdam/Philadelphia: John Benjamins.

Pollak, Johannes & Slominski, Peter (2003). "The Representative Quality of EU Treaty Reform: A Comparison Between the IGC and the Convention". Paper presented at the conference *Constitutionalism and Democratic Representation in the European Union*. Vienna, September 2003.

Reh, Christine & Wessels, Wolfgang (2002). "Towards an Innovative Mode of Treaty Reform?" *Collegium, 24* (Summer 2002), 17–24.

Schönlau, Justus (2003). "Conventional Wisdom? Comparing deliberative interaction in the European Conventions Mark I and II". Paper presented at the *CIDEL Zaragoza Workshop*, June 2003.

Weiler, Joseph H. H. (1999a). "Introduction: 'We will do, and hearken'". In J. H. H. Weiler (Ed.), *The Constitution of Europe. "Do the new Clothes have an Emperor?" and other essays on European integration* (pp. 3–9). Cambridge: Cambridge University Press.

Weiler, Joseph H. H. (1999b [1991]). "The transformation of Europe". In J. H. H. Weiler (Ed.), *The Constitution of Europe. "Do the new Clothes have an Emperor?" and other essays on European integration* (pp. 10–101). Cambridge: Cambridge University Press.

Weiss, Gilbert (2002). "Searching for Europe: The problem of legitimisation and representation in recent political speeches on Europe". *Journal of Language and Politics, 1*(1), 59–83.

Weiss, Gilbert & Wodak, Ruth (2000). "Debating Europe: Globalization rhetoric and European Union employment policies". In I. Bellier & T. M. Wilson (Eds.), *An Anthropology of the European Union. Building, Imagining and Experiencing the New Europe* (pp. 75–91). Oxford, New York: Berg.

Weiss, Gilbert & Wodak, Ruth (2003). "Introduction. Theory, Interdisciplinarity and Critical Discourse Analysis". In G. Weiss & R. Wodak (Eds.), *Critical Discourse Analysis. Theory and Interdisciplinarity* (pp. 1–34). London: Palgrave/MacMillan.

Wodak, Ruth & Weiss, Gilbert (2001). "'We are different than the Americans and the Japanese!' A critical discourse analysis of decision-making in European Union meetings about employment policies". In E. Weigand & M. Dascal (Eds.), *Negotiation and Power in Dialogic Interaction* (pp. 39–62). Amsterdam/Philadelphia: John Benjamins.

Wodak, Ruth & Weiss, Gilbert (2004). "Möglichkeiten und Grenzen der Diskursanalyse. Konstruktionen europäischer Identitäten". In O. Panagl & R. Wodak (Eds.), *Text und Kontext. Theoriemodelle und methodische Verfahren im transdisziplinären Vergleich* (pp. 67–85). Würzburg: Königshausen & Neumann.

Wodak, Ruth (2001). "The discourse-historical approach". In R. Wodak & M. Meyer (Eds.), *Methods of Critical Discourse Analysis* (pp. 63–94). London: Sage.

Wodak, Ruth (2004). "National and Transnational Identities: European and Other Identities Constructed in Interviews with EU Officials". In R. K. Herrmann, T. Risse-Kappen, & M. B. Brewer (Eds.), *Transnational Identities: Becoming European in the EU* (pp. 87–128). Lanham: Rowman & Littlefield.

CHAPTER 9

"It is not sufficient to have a moral basis, it has to be democratic too"

Constructing 'Europe' in Swedish media reports on the Austrian political situation in 2000*

Christoph Bärenreuter

University of Vienna

Introduction

Austrian domestic affairs rarely attract the attention of a wider international public. Apart from neighbouring German-speaking countries, the international media has little interest in the internal developments of Austrian political and societal life. In early 2000, however, the formation of a coalition government between the conservative Austrian People's Party (ÖVP; *Österreichische Volkspartei*) and the right-wing, populist Freedom Party (FPÖ; *Freiheitliche Partei Österreichs*) caused a major international stir. A fierce debate developed over whether the FPÖ, then headed by Jörg Haider, should be accepted in the government of a Member State of the European Union (EU), as the Party frequently made use of populist, racist and anti-Semitic discourse (Sedlak 2000; Pelinka & Wodak 2002). International politicians were quick to express their concern about the FPÖ's possible participation in the government, and the furore increased when the Portuguese Presidency of the EU released a statement on behalf of the other 14 Member States announcing a "joint-reaction [...] in case it is formed in Austria a Government integrating the FPÖ" (Tiersky 2001:217). In such an event, the following measures would be taken:

> – Governments of XIV Member States will not promote or accept any bilateral official contacts at political level with an Austrian Government integrating the FPÖ.

    – There will be no support in favor of Austrian candidates seeking positions in international organizations.
    – Austrian Ambassadors in EU capitals will only be received at a technical level. (ibid.)

When, on February 3rd, it became clear that the FPÖ would be represented in the new government, a press release was published, announcing that the "joint reaction" was put into action. In the press release, the following justification of these measures was given:

> The Portuguese Presidency of the EU Council will do its best, within its competence, to uphold the values and principles of humanism and democratic tolerance underlying the European project. FPÖ and its leader have repeatedly questioned said values and principles. (ibid.)

With this reference to certain values, which are said to be fundamental to European integration, a central element of the discursive construction of collective identities was addressed. One could thus, at first sight, interpret this statement as the expression of a common European identity. Yet, in the on-going public debate, the EU-14's measures and the justification given by the Presidency of the EU Council were evaluated very differently, reaching from clear support of the measures on the one hand, to the explicit rejection of the notion of "European values" per se on the other. Accordingly, no general statement can be made about whether the EU Presidency's appeal to the notion of European values contributed to the creation of a European identity. To arrive at more critical insights on the discursive mechanisms that were put into play, and what they can be thought to say about European identity, it is necessary to examine the ensuing discourses in European media. Besides simply appealing to "European values" in justifying the 14 EU Member States' measures, this specific media discourse provides an especially fruitful empirical case for the study of the discursive construction of European identities, as it makes us question how the European collective should be defined and who should belong to it. According to Schlesinger (1996), the construction of collective identities can be understood as the interplay of discourses of "auto-identification" and of "hetero-identification". While the former concept refers to discourses in which the particular characteristics of a certain group are central, the latter refers to discourses in which a collective is constructed by discriminating how "we" differ from "them". When applying this analytical distinction to the "*Causa Austria*", it becomes clear that elements of auto- and hetero-identification were interwoven in a way that complicated the distinction between an in-group and an out-group. *First*, the official justification of implementing measures against the Austrian government created a clear "other", i.e. the Austrian government including the FPÖ. *Second*, this other was contrasted with an in-group, i.e. those states adhering to the common European values. *Finally*, however, the "other" in this case did not come from outside the EU but was itself a Member State of the Union. It is especially this last condition that complicated the situation as it implied both a European "in-group," as constructed in the official justification of the measures, and an "other", which was also European, i.e. the Austrian government. How, then, was this situation discursively dealt with in the media? How was the appeal to European values by the "EU 14" reported on? And could these discourses contribute to the discursive creation of a European identity?

The aim of this article is to answer these questions in regard to Sweden. I will focus on how four major Swedish newspapers – *Aftonbladet*, *Dagens Nyheter*, *Expressen* and *Svenska Dagbladet* – discursively constructed "Europe" and whether a European identity was created in the reporting on the Austrian political situation.

One of the basic assumptions of this article, which will be spelled out below, is that discourses on European issues are closely intertwined with discourses on national identities and that they mutually influence each other. Therefore, it is also the aim of the paper to analyse how the discursive construction of Swedish national identity is related to the discourses on the *Causa Austria*.

Swedish media were chosen as an object of analysis due to several reasons: First, as the results of Eurobarometer surveys show, public opinion in Sweden is among the most EU-sceptic compared to other Member States. Second, during the last decades, the Austrian and the Swedish state maintained good relationships and cooperated, for example, in the field of military defence. These good relations are backed up by the fact that both states are neutral; in both states the Social Democrats have been the decisive political force in many years and both joined the European Union in the year 1995. The combination of Swedish EU-scepticism and the long-lasting good relationship between Austria and Sweden suggest a way of reporting that takes a critical stance towards the imposition of measures by the 14 EU Member States and which can thus be expected not to contribute to the discursive construction of a European identity. Third, however, we can presuppose that the kind of politics that Jörg Haider and the FPÖ stand for does not fit with Swedish narratives on democracy that are a central part of the Swedish national identity (cf. below). One could therefore assume that the proceedings of the 14 EU Member States were supported by claiming that they are necessary to protect democracy and the "European values". The influences that these divergent and specifically Swedish contexts exert on the discourse on the *Causa Austria* make Sweden a highly interesting case for the study of European identity construction in media discourses.

The newspapers that are included in the study are the social-democratic tabloid *Aftonbladet*, the liberal tabloid *Expressen*, the liberal broad-sheet *Dagens Nyheter* and the conservative broad-sheet *Svenska Dagbladet*. Before presenting the empirical results, I will first take up the question of how the relation between discourses on national and on European identities can be theorised. Thereby, a promising heuristic model, developed by Ole Wæver, will be used for explaining key characteristics of the discourse that is under scrutiny. In the next step, a brief overview will be given of the historical development of discourses on Swedish national identity and their relation to discourses on Europe. Finally, after the presentation of the empirical findings, these results will be tied back to Wæver's model.

The national and the European 'we'

In the early days of research on European integration, which took place in the 1950s, authors such as Karl Deutsch and Ernst Haas developed theories on the links between national identities and European integration. Their basic assumption was that this relation is characterised by an either/or logic. Haas understood European integration as a process in which the loyalties of political actors are shifted towards a new centre.

> Political integration is the process whereby political actors in several distinct national settings are persuaded to shift their loyalties, expectations and political activities toward a new centre, whose institutions possess or demand jurisdiction over the pre-existing national states. The end result of a process of political integration is a new political community, superimposed over the pre-existing ones.
> (Haas 1958:16)

In recent years, however, most research on the construction of European identities is based on the assumption that people are capable of having multiple identities, reflecting affiliations with, for example, gender, occupational groups, and regional, national or supranational entities (Kohli & Novak 2001). While this assumption is largely uncontested, the question of how to conceive of the relationship among these identities is the object of ongoing debates. As Risse shows, there are differing theoretical approaches to the conceptualisation of the relation between identities. He distinguishes four strands: First, identities

can be conceived of as being nested. According to this model, regional identities, for example, are contained in national identities, which in turn can be
nested in supra-national identities, such as European. Second, identities can be
"cross-cutting", meaning some members of identity group A can also be members of identity group B. However, not all members of A are also members
of B. Third, identities can be thought of as being separate, for example, when
private and professional affiliations are apart from one another. Risse's fourth
approach is the so-called "marble cake" concept. According to this concept

> the various components of an individual's identity cannot be neatly separated
> on different levels as both concepts of nestedness and of cross-cutting identi-
> ties imply. What if identity components influence each other, mesh and blend
> into each other?   (Risse 2004: 251f.)

This approach would seem to have much to offer for the study of the construction of European identities as it opens up a new field of inquiry to social
scientific research: i.e., the study of *how* exactly identities interact with each
other. For research focusing on the construction of European identities, one
of the central influencing variables is national identity with its specific historically rooted ideological implications. However, few theoretical attempts
were made to theorise the character of the mutual influence of discourses on
Europe and the national 'we'. A very auspicious approach recently was developed by the Danish political scientist and discourse analyst Ole Wæver. With
his background in the study of International Relations, Wæver's intention is
to explain the "longer lines of foreign policy" by applying discourse analysis
to discourses on political key concepts, such as the "state", the "nation", and
"Europe". At the same time, his model is a heuristic tool to address the exact
character of the relationship between national and European identities. He regards these identities as being in a relationship of mutual influence, prompting
him to consider

> how the nation/state identification is upheld by way of narratives on Europe,
> and conversely how Europe as a politically real concept is stabilised by its inner
> connections to other – maybe more powerful – we's.   (Wæver 2002: 25)

Wæver is operating with a notion of discourse that stems from Foucault (1972),
but also from the discourse theory of Laclau and Mouffe (1985). He perceives
discourse as being a "system for the formation of statements" which exerts a
structuring impact on "what can be said and what not" (ibid.: 29). In the current case, he considers the discursive constructions of state and nation as the
relevant basic structures that influence discourses on Europe. Thus, in order to

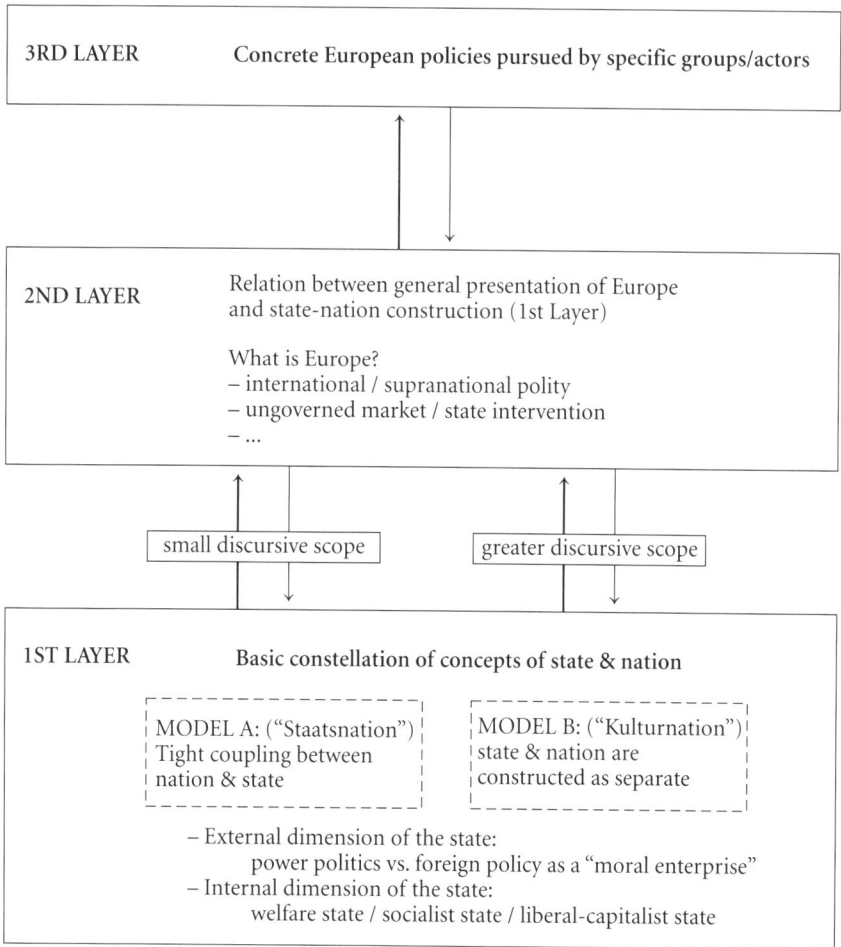

Figure 1. Theoretical model on the interaction between the discursive constructions of national identities and of 'Europe' (based on Wæver 2002)

understand the relation between discourses on state/nation and on "Europe", one has to take the specific characteristics of the definitions of these concepts into consideration (cf. below). For analysing how exactly discourses on state and nation influence the discursive construction of Europe, Wæver suggests an analytical framework that comprises three levels of analysis (see Figure 1).

The first – and "deepest" – layer of analysis "consists of the basic constellation of the concepts of state and nation. It poses the questions: what is the idea of the state, what is the idea of the nation, and how are the two tied together?"

(ibid.: 33) To be able to grasp the character of the discursive construction of the state and of the nation as well as their discursive connection, Wæver points to the ideal typical "French model" (*"Staatsnation"*), on the one hand, and the "German model" (*"Kulturnation"*) on the other. While in the French model the state and the nation are closely linked together, in the German model the two are thought of as being separate. To put it in the words of Brubaker:

> In the French tradition, the nation has been conceived in relation to the institutional and territorial frame of the state. [...] If the French understanding of nationhood has been state-centered and assimilationist, the German understanding has been *Volk*-centered and differentialist. Since national feeling developed before the nation-state, the German idea of the nation was not originally political, nor was it linked to the abstract idea of citizenship. This prepolitical German nation, this nation in search of a state, was conceived not as the bearer of universal political values, but as an organic cultural, linguistic, or racial community – as an irreducible particular *Volksgemeinschaft*. On this understanding, nationhood is an ethnocultural, not a political fact.
>
> (Brubaker 1992: 1)

This often used distinction between the two ideal typical concepts of the nation and its relation to the state has an important bearing on the discursive construction of national identities. Discourses on national identity that reflect a *Staatsnation*-understanding will focus on political notions that the state is said to stand for, on common moral concepts (*Wertvorstellungen*), state institutions, and a shared vision of political consciousness. A *Kulturnation*-understanding of national identity, on the other hand, will focus on ethnicity or culture as the *decisive* criteria for belonging to a nation. However, it should be kept in mind that these two concepts serve as ideal types and that in discourses on national identity, elements of *Staatsnation* and *Kulturnation* are frequently combined (cf. Wodak et al. 1998: 24ff.; Wodak 2001: 84f.). As Wæver points out, at this level of the heuristic model, not only the use of discursive elements of *Staatsnation* and *Kulturnation* should be taken into consideration, but also the discursive construction of the state's relation to other states and international organisations (external dimension) as well as the "state idea as projected 'backwards' onto its constituency" (internal dimension) (Wæver 2002: 36). To grasp the external dimension of the state, Wæver suggests asking how the state's relations to other countries and international organisations are understood. Is a state's foreign policy characterised by a "raison d'état logic" and "power politics" or is it rather considered as a "moral enterprise leading to, for example, peacekeeping and support for development policies?" (ibid.: 36). The state's "internal dimension", on the other hand, can be grasped, by analysing how the state defines its relation to its constituency. Here, Wæver names three cases in point that imply very different ways of discursively constructing the relation between the state and its constituency – the "welfare state, the socialist state and the liberal-capitalist state" (ibid.: 36).

For showing how these basic characteristics of the discursive construction of national identities influence discourses on Europe, one has to move further up in the model. At layer 2, the "relational position of the state/nation vis-à-vis Europe" (ibid.: 37) is at the centre of interest. As Wæver points out, the discursive constructions of state and nation from layer 1 have a "highly structuring impact on discourses on Europe" (ibid.: 37). Here the two models differ insofar as the German model, with its distinction between state and nation, offers more room to manoeuvre and discursively accommodate "Europe" than the French model. At the second layer of analysis, attention should be paid to how "Europe" is constructed at a general level (as opposed to discourses on day-to-day politics) and how this construction fits with the respective concepts of state/nation. Questions that help to grasp the general presentation of Europe comprise the following: "Is Europe an arena for intergovernmental cooperation between sovereign states? Is Europe a market ungoverned by state intervention? Is Europe integrating around a Western core? Is Europe all-European?" (ibid.: 38). As Wæver points out, discourses on Europe, in order to be successful, must be constructed in a way in which they are perceived as being in accordance with the basic constellation from layer 1. In other words, if the discursive construction of Europe is in conflict with the various national understandings of state and nation, it is likely that these European narratives will be rejected.[1] In such an event, pro-European discourses, in order to be successful, have to assure that this supposed threat is not "true" and that accession to the EU is thus not contradictory to (cultural) national self-understanding.

Lastly, on a third analytical layer, Wæver locates "the more specific European policies pursued by specific groups of actors, often political parties, thereby adding more specificity to the very general level of abstraction of level 2" (ibid.: 38). It is on this layer that most day-to-day discourses are located. Also, the reporting on the political developments in Austria can be counted among this group of discourses.

As Wæver points out, changes on the third layer are the smallest ones. Indeed this kind of change can be observed in everyday political debates when, for example, politicians change their line of argumentation concerning a particular political issue. Changes on the second layer already require a more profound change in the discursive structure and presuppose actors that try to reformulate the discursive connections between the basic definition of state/nation and Europe. To give a theoretical example, one can imagine a party that has rejected EU Membership for a long time, arguing that accession to an "imperialistic" EU would be incompatible with the country's policy of neutrality. Imagine that this party changes its policy with regard to EU accession and starts promoting accession to the EU, but at the same time adheres to the country's neutrality. To make this change possible, the discursive construction of "Europe," as presented by the party, has to change fundamentally. The new discursive construction of Europe will now have to offer a possibility of reconciling the country's neutrality with membership in the EU.

The most difficult to change, however, are discourses located on the first layer as the fundamental conceptions of state and nation tend to have a long history, only change gradually, and are often heavily laden with emotion. Though the three discursive layers are distinguished analytically, this does not imply that three distinct discourses can be found. "Rather, each discourse on Europe comprises – or articulates itself around – all three levels simultaneously" (ibid.; 33). However, I would add that the focus can be different depending on the text analyzed.

One of the strengths of Wæver's model is that it takes into consideration the *reciprocal* relationship between discourses on the national "we" and on "Europe". This means that his model not only allows for a theoretical approach to the influence that discourses on the state and the nation exert on the construction of Europe, but also acknowledges the possibility of European discourses impacting on the discursive construction of state and nation. In other words, if persistent discourses on Europe are not concordant with characteristics of the discursive construction of the national "we", a process can be triggered that may lead to a new discussion or even reformulation of the basic understanding of state and nation. An example of this is Austria's accession to the EU, which caused a new debate on the country's neutrality, a topic that for decades has remained central to Austrian national identity (cf. Kovács & Wodak 2003).

Another conclusion, central to the present study, can be drawn from this theoretical background: Despite the differing political editorial lines of the four newspapers that are under scrutiny here, it can be assumed that an investigation into the discourses about the Austrian political situation does not merely yield findings on the discursive constructions of Europe in these specific newspapers, but at the same time – and more importantly – will also deliver findings that are more *generally* valid for Swedish discourses on Europe. Though the editorial colour of the newspapers may have an influence on the actual reporting, it is here assumed that it is very likely that the four newspapers will refer to some basic common concepts that are central to Swedish national identity, which – theoretically speaking – can be found on the deeper layers of Wæver's model (cf. Wæver 2003:7). Here, Wæver takes inspiration of the discourse theory of Ernesto Laclau and Chantal Mouffe. According to these theorists, political adversaries in a given society (or – as in this case – newspapers with differing political lines), in their struggle for bringing their political notions to the fore, refer to shared "nodal points" that give a certain stability to the otherwise unfixed flux of meanings. In Wæver's model, these nodal points are the basic concepts of state and nation situated at layer 1. According to this view, political struggles can be understood as the attempt of political actors to promote their respective understandings of these central concepts and make it the dominant one (cf. e.g. Laclau & Mouffe 1985:112).

Wæver's heuristic model furthermore is a good example of interdisciplinary research, as it allows for the integration of political sciences and discourse analysis. Though his model itself does not provide concrete methods that can be applied for analyzing discourses, it nevertheless combines both, discourse theoretical and politico-theoretical assumptions in a way that can be translated into empirical research. Following the definition of Weiss and Wodak, interdisciplinarity is understood as a way of integrating different theoretical approaches and thereby creating "new holistic approaches" (Weiss & Wodak 2003:18). A necessary prerequisite for interdisciplinary research is thus the development of a "standardized transdisciplinary terminology" (ibid.). The aim of developing this kind of terminology is to generate a common understanding of analytical concepts, such as 'identity' that are used in different disciplines. In the particular case of this study, the social scientific concepts of national identity as well as European identity can be operationalized, using discourse analytical methods. Studying the discursive construction of these collective identities adds a level of analytical accuracy which can not be achieved when using classical political scientific methods. Conversely, for example, the use of the social scientific concepts of *Staats*nation or *Kultur*nation draws the attention of the applied linguist to differing characteristics of concepts of collective identity, both national and supranational/European (Wodak 2001). Furthermore, the focus on discursive structures, which is inherent to Wæver's model, allows the political scientist to actually make "something close to predictions" (Wæver 2002:28) on the probability of success of policies pursued by specific actors. The assumption here is that discourses with which actors try to promote their respective policies in order to be successful must relate to the basic concepts of state and nation in a convincing way as "it is always necessary for policy makers to be able to argue where 'this takes us' [...] and how it resonates with the state's 'vision of itself'" (Wæver 2002:27). To take up again the above example on Austrian neutrality and membership in the EU, actors promoting EU membership basically can choose between two strategies. Using the first strategy, they can attempt to discursively accommodate EU membership and Austrian neutrality by showing how membership in the EU can contribute to achieving the aims of neutral Austria. Following this strategy implies that the basic concepts of state and nation remain unchanged (layer 1), while merely changing their relationship to the EU. Alternatively, in the second option, political actors can try to reformulate the concepts of state and nation, for example, by claiming that neutrality is outdated and should be replaced by membership in NATO or a European defence system. This strategy, however, is a much harder to carry out, as it challenges well anchored narratives tied to Austrian national identity. As a consequence, one can assume that this kind of attempt, if not provided with a persuasive reformulation of discourses on state and nation, is likely to fail.

The Swedish concepts of state, nation and 'Europe'

In order to apply Wæver's heuristic tool to the study of the Swedish media discourse on the *Causa Austria*, one has to take into consideration the particularities of the definition state and nation in Sweden. Swedish national identity is still characterised by a tight coupling between the state and the nation. Central to this coupling is the notion of *folkhem*, i.e. the "people's home". Though the concept was first used by the Conservatives in the early 20th century, it was later successfully used by the Social Democrats to convey their understanding of the Swedish state and nation. The Social Democrats did not define themselves as a party based on class interests but rather presented themselves as a party of the *folk* (the people). Furthermore, the Marxist rejection of the state as a means of bourgeois domination was abandoned and substituted by a 'nation-state-nationalism' (Trägårdh 2002: 137). The combination of the Social Democrats' self-definition as a party of the *folk* on the one hand and the attempt to use the state to achieve the aims of the *folk* on the other resulted in a tight discursive coupling of the state and the people. At the same time, they presented the Swedish people as being intrinsically freedom-loving and democratic. According to this understanding, democracy was not simply a matter of institutional arrangements "but was rooted in the very soul of the people" (ibid.: 139). Starting from the 1930s, this construction of the Swedish state and the Swedish nation was increasingly contrasted by a negative depiction of Europe, which was turned into Sweden's 'other'. This mental demarcation was best captured by the 'four K's,' which in English would be the 'four C's.' According to this conceptualisation, Europe was the realm of Conservative, Capitalist, Catholic, and Colonial countries, while Sweden was perceived as being progressive, Social Democratic, Protestant, and anti-colonial with a well developed welfare-state (cf. Trägårdh 2002; Stråth 1993 and 2000).

By and large, this strong demarcation remained stable until the mid 1980s. At this critical time in Swedish history, a series of internal and external events, challenged both, the so-called 'Swedish model' and Sweden's relation towards Europe. The signing of the Single European Act in 1986 meant a big leap forward in European integration and gave new saliency to the question how Sweden should conceive of its relation with the European Community. Moreover, the collapse of the Soviet Union and the Communist Regimes in Eastern Europe deprived the concept of neutrality of much of its legitimacy and questioned Sweden's role in the international system. The economic crisis that hit Sweden in the early 1990s and the persistent claim of the Swedish Employers Association (SAF; *Svenska Arbetsgivareföreningen*; nowadays called *Svenskt Näringsliv*) to reorganise the state along neo-liberal lines also triggered new discussions on the Swedish welfare-state.

In the discussions prior to the accession of Sweden to the European Union in 1995, the various political parties referred to central concepts of Swedish national identity – such as the importance of democracy, the welfare system or gender equality – to argue both in favour and against Sweden's entry into the EU. The Left Party (*Vänsterpartiet*), for example, drew on the proclaimed democratic inferiority of Europe, while parts of the Social Democratic Party argued that Sweden would make the EU a 'living democracy' (Trägårdh 2002: 171; cf. ibid.; Weber 2001; Aylott 1999). The results of the referendum showed an only thin margin of 52,3% in favour of EU-accession. Since then, the Swedes remained to a large extent sceptical EU-citizens. According to the figures of *Eurobarometer 60* (p. 28), 50% of the Swedes say that their country has not benefited from EU-membership. This is the highest number among all member states. Furthermore, the rejection of the accession to the European Monetary Union in a referendum in September 2003 has shown a deep scepticism with regard to European integration prevailing in Sweden.

Empirical findings

Against this background of strong Euro-scepticism and given the special importance that "democracy" plays in discourses on Swedish national identity, investigating how the appeal "to uphold the values and principles of humanism and democratic tolerance" by the EU-14 was perceived in Swedish mainstream media, seems especially interesting.

The empirical study is based on a corpus of 1018 articles that were published in four major Swedish newspapers between January and September 2000. These newspapers are the social-democratic tabloid *Aftonbladet*, the liberal tabloid *Expressen*, the conservative quality newspaper *Svenska Dagbladet*, and Sweden's biggest daily, the liberal quality newspaper *Dagens Nyheter*. All articles were included that referred either to the political situation in Austria after the formation of a coalition government between the conservative People's Party (ÖVP) and the right-wing Freedom Party (FPÖ) or to the measures that were seized by the other 14 Member States. The articles were obtained from internet archives and saved electronically. For the analysis of the media discourse, the focus was on the contextualisation (for the concept of (re)contextulisation cf. Muntigl, Weiss, & Wodak 2000: 77ff.) of the events, the use of constructive and destructive strategies, as well as strategies of transformation (Wodak et al. 1998, 1999). Accordingly, central questions that were used for analysing the texts included the following: Which (historical, political, etc.) contexts were referred to in the texts? Which arguments, adverbs, adjectives were used to evaluate the proceedings of the EU-14 and the political situation in Austria respectively? What consequences of the measures were predicted? Could any discussion about "European values" be found? If yes, which stance is taken with regard to this notion? Was a common European *Erfahrungsraum* ('space of experience') or a common *Erwartungshorizont* ('horizon of expectation'; Koselleck 2000) constructed by postulating a common European understanding of historical events and of the future respectively? When posing these questions to the Swedish media texts on the *Causa Austria*, the answers will yield insights into the discursive construction of Europe in Sweden and will allow conclusions to be drawn on how Europe is discursively related to the Swedish understanding of state and nation. As the newspapers included in this study are the only four nation-wide dailies in Sweden, the results can be expected to reflect mainstream perceptions of Europe. In the following pages, some selected newspaper articles will be analysed in detail. The aim is to point out typical but also certain non-typical ways of how the four newspapers dealt with the *Causa Austria*. In the concluding part of this article, the findings of the empirical study will be tied back to the theoretical discussion above.

One possible way that one could expect the Swedish media to deal with the formation of government in Austria in the year 2000 and the ensuing sanctions by the other EU Member States is to follow the way of reasoning as given by the heads of the other EU Member States. Their reference to the importance of protecting the 'European values' implies an appeal to a common European identity. Indeed, a *few* articles can be found that follow this line of argumentation.

An example for this is an article published in the social-democratic tabloid *Aftonbladet* on February 1st, 2000 (p. 2).

> [...] Haider and the FPÖ have positioned themselves outside the democratic values which the EU was founded to protect and strengthen. [...] The EU can and should not form a government in Vienna. The Austrian's democratic elections have to be accepted. But the EU countries' decision is a justified warning to every democratic party within the community not to accept to collaborate on a government level with parties that discredit the EU's community of values, discriminate minorities and balance on the edge to fascism and nazism.[2]
>
> (*Aftonbladet*, February 1st, 2000, p. 2)

In this article, various strategies are used to construct a European identity. First, the FPÖ is depicted in a negative way and, second, set in opposition to a democratic Europe. Furthermore, a tension is recognised between the supranational reaction to domestic political developments in one country, on the one hand, and state sovereignty on the other. This tension, however, is, in the third strategy, solved in favour of the first by referring to the importance of protecting democracy and the "EU's community of values". Fourth, this argument is backed up by a historical reference to "fascism and nazism" grouped together as the negatively laden "other".

An article combining very similar strategic elements can be found on March 5th in the liberal broad sheet *Dagens Nyheter*. Once again, history serves as the background against which the argument is developed:

> [...] The Austrian FPÖ has dreadful similarities with a neo-nazi party. Its leader openly speaks about Adolf Hitler as his idol [...]. Austria is a little country and cannot threaten Europe alone. But what is happening in Austria threatens the future of the EU and of Europe. [...] To claim that all this is Austria's internal matter in which no one is allowed to intervene – this is not appropriate. [...] Democracies actually have the right to defend themselves. [...][3]
>
> (*Dagens Nyheter*, March 5, 2000, p. A4)

With the first line, the author paints a sinister picture of Haider and the FPÖ by almost equating the FPÖ with a neo-nazi party and by pointing to the ideological closeness of Haider and Hitler. Then the developments in Austria are given a European dimension by claiming that they "threaten the future of Europe". In the following phrase, the author touches upon a critical point in Swedish discourses on Europe, by once again addressing the question of state-sovereignty and by framing the developments as a problem for democracy. In this case, the 'intervention' in Austrian domestic matters is legitimised with reference to the right of democracies to "defend themselves". This kind of reconciling the question of state sovereignty with democracy is quite remarkable and, as will be shown below, rather untypical for Swedish discourses on Europe in general. All in all, in the few articles that follow this pattern, a kind of all-European democratic community is constructed which is contrasted with Haider / the FPÖ / Austria as Europe's 'other'. Though the line of argumentation used in these articles is suggested by the official legitimisation of the EU-14's measures, it is indeed the exception.

Aftonbladet's way of reporting proved to be especially interesting, as it combined both a positive evaluation of the diplomatic sanctions as well as a negative evaluation. The paper's editorials *exclusively* supported the proceedings of the EU-14, while articles in the paper's debate section were much more critical. This ambivalent way of reporting can be explained when taking the newspaper's social democratic editorial line into consideration. The Social Democratic Party in Sweden, as well as the Social Democratic electorate, is split up into supporters and opponents of European integration. The newspaper's handling of the *Causa Austria* can then be understood as an attempt to give balanced coverage of both sides.

In general, a very critical stance towards the proceedings of the EU-14 and the notion of European values was predominant in the four newspapers. For instance, an article from February 15th is a good example of *Aftonbladet's* negative way of reporting on the matter.

> [...] The EU, Austria and Haider are not Hitler and Europe 1931 and the intricate dilemma how and when the Union has the right to intervene in a sovereign country's inner life cannot be rejected with a historical cliché. [...] In practice it was actually a veto that the EU's big powers interposed with their threat of reprisals in the case that the Freedom Party would be taken into the government. A veto that the small countries joined due to the lack of an alternative. [...] I can hardly interpret the situation other than that the EU has usurped the dangerous rights to interpret, sentence and sanction a sovereign member country's election results [...]. Keeping democracy clean for sure is a good thing, but in the long run only few things are so harmful for democracy as political power's well-meaning arbitrariness. [...]⁴
> (*Aftonbladet*, February 15th, 2000, p. 16)

In this article, the references to history and the questions of state-sovereignty and democracy are used in a way diametrical to the previous examples. Here, the current situation is explicitly dissociated from any comparison with the 1930s, and the question whether the EU should have the right to intervene in national politics to "keep democracy clean" is answered in a clearly negative way. Furthermore, the sanctions of the EU-14 are presented as an initiative of the "EU's big powers," which the smaller countries only joined due to the lack of an alternative. This argument plays on a "David-Goliath" topos and serves to delegitimize the proceedings of the EU-14. Apparently, according to this article, the diplomatic measures against the Austrian government had little to do with the convinced defence of "European values".

The topic of democracy also occurs in many of the articles published by the liberal broad-sheet *Dagens Nyheter*. Here again, it is frequently used to criticise the proceedings of the EU-14. In an article from February 4th, for example, the following lines can be found:

> [...] The federally disposed can even see a positive development, that the EU takes an ever bigger responsibility for the political developments in the respective member states. Problems become European, not national. Austria concerns us just as much as Säffle and Mora [two Swedish provincial towns; C.B.]. The way to such a Europe, however, is long, and problems have to be dealt with in the reality in which they come up, not in a future vision. [...] Shouldn't the EU's democratic cement be strong enough to bring an obstinate Austria back on the track? I am inclined to think so.[5]
>
> (*Dagens Nyheter*, February 4th, 2000, p. A2)

As these excerpts show, this article plays on a set of disputed topics. Once more, the topic of state-sovereignty is raised and once more the sanctions are rejected. Only the "federally disposed" may see these developments as positive, according to the article. The author, however, rejects this interpretation and argues that European Integration does not yet legitimise this kind of politics. By stating, first, that the way to a kind of 'Europe,' in which national problems "become European," is still long and, second, that this is only a kind of "future vision," the author deprives the reference to Europe's future of its identity-creating potential. Indeed, by stressing the temporal distance, the irrelevance of this vision for contemporary politics is pointed out. At the end of the article, the topic of democracy is introduced by claiming that the developments in Austria are no threat to democracy in the EU ("democratic cement").

Another topic, also closely related to 'democracy', is given a prominent position in the liberal tabloid *Expressen*, namely, the lack of a European constitution. The following quotation from an article entitled "Democratic values without Democracy" provides an example:

[...] The affair is surely counterproductive. [...] There have been proposals that the EU should get hold of the power to resist the acts of individual member states, especially when it comes to the common defence and foreign policy. This is exactly what has happened this week, with the difference that it happens without a constitutional basis. Such, one should get hold of as soon as possible. The current lawless situation supports corruption and power politics at the expense of openness and equal treatment of small and big states. [...] But it is even more important that the loss of democracy at the national level is replaced by the Union. If the EU thinks that it can drive over the Member States' voters, the same voters have to be able to demand responsibility from the EU. They cannot do this today. If the EU is supposed to have such a big supra-national power as the heads of government have taken now, it has to be considered legitimate. It is not sufficient to have a moral basis, it has to be democratic too.[...][6]   (*Expressen*, February 3rd, 2000, p. 2)

A very similar line of argumentation can be found on March 3rd, p. 2:

[...] The EU's slightly anarchistic supra-nationality therefore must be regulated and has to get a working democratic mechanism. In other words: a constitution and increased power to the European Parliament.[7]
                                        (*Expressen*, March 3rd, 2000, p. 2)

Expressen's way of reporting is remarkable, as it combines a disapproving stance concerning the measures with a clearly expressed positive attitude to European integration. The latter is expressed by the claim for a European constitution that one "should get hold of as soon as possible". This claim, along with the reference to the importance of "openness and equal treatment of small and big states", resonate Swedish narratives of the "good state", an international system based on equality and law and – once more – on democracy. Again, the interweavement of discourses on the nation and of discourses on Europe can clearly be found in this example. Due to the combination of criticism concerning the concrete measures of the EU-14 and the claim for a European constitution, this article constructs the possibility of a future identification with the EU – an EU, one could say, which has certain important characteristics of the Swedish state.

Finally, the conservative *Svenska Dagbladet* was the most critical when it came to the evaluation of the proceedings of the 14 EU member states. For example, on February 1st, 2000, the following lines could be found:

The EU has not declared war against Austria. Not yet. But yesterday a conflict escalated that makes the relation between the EU's inter-governmental co-operation and the Member States topical. [...] The motive behind this action can easily be understood. Nevertheless the action is unprecedented and creates an unfortunate precedent: that it is possible to conduct single nations

> by supranational consensus. When will the EU perceive it as being moti-
> vated to intervene against internal political circumstances in other democratic
> Member States? [...][8]   (*Svenska Dagbladet*, Feb. 1st, 2000, p. 2)

Here, the criticism of the measures of the EU-14 is not mitigated by any positive reference to European integration. On the contrary ,*Svenska Dagbladet*
even uses the rhetoric of war to evaluate the situation. The topic of state-
sovereignty is addressed in a very direct way and the end statement ("When
will...?") even conjures the possibility of intervening with the domestic affairs
of other "democratic Member States", including Sweden.

As these examples have shown, the discourse on the *Causa Austria* in the
four newspapers very much evolved around a small number of key questions
all connected to the discursive construction of a European identity. No matter what stance the various newspapers took on the matter, the discussions
focused (1) on how to perceive of the relation between the state and the supra-
national polity of the EU, (2) on whether parallels to fascism and nazism can
be drawn, and (3) on the debate on the European values, especially on democracy. Though a small number of articles could be found in which constructive
strategies were applied, based on the support of the notion of European values,
the reference to a common "*Erfahrungsraum*" and the support of the supranational measures, the majority of the articles did not correspond to this pattern.
Rather, these topics were dealt with in a way that denied the democratic legitimacy of the EU-14's measures, thereby rejecting this kind of supranational way
of doing politics and, to a lesser extent, disclaimed the plausibility of references
to the national socialist past.

Conclusion

The empirical results of this study support the assumption that discourses on
European issues are closely intertwined with and influenced by discourses on
national identity. As has been pointed out above, Swedish national identity is
characterised by a tight discursive coupling between the nation and the state.
In this discursive connection, besides the welfare state, 'democracy' plays a
central role. As a result of the specific characteristics of the discursive construction of Swedish national identity, discourses touching upon topics – such
as democracy, the welfare state, or state sovereignty – directly affect the national self-understanding and thus become especially salient. In the discourse
on Austria's political situation in Austria in 2000, numerous arguments could

be found that, in one way or another, addressed the question of 'democracy' and state-sovereignty. In most cases, these references were used to criticise the proceeding of the 14 EU Member States. Though scepticism concerning the politics of the Austrian Freedom Party and its participation in the government prevailed, these concerns were frequently ruled out by the argument that the formation of government was the result of democratic elections. Furthermore, the measures of the EU 14 were often depicted as being an undemocratic, ad-hoc measure lacking political legitimacy that even can be a threat to national sovereignty. In this way, a picture of the European Union was created that presented Europe as being at odds with central characteristics of Swedish national identity. According to this perception, the proceeding of the 14 Member States was opposed to the "good and democratic" Swedish state. However, as pointed out above, a European identity can only develop if discourses on Europe succeed in showing how 'Europe' can be accommodated with the national 'we'. This kind of discursive accommodation could only be discerned in few articles. The EU in this particular discourse emerged as Sweden's 'other' so that there was only little room for the discursive construction of a European identity.

The results, however, also show that in the discourse on the *Causa Austria*, there was a possible way of accommodating Swedish national and European identity. *Expressen's* insistence on the necessity of a European constitution for compensating the "loss of democracy at the national level" illustrates a way in which Swedish narratives on democracy can be reconciled with discourses on Europe. According to this discourse, Europe has to become more like Sweden – i.e., more democratic – in order to become a site of identification. This finding corresponds to figures of *Eurobarometer*, according to which the Swedes clearly support the creation of a European constitution. For example, in spring 2002, according to *Eurobarometer 57*, 73% of the Swedes (as well as of the Dutch) declared that the EU should have a constitution. This figure was only topped by Italy, where 81% expressed their positive attitude towards a European constitution (cf. *Eurobarometer 57*, p. 67). Interestingly, this figure has dropped to a mere 63% in autumn 2003 (cf. *Eurobarometer 60*, p. 15), which means that the approval of a European constitution in 7 Member States of the EU is higher than in Sweden. This clear decrease in approval of a European constitution co-incides with the debates following the presentation of a European Constitution by the European Convention. It seems likely that in the course of the debate on the concrete design of a European constitution, the question of democracy and of the tension between state-sovereignty and supra-nationality led to an increasingly sceptical perception of the notion of a European constitution. This question should be dealt with in further discourse analytical research.

Notes

* This paper is based on some of the findings of my master thesis at the University of Vienna (cf. Bärenreuter 2002). I would like to thank Alexa Robertson and Ruth Wodak for their comments on earlier versions of the paper. I am also very grateful to Ruben Inion for his help in drawing the figure and to Thomas Nesbit for carefully reading this article.

1. To give an example from Austria, in the debate preceding the referendum on EU-accession in 1994, concerns were put forward that certain particularities of the Austrian version of the German language would get lost in the EU as they would be replaced by expressions from Germany. Pro-European Austrian politicians were quick to assure that this would not be the case and that measures would be taken to safeguard certain typical Austrian expressions.

2. *Aftonbladet*, February 1st, 2000, p. 2:

> [...] Haider och FPÖ har ställt sig vid sidan av de demokratiska värden som EU bildats för att värna och stärka. [...] EU kan och bör inte bilda regering i Wien. Österrikarnas demokratiska val måste respekteras. Men EU-ländernas beslut är en motiverad varning till varje demokratiskt parti inom gemenskapen att inte acceptera att i regeringsställning samarbeta med partier som diskrediterar EU:s värdegemenskap, diskriminerar minoriteter och balanserar på gränsen mot fascism och nazism.

3. *Dagens Nyheter*, March 5th, 2000, p. A4:

> [...] Det österrikiska FPÖ har otäcka likheter med ett nynazistiskt parti. Dess ledare talar öppet om Adolf Hitler som förebild [...]. Österrike är ett litet land och kann inte ensamt hota Europa. Men det som hände i Österrike hotar EU:s och Europas framtid. [...] Att hävda att detta är Österrikes inre angelägenhet som ingen får lägga sig i – det är inte rimligt. [...] Demokratier har faktiskt rätt att försvara sig. [...]

4. *Aftonbladet*, February 15th, 2000, p. 16:

> [...] EU, Österrike och Haider i dag är inte Hitler och Europa 1931 och det intrikata dilemmat hur och när Unionen har rätt att blanda sig i ett suveränt lands inre liv kan inte avfärdas med en historisk kliché. [...] I praktiken är det nämligen ett veto som EU:s stormakter lade in med sina hot om represalier i fall Frihetspartiet togs in i regeringen. Ett veto som de små länderna hakade på i brist på alternativ. [...] Jag har svårt att se annat än att EU har tagit sig vådliga rättigheter att uttolka, fördöma och sanktionera ett suveränt medlemslands valresultat [...] Demokratisk renhållning är förvisso en bra sak men i längden är få ting så skadliga för demokratin som maktens välmenande godtycke. [...]

5. *Dagens Nyheter*, February 4th, 2000, p. A2:

> [...] Den federalistiskt lagde kan också se en positiv utveckling där EU tar ett allt större ansvar för den politiska utvecklingen i de enskilda medlemsstaterna. Problemerna blir europeiska, inte nationella. Österrike berör oss lika mycket som Säffle eller Mora. Till ett sådant Europa är steget emellertid långt, och ett problem måste hanteras i den verklighet där det uppstår, inte i en framtide vision. [...] Borde inte

EU:s demokratiska kitt vara starkt nog för att få ett eventuellt motsträvigt Öster-
rike på rätt kurs igen utan symboldhandlingar och bestraffningar? Jag vill gärna
tro det.

6. *Expressen*, February 3rd, 2000, p. 2:

> [...] I sak är beslutet säket kontraproduktivt. [...] Det har också kommit förslag
> om att EU bör skaffa sig makt att stå emot enskilda medlems-länders handlin-
> gar, särksilt vad det gäller den gemensamma försvars- och utrikespolitiken. Det
> som har hänt denna vecka är precis detta, med den skillnaden att det sker utan
> en konstitution i botten. En sådan bör man snarast skaffa sig. Det nuvarande
> laglösa tillståndet gynnar korridorfiffel och stormaktspolitik på bekostnad av öp-
> penhet och lika behandling av små och stora stater. [...] Men än viktigare är
> att den nationella demokratieförlusten ersätts av en unionell. Om EU anser sig
> kunna köra över medlemsstaternas väljare, måste samma väljare kunna utkräva
> ansvar av EU. Det kann de inte i dag. Om EU ska ha så stor överstatlig makt som
> regeringscheferna nu tagit sig, måste denna uppfattas som legitim. Det räcker inte
> med en moralisk grund, den måste också vara demokratisk. [...]

7. *Expressen*, March 24th, 2000, p. 2:

> [...] EU:s lätt anarkistiska överstatlighet måste därför regleras och få en fungerande
> demokratisk mekanism. Med andra ord: en konstitution och ökad makt åt Europa-
> parlamentet.

8. *Svenska Dagbladet*, February 1st, 2000, p. 2:

> [...] EU har inte förklarat Österrike krig. Än. Men i går eskalerade en kon-
> flikt som aktualiserar förhållandet mellan det mellanstatlige smarabetet EU och
> medlemsländerna. [...] Motivet bakom denna EU-aktion är lättebegripligt. Inte
> desto mindre är aktion exempellös, och skapar ett olyckligt prejudikat: att det går
> för sig att genom överstatlig konsensus försöka styra enskilda nationer. När kom-
> mer EU att anse det motiverat att inskrida mot interna politiska förhållanden i
> andra demokratiska medlemsländer? [...]

References

Aylott, Nicholas (1999). *Swedish Social Democracy and European Integration. The People's Home on the Market*. Aldershot: Ashgate.

Bärenreuter, Christoph (2002). "It goes without saying that the EU shall stand for democratic principles, but the very method [...] is dubious". European Identity Construction in the Reporting of Swedish Newspaperson the political Situation in Austria in the Year 2000, unpublished master thesis, University of Vienna.

Brubaker, Rogers (1992). *Citizenship and Nationhood in France and Germany*. Cambridge: Harvard University Press.

Eurobarometer 57.
http://europa.eu.int/comm/public_opinion/archives/eb/eb57/eb57_en.pdf

Eurobarometer 60.
    http://europa.eu.int/comm/public_opinion/archives/eb/eb60/eb60_en.pdf

Foucault, Michel (1972). *The Archaeology of Knowledge*. London: Pantheon.

Haas, Ernst B. (1958). *The uniting of Europe. Political, social and economic forces 1950–1957*. Stanford: Stanford University Press.

Kohli, Martin & Novak, Mojca (2001). "Introduction. Will Europe work?" In M. Kohli & M. Novak (Eds.), *Will Europe work? Integration, employment and the social order* (pp. 1–17). London / New York: Routledge.

Koselleck, Reinhart (2000). *Vergangene Zukunft*. Frankfurt: Suhrkamp.

Kovács, András & Wodak, Ruth (2003). *NATO, Neutrality and National Identity. The case of Austria and Hungary*. Vienna: Böhlau.

Laclau, Ernesto & Mouffe, Chantal (1985). *Hegemony and Socialist Strategy. Towards a Radical Democratic Politics*. Verso: London.

Muntigl, Peter, Weiss, Gilbert, & Wodak, Ruth (2000). *European Union Discourses on Un/employment. An Interdisciplinary approach to employment policy-making and organizational change*. Amsterdam / Philadelphia: Benjamins.

Pelinka, Anton & Wodak, Ruth (Eds.). (2002). *"Dreck am Stecken". Politik der Ausgrenzung*. Vienna: Czernin.

Risse, Thomas (2004). "European Institutions and Identity Change: What Have We Learned?" In R. Herrmann, T. Risse, & M. Brewer (Eds.), *Transnational Identities. Becoming European in the EU* (pp. 247–271). Lanham: Rowman and Littlefield.

Schlesinger, Philip R. (1996). "Europeanisation and the Media: National Identity and the Public Sphere". In T. Slaatta (Ed.), *Media and the Transition of Collective Identities. JMK Report No. 18*. Oslo: Department of Media and Communication.

Sedlak, Maria (2000). "You Really do make an Unrespectable Foreigner Policy... Discourse on Ethnic Issues in the Austrian Parliament". In R. Wodak & T. A. van Dijk (Eds.), *Racism at the Top. Parliamentary Discourses on Ethnic Issues in Six European States* (pp. 107–168). Klagenfurt / Celovec: Drava.

Stråth, Bo (1993). *Folkhemmet mot Europa. Ett historiskt perspektiv på 90-talet*. Stockholm: Tiden.

Stråth, Bo (2000). "The Swedish Image of Europe as the Other". In B. Stråth (Ed.), *Europe and the Other and Europe as the Other* (pp. 359–383). Bruxelles et al.: Peter Lang.

Tiersky, Ronald (Ed.). (2001). *Euro-skepticism. A reader*. Lanham et al.: Rowman and Littlefield.

Trägårdh, Lars (2002). "Sweden and the EU. Welfare state nationalism and the spectre of 'Europe'". In L. Hansen & O. Wæver (Eds.), *European Integration and National Identity. The challenge of the Nordic states* (pp. 130–181). London / New York: Routledge.

Wæver, Ole (2002). "Identity, communities and foreign policy. Discourse analysis as foreign policy theory". In L. Hansen & O. Wæver (Eds.), *European Integration and National Identity. The challenge of the Nordic states* (pp. 20–49). London / New York: Routledge.

Wæver, Ole (2003). "European Integration and Security: Analysing French and German Discourses on State, Nation and Europe." Paper presented at the conference *Discourse theory – its empirical application and methodological self-reflections*, February 6–7 2003; Roskilde University.

Weber, Martin (2001). *Schweden und die Europäische Union. Europadebatte und Legitimität.* Baden-Baden: Nomos.

Weiss, Gilbert & Wodak, Ruth (2003). "Introduction: Theory, Interdisciplinarity and Critical Discourse Analysis". In G. Weiss & R. Wodak (Eds.), *Critical Discourse Analysis. Theory and Interdisciplinarity* (pp. 1–32). Houndmills / New York: Palgrave Macmillan.

Wodak, Ruth, de Cillia, Rudolf, Reisigl, Martin, Liebhart, Karin, Hofstätter, Klaus, & Kargl, Maria (1998). *Zur diskursiven Konstruktion nationaler Identität.* Frankfurt: Suhrkamp.

Wodak, Ruth, de Cillia, Rudolf, Reisigl, Martin, & Liebhart, Karin (1999). *The discursive construction of national identity.* Edinburgh: Edinburgh University Press.

Wodak, Ruth (2001). "Politikwissenschaft und Diskursanalyse: Diskurs in/der Politik". In A. S. Markovits & S. K. Rosenberger (Eds.), *Demokratie. Modus und Telos. Beiträge für Anton Pelinka* (pp. 75–98). Vienna et al.: Böhlau.

CHAPTER 10

Language, psychotherapy and client change

An interdisciplinary perspective

Peter Muntigl and Adam Horvath

University of Salzburg / Simon Fraser University

1. Introduction

The impetus for this project comes from the convergence of interests of two disciplines: Systemic Functional Linguistics (hereafter SFL) and psychotherapy research.[1] There is strong evidence in the psychotherapy research literature that a number of different forms of psychotherapeutic interventions do provide relief for psychological problems (Garfield & Bergin 1994; Luborsky, Singer, & Luborsky 1975; Shapiro & Shapiro 1982; Smith & Glass 1977; Smith, Glass, & Miller 1980). Whereas the over all evidence for efficacy of therapy is convincing, the same body of research also indicates that there is no empirical validity to claims linking one particular theoretically defined technique (such as interpretation, behavioral training etc.) as exclusively superior to other forms of interventions (Smith, Glass, & Miller 1980; Shapiro & Shapiro 1982; Wampold 2001). This finding has lead to the growing realization among psychotherapists, that available theories of psychotherapy and traditional research methodologies offer limited potential to further clarify the question: "How does psychotherapy facilitate client change?" Many believe that progress towards a better understanding of the phenomena of social and psychological problems lie in the detailed exploration of the discrete elements of the therapy process and in the identification of specific in-therapy events associated with client change (Rice & Greenberg 1984). It is argued that the identification of these "significant micro events" would lead to the specification of a number of processes that are operative in some form and context in all forms of effective therapy (Horvath & Luborsky 1993).

The interactive medium that is central to most psychotherapies is conversation. Yet research on conversation as the basic building block of the therapy process has been relatively slow in coming. Moreover the great majority of the available literature tends to examine therapeutic conversation as a method of conveying intended meanings rather than as a process that provides clients with new linguistic resources in order to change their social relationships. Similarly, systematic explorations of changes and developments in the discourse between therapist and client over the length of the therapy process have been generally neglected. More recently, however, the narrative aspect of therapy has been emphasized by theorists and explored by researchers (Anderson & Goolishian 1988; Tomm 1987a, 1987b, 1988; White & Epston 1990), but largely without having incorporated a linguistic and semiotic understanding of conversation as a form of social action.

Discourse analysts, on the other hand, are increasingly exploring how language, as a resource with which to make and negotiate meanings, plays an integral part in realizing the therapy process (for earlier seminal work see Davis 1986; Labov & Fanshel 1977; Peyrot 1987). Later discourse analytic studies have focussed on couples therapy (Buttny 1993, 1996, 1998; Edwards 1994, 1995; Kogan & Gale 1997), AIDS counselling (Peräkylä 1995; Silverman 1997), family therapy (Aronsson & Cederborg 1994; Grossen 1996), group therapy (Wodak 1986, 1996), psychiatric intake interviews (Bergmann 1992) and radio talk-show therapy (Gaik 1992).

More recent studies, however, have begun to specifically address linguistic change within therapy; that is, how problems get linguistically constructed and effaced, and how clients' linguistic resources can develop in therapy so that they are able to construct new and alternative stories about their experiences (Muntigl 2004a, 2004b). Thus we became convinced that therapy as discourse requires rigorous attention utilizing the conjoint, interdisciplinary understandings and resources of both disciplines: SFL and psychotherapy research.

2.   Three models of interdisciplinarity

There are a range of options and degrees of integration between disciplines that may be implemented when a plurality of perspectives are applied to a problem (see Weiss & Wodak 2003). Van Leeuwen (2003) proposes three different models that encapsulate different levels of integration in interdisciplinary work (for a similar view on degrees of discipline integration – called *trans*disciplinarity – see Halliday 2003 [1990]). As Table 1 shows, investiga-

Table 1. Three models of interdisciplinarity (source: van Leeuwen 2003)

	Orientation	Dependency	Valuation
Centralist model	Discipline-oriented	Autonomous disciplines	Disciplines not equally valued
Pluralist model	Problem-oriented	Autonomous disciplines	Disciplines equally valued
Integrationist model	Problem-oriented	Interdependent disciplines	Disciplines equally valued

tions may proceed from a *centralist*, *pluralist* or *integrationist* model. Centralist models are discipline-oriented. Other disciplines are used merely as tools to answer discipline-internal questions. Pluralist models, on the other hand, involve disciplines that have a shared interest in a certain problem or question. Whereas disciplines in this model are equally valued – that is, one discipline is not seen as subsidiary to another – they remain self-sufficient, and do not 'import' aspects from other disciplines. The third model is integrationist. The main feature that separates this model from the others is that disciplines are seen as interdependent. Here, problem-oriented investigations proceed from the assumption that a single discipline by itself does not contain the means to answer the research question. For this reason, an interdependent constellation of disciplines is needed.

The interdisciplinary models that van Leeuwen has proposed can be understood as 'pure' or 'ideal' forms. In practice, of course, such 'pure' forms do not exist. In all likelihood interdisciplinary work evolves over time in a non-linear fashion and in the process of evolution from time to time draws from all three models. For this reason, these models are best viewed along a continuum, in terms of *the degree* to which a certain approach may be identified as centralist, pluralist or integrationist.

The model that we are moving toward in this project is integrationist. We say that we are "moving toward" because our model does not yet reflect a full integration of both SFL and psychotherapy research. A cogent integration of theoretical understandings and technical resources, however, is a progressive and ongoing process involving the bringing together, adopting and modifying contributions of the host disciplines. When does this process reach the level of maturity where it can be recognized as truly interdependent? Our theoretical position is that in order to achieve a better understanding of the psychotherapy change process we need to draw from aspects of both linguistics and psychotherapy disciplines. We do not view one discipline as being merely a 'tool' for the other. Nor do we think, in addressing the process of client change, that these disciplines can remain autonomous, because: (1) in order to understand change in therapy, we need to understand the linguistic-semiotic process of how clients' develop their ability to use meaning-making resources; and (2) we need a more inclusive and detailed description of how contextual and social factors influence client change.

For example, in a more advanced integrationist model more must be said about clients' social relationships, and we will need also to include the relationship between the client and the therapist. In order to demonstrate how the resources of both linguistics and psychotherapy may be combined in an integrationist model to address the issue of therapeutic change, it is important to first review theories of the client change process during therapy, and to speculate on how both linguistic and psychotherapeutic theories may play a complementary role in conceptualizing change.

3.   Theories of change

Since our focus is on examining the semiotic change process in therapy, one could argue that we are privileging or even imposing an understanding of the discipline of linguistics over psychotherapy, and that our focus is more centralist than integrationist. However, there already exists a significant body of work within psychotherapy that recognizes the importance of language in the therapeutic process (Anderson & Goolishian 1988; McCleod 1997; McNamee & Gergen 1992; White & Epston 1990). These psychotherapists have argued that the main resources used to create and negotiate client change in the problem-solving/dissolving therapy process are based in language. Tomm's (1987a, 1987b, 1988) observations on the importance of therapist's questions, Anderson and Goolishian's (1988) view of the therapy process as a linguistic system, Stiles' (1992) taxonomy of verbal response modes and White and Epston's (1990) focus on the centrality of narrative are just a few examples of the growing recognition of the central role of language in therapy.

Nonetheless, most of these studies – with the exception of Stiles' (1992) speech act related work – have not taken advantage of the accomplishments in linguistic theory to help achieve more in-depth understandings of the kinds of interactions that take place during psychotherapeutic conversations. In other words, even though there is a growing awareness in the discipline of psychotherapy that the process of therapeutic change is grounded in the semiotic exchanges between therapist and client, this understanding has more or less stayed at a speculative and generalized level. Some reasons for this slow development seem to be a lack of an in-depth understanding of psychotherapy as a

semiotic process, and a lack of analytic tools available in the psychotherapy research community to analyze the semiotic process in a rigorous systematic way.
Thus we believe that if Rice and Greenberg's (1984) plea for more "fine-grained
descriptions of [these] moments of change" is taken seriously, rigorous and detailed attention must be given to how language is actually used during therapy.
More precisely, analysis must consider the interactive sequences of therapist-
client talk, the linguistic construction of the turns uttered during therapy and
how these linguistic meanings help to realize the therapy process.

3.1 Language: System and instance

In order to understand the role of language in the change process, a few observations need to be made about language. Halliday (1991, 1992) argues that
language needs to be examined from two perspectives: a *systems* perspective
and an *instance* perspective. In the former, language is construed as a meaning *potential*, as a system of meaning-making possibilities that we may draw
from in various contexts. In the latter, language refers to the specific instances
in which language is used. For Halliday, a *text* is an instance of language, and a
collection of texts produced within a culture constructs the system. As Halliday
(1999: 7) summarizes:

> What the learner has to do is to construe (that is, construct in the mind) a
> linguistic *system*. That is what is meant by "language as system": it is language
> as stored up energy. It is a language, or some specific aspect of a language, like
> the language of science, in the form of a *potential*, a resource that you draw on
> in reading and writing and speaking and listening – and a resource that you
> use for learning with. How do you construe this potential, and how do you use
> it when you've got it? You build it up, and you act it out, in the form of *text*.
> "Text" refers to all the *instances* of language that you listen to and read, and
> that you produce yourself in speaking and in writing.

Halliday's system-instance perspective on language can also explain how
change may come about. Using a 'weather' analogy, Halliday likens system to
'climate' and instance to 'weather'. Climate tends to be a relatively stable system,
and is realized in the pattern of weather instances over time. Climate, therefore,
is a statement of the probability of the temperature, wind velocity, humidity,
etc. of a given geographical region at a given time of year and day. In order to
bring about a change in climate, the over-all pattern of instances must change;
that is, for a given period of the year, temperature, humidity, etc. must deviate
from what was expected based on its probability of occurrence.

A similar perspective is taken on language. The language system is construed in terms of the probability that certain meaning-making resources are deployed in certain contexts of situation. A change in the system will amount to changes in the instances (i.e., texts). No one text will change the system, but patterned changes over time will. System and instance are not different phenomena; rather, they are the same phenomena seen from different observer perspectives at different time depths. The instance is the here-and-now unfolding of meanings in contexts of use, whereas the system is the pattern of meanings that have occurred in repeated instances. In sum, language is viewed as a culturally shared, dynamic open system that is constantly interacting with its social environment (Halliday 1991, 1992; Lemke 1984, 1995).

3.2 Semogenesis: Three perspectives on system change

In addressing the question of how systems change, Halliday (1991:41) proposes that there are three dynamics involved: (1) there is the history of the text, which include the meanings that unfold within a text; (2) there is the history of the individual, which includes the individual's developing ability to make meanings in different contexts; and (3) there is the history of the system itself: the evolving linguistic resources of a culture with which individuals may draw from to create texts. Halliday and Matthiessen (1999) refer to these three histories as *logogenesis*, *ontogenesis*, and *phylogenesis* respectively. Applying this model to the context of therapy, we use the term logogenesis to refer to the specific kinds of interactions that clients and therapists engage in over time to realize the therapy process. Client ontogenesis, on the other hand, refers to clients' developing linguistic practices during therapy. Lastly, phylogenesis refers to the evolving cultural practice of therapy itself. Therapy phylogenesis, then, would include the multitude of ways in which therapy has been practiced, is being practiced today, and the directions in which it may evolve.

A variety of practices have been usefully examined using this (SFL) approach including the fields of pedagogy (Christie 1997, 1998, 1999; Coffin 1997; Martin 1997, 1999a), politics (Muntigl 2002; Muntigl, Weiss, & Wodak 2000), media (Iedema, Feez, & White 1994), administration (Iedema 1995), therapy (Muntigl 2004a; 2004b) and child language (Cloran 1999; Halliday 1975; Hasan 1996; Painter 1984, 1999; Williams 1999).

3.3 Change in psychotherapy: A narrative perspective

Different theories of psychotherapy offer distinct hypotheses as to how client changes come about. For example, whereas behavioural theorists emphasize learning and extinction, psychodynamic formulations propose insight and catharses as the process leading to change. Although our longer term project hopes to locate the unique and common semiotic realizations associated with different kinds of therapy approaches, for this chapter we shall restrict our focus to the client change process as it is realized in narrative therapy. In their book "Narrative Means to Therapeutic Ends" White and Epston (1990) have suggested that change occurs when clients are able to re-author their lives and relationships in which they may construct more 'preferred' and alternative ways of living and acting in the world. White (2001) argues that clients often become stuck in negative identity claims in which they tend to identify problem attributes as stable and enduring features of their identity ("I am *inadequate, a failure, incompetent*"). The aim of narrative therapy, therefore, is to unpack these negative identity claims so that clients are able to produce "thick descriptions" of their lives and relationships. The term "thick description" is borrowed from Geertz (1973) and refers to multiple and contradictory formulations of experience. Change, then, is associated with a clients' ability to construe and act upon the social world in diverse (and perhaps contradictory) ways. With this expanded ability to make new meanings, clients are able to construct alternative formulations of the problem and alternative narratives of personal experience. By doing so, clients no longer identify themselves as the problem, and hence as an obstacle to change. Instead, they construe the problem as external to themselves ("the problem makes me" vs. "I am the problem"), and as something against which they may act; thus enabling them to act in more diverse and 'preferred' ways.

What we are proposing in this paper is that an examination of therapist-client discourse shows how a psychotherapy (in this case narrative) 'theory' is put into practice. In this discursive and semiotic view, theory corresponds to what people do in various contexts of situation. Or, in Halliday and Matthiessen's (1999:566) terms, a theory is a *sub-cultural model* that represents a more restricted set of situation types. Psychotherapy will most likely not be realized in 'everyday' situations; rather, it will be associated with specific activities (e.g., identifying problems), certain subject matters (e.g., problems), certain role relationships (i.e., therapist-client, confidant-confider, etc.) and certain modes such as face-to-face conversation. Furthermore, the situations in which psychotherapy is practiced will also be realized in certain language patterns. Halliday and Matthiessen (1999: 14) refer to this set of language patterns as a *sub- or domain potential*. The next section will demonstrate how a narrative therapists' linguistic practices realize a narrative 'theory', and play a dominant role in facilitating client development.

4.   An integrated view of the narrative therapy process

Some interesting bridging work between narrative therapy and SFL can be demonstrated by examining the activities of narrative therapy and the language used to realize those activities. It was mentioned before that narrative therapists aim to unpack clients' negative identity claims and help clients into producing "thick descriptions" of their lives and relationships. These narrative activities relate to client change in two ways. The first is through the genres used in narrative therapy, and the second is through the therapist's social actions that guide client behaviour. The important role of genre is addressed first.

4.1   Logogenesis: Genre and its relationship to client change

Semogenesis in narrative couples therapy has been explored in Muntigl (2004a, 2004b). From an examination of six conjoint sessions of narrative couples therapy involving a therapist (male) and one couple, it was found that problems were regularly constructed and effaced through a specific set of linguistic genres. Our interpretation of genre is taken from Ventola (1987) and Martin (1992, 1999b), in which genre is defined as "a staged, goal-oriented social process" (Martin 1992: 505). Genres are *social* processes because they are realized through interactions between speakers or between writers and readers. Genres are *goal-oriented* because the interactions realizing a genre orient towards an end-point. This end-point is not fixed or pre-determined, but is interactively negotiated. Finally, the *staging structure* of genres refers to the number of interactive functional steps needed to realize a genre's end-point. In SFL numerous genres have been identified in school and workplace environments such as stories, reports, descriptions, explanations, expositions, procedures, and discussions (see Martin 1997 for an overview).

Construing narrative therapy as a set of genres (or macro-genre) means that narrative therapy orients to an end point. This end point is, however, not known in advance. In the first therapy session, therapist and clients do not 'know' what will happen next. They do not, for instance, know how the problem will be construed or how the problem will be effaced. The *how* of problem construction and effacement unfolds through the unfolding interaction between therapist and clients. Although neither party has prior awareness of this logogenetic process, they still orient to the two most basic kinds of goal-oriented genres of therapy: problem construction and problem effacement (Muntigl 2004b). For the therapist and couple that were observed, these two goal oriented genres, the recursive construction and effacement of problems, were what drove the interaction forwards.

4.1.1 *Problem construction*

Problem construction consisted of two stages: Problem Identification and Problem Agency. The first stage of problem construction, Problem Identification, consisted of a client formulation followed by a therapist reformulation in which client behaviour became nominalized (e.g., I begin to feel like *I'm letting him down* → *this letting him down*). Ex. (1) is an instance of Problem Identification.

```
(1)²      01  W:   a:nd uh then (0.8) I begin to fee:l
     →    02       like I'm letting him down (1.0)
          03       cause I'm not enthusiastic about it
          04       an I: uh I don't wanna go out anyway (.)
          05       I don't wanna (1.0) yeah=
          06  T:   =mhm
                   .
                   .
                   .
          54  T:   okay su so so you started talking bout um (.)
     →    55       um this letting him down. (.)
```

In this stage, clients tended to negatively evaluate self or other's behaviour in terms of usualness (e.g., "I am *always* letting him down, doing it right, feeling badly"). The therapist tended to orient to these formulations of high usuality by nominalizing client's formulation (*this* letting him down, doing it right, feeling badly).

Subsequent to Problem Identification was Problem Agency. In this stage, problems were construed as Agents that caused clients to 'think' negative thoughts (e.g., this letting him down *makes you think* that…). In Ex. (2), T construes the problem (=this letting him down) as convincing F to think something.

(2)   T: so so the problem's tryin tuh convince <u>you::</u> that its <u>your</u> job tuh take
          on all this stuff

4.1.2 *Problem effacement*

In order for the second genre of therapy to occur, a problem (or problems) must first have been constructed; that is, once problems and their effects had been identified, therapy moved on to the identification of events that contrasted with the events caused by the problem. Effacing previously construed problems involved two stages: Identification of Alternative Events and Alternative Event and Client Agency. For example, if the 'problem' centred around *indecisiveness*, a contrasting event might involve an instance in which the client made a decision.

In Ex. (3), W narrates an episode in which she refuses a request from her family. In previous situations W would tend to comply with requests for fear that she might let someone down. What is significant about her ability to say *no* is that it contrasts with her previous problem-induced behaviour.

```
(3)        01  W:  =its been really i uh interesting the last couple of weeks
     →     02      .hh when I have simply said
     →     03      no::: .hh I'm not going to do tha::t
           04      (0.8)
           05  T:  you've done that?
           06  W:  I have done that hh heh heh .hh
           07      [an its difficult an ]
           08  T:  [(          )     ]
           09  W:  an as guilty I feel afterwards
           10      I kno::w I'll .hh
           11      that its the right thing for me tuh [say:: ]
     →     12  T:                                      [so so ]
     →     13      j just those simple words did you say
     →     14      no:: [I am ] not going to do that=
           15  W:       [ye::s ]
```

In lines 05 and 12–14, T reformulates W's newly articulated behaviour by emphasizing its significance. This emphasis is achieved by quoting W's prior formulation and by indicating surprise (*you've done that?*).

Following the first stage of problem effacement, the interaction proceeded to the second stage in which an alternative event (*no:: I am not going to do that*) or the client was construed as an Agent of client behaviour. In Ex. (4) the new behaviour (realized by 'that') is construed as opening up possibilities for W.

```
(4)   01  T:  =w what what does that op- what does that open up
      02      for you=
      03  W:  =.hh aw gee:: it opens up so many things
```

In sum, effacing problems translated into identifying behaviours that contrast with problem behaviours and construing these behaviours or clients, rather than the problem, as the Agents of client behaviour.

If a therapist (together with the clients) adheres to these genres of problem construction and effacement, clients' problems will likely undergo a specific kind of genesis. Our proposal is that genre acts as a constraint on meaning-making resources. Since narrative theory is described in terms of a sub-cultural model (i.e., narrative therapy is associated with specific social contexts), adhering to the practices of unpacking negative identity claims and clients' re-authoring of their lives and relationship will be associated with a specific set (i.e., subpotential) of language resources. This means that narrative therapy will draw from certain language resources and not others. Thus, problems, and the multitude of meanings or interpretation they are given, will be influenced by the genres in therapy.

4.2 Client ontogenesis: Scaffolding client change

By approaching therapy from logogenesis, we were able to provide an account of how problems semiotically came into being, and how they were interactively negotiated throughout the therapy sessions. Turning to client ontogenesis, we were then able to account for how clients made use of alternative meanings that became available during therapy, by formulating alternative and multiple descriptions of their lives and relationships. Thus, it was shown that clients were able to develop their repertoire of meaning-making resources in problem contexts. Clients were able to shift from negatively evaluating self and other's behaviour and describing negative behaviour as highly usual, to construing problems as Agents, to narrating instances of alternative behaviours, positively evaluating these alternative behaviours and construing themselves as Agents of alternative behaviours. A partial list of language features that comprise clients' beginning and developed semiotic repertoires is shown in Table 2. (For the complete list see Muntigl 2004b.)

Table 2. A comparison between clients' beginning and developed semiotic repertoires in the therapy context

Beginning semiotic repertoire	Developed semiotic repertoire
– negative evaluation of behaviour – problem behaviour highly usual	– problem behaviour as Agent – alternative behaviour as Agent / Client as Agent – positive evaluation of alternative behaviours

Whereas ontogenesis (semiotic development) is an ongoing life-long process, there are certain social contexts (e.g., therapy) that are specifically oriented to promote such changes. We find Basil Bernstein's (1971, 1990, 1996)
notion of *critical socializing contexts* or *pedagogic discourses* useful in conceptualizing how clients' semiotic development occurs within therapy. Although
the term *pedagogic* evokes a classroom setting, Bernstein (1996:17) explicitly
argued that other settings such as doctors' or counsellors' offices may also become sites for pedagogic practices. Central to Bernstein's model is the notion
that learners are scaffolded[3] into the mastery of new skills. In addition to having demonstrated that clients were able to deploy additional semiotic resources
as therapy progressed, it was also demonstrated that these meaning-making
resources were made available through a process of therapist scaffolding. Two
kinds of scaffolds proved central to this task: reformulations and questions. We
therefore claim that there are two perspectives that need be taken into account
when describing a therapist's theory in practice. First there are the genres that
characterize the therapy. Second are the scaffolding practices in which the therapist is able to influence the kinds of meanings that clients are to produce in
subsequent turns.

To view a therapist reformulation, let us revisit Ex. (1). W formulates that
she feels as if she is letting F down, when she is not enthusiastic about ac-
companying F when he wants to do something. A number of turns later in
the conversation T refers back to what W had talked about (i.e., *okay su so so
you started talking bout um (.) um this letting him down.*) by reformulating and
nominalizing W's prior formulation. In sum, W's formulation is moved to a
different level of abstraction from a clause to a noun.

```
(1)        01  W:  a:nd uh then (0.8) I begin to fee:l
      →    02      like I'm letting him down (1.0)
           03      cause I'm not enthusiastic about it
           04      an I: uh I don't wanna go out anyway (.)
           05      I don't wanna (1.0) yeah=
           06  T:  =mhm
                   .
                   .
                   .
      →    54  T:  okay su so so you started talking bout um (.)
      →    55      um this letting him down. (.)
```

Nominalizing client behaviour has been shown to play a central part in what
White and Epston (1990:38) would refer to as an externalizing conversation.

Through nominalization, the client becomes 'separated' from the problem. As a consequence, it becomes more difficult for clients to attribute the negative behaviour as a central part of their identity (for a discussion see Muntigl 2004a). In other words, *letting him down* is not an enduring feature that W must live with and accept for the rest of her life. By nominalization, T has taken the necessary steps to achieve this separation.

Nominalizing behaviour allows the behaviour to be placed in different participant roles such as Actor, Senser, Behaver, Goal (for a review of the different participant roles realized in different clause types see Halliday 1994: 106ff.). For instance, W's initial formulation of the problem in Ex. (1), *I begin to fee:l like I'm letting him down*, is a clause complex, and therefore does not realize a participant role. But once the clause complex becomes nominalized as *this letting him down* or *the problem*, it can participate with the elements within a clause. In Ex. (5) *the problem* (=this letting him down) is realized as an Agent that tries to put ideas in W's head and that convinces W of these ideas.

```
(5)    ›  01  T:  [well what ideas] has the problem tryin tuh put in your mind
          02       tuh tuh push you back=
          03  W:  =to put ki- to have him at my house
          04       an I will cook breakfast
          05       an I will do .hh all of these things
          06       tuh make them feel very comfortable at our our house
       → 07  T:  so so the problem's tryin tuh convince you::
          08       that its your job tuh take on all [this ] stuff
          09  W:                                     [yes ]
          10  T:  [becuz ] otherwise you'd be letting people down=
          11  W:  [yes    ]
          12  W:  =yes=
```

Examples (1) and (5) are both instances of therapist scaffolding. In Ex. (1) T uses a reformulation to reconstrue W's construal of her own experience and behaviour. W, therefore, is being apprenticed into interpreting behaviour as a 'thing' rather than as a clause. Furthermore, through the question and answer sequence in Ex. (5), T is able to introduce causal relationships between a problem (e.g., *this letting him down*) and the problem's effects (e.g., *its your job tuh take on all this stuff*). In other words, W is being mentored into setting up causal relations between problem behaviours that are not an integral part of herself and unwanted effects that are invited by problem behaviours.

Evidence for W having become scaffolded into using nominalization and causality in problems comes from W's independent use of these resources in later therapy sessions. This phenomenon is illustrated in Ex. (6) in which W construes her own behaviour in terms of a 'commanding' problem. W begins by formulating a series of events that described her behaviour prior to seeking therapy (e.g., *my stress levels were just too* high, *still .hh* trying to do:: everything, *perhaps not letting* them *do anything*). However, in line 11, W suddenly introduces the problem (i.e., I:: *my- the problem (0.8)* told me), and construes the problem as an Agent who commands W.

```
(6)        01  W:  .hh I've had alotta people telling me th(hh)ehat .hh
           02      u- y'know even before I went into:: any kind've therapy
           03      .hh becuz they could see:: (0.8)
           04      tha tum (0.8) that uh my stress levels were just too high
           05      .hh an I I wuz taking
           06      and still .hh trying to do:: everything (1.5)
           07      and perhaps not letting them do anything .hh
           08      neither were- really gave anybody a a good chance to
           09      .hh it wuz always (oh bum)
           10      y'see I've realized .hh (.)
      →    11      I:: my- the problem (0.8) told me
           12  C:  mhm=
      →    13  W:  =that I had tuh do it. (0.8)
      →    14      no one else could do it.
```

As a pedagogic discourse, therapy involves both regulation and instruction (Bernstein 1990). Furthermore, the pedagogic quality of therapy resides in the type of scaffolding used to guide client behaviour. Turning first to regulation, a sharp distinction can be made in terms of *who* has access to *what* resources. For instance, it is the therapist (and *not* the clients) who tends to draw on certain interpersonal resources such as questions and restatements. The therapist, for instance, reformulates what clients have said and asks questions that get clients to think of behaviour as a 'thing' that invites them into forming negative identity conclusions. The therapist's theory – in terms of a sub-cultural practice realized in a set of language patterns – orients him/her to draw on specific genres. In this sense the therapist is realizing himself as an expert on the therapeutic activity, by reformulating and essentially re-construing client experiences. Turning to the instructional aspect of therapy, the therapist strongly influenced the sequential unfolding of the therapy process (i.e., first problems are identified, then they are made agents, then clients identify alternative behaviours to the problem, etc.) and he influenced which meaning-making resources will be selected for problem construction. As was shown previously, the therapist's continued focus on nominalizing behaviour and the causal relations between problems and their effects led to the clients' ability to draw on these resources when effacing problems.

5.   Discussion: Which contextual factors influence change?

Based on our examination of narrative couples therapy, we are able to make the argument that the genres and stages of narrative therapy have been responsible for clients' semiotic change. Thus, the production of a certain genre will imply that certain kinds of actions/activities/meanings – as opposed to others – will be realized. The production of the narrative therapy genres means that problems will be identified and associated with agency. Furthermore, problems will be effaced by clients' formulation of alternative events and narratives.

So far, however, scant mention has been made of interpersonal relationship factors and what influence these factors might have on the change process. Psychotherapy research on *common factors* has shown that client characteristics, therapist qualities and relationship factors will be influential of change (Wampold 2001). Especially important is the therapeutic alliance, which includes the therapist's relationship to the couple and the couples' relationship to each other. The therapeutic relationship in general and the working alliance in particular has been shown to have a significant impact on therapy outcome (Horvath & Bedi 2002). Bordin (1994) has argued that the alliance between the therapist and clients is the factor that enables therapists to effectively implement the activities prescribed by specific theories of therapy. This argument can be understood as the claim that a 'good' alliance can provide the therapist with the means to better facilitate change.

An examination of therapist mentoring or scaffolding has shown that the interpersonal level was important, and this was partially demonstrated by therapists and clients' negotiation of authority and expertise through questions and reformulations. The concepts of *authority* and *expertise* form part of the contextual variable *tenor*.[4] Poynton (1985:76–77) argues that "**authority** is a function of socially-legitimated inherently unequal role relationships such as parent-child, teacher-child, employer-employee, or ruler-ruled", whereas "**expertise** is a matter of the extent to which an individual possesses knowledge or skill, e.g., the expert knitter compared with the novice, the nuclear physicist with the high school student beginning to study physics." It should be emphasized that authority and expertise are not inherent features of individuals, but are negotiated *between* individuals and are *realized in* semiotic systems such as language. A therapist-client relationship realizes unequal role relationships, *if and only if* we can demonstrate that therapists and clients have differential access to semiotic resources; that is, they must be using language in different ways. Turning first to authority, the therapist's reformulations of clients' experience, and his questions that implicate causality and negative client cognitions position him as the primary knower.[5] It is the therapist's and not the clients' construal of experience that ultimately gets taken up and worked with throughout the remaining therapy sessions. Expertise, on the other hand, refers to the kinds of ideational resources speakers have access to in a specific field of activity. In narrative therapy, for instance, expertise is demonstrated through the ability to identify problems through nominalization and to associate problems with agency.[6]

This formulation of expertise and authority, at first glance, runs counter to narrative oriented therapists' accounts of these variables. Anderson and Goolishian (1992), for instance, clearly state that *the client* is the expert in therapeutic conversations with a social constructionist orientation. The term *expert*, in Anderson and Goolishian's sense, refers specifically to *who* has most knowledge of *personal* experience. On this view the client knows more about his/her life and relationships than a therapist with whom the consultation is taking place. If expert is defined in these terms, then we certainly agree that the client is the expert of his/her own experience, that narrative practice does not discredit clients' formulations of their experience and that the conversations between narrative therapists and clients are collaborative as opposed to authoritative. However, if expertise is given Poynton's (1985) definition – access and ability to draw from semiotic resources in a given field of activity – then the therapist is the 'overall' expert. The therapist guided the conversation in terms of how the stages of the genres unfolded. Formulations of experience were nominalized/externalized and then associated with agency so that the influence of the problem in the client's life could be explored. The narrative therapist's role in guiding and directing clients in the course of therapy has been acknowledged by White (2000:98). He admits that therapists do direct the general course of conversation. But, he also points out that narrative therapists do not re-author clients' stories. It is clients who do that. The therapist 'knows' that problems *invite* 'unwanted' behaviours, but does not know what the problems consist of, or what will constitute a satisfactory re-authoring for the client. Thus, whereas narrative therapists provide a *frame* for re-authoring, clients provide their own "thick descriptions" of their lives and relationships. In some sense, then, a narrative therapist's expertise opens up a space for clients

STATUS $\rightarrow$ ⌈ equal
                      ⌊ unequal

TENOR $\rightarrow$

CONTACT $\rightarrow$ ⌈ involved
                       ⌊ distant

AFFECT[7] $\rightarrow$ ⌈ happiness
                          ├ security
                          ⌊ satisfaction

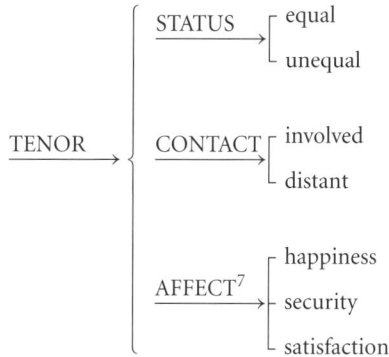

Figure 1. Three dimensions of tenor (adapted form Martin 1992:526)

to become better experts of their lives, how problems are influencing their lives and how they may, in turn, influence problems.

But are aspects of expertise and authority the only relevant interpersonal components in therapy in terms of *what* influences change? If we take Martin's (1992:526ff.) construal of the contextual variable *tenor* as a starting point, then there are two other important variables that we have neglected so far: *contact* and *affect*. Whereas contact specifies the degree of involvement between speaker/hearer and writer/reader, affect specifies the types of positive or negative emotional surges/dispositions that people may realize. Drawing from a slightly reworked system of affect from Martin (2000), affect involves three subsystems of meaning: dis/satisfaction, un/happiness and in/security. All three systems are depicted in Figure 1.

Martin's (1997, 2000) more recent model of affect is interpreted as a subsystem of the discourse semantic system of *appraisal*. Hence, affect is no longer construed as a contextual system, but as a linguistic system. Although we agree with Martin's move to view +/− happiness, security and satisfaction discourse semantically, the problem is that we are left with a fairly 'thin' description of tenor. Emotions such as happiness, hate, anger, confidence, etc. will influence social roles and relationships to some degree, yet status and contact do not seem to be equipped to account for this. It is, however, recognized within SFL that more extensive work needs to be done on affect, and that other disciplines such as social psychology or psychotherapy may provide some solutions. Commenting on the present system network for affect at the contextual level, Martin (1992:535) claims that "As with system networks in general, the account is a purely synoptic one, glossing over completely the elaborate interplay that charges relationships between speakers. For this, a dynamic account needs to be constructed, drawing on a large tradition of theory and practice in clinical and social psychology."

In our narrative therapy data we found that the way in which couples relate to each other or had previously related to each other influenced the therapy process. The aspect of 'relating' that was focused on primarily involved emotions, and so we drew mainly from the dimensions of affect that Martin (1992) had identified as making up part of tenor. We were thus interested in clients' degree of being 'happy', 'satisfied' and 'secure' with the relationship. For instance, one way in which dis/satisfaction may be construed is the degree to which the couple agrees[8] with one another, and whether or not this degree of agreement leads to happiness or unhappiness. Agreement or disagreement on its own is, of course, not an indicator of whether the relationship is positive or not, as much work on arguing has already shown (Goodwin 1983, 1990; Muntigl & Turnbull 1998; Schiffrin 1984). However, our guess is that arguments that lead to feelings of unhappiness tend not to be positive indicators of relationship outcome.

In order to show how negative affect may influence the course of therapy, we present an example of a couples' dissatisfaction and unhappiness that resulted from a bitter argument. The argument had occurred in the night just prior to the therapy session, and was precipitated by W's snoring. In Ex. (7) F recounts the snoring episode and how that led to *just lousy communication* between F and W (line 16). This conversation occurred in session five of couples therapy.

(7)	01	F:	well tuhday for example. (2.0) where we then y'know
	02		(1.5) I think she's I think Wendy's grumpy today.
	03		it all goes back to y'know <u>snoring</u> in the middle of the
	04		night sort've business (.) u::m (1.5) she asks are you
	05		going tuh shower. (1.0) well (1.2) my answer wuz at the
	06		moment? (2.0) uh which is flippant kinda
	07		[obviously] I'm obviously I'm not showering .hh
	08	T:	[mhm]
	09	E:	whadya <u>mean</u> (.) by that question
	10		.hh are you going to shower this week?
	11		<u>today</u> in the next half hour. (1.0) u::m y'know? (1.0)
	12		but she wuz offended that I didn't answer her question
	13		properly an I don't (.) I didn't have a question that I felt
	14		I could answer properly so .hh that's what we've been
	15		going through today an we go through that off an on (1.0)
→	16		is (.) just lousy communication (1.2) u::m (1.0)
→	17		I don't understand her question or she doesn't

$\rightarrow$ 18   underst(hh)e(h)hand my answer
  19 T: mhm
  20 E: uh an vice versa
$\rightarrow$ 21 T: mhm .hh so you <u>know</u> that's lousy communication.

Approximately 20 lines later W recounts a slightly different episode in which it was F's *violent swearing an violent anger* (lines 72–73) at W's snoring that precipitated the communication breakdown. As a consequence, W lists a number of effects such as *my defenses are dow:n* (line 44), *I've messed up (.) a lot* (line 45), and *very depressed* (line 48) that resulted from the argument and the 'swearing episode'.

(8)   43 W: w(hh)ell I(hhh) I at that point when its at that point
$\rightarrow$ 44   then (1.0) I <u>all</u> my defenses are dow:n like I .hh
$\rightarrow$ 45   I really feel like <u>I've</u> messed up (.) a lot and that I:: (1.8)
       46   I didn't ask the question properly.
       47   therefore we're in this now (1.2) u::m nothing u
$\rightarrow$ 48   an there I get very <u>depressed</u> (1.5) u::h (1.5)
       49   and I I jus simply can't <u>deal</u> with any of this.
       50   I didn't wanna come today? .hh I didn't think
       51   that there would any point in coming today? (0.8)
                 .
                 .
                 .
       68   if Fred's bother- if s if Fred's snoring
       69   bothers me I quietly get up (.) an go to the other room.
       70   .hh but when <u>my</u> snoring bothered <u>Fred</u> last <u>night</u>
       71   he couldn't (.) wake me or:: something .hh an I woke <u>up</u>
$\rightarrow$ 72   (.) to:: this (.) in <u>my</u> mind my m my uh of's of's violent
$\rightarrow$ 73   swearing an violent <u>anger</u> tuh me.
       74   (0.8)
$\rightarrow$ 75 T: y y you experienced Fred as being violently angry
       76   towards [you.]
$\rightarrow$ 77 W: [yes] (.) becuz he wuz using language .hh an (.)
       78   then I got up an went to the other an went tuh sleep. (1.0)
$\rightarrow$ 79   .hh (1.0) (hh)and that's what started the whole hhhh day
$\rightarrow$ 80   (0.8) so (.) w we weren't communicating .hh
       81   he should've maybe stayed in the other room
       82   or <u>I</u> should stayed in the other room or .hh
$\rightarrow$ 83   something should've happened but it it didn't work a tall.

Towards the end of W's recount, she laments in line 79 that *that's what started the whole hhhh day* and that, even though there were other possibilities for acting differently such as one person remaining in a separate room, nothing seemed to work (i.e., *but it it didn't work a tall*). Although the unhappiness and dissatisfaction that resulted from the previous night can be palpably felt by re-viewing the transcript, more needs to be said in terms of how this unhappiness and dissatisfaction influences ontogenesis. This disagreement and negative af-fect occurred in session 5. In the prior session, clients were well on their way to effacing problems; that is, they had left problem construction behind, and were at that point producing a new genre in which they were formulating alternative stories that demonstrated additional ways in which they may act for themselves and with others. Session five, therefore, marked a regression. The 'snoring' episode demonstrated that they were not able to deploy the newly acquired semiotic resources from therapy to deal with the problem. As Ex. (9) shows, W construed the 'snoring' event in terms of W making wrong or incorrect statements and F being smarter and quicker than her. In lines 19–20, T refor-mulates W's recount through nominalization (*this notion of you being wrong*). As a consequence, the therapist and the couple moved back into the problem construction genre, in which problems were identified through nominaliza-tion and the influence of the problem in the couples' lives and relationships were explored.

```
(9)       01  W:  well I get I I I feel I'm a victim (.) of someone who's
          02      .hh I feel I'm a victim? o::f someone who's jus smarter
          03      than me. (1.0) quicker than me. (.) someone who:: (1.0)
          04      he- i jus knows more than me. (0.8) I don't know as
    →     05      much? (.) I say something when I say it wro::ng (.) I say
          06      it incorrectly .hh an I feel badly about it an my only way
          07      of (1.5) of of (1.0) making myself feel (0.8) a little
          08      who::le
          09  T:  mhm
          10      (1.0)
          11  W:  is to s:: is to (.) say (1.2) is to try'n get im:: some way an
          12      that (.) an becuz I can't do it with .hh I can't do it with uh
          13      (1.2) with words becuz I'm not good at that.
          14  T:  so you're not so angry with with Fred'n what he said its
          15      what it brings up in you (.) these notions that in some
          16      way (.) u::h becuz he
          17      [doesn't answer your question ]
          18  W:  [exa::ctly I                  ] that ri::ght=
```

19 T: =its its uh something about <u>me</u> that I'm wrong so
→ 20   [you're really] <u>angry</u> with this notion of you being wrong
21 W: [yeah   ]

In sum, couples' disagreements that lead to unhappiness and dissatisfaction illustrate that clients' developed semiotic resources from therapy are either too new – and hence they need more time to effectively deploy them in problem contexts – or insufficient to deal with new problems. It should also be mentioned that a sharp distinction should be made between the clients' relationship *in* therapy and the clients' relationship *outside* of therapy. In couples' therapy the *in therapy* relationship is further complicated because we need to take into consideration the relationship *between* the clients as well as the relation of the clients with the therapist. We have just explored the impact of something that happened outside of therapy to the therapy process. The effect of this was to derail the generic process, thereby putting a halt to problem effacement. However, because the relationship between the clients during therapy moved toward satisfaction and happiness (not shown in above transcript), they were able to move back to problem effacement in the latter part of the session. More research is needed to capture this complex interplay between relationship factors within and outside of therapy and the effects these values will have on change.

6. Conclusion: Bridging the 2 disciplines

To close this chapter, we would like to return to the theme of interdisciplinarity and speculate on the kinds of bridging that we have attempted to do with respect to client change. What we have done could, arguably, be seen from a centralist, pluralist or integrationist model. From a centralist perspective, either discipline may be seen as being a tool for the other. Narrative therapy could, for instance, benefit from a close linguistic examination of psychotherapy conversations, in order to fine-tune therapeutic practices. SFL would then be reduced to a tool for modifying the language used to realize narrative therapy activities. SFL could also import insights made in narrative therapy and psychotherapy research to flesh out the tenor variable. Specifically, research on the therapeutic alliance could add past/present relationship qualities in terms of satisfaction and happiness to the variables *status* and *contact*. Doing this would certainly find support in developing the aims of SFL in describing and accounting for various aspects of social life.

If a pluralist approach had been taken, developments in either discipline would have resulted without any importing from the neighbor discipline. This would have meant that insights from either psychotherapy or linguistics would have to be re-interpreted within the host model. As an example, SFL could take the insights from alliance theory without necessarily importing the language of psychotherapy. In this way, SFL would retain its autonomy. By the same token, psychotherapy could adopt the insight that language is central to how we construct experience – an insight that has largely been adopted in social constructionist research, without, however, drawing from linguistic theory or linguistic categories. If the disciplines are to remain autonomous, how then does a pluralist approach work in practice? One way would be the assembly-line method; First therapy is analyzed in terms of linguistics, psychotherapists then take these results and add a layer of psychotherapeutic interpretation to it – and, if sociologists are also involved, they, in turn, can add a further layer of sociological analysis.

Finally, an integrationist perspective would have meant that both perspectives are needed to address the issue under investigation. However, rather than being an assembly-line approach, integrationist models try to make links between the disciplines. For example, our integrationist approach that examines client change recognizes that the linguistic and relationship level are equally important. We have tried to capture these two aspects under a more general *semiotic* level, which basically means that both language and relationships are semiotic systems, albeit at different orders of abstraction. Language plays a major part in realizing relationships, and relationship qualities constrain the kinds of meanings that relationships can and will realize.

One nagging question about integrationist models is what do these models become when they have been truly integrated? Do they become a new discipline? Or are they still able to retain their autonomy? If this work continues in the SFL tradition, then perhaps both questions will apply. For, SFL may evolve by creating more contextual variables that may better account for functional varieties of language (or *registers*). Psychotherapy research may also evolve in a unique way by integrating the role of language in a conception of psychological processes. But we think the main point is that there will be more bridges and connections between the theories. Our hope is that this will ultimately help us in learning more about the client change process in particular, and about ontogenesis in general.

Notes

1. Psychotherapy research is a research tradition that is not bound to any single psychotherapy approach. Psychotherapy research may focus on any number of psychotherapy approaches such as cognitive-behavioural, experiential, narrative, strategic, etc. (For an overview of psychotherapy research see Garfield & Bergin 1994.)

2. The left-most column of each example is reserved for highlighting important material under discussion. Arrowed symbols (i.e., →) are used for this purpose. The second column refers to line numbers. In the third column, speakers are identified (i.e., T = Therapist; F = Fred; W = Wendy). Names for speakers are pseudonyms to protect the identity of the clients and therapist. The fourth and last column contains the graphological recordings of speakers' phonological output. In addition, speakers' turns are segmented into clauses. The transcription notation used is taken from Atkinson and Heritage (1984:ix–xiv).

3. The term *scaffolding* was promulgated by Bruner (1986), and draws extensively from the ideas of Vygotsky (1978). Scaffolding may be described as "guidance through interaction in the context of shared experience" (Martin 1999a:126). It should be noted that Bernstein did not, to our knowledge, make use of this term.

4. In Halliday's (1978) framework, the context of situation is organized by three dimensions: *Field, Tenor* and *Mode*. Field refers to the social activity and subject matter, Tenor to the social roles of the interactants and Mode to the way in which semiotic resources are being deployed (e.g., channel, medium).

5. Labov and Fanshel (1977:100) refer to activities in which something is known to speaker A, but not to B as *A-events*.

6. Martin (1992:523–536) offers a slightly different interpretation of authority and expertise. Poynton's *expertise* is re-classified by Martin as *authority*, and Poynton's *authority* as *status*. For Martin (1992), status is an overarching concept that also includes terms such as *control, prominence* and *power*.

7. Not included in this system network is polarity, which would then account for unhappiness, insecurity and dissatisfaction.

8. Other linguistic realizations of Affect include exclamatives, attitudinals, amplified structures, suffixation, reduplication, swearing, attitudinal lexis, rhythm, rate and pitch (Poynton 1985:81).

References

Anderson, Harlene & Goolishian, Harold (1988). "Human systems as linguistic systems: Preliminary and evolving ideas about the implications for clinical therapy". *Family Process, 27,* 371–393.

Anderson, Harlene & Goolishian, Harold (1992). "The client is the expert: A not-knowing approach to therapy". In S. McNamee & K. Gergen (Eds.), *Therapy as Social Construction* (pp. 25–39). London: Sage.

Aronsson, Karin & Cederberg, Ann-Christian (1994). "Conarration and voice in family therapy: Voicing, devoicing and orchestration". *Text, 14*(3), 345–370.

Atkinson, J. Maxwell & Heritage, John (1984). *Structures of Social Action: Studies in Conversation Analysis*. Cambridge: Cambridge University Press.

Bergmann, Jörg (1992). "Veiled morality: Notes on discretion in psychiatry". In P. Drew & J. Heritage (Eds.), *Talk at Work: Interaction in Institutional Settings* (pp. 137–162). Cambridge: Cambridge University Press.

Bernstein, Basil (1971). *Class, Codes and Control, Vol. I. Theoretical Studies Towards a Sociology of Language*. London: Routledge.

Bernstein, Basil (1977). *Class, Codes and Control, Vol. III* (2nd ed.). London: Routledge.

Bernstein, Basil (1990). *The Structuring of Pedagogic Discourse, Vol. 4*. London: Routledge.

Bernstein, Basil (1996). *Pedagogy, Symbolic Control and Identity*. London: Taylor & Francis.

Bordin, E. S. (1994). "Theory and research on the therapeutic working alliance: New directions". In A. O. Horvath & L. S. Greenberg (Eds.), *The Working Alliance: Theory, Research, and Practice* (pp. 13–37). New York: Wiley.

Bruner, Jerome (1986). *Actual Minds, Possible Worlds*. Cambridge: Harvard University Press.

Buttny, Richard (1993). *Social Accountability in Communication*. London: Sage.

Buttny, Richard (1996). "Clients' and therapists joint construction of the clients' problem". *Research on Language and Social Interaction, 29*(2), 125–153.

Buttny, Richard (1998). "Putting prior talk into context: Reported speech and the reporting context". *Research on Language and Social Interaction, 31*(1), 45–58.

Christie, Frances (1997). "Curriculum macrogenres as forms of initiation into a culture". In F. Christie & J. R. Martin (Eds.), *Genres and Institutions* (pp. 134–160). London: Cassell.

Christie, Frances (1998). "Science and apprenticeship: The pedagogic discourse". In J. R. Martin & R. Veel (Eds.), *Reading Science: Critical and Functional Perspectives on Discourses of Science* (pp. 152–177). London & New York: Routledge.

Christie, Frances (1999). "The pedagogic device and the teaching of English". In F. Christie (Ed.), *Pedagogy and the Shaping of Consciousness: Linguistic and Social Processes* (pp. 156–184). London & New York: Continuum.

Cloran, Carmel (1999). "Contexts for learning". In F. Christie (Ed.), *Pedagogy and the shaping of consciousness: Linguistic and social Processes* (pp. 31–65). London & New York: Continuum.

Coffin, Caroline (1997). "Constructing and giving value to the past: An investigation into secondary school history". In F. Christie & J. R. Martin (Eds.), *Genres and Institutions* (pp. 196–230). London: Cassell.

Davis, Kathy (1986). "The process of problem (re)formulation in psychotherapy". *Sociology of Health and Illness, 8*, 44–74.

Edwards, Derek (1994). "Script formulations: A study of event descriptions in conversation". *Journal of Language and Social Psychology, 13*, 211–247.

Edwards, Derek (1995). "Two to tango: Script formulations, dispositions, and rhetorical symmetry in relationship troubles talk". *Research on Language and Social Interaction, 28*(4), 319–350.

Gaik, Frank (1992). "Radio talk-show therapy and the pragmatics of possible worlds". In A. Duranti & C. Goodwin (Eds.), *Rethinking Context: Language as an Interactive Phenomenon* (pp. 271–289). Cambridge: Cambridge University Press.

Garfield, S. L. & Bergin, A. E. (1994). *Handbook of Psychotherapy and Behavior Change* (4th ed.). New York: Wiley.

Geertz, Clifford (1973). "Thick Description: Toward an interpretive theory of culture". In C. Geertz (Ed.), *The Interpretation of Cultures*. New York: Basic Books.

Goodwin, Marjorie Harness (1983). "Aggravated correction and disagreement in children's conversations". *Journal of Pragmatics, 7*, 657–677.

Goodwin, Marjorie Harness (1990). *He-said-she-said: Talk as Social Organization among Black Children*. Bloomington and Indianapolis: Indiana University Press.

Grossen, Michele (1996). "Counselling and gatekeeping: Definitions of the problem and situation in a first therapeutic interview". *Text, 16*(2), 161–198.

Halliday, M. A. K. (1975). *Learning how to Mean*. London: Edward Arnold.

Halliday, M. A. K. (1978). *Language as a Social Semiotic*. London. Edward Arnold.

Halliday, M. A. K. (1991). "Towards probabilistic interpretations". In E. Ventola (Ed.), *Recent Systemic and other Functional Views on Language* (pp. 39–61). Berlin: Mouton de Gruyter.

Halliday, M. A. K. (1992). "How do you mean?". In M. Davies & L. Ravelli (Eds.), *Advances in Systemic Linguistics* (pp. 20–35). London: Pinter.

Halliday, M. A. K. (1994). *An Introduction to Functional Grammar* (2nd ed.). London: Edward Arnold.

Halliday, M. A. K. (1999). "The notion of 'context' in language education". In M. Ghadessy (Ed.), *Text and Context in Functional Linguistics* (pp. 1–24). Amsterdam: Benjamins.

Halliday, M. A. K. (2003 [1990]). "New ways of meaning: the challenge to applied linguistics". In J. Webster (Ed.), *On Language and Linguistics* [Vol. 3 in the Collected Works of M. A. K. Halliday] (pp. 139–174). London: Continuum.

Halliday, M. A. K. & Matthiessen, M. I. M. (1999). *Construing Experience through Meaning: A Language-Based Approach to Cognition*. London: Cassell.

Hasan, Ruqaiya (1996). "The ontogenesis of ideology: an interpretation of mother-child talk". In C. Cloran, D. Butt, & G. Williams (Eds.), *Ways of saying: ways of meaning, Selected papers of Ruqaiya Hasan* (pp. 133–151). London: Cassell.

Horvath, A. O. & Bedi, R. P. (2002). "The Alliance". In J. Norcross (Ed.), *Psychotherapy Relationships That Work: Therapist Contributions and Responsiveness to Patients* (pp. 37–70). New York: Oxford University Press.

Horvath, A. O. & Luborsky, L. (1993). "The role of the therapeutic alliance in psychotherapy". *Journal of Consulting and Clinical Psychology, 61*, 561–573.

Iedema, R. (1995). *Administration Literacy* (*Write it Right Literacy in Industry Research Project – Stage 3*). Sydney: Metropolitan East Disadvantaged Schools Program.

Iedema, R., Feez, S., & White, P. (1994). *Media Literacy* (*Write it Right Literacy in Industry Research Project – Stage 2*). Sydney: Metropolitan East Disadvantaged Schools Program.

Kogan, Steven & Gale, Jerry (1997). "Decentering therapy: Textual analysis of a narrative therapy session". *Family Process, 36*, 101–126.

Labov, William & Fanshel, David (1977). *Therapeutic Discourse: Psychotherapy as Conversation*. New York: Academic Press.

Lemke, Jay (1984). *Semiotic and Education*. Toronto: Victoria University.

Lemke, Jay (1995). *Textual Politics: Discourse and Social Dynamics*. London: Taylor & Francis.

Luborsky, L., Singer, B., & Luborsky, L. (1975). "Comparative studies of psychotherapies; "Is it true that everybody has won and all must have prizes?"" *AGP, 32*, 995–1008.

McNamee, Sheila & Gergen, Kenneth (1992). *Therapy as Social Construction*. London: Sage.

McLeod, John (1997). *Narrative and Psychotherapy*. London: Sage.

Martin, J. R. (1992). *English Text*. Amsterdam: John Benjamins.

Martin, J. R. (1997). "Analyzing genre: Functional parameters". In F. Christie & J. R. Martin (Eds.), *Genres and Institutions* (pp. 3–39). London: Cassell.

Martin, J. R. (1999a). "Mentoring semogenesis: 'genre-based' literacy pedagogy". In F. Christie (Ed.), *Pedagogy and the Shaping of Consciousness: Linguistic and Social Processes* (pp. 31–65). London & New York: Continuum.

Martin, J. R. (1999b). "Modelling context: A crooked path of progress in contextual linguistics". In M. Ghadessy (Ed.), *Text and Context in Functional Linguistics* (pp. 25–61). Amsterdam: Benjamins.

Martin, J. R. (2000). "Beyond exchange: APPRAISAL systems in English". In S. Huston & G. Thompson (Eds.), *Evaluation in Text: Authorial Stance and the Construction of Discourse* (pp. 142–175). Oxford: Oxford University Press.

Muntigl, Peter (2002). "The language of EU employment policy". *Text, 22*(3), 393–441. (Special Issue on Discourses of Un/employment.)

Muntigl, Peter (2004a). "Ontogenesis in narrative therapy: A linguistic-semiotic examination of client change". *Family Process, 43*(1), 109–131.

Muntigl, Peter (2004b). *Narrative Counselling: Social and Linguistic Processes of Change*. Amsterdam: John Benjamins.

Muntigl, Peter & Turnbull, William (1998). "Conversational Structure and Facework in Arguing". *Journal of Pragmatics, 29*, 225–256.

Muntigl, Peter, Weiss, Gilbert, & Wodak, Ruth (2000). *EU discourses on Unemployment: An Interdisciplinary Approach to Employment Policy-making and Organizational Change*. Amsterdam & Philadelphia: John Benjamins.

Painter, Clare (1984). *Into the Mother Tongue: A Case Study of Early Language Development*. London: Pinter.

Painter, Clare (1999). *Learning through Language in Early Childhood*. London & New York: Continuum.

Peräkylä, Anssi (1995). *Aids Counselling: Institutional Interaction and Clinical Practice*. Cambridge: Cambridge University Press.

Peyrot, Mark (1987). "Circumspection in psychotherapy: Structures and strategies of counsellor client interaction". *Semiotica, 65*(3/4), 249–268.

Poynton, Cate (1985). *Language and Gender: Making the Difference*. Victoria: Deakin University Press.

Rice, Laura & Greenberg, Leslie (1984). *Patterns of Change: Intensive Analysis of Psychotherapy Process*. New York: Guilford.

Schiffrin, Deborah (1984). "Jewish argument as sociability". *Language in Society, 13*, 311–335.

Shapiro, D. A. & Shapiro, D. (1982). "Meta-analysis of comparative therapy outcome studies". *Psychological Bulletin, 92*, 181–204.

Silverman, David (1997). *Discourses of Counselling*. London: Sage.

Smith, M. L. & Glass, G. V. (1977). "Meta-analysis of psychotherapy outcome studies". *American Psychologist, 32,* 752–760.

Smith, M. L., Glass, G. V., & Miller, T. I. (1980). *The Benefits of Psychotherapy.* Baltimore: John Hopkins University Press.

Stiles, William (1992). *Describing Talk: A Taxonomy of Verbal Response Modes.* London: Sage.

Tomm, Karl (1987a). "Interventive interviewing: Part 1. Strategizing as a fourth Guideline for the therapist". *Family Process, 26,* 3–13.

Tomm, Karl (1987b). "Interventive interviewing: Part II. Reflexive questioning as a means to enable self-healing". *Family Process, 26,* 167–183.

Tomm, Karl (1988). "Interventive interviewing: Part III. Intending to ask lineal, circular. or reflexive questions?" *Family Process, 27,* 1–15.

van Leeuwen, Theo (2003). "Three models of interdisciplinarity". Paper read at the International Symposium *A New Research Agenda in (Critical) Discourse Analysis: Theory & Interdisciplinarity.* Vienna, Austria, March 2003.

Ventola, Eija (1987). *The Structure of Social Interaction: A Systemic Approach to the Semiotics of Service Encounters.* London: Pinter.

Vygotsky, L. S. (1978). *Mind in Society.* Cambridge: Harvard University Press.

Wampold, Bruce (2001). *The Great Psychotherapy Debate: Models, Methods and Findings.* NJ: Lawrence Erlbaum Associates.

Weiss, Gilbert & Wodak, Ruth (Eds.). (2003). *Critical Discourse Analysis: Theory and Interdisciplinarity.* New York: Palgrave Macmillan.

White, Michael (2000). *Reflections on Narrative Practice.* Adelaide: Dulwich Centre Publications.

White, Michael (2001). "Narrative practice and the unpacking of identity conclusions". *Gecko: A journal of deconstruction and narrative practice.* (Website, pp. 1–13: http://www.dulwichcentre.com.au/narrativepractice.html)

White, Michael & Epston, David (1990). *Narrative Means to Therapeutic Ends.* New York: Norton.

Williams, Geoff (1999). "The pedagogic device and the production of pedagogic discourse: a case example in early literacy education". In F. Christie (Ed.), *Pedagogy and the shaping of consciousness: Linguistic and social Processes* (pp. 88–122). London & New York: Continuum.

Wodak, Ruth (1986). *Language Behaviour in Therapy Groups.* Los Angeles: University of California Press.

Wodak, Ruth (1996). *Disorders of Discourse.* London: Longman.

Part III

Inside and outside traditional disciplines

CHAPTER 11

Anthropology of institutions and discourse analysis

Looking into interdisciplinarity*

Irène Bellier

Maison des Sciences de l'Homme, LAIOS, CNRS

Introduction

In order to study European or other powerful institutions, political anthropologists have to conceptually adjust the modes of investigation and analysis they experience in very distinct kinds of fieldwork. This is especially true for putting in relation various elements which are useful to answer the question raised by Mary Douglas: "how do institutions think?" (1986), for deepening a central hypothesis regarding the influence political institutions have on social and cultural developments. This issue is closely related to discourse analysis since oral statements and written documents constitute material proofs of an organizational "thinking activity". But it also involves other dimensions, which are related to the observation of collective and individual practices the anthropologist is familiar with, in order to clarify what s/he defines as an "object" and the position of the "subject" in question: for instance, to qualify "who" the organization is. It also raises the issue of the position individuals have within a cultural context, a matter on which we focus to make salient the categories through which members of a particular society – be it an organization or anything else – represent the world, enter in a process of classification, or conceptualize their relations with others. As a consequence, the methodology the researcher uses to engage in the field of discourse analysis varies, the anthropologist paying maybe less attention to the formal content and structure of a discourse than to its conditions of production and the many parameters which explain a lexical choice, especially when discourses are studied in multilingual settings such as the European Commission (EC) or the United Nations (UN).

For many years, institutions as organizations have not been central to the anthropological project and their current study poses the question of interdisciplinarity. Anthropology has long been a discipline associated with the study of cultures and the concept of "otherness", targeting far and distant worlds (ethnic groups, clans, tribes and so forth) as well as remote societies and cultures. Hence, modern institutions of the developed world were not considered as a priority. But putting them outside of the anthropological project meant that entire aspects of modern, developed, contemporary societies escaped, as if anthropology were a science of the past and lost peoples. Opposed to this dichotomy in the field of Human Sciences, a growing number of researchers decided to focus on what has been called "new objects" (Sciences Humaines 1998), and recent studies undertaken by European and US anthropologists proved that ethnography and the anthropological methodology are quite appropriate to studying administrative and political organizations as power-related social and cultural places.

Consequently, taking institutions as scientific objects – as sociologists, political scientists, linguists, psychoanalysts or economists do – leads anthropologists to redefine their position towards other human sciences, especially on two points: the definition of the field and the determination of the object. The movement towards more reflexivity, so as to consider the impact of subjectivity on our studies, induces interesting changes in the modes of writing, with the production of less authoritarian texts and a greater attention to contextualization. This emphasis contributes to a better qualification of the institutional process as we consider for analysis not only the outcome of a particular organization but also the whole process that systematically involves the agents into the production of the institution's voice. Interdisciplinarity allows the development of a dialogue not only about the results of the research but also in terms of the methodology used for analyzing the different aspects of social constructions and organizations and the roles individuals play inside them. There exists a variety of tools that have different qualities and impact on the results of research – such as direct collection of data or second hands data, individuals' interviews, enquiries or poles, qualitative or quantitative analysis, working in the field or in the office.

After a short presentation of the ethnographic settings of a case study in the UN together with references to previous studies conducted on European institutions, I would like to open a discussion on three domains, in order to engage the debate on anthropology's and linguistics' distinct approaches of discourse practices: one is the process of thinking in institutions, the second one concerns the production of discourses in a multinational environment, the third one relates to the partition of objects and interdisciplinarity.

Studying a working group in the United Nations

The recent case study I undertook is useful for engaging the debate on some variations that can be observed between linguistics and anthropology on discourse analysis. Since 1982, there exists a UN working group on Indigenous Populations, whose experts – seconded by the Human Rights Commission – produced, ten years ago, a project of a declaration for the Rights of Indigenous Peoples. In 1995, the General Assembly set up an open-ended intersession work group on the project of declaration, which involves indigenous representatives and government delegates. In 2000, a Permanent Forum on Indigenous Issues next to the Social and Economic Council was set up. Within 20 years, Indigenous Peoples who are largely marginalized and unheard in their respective States, received greater attention in the UN system. Thousands of indigenous representatives attend these sessions every year. The movement, originated at the international level and characterized by its discursive nature, started to have an influence in the countries where indigenous peoples live.

Discourses in the UN

The production of discourses in this international arena is especially interesting to study as it engages speakers and representatives from very distinct origins and cultural backgrounds. It is indeed a place where the conditions of production of texts that join the corpus of international law can be observed. Discourses are what political and administrative institutions produce continuously and sociolinguists have taken on the charge of analyzing them, in multiple situations (see for instance Muntigl, Weiss, & Wodak 2000[1]). The discourse of and in institutions corresponds to distinct genres and they are formulated according to several modalities, from formal contexts to informal ones. Interestingly, informality seems to be central in very official places, generating a paradox, as formal rules are also extremely important for the production of the final text. As informal sessions often precede and follow formal gatherings of ministers or diplomats, they serve to prepare the adoption of whatever decision is taken in the formal sessions. What surprised me is the fact that a stage of "informal-informal session" has even been invented, as I could see in the UN where I have been following the three working groups and forums related to Indigenous Peoples situations and development.[2] What does the duplication of informality mean in the context of the working group on the draft project of the Declaration of Indigenous Peoples Rights (WGDD)? "Informal informal" is a curious form, first of all, because none of the actors involved in the session knew what it really meant besides the fact that no decision was to be taken then. This particular meeting was taking place after seven fruitless sessions of that same working group, hence contributing to the fixation of identities and positions. As I could attend the meeting, and see by myself how different it was from other informal meetings, I realized that this expression carries more meaning than what the words imply.

Firstly, it meant the choice of a less intimidating physical location than the Room of the General Assembly in which the other meetings are held. To clear the context for the reader, imagine a small working room of the large UN building in Geneva, in which about 260 Indigenous Representatives and 76 State Delegates (a significant distribution of roles is defined by the choice of the label "representative" or "delegate") were invited to sit, side by side, in a non protocol order, and face to face, without displaying their identity. Secondly, it was proposed by the President of the working group to bring closer opposite partners of a tough negotiation. The desired impact of this "informal-informal" procedure was for the President to let speeches flow more easily. It was an ultimate move to overcome the freezing of official discussions, on the morning of the final day of the period opened, the last year before the expiry date when the working group was supposed to give its resolution regarding the precise writing of (and language used by) the Declaration of the Rights of Indigenous Peoples. The result was so conform to the Presidential expectations that even emotional statements were made, to the surprise of the members of this assembly who usually control themselves within institutional limits. Mixing the participants in such a way was a real change compared to ordinary situations taking place in the plenary room, where people sit by rows, the first ones being reserved for the governments whose delegates sit in the alphabetical order of their country, the following ones being taken by NGOs and indigenous representatives, as they want. The distribution of the indigenous representatives in the usual room attests the development of regional affinities which are a demonstration of some of the means taken to reinforce the peculiar position of the indigenous peoples: indeed, breaking the isolation within the nation state borders is one vector of their empowerment.

From the changing context of discussion we can deduce that the observation of the conditions of production of indigenous discourse at the UN is quite enlightening. Most of the time, all attendants face the Presidential tribune, where the General Secretariat officers are also sitting. As a consequence, in the formal or informal sessions that take place in the main room, indigenous peoples representatives and governments delegates never face each other. Their respective discourses are not directed to each other to solve a particular situation, but to a common universal representation, highly detached from the grounds of reality, which is involved in the definition of a supranational kind of a law. On the contrary, in the "informal informal" session, the fact that they are facing each other at a very short distance breaks the rules and forces the participants to face the evidence: an effort must be made to guarantee a fruitful negotiation. State delegates as well as indigenous representatives must make a move to find an agreement on the wording of the 45 articles of the declaration. Reality must be considered directly, and that is evidenced by the direct involvement of the representatives and delegates.

People's interactions are significant for the construction of a discourse. But the same discourse can be analyzed from very different angles. This is why, as argued by Muntigl, Weiss and Wodak (op. cit.: 3) "a variety of methods is needed in order to examine an issue from a variety of perspectives".

Reports, authors and voices

One example will serve me to draw the attention to the problem of analyzing a discourse as an outcome without being informed of the previous stages, as the linguist Dominique Maingueneau does when he analyses, though very interestingly, the reports produced by international organizations (2002: 119–132). I will discuss several points he pushes forward, so as to show the gap between (his) linguistic and (my) anthropological approaches, and hence the need for complementary work. To begin with, Maingueneau claims his interest for the "modes of enunciation", putting the relationship between places and speeches as central to his approach. He introduces the concept of "a discursive community" which designates "the groups which exist only because of, and through the enunciation of the texts they produce and release" (p. 124). But he does not consider as necessary for his analysis the presence of real speakers. This absence gives a weird echo to the concept of community he pushes forward. Such a community – with no real, referenced people, no speakers – sounds virtual for an anthropologist: likely to be true as we can imagine who they are, but rather undefined and usually designated through general terms such as global references to international organizations or the notion of a community of experts, addressing a public at large, etc. With this limit, the concept of "discursive community" is both interesting – it exemplifies the collective character of the discourse production – and frustrating; it subsumes into one indefinite whole the particular sources which constitute the ideological background of discourses.

Later, Maingueneau stresses the notion of "author", a character he attributes to the names presented in the reports, who are usually those of the President and the members of the team in charge of writing the report. And he links up the notion of author to that of authority. Who is the author is not a simple question in the context of institutions. The position of author is certainly defined as a signature, but the expert capacity, which legitimizes a report's authorship, does not derive from one's own quality only (which explains why s/he has been appointed, or elected there): it is also taken from external sources. For what I have seen in the UN working group, whose reports are indeed written by the President of the group with the help of the "experts",[3] there is a continuous flow of exchanges between an increasing number of actors who constitute as many "non authorized sources". Here, I would include all those individuals who attend the annual and inter-session meetings and circulate ideas, but do not transmit their input on written supports to the General Secretariat. Their names disappear but, from the observation of situated discussions, we know that their ideas can be inserted in the report under different forms. To illustrate this point, let us take another example of a complex situation of authorship, which is the case of the "special rapporteur on the situation of Human Rights and the fundamental freedoms of Indigenous People". The person, presently a renowned Mexican professor of sociology, is especially appointed by the UN General Assembly to make investigations, write the annual report denunciating crimes and situations of rights deprivation. He bases his remarks on what he has personally witnessed and on data that have been transmitted to him. Some of these data appear explicitly in the annex to the report, but precise names must be hidden to avoid government repression. Furthermore, to limit the report to the number of pages allowed by the institution, many references disappear. If the rapporteur is to be considered as the author, a status that engages his responsibility, how the position of author is constructed in the international organization remains a matter of investigation, especially because of the circulation of information whose origin can be either ignored, either collectivized. Both for the anthropologist who cares about how things are done, as for the linguists engaged in critical discourse analyses, authorship does not only imply signature. It is a matter of observation that "other voices" challenge the position of author, as an individual, as a collective, or as a collection of individuals. The working group allows us to observe how the relation between authorship and authority is created. The main task of the working group's President is to keep the expression of these voices under control not repressing them but allowing them a limited time and a formal support that frames their expansion. It is both a matter of physical behaviour and capacity to lead the working group and a matter of interpretation of the messages carried by the many voices who are part of the collective work. The study of all these sources contributes to clarify how texts are constructed, and I would assume that, in the context of this group, their particular efficiency derives from the circulation of the words between the authors, precisely the President of the group as the writing author and figure of authority, and the members of the group who are the oral authors and sources of ideas. The conversion of discourses into texts explains the value acquired by some expressions which become keywords for a while, before progressively losing power and becoming obsolete. Here, the research done by Ruth Wodak on un/employment and globalization, based on the working operations of the European Competitiveness Advisory Group, must be quoted as she carefully deconstructs the discourses to answer a question central to her: "Does the final version of the policy paper manifest a consensus or only the opinion which was "strongest" in the debate?" (Wodak 2000:79). For her analyses she uses the Bakhtinian concept of voices (1981) to identify the participants and see how they engage in the process of recontextualization of topical issues.

Along with the identification of the many voices lying behind the author of a UN report, one should pay attention to the question of the languages in which the UN discourses and reports are formulated. Maingueneau pays attention to the linguistic code operating in multinational settings, adopting the concept of "translinguistic discursive community"[4] defined by Jean Claude Beacco. He considers that "International organizations reports are genres of texts which, certainly, are written in French, English or whatever other language, but which, legally, are not written in French, English or any other natural language, but in the generalized convertibility of Humanity's multiple languages" (Maingueneau 2002:128, my translation). Though we may understand that a generalized convertibility affects the precision of the language used, some ethnographic data would, in that case, be very appropriate to see how translinguistic that community is which he refers to. No details are provided by the analyst, only general considerations. Which language does the author of a report use? The reader does not know what the UN linguistic rules are, nor if individuals (one of the multiple voices engaged in the UN production of discourse) speak, one, two or twenty languages, express themselves in dominant, minority or repressed languages, according to a popular or high-class genre, etc. This information would be important. For instance, in the three Working Groups and Permanent Forum on Indigenous Issues, indigenous languages which are "natural languages", are never used in any kind of reports, notwithstanding the efforts undertaken by the representatives of different regions of the world, to introduce orally a few words (usually terms of address for opening and closing their speeches) to mark their diversity and identity. Part of the misunderstandings slowing down the negotiations on the wording of the declaration can be related to the different visions of reality, which cannot be expressed properly in the languages used by the speakers.

Slowly the participants of the working group come to know each other's points of view and negotiating positions. After a while, something completely strange at the beginning, a local invention like the name of a program or a reference to customary legal practices, sounds familiar: a process of naturalization has taken place. The meanings become fixed. However, imprecision sometimes remains high. And that imprecision is exactly what should be investigated. A task taken on by Wodak when she focuses on the ongoing process: "The recontextualization takes place from the dialogic to the monologic, from verbal to written interaction, from concrete to abstract, from vertical to horizontal, many voices in the Bakhtinian sense get condensed to a single voice or to two distinguishable voices in our case, the voice of the employers and the voice of the trade unions" (Wodak 2000: 78).

Such a process cannot be seen by an outsider, even less if one considers only the final result of linguistic operations, as the report. The choice of sources and the methodology obviously condition the proposed analysis. Working on official reports, only when they become public, leads to a number of considerations which, in the case mentioned above, does not allow the researcher to consider the previous stages, nor to make a difference to other kinds of writings. Nevertheless, there are interesting distinctions to be made within a typology of reports, such as Green or White books, communications, blue print, etc. that look like reports but are not reports. The alchemy of reports escapes common understanding and their distinctive format should be analyzed. If one considers only the report process in the UN, let us mention that pre-report sessions take place before the consolidation of the written aspect of the report which, in the case of the Permanent Forum on Indigenous Issues (PFII), constitutes the author as a collective – even though a President has been elected among the Indigenous experts to assume responsibility for the forum. How can the process thus be described?

During brief meetings held at morning and evening hours of the ten an-nual PFII session official days, before and after the public sessions take place, the eight (elected) Indigenous and eight (appointed) government experts dis-cuss the pieces of the report they will adopt progressively and publicly. Their position is formed after a larger debate, the extent and the content of which has involved, in the exchange of ideas, all the non-expert participants (about a thousand indigenous representatives previously accredited by the UN and a hundred states delegates). One element of the game allows the simple represen-tatives (not so called experts) who are not in charge of the writing, to see their ideas taken in consideration by the experts, and therefore to figure somehow in the report. In the case of indigenous peoples, such a mechanism contributes to the feeling of having become political actors. These moments before and around the finalization of the report explain how individuals, in an active dis-cursive situation choose words and impose ideas. This is what constitutes them as authors.

Researchers in or out?

As researchers, we are confronted with a dilemma. How can we properly take into consideration all these individuals whose contribution as authors is usu-ally not acknowledged? On the one hand, their precise participation cannot be detailed and, on the other hand, the internal process of collective thinking is not always disclosed. In that case, the annual attendance of the Indige-nous Working Groups concerns more than a thousand representatives from all around the world, whose affiliations to registered organizations are mentioned in the annex of the report. Individual names figure in a list of attendance given to the participants only, but not in the official report. Half of these representa-tives actively take the floor and distribute their declarations, hence contributing to their identification as possible authors. The problem remains open for all sit-uations when the individuals cannot be classified and are reduced to a title or a position. In that debate between the linguists who propose interesting concep-tualizations of international discourses and the anthropologists for whom the discursive community referred to needs to be related to real people, a question becomes salient. How do we solve the contradiction between too high abstrac-tions – as models leave individual performances outside the focus – and too concrete presentations which does not render justice to a complexity that is not easily imagined? Scientific tools, which contribute to a reduction of diversity into something observable for the anthropologist, analyzable for the linguist, finally constitute two facets of the same object. As we are usually limited by space, analytical choice becomes a priority. As Wodak puts it, "I have decided to focus on several central research questions in this chapter... and leave other possible studies of this material to future work" (ibid.: 77). That kind of scientific choice has to be admitted even though it renders a global understanding of complex issues more difficult.

But how do we appreciate the reduction of analyses that results from the fact that powerful institutions do not open their doors widely to all kinds of observations? Do we have to avoid them, hence complying with their sense of secrecy and opacity, or to diplomatically force their doors? As I dealt with that aspect in another paper (Bellier 2001), I would only like to suggest here that the outsider position introduces a very critical bias regarding the conclusions that can be drawn on UN or any other organizational reports. For instance, Maingueneau poses a very interesting question: "do these reports of international organizations define a genre which would characterize a new constituent discourse?" (2002: 130, my translation). For me, as an anthropologist, without considering the actual personality of the individuals who are engaged in the production of the discourse, without observing the kind of emotions that lay behind the wording of a particular sentence, without knowing the arguments which have been exchanged before the final text is agreed upon, the researcher is not allowed to qualify the constitutive character of the assembly and of the text it produces.

Rivalries reign between international agencies, but essential to Maingueneau is the fact that the institution masks the conflicts, or only lets the experts (who know how to read between the lines) be aware of their existence. It is a sign through which it constructs a legitimacy: "One has to distinguish oneself from the others to affirm one's identity, but one must not distinguish oneself in order to speak as an authorized entity, to embody Authority itself" (ibid.: 131, my translation). For the anthropologist, that is not valid. How identity is constructed as authority, and authority as authorship, corresponds to a process based not only on what is masked, to protect the interest of the organization, be it a political party, a trade union, the UN or the European Commission. What accounts for our understanding of authority are also the processes through which the words and meanings circulate and through which the expression of differences is being repressed. We all know that an organization like the UN tries to constitute itself as an authority but failures to support this authority come both from internal criticisms, for instance the USA, and from external ones. Once the figure of authority is contested, what is the status of the text? Is it a constitutive one, as if its power were self contained and indivisible? Are we not confronted with a hybrid between what is supposed to address the whole (the purpose of universal principles) and something that is understood only by a part (who know how to deal with such texts), a division that cannot qualify such a document? Similar issues are dealt with by Wodak when she analyses the construction of a policy paper as progressing from conflict to consensus. She suggests that the Committee she studied "provides a stage for such ideological debates, a public space where different ideologies and opinions can meet and negotiations take place" (2000: 114). This raises a new question, to conclude this part: How can we understand an organization which provides a space for dialogue but leaves the decision making system behind closed doors?

Discourses in a multicultural environment: The problem of unity and diversity

In different multilingual situations in the EU or the UN, one of the problems related to the multiplicity of languages is the need of a common language that will be used to agree upon the formalization of concepts. The question is to know whether this common language comes from a dominant language, such as English, or if it results from a mix between different languages, such as a jargon. This makes a difference for the constitution of a translinguistic discursive community, whose features do not follow the same path in the UN or the EU surroundings. In the UN, most of the new words and concepts are introduced and circulate in a dominant language which becomes central, actually English, because it is the most commonly shared language in all the regions of the world (Swaan 2001). The reports are released in six official languages and the translation is carefully checked. In the EU, which acknowledges 20 languages, new words are being introduced through contacts with UN organizations and also through the Commission, a central organization in the EU system, whose agents experience the day-to-day fact of working together in three and more languages (cf. Bellier 2001; Phillipson 2003). As I could judge from direct observation, a process of linguistic invention is stimulated, a jargon created, which feeds the perception that the EU world is far away from local and national realities. As the meaning of international words and European expressions takes time to be stabilized through translation in several languages, one has the impression – when interviewing officials – to be constantly looking after "a floating significant"; it is the case for instance with the notions of "community interest", of "acquis communautaire" or "diversity". The language of the institution influences the mental images of Europe, a process I would like to present on the basis of the analysis I carried out in the EU over the last decade.

The study of the Commission as an integrated institution, acting for "the Community and its member States", source of the European initiative and guardian of its legal implementation, poses the question of the relationships between State and Nation, which determines the fixation of what is called an "official language". The link is currently being weakened by the status of member states, the displacement of sovereignty and the slow formation of a European consciousness. Such a process stimulates thoughts on the existence of a pluralistic model in Europe, as a means to avoid the reproduction of the unitary state model, of that sort which led arrogant nationalisms to terrible wars. The variety of languages, cultures and social habitus made Europe an attractive continent but European societies are now facing a crucial period of reduction of that diversity due to the construction of the European Union. As it corresponds to the process of institutionalization, I want to concentrate here on the problem of the "voice of the institution", especially because it takes birth within a multicultural context.

What is the voice of the Commission? This notion of voice, a Bakhtinian one, and one that is also explicitly used by the media (at least in France), reflects the personification of an abstract entity and organized collectivity, because we commonly say "the French voice" or "the Austrian voice" when referring to the voice of the government. The present popular formula derives from the international stage of negotiation where States are given a voice and vote – "one country, one voice" (UN), "one voice one dollar" (IMF), or "one voice ten votes" (EU): different formulas are experimented in international organizations. The voice of an institution does not relate to the question of tone, style and content. One does not care, in this context, if the voice is male or female for instance, and the age of the "voicer" is not important either. But it is interesting to know how it is formed within given structures and what language the institution speaks.

In the case of the Commission, linguistic regulations and the decision to adopt three working languages give part of the answer: French, English and German. Another part is given by the observation of linguistic practices and the fact that a creative jargon, barely understandable for outsiders, is formed within the organization and is spreading out of it in national/European related circles that in one moment constitute "epistemic communities", in which civil servants and experts collect ideas.[5]

To qualify the production of "voice", one should take into account the fact that it is rooted within the organization of professional relations, in a larger political system looking forward to its unity. Behind the voice formation, is the issue of representation and the will to reduce the expression of diversity of interests, of languages and, in the case of States and governments, of peoples. However, the institutional voice is not disembodied nor is it detached from reality as we could imagine by studying the linguistic code operation. In the case of the Commission, we can admit that it speaks through the voices of its representatives and their personality, competence and performance contribute to its public image. It speaks its own language, this is why the figure of the representative is also important. The Commission's voice is formed within the services as a means to solve the multiple contradictions inherited from a complex structure, to forge the capacity to occupy a position at the cross roads of several influences. Among them, are the national cultures and languages, which inform us about different possibilities for conceptualizing the same object. Presently, we can say that for Europe's sake, the Commission tries to speak for itself and to the Union members, before it speaks for all of them on the international arena. That is due to their mandate. It is only in particular sectors, like trade or agriculture policies, that the European Commission receives a mandate from the Ministers for speaking on behalf of the member states, in WTO negotiations, for instance.

Up to this point, the question is to know whether the Commission's voice is the EU voice, a problem that is linked to the conceptualization of Europe and the organization of the Convention. The European voice is inaudible when it does not carry the agreement of all its parts. It is poorly defined because of political disagreements among member states which argue about representations of the world, and also because it is formed through exchanges that take place in several languages and forums. A European voice to express unity takes time to be forged: the meanings of the words are defined at the minimum most consensual cost, this process limits the free circulation of ideas. Indeed, one can notice that while national and European powers are challenging each other, political debates do not really touch society. As a result, the EU does not only suffer from its diversity of languages, which to my eyes is a richness that prevents it from speaking only one dominant language. In that period of enlargement and redefinition of the EU project, the "New Europe" is also experiencing a kind of "neutral stage", as Roland Barthes puts it referring to "neutral" in politics as "a non-operating operation", following Maurice Blanchot's definition (in Barthes 2002). It may though come out of that period of latency, with the reintroduction of real ideological controversies, such as regarding the place of God in the European constitution or the effect of liberalism on social structures.

Behind the question of voice lies the issue of the representations of the world, of European unity as a means to build a position in the world: something related to the notion of constitutive discourses. The question of the language spoken is one aspect, that of the content is another, more important one. It relates to the European project, its definition and perception by all sectors of society. Similar questions can be posed for the UN's voice, having in mind the organisational and political differences that exist between the EU and UN. This is why critical discourse analysts and political anthropologists engage themselves in the study of organizational practices.

Thinking process: Content and values in political institutions

Executive manners and procedural movements are the other side of the transnational discourses that Beatrice Steiner defines as forming the "language of cotton".[6] At supra-national levels, officials' discourses are often, if not always, intentional: most of them are written and they acquire a definite style when they come to the last stage of their officialization. Because discourses are more often contested than practices – that come under scrutiny only when they need to be reformed, when a scandal is sanctioned (think for instance of the Commission's dismissal after the Cresson Affair which led to an internal reform of the EU administration) or when they are seen as inferior and not adequate to a dominant model (the case of Eastern European administrative practices before accession) – the content of official documents tend to be limited to what has been agreed, letting aside sources of disagreement. This is especially salient in the EU context where decisions are taken by consensus, through a process of bargaining (Hoffmann & Keohane 1991) and compromise (Abélès & Bellier 1996). The culture of compromise is worth considering because it stimulates the invention of European categories; but it does not contribute to give meaning to the machinery. Closer scrutiny of the relations between what deciders say and what they do, is therefore a priority. It means that we do not only have to take the temporal dimension into account, as Wodak does, but also to explore different scenes, on the line suggested by Marcus with his concept of multi-sited ethnography (1995).

Where is the gap? On the one side, official discourses are available for analysis, but internal negotiations and day-to-day practices related to discourse production or to the policy field, are difficult to observe, as already stated. On the other side, institutions produce a dominant discourse. Their agents contribute to formalizing their voice, the policy orientation for instance, even though (or maybe because) they have a blind perception of the people they reach. As Wodak puts it, the question is to know what the functions of a European committee are and why so much energy is invested into a policy paper, which may not be read by the audience it addresses (Wodak 2000: 113). Euro civil servants themselves say it clearly: "we are cut off from realities". My question therefore is: what reality do we, as social researchers, focus on?

To answer it partly, let us consider the negotiation process established between the European Union and the Eastern and Central European countries. Following up the internal discussions and reading the texts that are put on the European web sites, we are confronted with the affirmation of the Western superiority to define rules, laws, norms, and institutions. Respectively, the negation of the idiosyncratic capacity of these countries to propose an alternate model can be observed, so much that their ambivalent position regarding EU and NATO surprised many observers. Like a dominant rumour, it is assumed that Eastern and Central European countries will gain from accessing the Union, even though the process of transformation induced by the shift to a liberal market economy has serious social consequences in the short and medium term. The dominant organizational discourses hide the hard reality of social and political facts, which reveal themselves slowly, for example the intergovernmental conference for adopting a European constitution where no consensus could be reached.

The EU position is one of authority and the Commission's task is to clarify the rules for the newcomers, not to redefine them through the mobilization of a new discourse. It is that position I want to put into question now, with a small case study. As academics, we have time to think about the notion of "merit" that has been put forward to sanction the order of accession of the newcomers in the EU: as agreed by the Council of Ministers, "they will join the EU on the basis of their own merit". What does this notion mean? "Merit" is not a technical characterization but a qualification imposed by the EC, which constituted itself as the figure of authority to fix the conditions, the targets and the means of accession. This notion of "merit" has been put forward to replace the initial division in "first" and "second wave", used to distinguish the countries closer to the EU system from those still far from it. As this hierarchical ranking was resented by the candidate countries, a set of criteria – supposed to be more objective – was defined in Copenhagen (1993, summit of the Heads of States and Governments). The notion of "merit" was later introduced by the Commission to legitimize the fact that economic and political transformations were parts of a complex and painful process. The European dominant discourse declares that Eastern and Central European countries deserve to join the EU because (and when) they make the necessary efforts and, in doing so, prove their capacity to support EU rules. What do these efforts, related to the above notion of merit, consist of?

It means that accessing countries will have transposed in their national systems the "*acquis communautaire*", about 150 000 pages of legal texts corresponding to the different sectors of EU policies, which have been previously discussed and negotiated by chapters. It also means that they will not only have transposed EC laws but also performed deep changes to support accession and prepare the population to a change of status. For describing that process, which has taken place before, the word "screening" was used to identify the situation in each country, and define the places where the changes should be undertaken; a "strategy" has been designed to accompany the production of efforts and check the positions. Under the close attention of the Commission's agents, who mediate discourses and write reports, a disciplinary control has been exerted that led to the final statements given to the Council of Ministers. To conclude that stage, the political institution agreed, in Copenhagen 2002, to give a date for the entry of some countries, refusing it to others: Bulgaria and Rumania remain in negotiations, and accession procedures have not been opened yet for Turkey (see Bellier 2004).

With that example, we realize that more than ten years have been necessary to reach the final step, that a number of individuals and institutions have been involved in the process, and that the notion of "merit" might as well be a reflexive one, forged by the Commission's agents to think about their own involvement (for the positive change of these countries). At no moment, the value of this notion of "merit" seems to be questioned. It is based on implicit considerations on the value of progress, the superiority of European Western development and structures, and on explicit ones based on the experimentation of new pedagogical forms to learn "good practices" such as twinning, benchmarking, ranking, etc.

Let us continue for a while with the case of the Commission (a central institution), and make more comments on texts related to the enlargement process. It is instructive to confront these texts – which are produced and published on the web site – to some discourses of individuals in direct interviews. From the texts, we understand that for the Commission as well as for the Council of Ministers, strategies to reach the objectives, measurement of the steps, efforts and calculations of all sorts are what matter the most (Bellier 2004). This is reflected in the vocabulary chosen (strategy, roadmap, deadlines, etc.) the repetition of which in the documents is a good indicator that a battle is going on to replace cold war and the communist print by an effort to make capitalism the source of the right transformation of Eastern and Central European countries. Through the observation of how the agents feel when they are working in such an organization, of how disciplined they are, and how they express their commitment in the organizational goal, we see that interferences of measurement with the working process weigh upon the representations they produce. When European officials express common views (meaning that they can be expressed by many other people) like this one in the External Affairs DG, who says "we are submitted to the 'primacy of the chronogramme'", or that one in the Regional Policies DG who states "we drive with no rear view mirror",[7] we realize that the organization is powerful – it imposes a control on time – and it does not act rationally – it goes ahead without control. The two images stress, the first one, a lack of autonomy of the agents, and the second one, the fact that they are cut off from surrounding realities, which they can only imagine. On the one hand, the organization has a coercive strength, time schedule becomes a common obsession, on the other hand they lack spatial references and have the future as sole line of horizon (see Abélès, Bellier, & McDonald 1993).

The demand for pluridisciplinarity

The period from 1989 (fall of the Berlin Wall) to 2004 (EU enlargement) is extremely interesting to analyze for social and human scientists, and we can document what has changed in Europeans practices and discourse. But it is difficult for any of us to have a global view of such changes. Analytical work must necessarily be done by teams of researchers, from different disciplines, on multiple sites, with the development of interdisciplinarity that presupposes a harmonization of our tools. What we actually see is what I call "a migration of concepts" to which some attention must be paid, not to protect disciplinary walls but to be sure that we use those concepts properly. Disciplines do not have the same definition of what a scientific object is, and the notion of context varies according to history, linguistics or anthropology. What changes are being introduced by this "migration of concepts"? Does it stimulate new thinking avenues or does it lead to confusion?

At the turn of the millenium, how do we participate in a global understanding of politics? For anthropologists, the question is important because globalization affects the definition of the relationships with "others". The border line no longer follows geographical landmarks, peoples of the world are mutually dependent and more related to each other than ever, through diasporas, economic and cultural flows though they are certainly not equal regarding economic and power conditions. Similar observations can be made for organizations that are part of a system and are mutually dependent within the borders of nation states and outside them. Yet, borders have not disappeared, and the process of classification, which leads to categories of thoughts, that serve to fix policy orientations, arrange groups, define interest relations, and elaborate conditions for association or exclusion, is extremely sophisticated.

Multiple models have been explored to organize relations and structures, from organic to mechanic solidarity (Durkheim), from the theory of dependence to that of liberalization but we do have some difficulties to qualify what is going on. If we take only some of the expressions that have been popularized in political discourses after having been invented in multinational organizations, we observe a growing level of loose definitions. The concept of "good governance" is stabilized in several languages with a rather indefinite content, mainly structured around an opposition to "bad governance", the significance of which is pointed out by denunciating the weight of bureaucracy, the corruption of the elite, the non respect of Human rights, etc. The notion of "sustainable development", also very fashionable, creates even more problems as it gave birth to a divorce between "sustainable" which is used for anything in the future, and "development" the meaning of which is exhausted. Sustainable development resembles to a chimera – people realizing that it does not involve only State responsibility but that of all actors. To make it performative in the many contexts in which it is used (like "sustainable tourism", "sustainable food", "sustainable research", "sustainable citizenship"...) new concepts are invented such as that of "Corporate Social Responsability" (CSR), or the extraordinary concept of "global compact" that has been formalized in the UN to associate the firms who declare themselves interested in a positive evaluation of the social and environmental impact of their activities (Sybille Van der Hove 2003).

Listening and analyzing institutional discourses confront researchers with the variability of these categories, which reflects the instability of the political field. In front of the proliferation of institutional concepts which contribute to structuring political discourses but are used in many situations, most of them not being defined as political ones, we have a problem of identification of the communities of speakers – the producers or inventors of words – and of the public concerned, which is sometimes composed of the same speakers – in that case discourses circulate in a closed system. Such a lack of precision has important consequences regarding the impact of discourses. How can we build a dynamic model that would clarify the meaning of the metaphors related to time acceleration, circulation of flows, social fragmentation and individual flexibility, present in the European context, represented at the UN levels, and observable at local levels? Different temporalities and spatial references, multiple scale values, numbers of languages, the complexity of the translation and communication systems, the existence of shared ideologies and historical oppositions characterize the study of the European institutions. The analytical representation of that complexity requires the collaboration of all human sciences.

While doing fieldwork in several administrative institutions, I could notice that due to the acceleration of the process of change, the time of "sustainable" thought (that could be expected from leading institutions) is giving way to that of "executive" thought. This is partly induced by the fact that what is generally expected from an institution is not that it is a thinking organization but an efficient one, and that this efficiency can be measured: a chance for quantitavists. But the existing gap between the mandate of the institution – which defines its *raison d'être* – and the collective practices – which give it the means to fulfil this mandate – is not measured as such. For instance, how close to its mission is the Commission when it accepts a single dominant language as the European working language? A language that is not only English but also that of economics, management, accountability and liberalism. The answer requires arguments rather than figures, with a philosophical orientation about the function of communication rather than an economic one based only on budget deliberation.

The anthropologist, completing the interviews with multiple observations done in a variety of contexts, realizes that European agents have no time for thinking (as they say), even on their own condition (when condition means career, the trade unions are in charge of it). In other words, they are not compelled to engage in a reflexive process, in spite of the fact that most senior officials have an impressive university pedigree. It seems they are themselves taken by the spillover effect that makes European things go ahead (Keohane & Hoffmann 1991). Unlike the agents of the European Commission who are worried not to have time to think about what they do and communicate their unique experience to the outside world (Bellier 2004), those of the UN, who are working in the Permanent Forum secretariat office engage their energy to communicate with indigenous representatives and the outside world. The agents of the EU have no time left to appreciate what has been done while the agents of the UN have no means to get the things done. Together, these officials are engaged in the production of texts and discourses and live out of the reports transmitted to them. Is this what recipients of the policies designed therein are asking for: a review of the processes to check the balance?

Participant observation reveals the many differences that exist between the organizations, and this helps to better conceptualize the analyses of discourses, texts and reports. Knowing the social conditions of the production of institutional discourses puts him/her in front of a contradiction between, on the one hand, the domain of the agents who are well educated but do not have time to think and nevertheless produce texts, discourses, recommendations etc. and, on the other hand, the institutions as a whole (authority) who produce ideas without being identified as the right place for the production of knowledge. Interestingly, this is reflected by internal self-representations, for the Euro civil servants consider themselves as technicians rather than intellectuals, as well as by external representations, which present them as bureaucrats. In the UN, in the arena dealing with indigenous issues, intellectuals are associated to the process as experts whose reports are used to debate at political levels, but their "efficiency" is nil.

In order to deepen the analyses by comparing the present state of observations with the past, as it appears in reports, archives or other kind of documents, the researcher collects papers, references, and is soon overwhelmed by the massive character of text production in such an organization. These characteristics contribute to define European institutions or the UN as thinking organizations not because they might propose constitutive discourses – that would be reserved to only one kind of text production – but because they constitute the basis for developing dialogue between different circles of people, from the reduced number of experts, to a larger number of civil society representatives, and because they impose orientations by building an authority position.

Conclusion

How do institutions think? I tried to answer this question, through the observation of practices in European and United Nations premises, and also through the study of texts and discourses from many different sources, corresponding to distinct genres. From this comparative perspective, differences emerge. The European Commission is a world of ideas and a place where so many different systems coincide that none of them dominate, letting space for the formulation of a composite model: that of hybridization, that of multilingual exchanges, that of a continuous recycling of speeches. Taking language as an object of study, and discourses as sources, observing practices and reading second generation literature, we are confronted with excessive materials when dealing with European matters. This is how I started working on the political meaning of words, something that is especially important in a multinational environment, where values and representations of norms vary. It is difficult to analyze European discourses not only because of the distinct languages which characterize them – the EU constitutes "a discursive translinguistic community" – nor because of the quantity of texts produced by an organization like the EC. The main reason is that of the complex relations between the content of the discourses, their conditions of production and their effects, upstream and downstream. Similar properties can be identified in the UN working group I am currently studying but, as a matter of fact, the groups dealing with Indigenous affairs are much more integrated and the topics they dealt with more coherently related. The production of meetings minutes thanks to a support NGO and their free circulation on the web, are of considerable importance not only for keeping record of what has been said, but also for relating the progress made in different places to the discourses that can be heard at a given moment.

In European matters, it is extremely difficult to bridge the gap between the different sources and the multiple times of enunciation that characterize the institutional production. Directives take years to be adopted; issues are discussed in many different forums before getting a kind of formalization somewhere; people producing data are not equally accessible to interviews and the minutes of the meetings not openly delivered. We find traces of a European dynamic in the domain of institutional semantics: the place where collective meanings are being cooked. When you observe a session of the Council of ministers, or a working group, you enter the kitchen and you learn that many elements are already transformed before getting there. You see how people juggle with words. Declarations are codified, but implicit meanings circulate actively. Intellectually, precision is crucial to the construction of discourses and one may have the impression that this is what state representatives do when they discuss the position of a coma, or the choice of an expression rather than another one; but politically, a number of undefined categories are preferred to give space to interpretations in the legal or state systems.

As objects of anthropological scrutiny, European, or other international institutions raise specific questions. A greater attention has been paid from our side to the study of institutions as microcosms, with specific rules, languages, customs, policies; observing on the one hand the symbolic vacuum and the multiplication of mini rituals to fill the vacuum and, on the other hand, the relationship with the surrounding world, in a kind of ecological approach. Making that visible may explain why people, and European citizens in particular, do not have a clear representation of what Europe is. It raises the question of what kinds of discourse do actually reach the citizen and to whom the European discourses we analyze are directed, discourses that we se-lect among a collection and that we take from participation in the meetings or from computer downloading. What is at stake is a greater comprehension of the relationship between political institutions and the social world.

Human sciences, anthropology as well, have evolved theoretically and em-pirically, but their relative positions have changed in the field of research. We can see how limited their place is in the European Research and Develop-ment frameworks, and how restrictive the role assigned to them to answer institutional demands. Of 7 priorities of the latest Framework only one con-cerns human sciences and it is targeted at "Governance and citizenship". The issue is certainly crucial for the EU but it seriously reduces the domain of hu-man sciences. Though some experts consider that human sciences are welcome in European research, through that gate at least, it seems to me that funda-mental research in Humanities is facing a clear limitation as it is allotted one sector only.

If we take again the case of the 5th and 6th Common Research and Devel-opment Frameworks that contribute to the redefinition of the European Space of Research, we see that the calls are very precisely written, in order to define what is expected from the researchers in terms of scientific content, feasibility, dissemination and finances. The control over the appropriateness of intentions and means is so strict that there is no space for a research beyond limits, beyond the limits that have been fixed through bureaucratic procedures; the system of evaluation is supposed to be fair and neutral; and the researcher is assigned a niche to fill; that is a justification of the credits given. If that is the future of "a knowledge society" – to recall the title of the 1995 report the EC listing the changes to be implemented in Europe, such as flexibility, management of three languages, harmonization of education and working systems, etc., – we are very close to the technocratic world anticipated by Roland Barthes. Ideology as rep-resentation of power is also what should be analyzed in institutional discourses, as technical orders are not deprived of political effects. Social scientists should be aware of the restriction of thought that results from a process which drains intelligent resources to the European level, as a positive dimension of the free circulation of people, but does not lead them to go beyond the lines. A number of consequences can be pointed out. Fundamental and independent research is challenged by technical applied research. For intellectuals, and we can take the French "new philosophers" as an illustration, the game seems to be above, next to the politicians and the media, to influence the decision centres and consol-idate an elite position rather than below where are the subalterns, the people who are confronted with a number of changes they cannot control. Direct collection of data on the field suffers from such an orientation, though a better understanding of the present-day reality of people is needed, in a time of accelerated technological changes. Competition as a means to select the best became the rule and (a certain degree of) association with decision power remains the best way to get funded, not because of any kind of corruption but because of a proximity to those places where the circulation of concepts is activated and to the people who launch them. Such a mechanism leads to controlling even the conditions of any possible criticism and contributes to isolate researchers from society.

The importance of such a gap might be considered in relation to the definition of the "ideosphere" which Roland Barthes gave in a seminar in the "Collège de France" in 1977–1978, and the reference he made to "the icy and civilized barbarianism of pure technocracy" (2002, lecture no. 7). For him, this image designated the possible existence of a world in which the absence of ideology as a system of representations is proved by the absence of any discourse mediating the access to reality. Such a situation would be defined by the absence of sublimation, with no possible reversal of that crude destiny: people speak of cars, computers, video games, good governance, etc; they express needs, in a kind of neutral situation. Something like this is at stake when the Commission (together with the experts needed to design the program and the ministers who approve it) says on the basis of technical arguments: "this is what Europe needs for research and this is how we want researchers to operate". But we should not forget that we are in a political process and that technical arguments are not the sole factors accounting for the design of a scientific field. "How institutions think" should be clearly taken as an objective for interdisciplinary research, not only because linguistics, anthropology, economics and political science are concerned by the object "institution", the definition of which varies according to several indicators, but because it affects society and the capacity human sciences have to answer social demands.

Notes

* I would like to thank Aziliz Gouez and Flora Bolter who carefully checked the English version of this text.

1. "Discursive resources such as talk and print provide the basic means with which policies are constructed, negotiated and rendered into an enduring form", Muntigl (2000: 1).

2. The Working Group on Indigenous Populations (WGIP) and the Working Group on the Draft declaration of the Rights of Indigenous Peoples (WGDD) in Geneva, the Permanent Forum for Indigenous Affairs (PFII) in New York.

3. In the Working Group on Indigenous Peoples (WGIP), the five experts (members of the Human Rights Sub Commission for the protection of Minorities) are chosen by the States represented in the UN, on a regional basis (Europe, Asia, Africa, America, Russia) to attend the meetings of that group, participate in the Commission of Human Rights and other organizational meetings and work together with the General Secretariat to produce the reports. In the working group on the draft declaration there is no expert as such. In the Permanent Forum for Indigenous Affairs (New York), eight experts are elected for a three year period by indigenous organizations on a regional basis, and eight are appointed by the government according to the same principle of world wide representation.

4. Langages, nr. 105:8–27, in Maingueneau (op. cit.:129).

5. This capacity was explained to me by a European member of the UNDP, in New York, who related her office which she considered a "world think tank" to academic US and European intellectual resources.

6. "An elegant way to avoid speaking one's mind, to hide what one doesn't want to say, this 'language of cotton' must constantly renew its vocabulary. The creation of new words (…), as well as the use of words borrowed from various specialized jargons (psychology, history, natural sciences) will give the speaker the opportunity to never be caught short of an answer" (2002:199). [*"Elégant moyen de tourner autour du pot, de cacher ce que l'on ne tient pas à dire, la langue de coton est constamment appelée à renouveler le stock de son vocabulaire. La création de nouveaux mots… et l'emprunt à différents registres spécialisés (psychologie, histoire, sciences naturelles) donneront à l'orateur l'occasion de ne jamais être pris de court"* (2002:199)].

7. Interview, Commission DG 1, 1993.

References

Abélès, M., Bellier, I., & McDonald, M. (1993). *An anthropological approach to the Commission.* Brussels: mimeo.

Abélès, M. & Bellier, I. (1996). "Du compromis culturel à la culture politique du compromis". *Revue Française de Science Politique, 46*(3), 431–456.

Barthes, R. (2002). *Le neutre.* Séminaire au collège de France (1977–1978), CD-Rom. Paris: Le Seuil.

Bellier, I. (2001). "In and out, fieldwork in a political space: the case of the European Commission". *Österreichische Zeitschrift für Politikwissenschaft, 31*(2), 205–216.

Bellier, I. (2004). "The European Commission, between the 'acquis communautaire' and enlargement". In D. Dimitrakopoulos (Ed.), *The Changing European Commission* (pp. 138–150). Manchester and New York: Manchester University Press.

Douglas, M. ([1986] 1999). *Comment pensent les institutions.* Paris: La découverte / M.A.U.S.S.

Hoffmann, S. & Keohane, R. O. (Eds.) (1991). *The New European Community. Decision-making and institution change*. Boulder: Westview Press.

Maingueneau, D. (2002). "Les rapports des organisations internationales: un discours constituant". In G. Rist (Ed.), *Les mots du pouvoir, sens et non sens de la rhétorique internationale* (pp. 119–132). Paris: PUF et Genève Nouveaux Cahiers de l'IED.

Marcus, G. (1995). "Ethnography in/of the World system: the Emergence of multi-sited ethnography". *Annual Review of Anthropology, 24*, 95–117.

Muntigl, P., Weiss, G., & Wodak, R. (2000). *European Union Discourses on Un/employment. An interdisciplinary approach to employment policy making and organizational change*. Amsterdam/Philadelphia: John Benjamins Publishing Company.

Phillipson, R. (2003). *English Only Europe, Challenging Language Policy*. London and New York: Routledge.

Sciences Humaines, décembre 1998 / janvier 1999, no. 23. *Anthropologie, nouveau terrain, nouveaux objets*. Paris.

Steiner, B. (2002). "De la langue de bois à la langue de coton; les mots du pouvoir". In Gilbert Rist (Ed.), *Les mots du pouvoir, sens et non sens de la rhétorique internationale* (pp. 193–208). Paris: PUF et Genève Nouveaux Cahiers de l'IED.

Swaan, A. de (2001). *Words of the world, the global language system*. Cambridge: Polity.

Van der Hove, S. (2003). "Approches institutionnelles de la responsabilité sociale des entreprises". In G. Froger, M. O. Blanc, & P. Schembri (Eds.), *Développement durable: quelle dynamique?* (pp. 61–81). Paris: Cahier du Gemdev 29.

Wodak, R. (2000). "From conflict to consensus. The co-construction of a policy paper". In P. Muntigl, G. Weiss, & R. Wodak, *European Union Discourses on Un/employment. An interdisciplinary approach to employment policy making and organizational change* (pp. 73–114). Amsterdam/Philadelphia: John Benjamins.

CHAPTER 12

The role of a political identity code in defining the boundaries of public and private*

The example of latent antisemitism

András Kovács
Central European University

Text and talk, subjects of Critical Discourse Analysis, can be of a public or a private nature. If we further consider language to be a form of social practice, we must be aware of the enormous differences between public and private communicative practices. If the purpose of the analysis is to deconstruct the hidden or latent social structures behind spoken and written texts, the ideological underpinnings of discoursive practices, it can not be irrelevant whether the subject of analysis belongs to the public or private realm of communication. The aim of this case study is to demonstrate, how empirical social science can contribute to revealing in which ways people define the borders of public and private communication, and what the consequences of this definition for their communicative behavior might be. My central thesis is that political identity plays an important role in this process of definition.

Those who study everyday communication know that people evaluate the situation in which they will communicate with their partners before such interaction actually begins. In this evaluation they primarily determine whether they should follow the rules of public or private communication. The act of communication occurs through constant re-evaluation of the situation, the goal of which is to develop a consensus about the public or private nature of the interaction engaged in. Such an evaluation of the private or public nature of an interaction is perhaps the most salient case of defining the borders of public and private spheres.

As researchers dealing with latent public opinion have shown (Angelusz 1996:9–39), the main factor determining whether opinions are hidden or clearly manifested is the political and social system, mainly through the structure of the public realm. On the one hand, opinions may be hard to identify in the course of research because the members of the society in question don't readily form opinions about relevant subjects. On the other hand, the difficulty may stem from the fact that certain individuals in society hide their opinions on account of "a refined attempt to seek psychological advantage, existential dependence, or a fear of the harder social consequences" (ibid.:21). Even in advanced democratic societies with well-functioning public realms, racial, religious, and other group prejudices belong in a category of opinions that are often kept hidden because their public expression would amount to an open breach of the consensus rejecting such views. As in the case of any other form of illegitimate public behavior, this would give rise to psychological conflicts and possibly even personal disadvantage. This observation has been verified by a series of empirical researches.

Research on prejudice – and on antisemitism in particular – has revealed a strong latency pressure: respondents consider it risky to express anti-Jewish opinions. For example, in the course of a survey performed in Austria in the summer of 1991, 27% of respondents avoided making a response when they were asked whether the number of Jews in influential positions should be limited, while 31% refused to take a position on whether a law should regulate the amount of property or land obtainable by Austrian Jews (Karmasin 1992:31–34). In Germany, in 1989, 20% of respondents in a survey agreed with the statement "if I am talking about Jews, I am always very careful, because it is very easy to get your fingers burnt", while 15% stated that "I don't tell just anybody what I think about Jews" (Bergmann & Erb 1991b:280). This same statement was accepted by 25% of respondents in a 1993 survey of Hungarian university students, while 52% of the same students thought that "if you say something bad about Jews, you are immediately branded an antisemite" (Kovács 1997:58).

Using Luhman's definition of latency (Luhmann 1984:458), scholars concerned with the problem distinguish between two forms of latency. They speak of conscious or factual latency where people have no developed opinions about certain issues, and of communicative or functional latency where participants in the communication hide their real opinions (Bergmann & Erb 1986, 1991; Bellers 1990). Opinions may be concealed in two ways: it may be that respondents avoid addressing a problem even though they do hold opinions; but it is also possible that they declare views that are not their real ones. Two types of motivation may explain why a respondent avoids answering questions of a survey. It may be that some people really have no developed opinions about the issues raised; the problems of the survey are of no interest to them. But it is also possible that the refusal to give a full answer is a means of hiding opinions. Using Luhman's categories, the first group is characterised by factual latency, and the second group by communication latency. Gilljam and Granberg call the former "real nonattitudes or true negatives", and the latter "pseudo-nonattitudes or false negatives" (Gilljam & Granberg 1993: 349).

As we know, the *public* expression of racial, religious or ethnic prejudices is condemned in Hungary – just as it is in every civilized state in the world – and yet there are still groups virtually everywhere in society who are not afraid to express such prejudice, even in public. However, research on latency also shows us that in situations defined as public many will hide their opinions if asked to answer touchy questions about such feelings as antipathy toward Jews. Why is it, then, that some people openly admit their non-conformist antisemitic views in public, while others are afraid to do so? How are the boundaries socially defined between public and private communication in such cases? Among other things, we looked for an answer to this question in the course of research carried out on antisemitic prejudices in Hungary in 1995 (cf. Kovács 1999).

From our point of view the most important issue is whether or not the feeling of latency pressure induces respondents to hide their real opinions in the course of the interviews. Obviously this will depend on whether respondents consider the sociological interview to be public discourse (in which case they might tend to express socially approved, conformist opinions) or a form of communication that is similar to a private discussion (in which case they might tend to say what they really think even about the sensitive issues). There is no general theoretical answer to this question. The interview situation can be seen both, private and public, depending mainly on political factors. Bergmann and Erb concluded that, while about one-quarter of respondents strongly felt latency pressure, it was primarily the antisemites – those who otherwise did not hide their opinions in the course of the survey – who considered the expression of anti-Jewish views to be risky. According to Bergmann and Erb, who found that 12% of the whole population was very antisemitic and 7% extremely antisemitic, at most a further 4% of the surveyed population could be hidden or latent antisemites (Bergmann & Erb 1991b: 282).

The 1993 survey of a representative sample of Hungarian university and college students produced similar results. It was shown that those who gave antisemitic answers in the course of the interview felt the strongest latency pressure, and that this did not stop them from openly expressing their opinions in the interview-situation. On the basis of the results of the survey, I calculated that 7% of the students were extremely antisemitic, 18% were antisemitic, and a further maximum of 9% (but probably less) were latent antisemites (Kovács 1997:59, 62). Róbert Angelusz, on the other hand, discovered higher levels of latent antisemitism following a national survey of a representative sample: over and above the 12% of openly antisemitic respondents, he identified a further 12% as latent antisemites (Angelusz 1996:211).

Based on a survey we carried out on a representative sample of the Hungarian adult population in 1995, we attempted to determine who might be considered antisemites who attempt to hide their views in public. The method we used was based on three theoretical preconceptions. According to the theory of "*the spiral of silence*" people in communication try to judge whether open expression of their views would provoke conflict with uncomfortable psychological consequences. Those who feel they hold a minority opinion in society often tend to avoid to say what they really think (see Noelle-Neumann 1980; Angelusz 1996). Therefore we first attempted to see who might feel that open expression of anti-Jewish views is illegitimate, and who might believe that a ban on the expression of such views is valid for them personally. Next, using the theory of "*pluralistic ignorance*" (see Fields & Schumann 1976; Crosby, Bromley, & Saxe 1980; Bergmann & Erb 1991; Angelusz 1996b) we examined how powerful the various respondents consider antisemitism to be in society, and – on the basis of their position on the antisemitism scale – whether they see themselves belonging to what they consider to be the majority or the minority. This analysis is important if we wish to estimate latency, because previous research has shown that certain groups react to the latency pressure by projecting their real opinions on to other people, in particular on to "the majority of society" (Angelusz 1996b:205). Finally, we assessed whether individual respondents consider a series of statements expressing to a greater or lesser extent antisemitic views to be antisemitic or not. We may consider the negative responses to indicate latency, because – in correspondence with the theory of *cognitive dissonance* – respondents may be able to dissolve the tension stemming from the illegitimate nature of their suppressed antisemitic views, by declaring these views to be non-antisemitic (i.e. legitimate). As a next step indices were prepared from the responses to the three groups of questions which were then used as indicators of latency. The distribution of responses and the indices are shown in the first six tables in the Appendix.

In order to define the latent antisemite group we created a new index by combining the three latency indices. The maximum possible score on the

index was 11, which respondents reached if they agreed with all three statements measuring latency, were of the opinion that there are many antisemites
in the country, and considered at most three of the antisemitic statements to
be antisemitic.[1]

Naturally we suspected that respondents were hiding antisemitic views
only when they reached a high score on the Latency Index, and, at the same
time, they had been included in the group of non-antisemites based upon
their responses to other questions.[2] As the results show, the antisemites feel
the latency-pressure much more strongly than the non-antisemites, and yet in
the course of the interviews most of them did not conceal their views and thus,
on the basis of their responses, were placed in the antisemitic group. (58% of
extreme antisemites and 58% of antisemites felt strong latency pressure, while
only 14% of non antisemites felt such pressure).

However, we cannot ignore the fact that approximately one-half of the
group that showed strong latency on the cumulative latency index proved to
be non antisemites (Table 8). In the interest, then, of seeing whether prejudice was hidden underneath latency we had to compare two groups: non
antisemites with a low latency index, and non antisemites with a high latency
index. This comparison showed that the non antisemites who reached high
values on the scale differ in the same dimensions from those who reached low
values, as in general differentiated between antisemites and non antisemites.
With regard to the social and demographic indicators, among members of the
group displaying a high latency, there were significantly greater numbers of
Budapest residents, those who were born in Budapest, and those whose parents were from Budapest, as well as of the relatively well-educated. Those with
high latency scores are more similar in terms of their attitudes to the antisemites than to the non-antisemites who were placed in the same group on
the antisemitism scale: among the former group xenophobia and anomie are
significantly stronger than among the latter.

From the point of view of our recent subject, an especially interesting characteristic appeared with regards to the group considered latent antisemites. In
the course of our survey we distinguished two frustrated and anomic social
groups on the basis of a combination of various attitudes. The "right-wing
frustrated" comprised respondents who – when we asked them about the state
of things after the collapse of the Communist system – agreed with opinions
revealing high levels of personal frustration and strong feelings of anomie, and,
at the same time, they were also characterized by strong national and religious
sentiments and a conservative outlook on life. The "left-wing frustrated" comprised respondents with high levels of personal frustration and anomie as well,

but they strongly rejected national and religious sentiments. This group's members, in addition to being personally frustrated, were characterized by feelings of loss of norms, social victimization, a lack of trust of democratic institutions and politics, as well as a nostalgia for the socialist past. The majority of the group also said in 1995 they would support leftist parties (Hungarian Socialist Party, The Workers' Party) that reject antisemitism in their public ideologies (cf. Kovács 1999: 44–48).[3]

In short, left and right-wing antisemites judge the freedom to express anti-Jewish feelings differently. Right-wingers speak openly, while leftists try to conceal their antisemitic views. Researchers have identified four spheres of differing degrees of freedom of expression. The "free" sphere is characterized by a lack of institutional or psychological blocks to the open expression of views arrived at in private. There is also a great deal of freedom of expression in the "quasi-free" sphere. It is generally accepted that the development of views about any given issue in this sphere is the individual's business. However, there are certain social mechanisms, and delicate psychological tools of reward and punishment, that show the individual what the "more acceptable" opinion choice is. This is why the open expression of "quasi-free" opinion is somewhat risky. In the case of "preferred" and "required" spheres of opinions much stronger sanctions set the boundary between "expected" and "undesirable" opinions (Angelusz 1996b: 22). It appears, then, that right-wing antisemites judge the expression of antisemitic views to be "free", whereas left-wing antisemites rather consider such views to belong to the "quasi-free" sphere.

The phenomenon we observe here is not new to social science. Already in 1948, in his essay on antisemitism, the Hungarian István Bibó writes about the "severely moral" type, who smothers his spontaneous antisemitism under the pressure of moral imperatives (Bibó 1986: 702–703). In *The Authoritarian Personality* Adorno and his colleagues identified the same phenomenon. On the "F" scale they observed a "rigid low scorer" type, a "…syndrome … in which the absence of prejudice, instead of being based on concrete experience and integrated within the personality, is derived from general, external, ideological patterns" (Adorno et al. 1969: 771–772).

A great many factors may play a role in the determination of the boundaries between private and public speech, internalized ideological values are one of them. In strict sense private communication – using the concepts of Alfred Schutz – is only the face-to-face communication between consociates mutually involved in each other's biographies (Schutz 1962: 15–16). In all other communicative situations the partners must make a judgement about the level of public nature of the intended communicative act and about the degree of freedom of communication on the given level. This degree of freedom is strongly influenced by the nature of the political system.

In undemocratic societies, for instance, the officially sanctioned viewpoint often strongly determines what personal opinions citizens are willing to publicly express. It is to be expected that first of all "preferred" and "required" opinions appear in public. In democratic conditions the consensus of norms on the different levels of communication has a similar controlling effect. During ordinary interaction in everyday life role expectations put pressure on those interacting, and drives their communicative behavior in the direction of role conformity. In case of interactions in which the actors appear as representatives of groups their communicative behavior is controlled by the set of norms of their reference group. The public acceptance of them functions as identity code, as a marker of belonging to the group. On a societal level the construct "norm consensus" is disseminated by public institutions and the media.

Social actors define the dividing line between public and private on the one hand on the basis of the degree of experienced consensus in everyday communication, and on the other hand in the institutional forums representing public opinion on the given communicative level. In the definition the distance social actors notice between these two spheres of opinion plays a decisive role. It seems that left- and right-wing antisemites judge this distance differently. Leftist antisemites are much more sensitive to latency pressure which indicates that they feel a much larger distance between their private views and the public norms of their group, then the right-wingers. In the case of leftist latent antisemites, as was the case with Adorno's group of rigid low scorers, a code of political identity is influencing decisively the degree of freedom of expression of opinion.

The novelty of the modern antisemitic ideology born in the 19th century lies in the symbolic meaning imposed on the "Jewish Question". Taking an antisemitic or anti-antisemitic position enabled individuals to express political and cultural identity in a panoply of political, moral and cultural conflicts (cf. Volkov 1978; Rürup 1987). As a result of this mechanism of encoding if someone expressed antisemitic views, it was more or less easy to intuit that person's views on a whole range of political and cultural issues might have had virtually nothing to do with the status and role of Jews in the society but they had to do something with anticapitalism. As Shulamit Volkov demonstrated, from the last third of the 19th century onward antisemitism functioned as a cultural code.

Because of the radical and anticapitalist nature of modern antisemitism, until the last decade of the 19th century the question of whether antisemitism would become an organic part of the anticapitalist canon of the workers' movement was an open question. But finally the social democracy of the II. Internationale joined the "emancipation" camp in opposition to the "Jewish question" camp. In the cognitive process that occurred in the decades following 1890 the marker – position on the "Jewish question" – was attached to the mark – position in political-cultural camps – and as a result followers of the leftist movement learned to use their position on the "Jewish question" as a code to express their identity in public. In leftist elite speech anti-antisemitism became a factor of identity, and antisemitic sentiments among the party faithful became unfit for public expression. In his Buchenwald novel, "Quelle beau dimanche", Jorge Semprun describes how antisemitism broke out of a German communist worker interned in the camp, and how it was driven back into the personal sphere of irrational hatred by a comrade "trying to re-build the security walls of his earlier common sense". This is exactly the way, how the self-control of Adorno's rigid low scorers works as well. And it is a well-established fact that the anti-antisemitic identity code was applied by communist parties who used antifascism as source of self-legitimation even when they exploited antisemitic sentiments for tactical reasons, or even directly engaged in antisemitic politics.

Our survey shows that antisemitism continues to function as a code today: it draws a symbolic line between politico-cultural camps, and is one of the most easily comprehended tools in the establishment of public political and cultural identity. As such it defines the boundaries of public and private for those for whom belonging to one camp or another is an organic part of their public identity.

Notes

* A previous version of this article has been published in *Social Research*, Vol. 69(1), Spring 2002, pp. 179–194.

1. Possible scores on the latency-index: 0 (none of the statements is true) – 3 (all three statements are true); possible scores on the estimate-index: 1 (there are very few antisemites) – 4 (there are very many antisemites); possible scores on the denial-index: 1 (7–14 statements are antisemitic) – 4 (0–3 statements are antisemitic).

2. We developed our three independent scales to measure anti-Semitism based upon the most widespread versions of prejudice theory. We measured the content of anti-Jewish prejudices, the degree of their emotionality, the willingness to discriminate against Jews. After this, based on the values reached on the three scales, we categorized respondents into groups of differing degrees of prejudices. The results of our categorization are displayed in the following table.

	N	%
Non antisemite	420	29
stereotyper	478	32
antisemite	246	17
extreme antisemite	116	8
unclassifiable	213	14
Total	1473	100

3. Our observations agree with the findings by Enyedi, Erős and Fabian, who in the course of their empirical study of authoritarianism in 1994 measured a relatively high F-scale value among voters supporting the left-wing of the political spectrum, a finding that was a causal factor for anti-Semitic prejudices (Enyedi, Erős, & Fabian 1997).

References

Adorno, Theodor W. et al. (1969). *The Authoritarian Personality*. New York: W.W. Norton.

Angelusz, Robert (1996a). "A rejtőzködéstől a megnyilatkozásig" (From concealment to expression). In R. Angelusz (Ed.), *Optikai csalódások* (pp. 9–49). Budapest: Pesti Szalon.

Angelusz, Robert (1996b). "Optikai csalódások" (Optical illusions). In R. Angelusz (Ed.), *Optikai csalódások* (pp. 168–212). Budapest: Pesti Szalon.

Bellers, Jürgen (1990). "Moralkommunikation und Kommunikationsmoral. Über Kommunikationslatenzen, Antisemitismus und politisches System". In W. Bergmann & R. Erb (Eds.), *Antisemitismus in der politischen Kultur nach 1945* (pp. 278–291). Opladen: Leske und Budrich.

Bergmann, Werner & Erb, Rainer (1986). "Kommunikationslatenz, Moral und öffentliche Meinung". *Kölner Zeitschrift für Soziologie und Sozialpsychologie, 38*, 223–246.

Bergmann, Werner & Erb, Rainer (1991a). "Mir ist das Thema Juden irgendwie unangenehm. Kommunikationslatenz und die Wahrnehmung des Meinungsklimas im Fall des Antisemitismus." *Kölner Zeitschrift für Soziologie und Sozialpsychologie, 43*(3) 1991, 502–519.

Bergmann, Werner & Erb, Rainer (1991b). *Antisemitismus in der Bundesrepublik Deutschland. Ergebnisse der empirischen Forschung von 1946–1989.* Opladen: Leske und Budrich.

Bibó, István (1986). "Zsidókérdés Magyarországon 1944 után." ("The "Jewish Question" in Hungary after 1944.") In B. István (Ed.), *Válogatott tanulmányok, 2. Kötet* (pp. 623–797). Budapest: Magvető.

Enyedi, Zsolt, Erős, Ferenc, & Fábián, Zoltan (1997). *Authoritarianism and the political spectrum in Hungary.* Collegium Budapest, Discussion Paper Series, No. 40.

Crosby, Faye, Bromley, Stephanie, & Saxe, Leonard (1980). "Recent unobstrusive studies of black and white discrimination and prejudice. A literature review." *Psychological Bulletin, 87*, 546–563.

Fields, James M. & Schumann, Howard (1976). "Public beliefs about the believes of the public". *Public Opinion Quarterly, 40,* 427–448.

Gilljam, Mikael & Granberg, Donald (1993). "Should we take don't know for an answer?" *Public Opinion Quarterly, 57,* 348–357.

Karmasin, Franz (1992). "Austrian attitudes toward Jews, Israel, and the Holocaust". In American Jewish Committee (Ed.), *Working Papers on Contemporary Antisemitism.* New York.

Kovács, András (1997). *A különbség köztünk van. Az antiszemitizmus és a fiatal elit* (The difference is between us. Antisemitism and the young elite). Budapest: Cserépfalvi.

Kovács, András (1999). "Antisemitic Prejudices in Contemporary Hungary. Analysis of Current Trends in Antisemitism." *Acta no. 16. The Vidal Sasson International Center for Study of Antisemitism,* The Hebrew University of Jerusalem.

Luhmann, Niklas (1984). *Soziale Systeme. Grundriss einer allgemeinen Theorie.* Frankfurt a. M.: Suhrkamp.

Noelle-Neumann, Elisabeth (1980). *Die Schweigespirale. Öffentliche Meinung – unsere soziale Haut.* München/Zürich: R. Piper.

Rürup, Reinhard (1987). "Die 'Judenfrage' der bürgerlichen Gesellschaft und die Entstehung des modernen Antisemitismus." In R. Rürup (Ed.), *Emanzipation und Antisemitismus* (pp. 93–119). Frankfurt a. M.: Fischer.

Schütz, Alfred (1962). *Collected Papers, Vol. 1.* Ed. by M. Natanson. The Hague et al.: Martinus Nijhof Publishers.

Volkov, Shulamit (1978). "Antisemitism as cultural code." *Leo Baeck Institute Yearbook, XXIII,* 25–45.

Appendix

Table 1. The feeling of latency pressure (percentage)

	true	false	don't know/no response
…I don't tell just anyone what I think about Jews	29	62	9
…I think many people don't dare say openly what they think about Jews	54	35	11
…if you say something bad about Jews, you are immediately branded an antisemite	44	41	15

Table 2. Latency-index (percentage)

none of the statements is true	29
one of the statements is true	29
two of the statements are true	29
all three statements are true	13

Table 3. Estimates of the strength of anti-semitism (percentage)

	very many (4)	many (3)	few (2)	very few (1)	don't know/no response (0)
In Hungary today, how many people do you think are hostile to the Jews?	2	23	48	16	11
And how many people might want to limit the influence of Jews in the country?	2	23	46	16	13
And how many people think it would be better if Jews were to emigrate?	1	17	44	24	14

Table 4. Estimate-index based on the sum of responses to the three questions (percentage)

there are very few antisemites (1–3 points)	15
there are few antisemites (4–6 points)	48
there are many antisemites (7–8 points)	14
there are very many antisemites (9–12 points)	14
unable to guess (0 points)	9

Table 5. Is someone an antisemite if they … (percentage)

	antisemite	non-antisemite	don't know/no response
always seek to know who is Jewish in their surrounding	23	66	11
don't consider Jews living in Hungary to be Hungarians	57	31	12
wouldn't marry a Jew	52	36	12
want to limit the number of Jews in certain professions	67	22	11
think that Jews can never become full Hungarians whatever the conditions	60	28	12
think that Jews have recognisable features	19	70	11
think that the murder of Christ is the unforgivable sin of the Jews	37	42	21
think that Jews should be encouraged to emigrate from Hungary	77	13	10
think that the interests of Jews in Hungary are very different from the interests of non-Jews	35	50	15
think that Jews are no longer capable of integrating into Hungarian society	48	38	14
think that the crimes committed against the Jews were no greater than those against the victims of Communism	30	51	19
think that Jews are responsible for the period of Communist rule in Hungary	45	34	21
think that Jews divide and weaken nations that accept them	65	21	14
think that Jews are hostile to the Christian faith	42	39	19

Table 6. Index of denial of antisemitism (percentage)

0–3 statements were antisemitic	23
4–6 statements were antisemitic	25
7–9 statements were antisemitic	28
10–14 statements were antisemitic	24

Table 7. Combined latency index

N		percentage	
non-latent	661	(index score of 2–5)	45
somewhat latent	521	(index score of 6–7)	36
latent	277	(index score of 8–11)	19

Table 8. Latency and anti-semitism (percentage)

	non-latent	somewhat latent	latent
non-antisemite	88	72	30
antisemite	11	21	25
extreme antisemite	2	7	25
	100	100	100

CHAPTER 13

Social order and disorder

Institutions, policy paradigms and discourses:
An interdisciplinary approach

Tom R. Burns and Marcus Carson
Uppsala University / University of Stockholm

1. Introduction

Institutional crisis evokes particular discourses. Some of these discourses are formulated in terms of the conceptions, values, and principles of the prevailing institutional paradigm. Critique may also emerge *external* to the institutional paradigm, and may entail criticism of key components of the institution – or of the paradigm itself. Critics may propose alternatives that break with the prevailing arrangements and their particular norms, social relationships, cognitive categories and assumptions. This involves a different type of discourse and rhetoric than that formulated from *within* an established order. The latter is generally compatible with the institutional paradigm and its corresponding organizational arrangements. For instance, such discourses may include references to idealized performances or other types of normative action, goal achievements, and characterizations of developments as right and proper according to established paradigmatic principles. The situation described is one of normality. In contrast, under conditions of *ab-normality* and crisis, effective opposition may facilitate a paradigm shift and the establishment over time of new arrangements and practices. Such change processes are characterized by entrepreneurship and charisma. In general, societal institutions and the paradigms upon which they are modeled are often remarkably robust, and most likely to undergo change only under extreme circumstances that include institutional crisis.

This chapter focuses on the concepts of *institution*, *paradigm*, and *discourse* and their interrelationships. It goes on to identify particular types of discourses in connection with institutional crisis or major malfunctioning of an institution. Finally, it identifies several common patterns of emerging paradigms, paradigm competition, and paradigm shifts. In our framework, the socio-cognitive and discursive dimensions are related to institutional and political dimensions. The approach outlined here stresses *rule-based cognitive processes such as framing, contextualizing, and classifying objects, persons, and actions in a relevant or meaningful way* (Burns & Engdahl 1998a, 1998b; Burns & Carson 2002; Burns & Gomolinska 2000, 2001; Carson 1999, 2000a, 2004; Nylander 2000). It also considers the production of meaningful accounts, discourses, and commentaries in the context of a given institution or institutional arrangement.

Our approach combines institutional theory with cognitive science and discourse analysis – fields that are typically separated. The separation can be observed in the different journals; the different conferences for the fields; different associations; and in the weak overlap of authors engaged in the different areas. We believe that the investigation and analysis of social phenomena needs each of the three scientific traditions. In particular, theoretical and methodological efforts are required to integrate the institutional with cognitive and discursive analyses (see Burns & Carson 2002; Weiss & Wodak 2003; Wodak & van Dijk 2000). This article is an effort to contribute systematically to such transdisciplinary integration.

2.   Institutions and institutional arrangements

An institution is a complex of relationships, roles, and norms, which constitute and regulate recurring interaction processes among participants in socially defined settings or domains. Any institution organizing people in such relationships may be conceptualized as an authoritative complex of rules or a *rule regime* (Burns et al. 1985; Burns & Flam 1987). Institutions are exemplified, for instance, by the family, the firm, a government agency, markets, democratic associations, and religious communities. Each structures and regulates social interactions in particular ways; there is a particular interaction logic to a given institution. Each institution as a rule regime provides a systematic, meaningful basis for actors to orient to one another and to organize and regulate their interactions, to frame, interpret, and to analyze their performances, and to produce commentaries and discourses, criticisms and justifications. Such a regime consists of a cluster of social relationships, roles, norms "rules of the game", etc. The system specifies generally who may or should participate, who is excluded, who may or should do what, when, where, and how it should be done, and in relation to whom. It organizes specified actor categories or roles vis-à-vis one another and defines their rights and obligations – including rules of command and obedience – and their access to and control over human and material resources.

More precisely: (1) An institution defines and constitutes a particular social order. It delineates positions and relationships, in part defining the actors (individuals and collectives) that are the legitimate or appropriate participants (who must, may, or might participate) in the domain, their rights and obligations vis-à-vis one another, and their access to and control over resources. In short, it consists of a system of authority and power. (2) It organizes, coordinates, and regulates social interaction in a particular domain or domains, defining contexts – specific settings and times – for constituting the institutional domain or sphere. (3) It provides a normative basis for appropriate behavior, including the roles of the participants in that setting – their interactions and institutionalized games – taking place in the institutional domain. (4) The rule complex provides a cognitive basis for knowledgeable participants to interpret, understand and make sense of what goes on in the institutional domain. (5) It also provides core values, norms and beliefs that are referred to in normative discourses, the giving and asking of accounts, the criticism and exoneration of actions and outcomes in the institutional domain. Finally, (6) an institution defines a complex of potential normative equilibria, which function as "focal points" or "coordinators" (Schelling 1963; Burns & Gomolinska 2001; Burns & Roszkowska 2003). The actors engaged in a given institution use their institutional knowledge of relationships, roles, norms, and procedures to guide and organize their perceptions, actions and interactions. Institutional knowledge is also used to understand and interpret what is going on, to plan and simulate scenarios, and to refer to in making commentaries and in giving and asking for accounts.

In this article, we focus on three *subcomplexes*, or components of an institutional regime. The first is the *organizing subcomplex* – the rules that define roles, relations, norms, and procedures. The second complex consists of the problem-solving or *policy paradigm*. The third is the *discursive complex*, which consists of the forms, expressions, etc., for institutional discourses concerning the organization, performances, and goal achievements; included here are the questions that accounts are to answer and the accounts themselves.

INSTITUTION

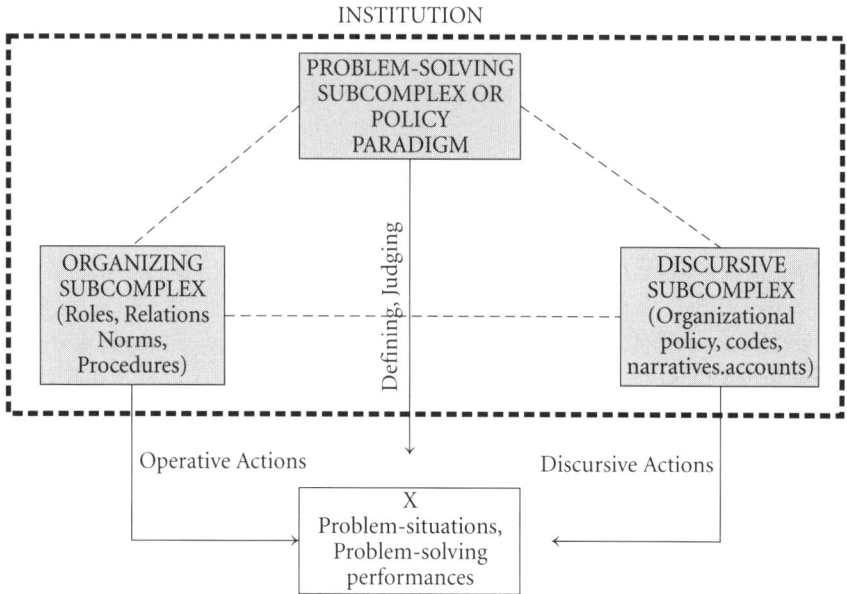

Figure 1. An institution and its core subcomplexes

These three interrelated core complexes of an institution are activated and applied with respect to concrete problem-situations or classes of problems, and can be represented as shown in Figure 1.[1]

Most modern institutions, such as business enterprises, government agencies, democratic associations, religious congregations, scientific communities, or markets, are organized and regulated in relatively *separate autonomous spheres or domains.* Each is distinguishable from others on the basis of distinctive rule complexes, each of which contributes to making up a specific moral order operating in terms of its own rationality or social logic. The actors engaged in an institutional domain are oriented to the rule system(s) that has (have) legitimacy in the context and utilize it (them) in coordinating, regulating, and talking about their social transactions.

Many modern social organizations consist of *multi-institutional complexes.* These combine, for instance, different types of institutionalized relationships such as market, administration, professional, and democratic association – each in a particular domain. They may also combine various types of informal networks. When different institutional types are linked or integrated into multi-institutional complexes, the resultant structure necessarily entails gaps and zones of incongruence and tension at the interfaces of the different organizing modes and social relationships (Machado 1998; Machado & Burns 1998). For instance, a modern university consists of scientific and scholarly communities, administration, democratic bodies with elected leaders, and both internal and external market relationships. Such diverse organizing modes are common in most complex organizations or inter-institutional complexes. Rule system theory identifies several of the types of institutional strategies and arrangements to deal with contradiction and potential conflicts in complex, heterogeneous institutional arrangements (Machado & Burns 1998). These include rituals, non-task-oriented discourses, and mediating or buffer roles that actors develop and institutionalize. Moreover, the theory suggests that social order – the shaping of congruent, meaningful experiences and interactions – in complex organizations, as in most social life, is built on more than rational considerations. It is also built on non-rational foundations such as rituals and non-instrumental discourses. These contribute to maintaining social order and providing the stable context that is essential for most "rational" decision-making and action.

3.   Institutional problem-solving paradigms

As actors engage in judgment, planning, interpreting, innovating, and applying rules in a given institutional domain or field of interaction, institutional rule knowledge is combined with other types of knowledge. Such organization of rule knowledge and its applications is accomplished through a shared cognitive-normative framework which we refer to as the institutional *paradigm:* the problem-solving, or *policy subcomplex* (see Figure 1) (other works using paradigm in this sense include Carson 2000a, 2000b, 2004; Dosi 1984; Gitahy 2000; Hall 1993; Perez 1985).[2] It provides people with a cognitive model with which to organize information, and to both define and attempt to solve concrete problems of performance, production, and goal achievement in a given institutional domain. The *paradigm* – associated with a particular institution – is a cognitive-normative framework, used by institutional actors in their concrete judgments and interactions to define problems, problem-solving strategies, and solutions.[3] Paradigms incorporate complexes of beliefs, classification schemes, normative ideas, and rules of thumb, and these are used in conceptualizing and judging key institutional situations and processes, relevant problems, and possible solutions for dealing with key problems.

The organizing subcomplex and paradigm, as subcomplexes of an institution, are obviously intertwined, but they are each affected in different ways in change processes – particularly those driven by tangible institutional problems. If, on the one hand, actors have a great investment in protecting the concrete organizational arrangements themselves – for reasons such as the desire to preserve power, security, or predictability – rules are tightened, enforcement mechanisms are deployed, and may even be strengthened (as in Michels's Iron Law of Oligarchy 1962). There is an emphasis on protecting ideas and principles that are already materialized, and sometimes this is done at great cost and to the detriment of the long-term functioning of the institution. If, on the other hand, actors have – or would like to make – a much greater investment in effectively solving problem(s) than the institutional organization and its operating paradigm have managed, the actions taken are quite different. Rules are consciously broken in spite of possible or likely sanctions, supporters are rallied around possibilities rather than certainties, and short-term, material interests may be set aside in favor of imagined or envisioned long-term opportunities. There is a substantial shift in risk-taking orientations and in the readiness to transform conditions.

A paradigm, as a collectively produced and maintained construction, is usually changed with reluctance – collective identities and interests, including material interests, are often closely associated with it. This contributes to making difficult changes that participants judge to alter the core elements that give them and their concrete institutional practices their identity, status, and power. A paradigm whose core principles, values, and normative practices are deeply embodied in concrete institutional and identity-giving practices will tend to be durable and resilient.

4. The gaps and anomalies of institutional paradigms

An institutional paradigm is used in the process of identifying, defining and classifying institutional problems (and "non-problems"), potential solutions to such problems (including the use of appropriate and effective technologies and techniques), and source(s) of authority in the institutional arrangement. These judgments play a key role in the giving and asking of accounts and in justifying or legitimizing actions.

Each paradigm is grounded in a particular set of fundamental assumptions and beliefs about reality that a group of actors shares.[4] It forms the framework for organizing their perceptions, judgments, and action that determines which phenomena are included in the picture – and which are excluded (Kuhn 1970; Lakoff & Johnson 1980). It is also the basis for operationally assigning values to certain actions and conditions, and encouraging and pursuing certain activities (or discouraging or even prohibiting others).[5]

Much of the day-to-day work of actors in a given institutional arrangement has the effect of cementing and normalizing the paradigm in a sense similar to what Kuhn (1970) characterized as "normal science," and we refer to as *normality*. Problems appear manageable, there is a high degree of consensus, and there is no sense of crisis or bold challenge. Because a paradigm necessarily focuses attention on certain phenomena while obscuring others – it is used to select and also restructure data so that they fit within the framework of its basic assumptions, categories, and rules.[6] Because of paradigm selectivity, inherent biases in its rules of interpretation, and its inherent limitations, the actors utilizing a given paradigm will experience difficulties in understanding, explaining, or knowing how to manage some types of situation or problem. Some of these problems arise in connection with – or as a by-product of, actions guided by the paradigm itself. That is, meaningful action – viewed from the perspective of the paradigm – generates anomalies and failures that some participants define as "problems" (Spector & Kitsuse 1987). Such problems are not only cognitive; they are also practical. Problems fail to be adequately addressed, and goals are not achieved. The stage is set for entrepreneurial actors to suggest new approaches and solutions, although these need not be initially radical.

One institutional paradigm can be distinguished from another in that it entails a distinctly different, and often incommensurable, way of framing, conceptualizing, judging, and acting in relation to particular classes of "problems" and "issues." Incommensurability refers to core paradigmatic elements rather than routine adjustments and corrections (and can be likened to the cognitive switching that occurs with figure-ground images). The properties of two distinct phenomena are present, but focusing on one involves making the other a secondary property – or obscures it altogether. This becomes particularly important when actors guided by alternative paradigms compete with one another or each tries to impose her respective paradigm in a given institutional domain. Two competing institutional paradigms – each with its reality-defining features and discourses – may embrace competing organizational modes or decision-making principles, for instance, "bureaucratic hierarchy" versus "democratic procedure," or "market problem-solving" versus "welfare" or "re-distributive" problem-solving" (see later).[7] While these may coexist within a single institution, one or the other is accorded primacy during conditions of stability. As we discuss below, conditions of instability are characterized by figure-ground switching in core paradigmatic elements and can be identified through the specific discourses that express these competing orientations.

5.   Institutional paradigms expressed in key discourses

An institutional paradigm is communicated through discourses – both descriptive narratives and conceptual forms – and through social action and interaction.[8] These discourses and actions define social problems and potential solution complexes, and suggest the assignment of authority and responsibility in a given or appropriate area of activity. Through their characterizations of goals and purposes, and accounts of institutional performance – successes as well as failures – actors in a given institution express or reveal their common paradigm. It is the framework through which they perceive and judge the world, and organize, understand, and regulate their activities in the institutional domain.

Particular institutional discourses, serving as a means of describing, interpreting, and dealing with real problems and issues, are inspired and organized – directed and purposeful – on the basis of the institutional paradigm. The discourses indicate, among other things, parameters of appropriate problems, solutions to problems, and evaluation of performances. For instance, they may concern whether the current performance or status of the institution represents improvement or deterioration over earlier performance or status. In general, an institutional paradigm encompasses a range of institutional practices and strategies for addressing issues considered to be problems, and for defining or establishing authority for how to address various types of problems.

5.1 Key components of discourse

Paradigms are articulated, in part, through discourses concerning institutional "problems," or "threats" and "crisis", the expressed distribution of institutional "authority and responsibility", the distribution of "expert authority", and "appropriate solutions" to deal with defined problems. The discourses refer to written rules and laws, and basic socio-cognitive principles that define the location and characteristics of authority, and set(s) of institutional strategies and practices for dealing with specific types of problems and issues (concerning public policy areas, see Sutton 1998; Carson 2000a, 2000b, 2004). The approach outlined here analyzes the ways in which discourses, on the one hand, express and articulate a public policy paradigm, and, on the other hand, frame and define reality (see, for example, Spector & Kitsuse 1987; Hardy & Phillips 1999; Kemeny 1999).

Public policy or problem-solving discourses can be analyzed in terms of *the categories or complexes of defining rules they contain* (Carson 1999, 2000a, 2000b; Sutton 1998):

(1) *Problem/issue complex* – defines and characterizes key issues/problems, including characterizations of who is affected and how, and the broad categorizations of the nature of an issue or problem as social, moral, economic, political, etc. Here we find *causal narratives* – or narratives and statements that contain either implicit or explicit assumptions about the sources of major problems, as well as *narratives of threat* which indicate or describe who is affected and the likely consequences if the problems are not addressed.

(2) *Distribution of problem solving authority and responsibility* – defines who is the authority with formal or informal responsibility for addressing and/or resolving key issues and problems. On a more systemic level, it defines where the location and distribution of appropriate problem-solving responsibility and authority lies in the organization or institutional arrangement. This refers, among other things, to institutional authority with the responsibility for taking specific corrective action and having legitimacy for making policy. This is related to expertise, as discussed below, but equally important, it is grounded in the social roles and norms for determining who should be empowered to pass judgment, adopt new problem-solving strategies, or initiate necessary action on behalf of the institution.

(3) *Distribution of expert authority* – defines the location and distribution of legitimate sources considered knowledgeable and authoritative on the issue or issues. It also defines who has the legitimacy to explain the causes and solutions of any particular relevant problem.

(4) *Solution complex* – defines the form and range of acceptable solutions to institutional problems. Solution complexes include the particular way(s) in which the resolution of an issue or problem should be constructed, including the use of appropriate, available institutional practices, technologies, and strategies. Problems are often deliberately defined in ways that permit an issue to land in particular parts of an institutional apparatus (Nylander 2000). This, in turn, dictates the range of both possible and likely responses (Sutton 1998).

6.   Systemic problems and types of discourse

Particular discourses in an institutional context relate to key dimensions in the paradigm: types of problems, solutions, distribution of responsibility and authority, and location and forms of appropriate expertise. They are generated in the institutional context, relating to what is normal or expected – and also in response to threats and deviation. Another way of putting this is that discourses are patterned with respect to the functioning (and malfunctioning) of the institution. Moreover, when there are institutional transformations in connection with paradigmatic shifts, discourses are also transformed, e.g. as occurred in the "velvet revolutions" of Eastern Central Europe (Burns 2002; Burns & Carson 2002). A central principle in our analysis is that the formulation and diffusion of significant new paradigms accompany and underlie many, if not most, radical reforms and structural revolutions. They provide new points of departure for conceptualizing, organizing, and normalizing institutional orders and generating new discourses.[9]

In general, major paradigm adjustments, or even paradigm replacement, may be preceded by changes in the discourses as well as in the organization and practices of the institution. In the perspective of some of our previous work (Burns & Carson 2002; Carson 2000a, 2000b), this is all relatively straightforward – and may only articulate conventional knowledge. Our aim here is to go a step further by identifying particular types of discourses in connection with institutional crisis, including major failings or malfunctioning of the institution. Any institution is faced with problem situations, types of problems or tasks in the course of its functioning, some of which are experienced or defined as "crisis".

In some of the research drawing on social systems theory (Burns 2004; Burns et al. 2002; Burns et al. 1985; Burns & Flam 1987; Burns et al. 2003), one may distinguish conditions that are problematic. Of particular interest are cases so problematic that they threaten substantial destabilization and disorder – a type of institutional crisis. The characteristic feature of crisis situations is that a failure or instability develops in areas that an institution is expected to deal with and control, and the problem is found to be neither understandable and analyzable nor controllable within the established paradigmatic framework. Another type of major problem or crisis arises when there is intense, destabilizing social conflict among institutional groups, for instance, capital and labor, or key professional groups in an institution such as a medical or university system.[10] This may be referred to as social dis-integration. In sum, there are different types of problematic situations, and these typically involve very different but characteristic discourses, as we outline below.

For the purposes of our analysis here, we distinguish 4 ideal-type situations with the dominant types of discourses likely to appear in these diverse situations. Let X symbolize such situations – types of problems or tasks – that agents involved in the institution, or responsible for its performance, should address and deal with. That is, they are the objects of attention and problem definition.

(A) *Discourses of normality.* High knowledge levels with respect to X are combined with high solidarity and value convergence (consonance) on the specific issue or problem X. Knowledge is available within the established paradigm to distinguish problems and solutions. The actors believe (and demonstrate) that they have an effective paradigm. They are capable of identifying and solving typical problems and are unified or express solidarity in doing this. Risk is calculable and presumably controllable. Guiding assumptions and core principles are not threatened. The process, or phenomenon X is known and "controllable". Failings and accidents are, in general, knowable, in some cases even calculable and predictable. More complex problems and actions may even arise which the established paradigm is believed to readily and systematically address. In other words, the overall system is well understood and established and derivable knowledge can be brought to bear to address any issues or problems.[11] Under these conditions, the institutional complex tends to be stable.

Three types of crisis conditions are characterizable by conditions of ignorance and lack of control and/or social conflict, which make for particular types of discourse:

(B) *Uncertainty and discovery discourses under conditions of social integration.* In this type of situation, there is cohesion and social integration (as in (A)) but a high degree of uncertainty about the nature of the problem and measures to deal with it. In other words, there is some significant form of system malfunction, but social integration and order continue to hold. Here the institutional actors' discourses refer to problems of high uncertainty and ignorance. They activate procedures and strategies of discovery, and they engage in corresponding discourses. There is consensus about the institutional authority and procedures essential to obtaining necessary knowledge for correcting malfunctioning and ineffective performance. For instance, key groups in the health care system may feel highly uncertain about human cloning and that a decision about the appropriateness or the impact of human cloning cannot be made currently. At the same time, the uncertainty is mitigated by continued basic agreement (and certainty) about the procedures (and the agents involved) to determine the nature of the problem and how eventually to solve it. A consensus about the way to achieve an optimum level of knowledge needed for correct decision and action contributes to relative paradigmatic and institutional stability. In sum, type B crisis conditions are characterized by consensus about who defines the problem(s) and solution(s), and generally how to proceed, although there is a strong sense of a lack of necessary, immediate knowledge.

This situation is not completely unproblematic, however. A high level of social cohesiveness may contribute to an emerging crisis by impeding those involved in the institution from conceiving of radically new solutions. Alternatively, while their problem solving efforts are initially cooperative, there is some risk that in the course of exploring and developing solutions, differences emerge that result in intense social conflict. In general, a sense of relative certainty about the efficacy of the institutional arrangements may be maintained, but disagreement about the specific phenomenon may grow so that a type (B) situation develops the characteristics of type C (discussed below). In such cases, the B situation is transformed into a type (C) or (D) situation (in the case, for instance, groups within the institution develop entirely divergent knowledge systems, beliefs and value orientations).

(C) *Oppositional normative discourses.* In this type of problem situation, there are intense conflicts over one or more components of a paradigm, or over different paradigms; for instance, there are conflicts about particular beliefs and values, or conflicts over who should be responsible and exercise authority. This might involve, for instance, religious versus scientific authority (or, under communist regimes, "red versus expert"). There might be a high level of established, agreed-upon knowledge but opposing values, e.g., in the case of abortion, cloning, construction of a large-scale socio-technical project such as an airport, nuclear energy facility, etc. In a medical context, contentious issues may arise from allowing euthanasia or performing abortion in hospitals. The staff becomes split. There is a "great normative divide" concerning value judgments of what is good or bad.

Such polarization (and, therefore, low social integration) obtains at the same time that there are conditions of relative certainty about the facts of the issue and about the capability of being able to control the problem. But there is a lack of value convergence and solidarity with respect to the specific issue or problem.

Examples, as indicated earlier, are pointed up by intense normative conflicts as in the case of some religious conflicts, or passionate political conflicts

(Berger 1998:367), for instance, in the struggle over abortion in the USA and elsewhere; or, over genital mutilation in France, Sweden, and other parts of Europe with significant African immigration (one cannot "split the difference" in the positions between those who believe that abortion is murder and those who understand it as a woman's right to control her own body); or, over the status of Islamic religious law in countries with substantial Muslim populations (compromises are difficult between those who believe that God's law supersedes any democratic decisionmaking and those committed to submitting their beliefs to the democratic process).

The risk in type C situations is that the highly polarized conflicts will block effective negotiations and compromises and possibly escalate into intense, even violent conflict. However, if a transcending principle is found around which to negotiate a compromise, conditions may be stabilized, leading to situation (A). One historical example of this was the Treaty of Westphalia (1648), which brought to an end European religious wars by determining that the religion of a region was the religion of its Prince. A very different, contemporary example is the merging of seemingly incompatible concepts into the notion of "sustainable development" (although some degree of contention remains as to exactly what constitutes sustainable development).

(D) *Chaos and transformative discourses.* The discourses in this type of situation characterize conditions of social disintegration (fragmentation and lack of solidarity) in which at the same time actors feel ignorant, or in which other significant actors fundamentally contest the content or form of established knowledge. Uncertainty is intensified, at least on the collective level, because important groups subscribe to divergent ideas about the very nature of the problem(s) and what to do about them. Different ontologies, epistemologies, and methods – which may be connected with identities – are brought to bear. Everything can happen in such an unstable, even revolutionary situation. The core principles in dispute might include, for example, the kind of production regime considered most just or efficient, or the type of political/policymaking form considered most legitimate or effective: a competition for instance, between different forms of government ranging from democracy to dictatorship.

The conditions under which type (D) discourses occur can be characterized as *contentious uncertainty*, reflected in low social integration and low certainty about the nature of the problem or what is to be done about it. Such conditions are likely to emerge in situations in which elites feel unable to adopt a new paradigm in order to retain social order (and their positions of power), or under which the elites are discredited to such an extent that they and the existing social order are unacceptable to the participants regardless of the policy paradigm adopted (see Burns & Carson 2002).

Under conditions of contentious uncertainty, the discourses are of chaos and confusion. Discourses of indifference or resignation to performance failings may also be commonplace. "Nothing can be done," in part because of lack of solidarity, in part because of ignorance and/or lack of controls over the relevant policy area (X). Under such conditions, individuals and subgroups adjust and adapt "as best they can." Given the social conditions (the low level of social integration), there is a common feeling that they themselves are in no position to establish a new order.

In sum, here one finds discourses about chaos and deep societal crisis, not only in terms of knowledge but in terms of profound cleavages in the society. One of the common responses is to call for a dictator to establish an order (the Hobbesian solution). There may be related discourses about returning to a "Golden Age" *or* establishing a "New Age", based on a new paradigm constructed around an alternative complex of core principles and assumptions.[12]

The ideal type situations outlined above obviously define extremes. In reality, there are varying degrees of system ignorance and of social dis-integration, and successes or failures in one institutional domain will have effects on other related domains. Moreover, the seriousness of X may vary. As we indicated earlier, however, we are most interested here in not only system failures considered serious by the groups involved, but also in group conflicts that are intense and disruptive of institutional functioning.

Our basic argument is that the form and content of discourses differ substantially in these different problem-situations. (1) The discourses in type (A) situations of consensus and certainty are discourses of "normality". In such circumstances, "we know what the problem is and how to deal with it." Problems are recognized and dealt with in established ways. Even if in some cases, investigation and analysis are required (conducted by experts) to deal with the specifics, the situation is basically in order. (2) Type (B) situations of *consensus uncertainty* entail discourses about ignorance concerning what has gone wrong and what has to be done. There remains general agreement about the "authorities" and experts who will deal with the problem situation. (3) Type (C) conditions of *contentious certainty* entail discourses of conflicting explanations pertaining to a body of agreed-upon knowledge. Such conditions reflect disagreement about the existing social order or a proposed order – for instance, the values or operating assumptions of some differ from those that

Table 1. Different types of problem situations and their characteristic discourses

		Degree of social integration	
		High Social Integration/Solidarity, for instance high value consensus.	Low Social Integration/Solidarity, for instance, low value consensus.
Degree of system knowledge and control	High level of knowledge and control, for instance, high certainty (about the problem and how to deal with).	(A) "Consensus certainty" Discourses of normality, certainty, and consensus.	(C) **"Contentious certainty"** Normative discourses in relation to well-known situations. Cleavage and opposition among key groups who are each highly certain about X and how to act with respect to it.
	Low knowledge and control, for instance, low certainty (about the problem and how to deal with them).	(B) **"Consensus uncertainty"** Discourses of Uncertainty and Discovery-mode Discourses, about which there are common understandings and commitments.	(D) **"Contentious uncertainty"** Chaos. Cleavage and opposition among groups who are highly uncertain about X and how to deal with it. Transformative discourses, but no consensus about these.

are established and institutionalized. (4) Type (D) conditions entail *contentious uncertainty*: the combination of types (B) and (C).

Situations (B), (C), and (D) are therefore "problematic situations" of different types. They tend to lead, under some conditions, to initiatives for institutional change and transformation. Two major dimensions can be shown to underlie many cases of the four ideal type situations, the situation of normality and the three types of crisis situation. The dimensions are the degree of system knowledge and control (as a basis of stabilization) and the degree of alienation and disruptive conflict among groups of individuals. Different types of problem or problem-situation can therefore be distinguished by analysis of these two dimensions: (i) the level of system knowledge/certainty apparently available within the paradigm employed to define problems and solutions; (ii) the degree of social integration and consensus within the institution about the paradigm (low convergence or consensus refers to social settings where there are competing values or paradigms, or intense disagreement about the validity or usefulness of an established paradigm). Four possible discursive situations can then be distinguished and, in each type of situation, the form and content of the discourses generated differ substantially.

Table 1 summarizes in large part the discussion of the different types of problem situation. The following sections consider institutional change, in part paradigm shift and discursive transformation. The discourses in use emphasize the need to deal with, on the one hand, a high degree of contentiousness and cleavage; or on the other, the lack of sufficient or optimal knowledge vis-à-vis the problem situation(s) X and the need of the group (or organization) to find solutions.

7.   The dynamics of interrelated subcomplexes

Institutional change entails changes in the rules and/or enforcement activities so that different patterns of action and interaction are encouraged and generated (Burns et al. 1985; Burns & Flam 1987; Levi 1990). Such changes may be initiated by a variety of social agents.[13] For instance, an elite may "legislate" an institutional change, or a social movement may bring about change through coming to direct power or effectively pressuring and negotiating with a power elite. Changes may also be brought about through more dispersed processes, e.g. where an actor discovers a new technical or performance strategy and others copy the strategy. In this manner, rule innovation diffuses through social networks of communication and exchange.

In general, several mechanisms explain rule regime formation and change (Burns & Carson 2002; Burns & Flam 1987): (a) Key actors or groups in an institution encounter normative failure or gaps in applying a rule system in an appropriate domain and try to overcome the failure or gap. Such a development may arise because of the emergence and influence of new social values. For example, the rise of more radical egalitarianism or the spread of the normative idea of citizen autonomy may draw attention to particular legal and normative limitations in the society, which gives purchase to demands for new legislation and institutional arrangements such as advancing gender equality. (b) Actors mobilize and struggle to realize what they consider an institutional ideal. One example would be where actors pursue a principle of distributive justice or common good that they believe can be more effectively or more reliably realized through reforming institutional arrangements. (c) Self-interest is a well-known and common motivator underlying initiatives to establish new policies, laws, or institutional arrangements. Self-interest refers in this instance to the pursuit of opportunities to make gains or to avoid losses through changing rules.

New technological developments often expose the limitations of existing laws and institutional arrangements. In the area of contemporary information technologies, existing laws concerning intellectual property rights have proven inadequate and have led to a number of reform efforts. Another example concerns Internet-related developments that have led to demands for increased regulation, because of the ready availability on the World Wide Web of pornography, or of political extremist and racist websites, among other problems. New medical technologies – organ transplantation, life support technologies, and the new genetics – also call for new normative principles, legislation, and institutional arrangements (Machado 1998; Machado & Burns 2000, 2001). In these and similar cases, rule formation and development must be seen as a form of *normatively guided problem-solving.*

Power, knowledge, interests, and values are key ingredients in institutional transformation. The power of elites to mobilize resources including wealth, legislative authority, and legal or coercive powers to maintain or change institutional orders is, of course, critical. But emerging groups and movements may also manage to mobilize sufficient power resources with which to challenge established elites, and to force or negotiate institutional change. The interaction between the establishment and challenging groups or movements is a major factor in institutional dynamics (Andersen & Burns 1992; Baumgartner & Burns 1984; Flam 1994; Woodward et al. 1984). Such power mobilizations and conflicts are fueled by actors' material interests as well as ideal interests reflected in the particular paradigm to establish and maintain "right and proper" institutional arrangements.

A *paradigm shift* implies a change in all or part of the core of an established paradigm, in particular, key organizing principles, normative ideas, and expectations regarding social relationships (see "Key components" above). For instance, in the context of major crisis (in terms of system failures as well as intensifying social conflict), communist society was transformed into a more liberal type of society in a number of former communist countries. A paradigm shift and institutional transformation entailed emphasis being put on introducing market principles, civil rights, and democratic multi-party systems. Of course, the concrete realization of such shifts required learning the practicalities of making the new institutions operate properly, that is, a certain development of the "semantics" and "pragmatics" of the new rule regimes also had to take place.

In addition, *shifts in discourse took place in many of the former commu-nist countries in connection with the transformation of several key paradigmatic components*: (1) There was a shift in value expressions and in the definition of the major problems facing the economy and society as a whole. Stress was placed on such values as "liberating production" and "increasing productiv-ity and wealth" rather than on "state ownership of the means of production," "planned economy," "equality of distribution" or "rational central control." "Opposition to Socialism" and "bourgeois economic behavior," ceased to be seen as threats to a well-functioning economy and society; "state ownership", "state controls", and "monopoly powers" – characteristic of a command econ-omy and the one party state – replaced them as threats. (2) The appropriate solutions for the economy were market reforms in terms of "free enterprise", "privatization", "private initiative", "entrepreneurship", or "positive investment conditions". Solutions for the polity were expressed in terms of "democrati-zation" and "political pluralism" in the form of independent, multiple parties and competitive politics. The role of the state should then become more reg-ulatory rather than controlling in detail. In the case of the economy, for in-stance – rather than the party-state deciding the quantities and distribution of goods and services as well as prices and wages – independent, decentralized enterprises were to assume responsibility and authority to make plans and to determine quantities and qualities of goods and services as well as prices. Thus, solutions to economic problems were not to be expected solely or largely from the state, but from enterprises and market mechanisms. State organized "so-lutions" would then concern only a few, select areas such as monetary policy, competition policy, research and development policy. The policy measures to be taken were to operate rather indirectly (for instance, monetary policy) rather than directly and in detail (price and wage controls, national production plans, or detailed regulation of imports and exports). (3) Expertise would not be em-bodied in the political leadership or the "vanguard party" which was assumed to have a monopoly of "historical truth" but in specialized professional experts such as economists, lawyers, and business leaders – among whom knowledge is dispersed.

8. The dynamics of policy paradigms, paradigm competition, and paradigm shifts and related discourses

What is it that gives a policy paradigm weight and importance and draws ad-herents to it – beyond the role of power and the distribution of resources to attract or buy-up supporters? First, the conceptualization of how a particular institution or institutional arrangement should work and the courses of action it recommends (in a particular sphere, i.e., welfare, health care, governance, etc.) must be sufficiently plausible and compelling to attract adherents from other, competing paradigms. Part of what makes any paradigm compelling is that it more satisfactorily addresses urgent and currently unsolvable institutional problems and formulates this in a language – in terms and concepts – that resonate with or relate to core values of society: "equality," "democracy," "justice or fairness," "efficiency," "rationality," etc. Second, it must offer an apparently coherent approach to the phenomena (designated as problems) that it addresses. It allows for "open-endedness," permitting the application of the paradigm to both a broad range of recognized institutional problems and those not yet defined. What makes this open-endedness compelling is not certainty, but possibility and promise. But there is also a strong belief ("certainty") that any current uncertainty will be resolved. For instance, the "state welfare" paradigm of Scandinavia and a number of other European countries addressed itself to persistent problems of poverty and mal-distribution of resources that the conservative and liberal paradigmatic thinking of the early 20th century had failed to satisfactorily address or account for. In a similar vein, we can consider the nature of the contest between the agents who promote particular paradigms, the means and standards by which a paradigm gains prominence, and the kinds of benefits awarded to those whose paradigm prevails. These are particularly salient in the way in which resources are marshaled behind one or another paradigm, in claims-making activities, and in the eventual fate of discarded paradigms.

8.1 Paradigmatic phases and paradigm shifts

The relationship between a policy paradigm and its institutional embodiment has a direct effect on the various possibilities and probabilities for change; it presents actors with concrete opportunities for (and obstacles to) action. The character of this relationship follows certain regular patterns. Any paradigm has developmental periods (also, see Kuhn 1970:92–134), which can be characterized as distinct phases in a life cycle. Three discrete phases can be identified based on the processes that most strongly characterize each phase, which are identified here as *emergence, institutionalization, and reification*. Particular conditions and processes are characteristic of each phase, and they are vulnerable to challenge in distinctly different ways and to differing degrees.

Emergence. This initial phase is characterized by the emergence of a reconceptualization of possible guiding principles. This represents a realization of the possibility of reordering or redefining guiding principles in response to crisis or radically new conditions that create an opening: for instance, radical novelty, or pressing social problems not adequately explained and accounted for by the currently established paradigm. As the new complex of ideas and principles becomes more systematized, a new paradigm emerges. This represents a challenge to the existing conceptual order, and as such, is typically not readily embraced. The initial rejection is in part a function of individual, organizational, and institutional investment in the established paradigm, and in part the inherent difficulties in conceptualizing and accepting dramatic change.

In all social systems, there is some measure of resistance to substantial change in the social order. This may take the form of attempts at "eliminating" challenging critique, ideas, and paradigms. In authoritarian systems, for instance, preservation of the social order is accomplished using means of coercion – even state terrorism. In more open, democratic societies, the process involves the use of ridicule, de-legitimation through referrals to "unscientific" or "utopian" ideas, etc. There is a spectrum of strategies ranging from attempting to crush the new paradigm on the one hand, to co-opting it on the other, adopting pieces of it and taking credit for the successes it may produce. Both of these polar strategies contain their own particular hazards for the actors who seek to preserve an established order and the paradigm upon which it is built.

In the replacement of one paradigm with another, those who have not "invested" in the old paradigm or the institutions that promoted it are likely to be more open to persuasion and pressures from others, other things being equal. This would include, for example, those who have not already deeply invested in careers or power based on the established paradigm, or those who are profoundly engaged in addressing unresolved problems and anomalies rather than in protecting the "infallibility" of a particular institution. For some, of course, the conceptual or institutional change is too great; they are eventually marginalized or simply die out.

In the context of public policy, novelty can be seen as the socially-defined problems that are either inadequately addressed under the existing paradigm, or those that may even arise from the ways in which the institutionalization of the dominant paradigm structures social action. The new paradigm provides a plausible explanation for the particular social problems (novelty) that are observed, including causal relationships and the likely consequences of a failure to address the problem. In providing these interpretations, the newly emerging paradigm also frames the possibilities for solution to the problem and the definitions of success, and identifies the particular actors who are seen as legitimate authorities for producing information or taking action.

The new paradigm gains a foothold by virtue of its ability to explain and offer plausible remedies for social problems that are unresolvable by the old. However, this is clearly not sufficient to anchor the paradigm and enable its expansion and widespread adoption. This process takes place through the successful realization of elements of the new paradigm in social institutions.[14]

But the greatest dangers to the challenging paradigm at this stage are, (a) that the irresolvable problem will disappear, leaving the challenger without an opening, or (b) that the realization of any significant paradigmatic elements will be blocked, depriving its proponents of the concrete evidence necessary to offer proof that the remedies offered are capable of delivering on the paradigmatic promises. Thus, the incremental, perhaps strategically sequenced institutionalization of the challenging paradigm is an essential process if the paradigm is to gain adherents and prevail.

Institutionalization. In this middle phase, the replacement of the old paradigmatic principles with the new takes place. This paradigmatic shift takes hold as the new principles and the methods and practices built around them are systematized, expanded, and institutionalized beyond initial experiments. Of great significance is when the realization of paradigmatic principles delivers the promised result. This not only has a reinforcing influence on paradigmatic beliefs, but also provides the credibility and momentum that help support the institutionalization of additional paradigmatic elements. The foundation of paradigmatic support begins to shift to a relative balance between the power of compelling ideas and the power of institutional structure, perhaps reflecting a shift from the idealism of the challenger to a pragmatism rooted in the need to deliver on promises made and being in position to attempt to do so. The conceptual framework is systematically applied to a widening array of problems, defining new problems to which it is particularly sensitive. Leadership is increasingly as likely to be bureaucratic as charismatic, and the movement within or into the institutional structure becomes more restricted as actors begin to concern themselves as much with protecting what they have achieved as reaching to realize the dreams that once inspired them. A potential weakness of this phase of relative balance and strength is that key elements of the paradigmatic promises will be kept, and dreams will be achieved without renewing and modernizing some idealized vision. New adherents may be attracted less by visions of the better society that could be made possible, and more by the practical benefits of alignment with the current regime. While these are not mutually exclusive, this middle phase is market by a distinct shift in the balance between idealism and pragmatism in their role of attracting and holding adherents. Weaknesses also begin to emerge more concretely, as the paradigm's limitations are established through its increasingly broad application and practice.

Reification. The old paradigm is sufficiently developed and broadly applied to have exposed some of its inherent shortcomings, weaknesses, and inconsistencies. The problems for which the paradigm provided the conceptual structure for solutions have been either resolved and therefore faded from the immediate consciousness of many, or proven themselves resistant to solutions developed on the basis of the paradigm. Additional problems arise from incompatibilities between core principles and marginal, situational adjustments in practices. The inability to accommodate an expanding array of novelties is represented by gaps and inconsistencies between paradigmatically informed expectations and empirical reality. Instead of using the power of ideas through persuasion, inspiration, and building consensus, adherent address problems and challenges by wielding institutional power, including sanctions and penalties. Robert Michels' (1962) characterized these processes in great detail in his study of the powerful tendency toward oligarchy in ideals-driven organizations.

Nevertheless, the efficacy of the established paradigm and the practices of the actors who wield institutional power are likely to be subject to questioning – although it may in the face of authoritarian power and controls, operate underground, and entail much hypocrisy and cynicism. In the case of public policy, a sufficiently large body of unresolved problems or undesirable side effects (as well as possibly authoritarian measures) helps to raise doubts about the efficacy or advisability of solutions guided by the paradigm in question. Some (it may be a few, some, or many) seek out or try to develop a new paradigm to explain and respond to the new or re-newed social problems, failures, and inconsistencies. Depending in part upon the power and vitality of the mature paradigm, in part upon the external conditions that helped produce unresolvable problems, and in part on the strategies and resources employed by the challengers, the introduction and support for a new paradigm may eventually lead to the modification or replacement of the established paradigm. Paradigmatic modification is distinguished from paradigmatic shift by whether the change takes place in peripheral rules and practices, or in core principles.

As already pointed out, some of the phase-bound challenges faced here are expressions of the powerful organizational tendencies observed by Michels (1962), in which the pursuit of utopian dreams is superseded first by the need to deliver on promises, then by the desire to stay in power – both to protect the faithful and to be in position once a new utopia is found or constructed. Weber (1946) described this general pattern in terms of traditional leadership being challenged and replaced by charismatic leadership, which itself becomes (or is eventually replaced by) bureaucratic leadership. The bureaucratic system takes on the reified characteristics of the traditional, and the cycle continues.

Acknowledgement

We are grateful to Nora Machado for her valuable comments and suggestions, in particular with respect to the development of the models in Figure 1 and Table 1.

Notes

1. There is a meta-paradigm, which provides the core for constructing the institution (and its subcomplexes).

2. This is a usage which differs substantially from Kuhn's (1970) notion of "scientific paradigm" which refers to a theoretical model or framework for representing and explaining empirical phenomena, the theoretical and methodological rules to be followed, the instruments to be used, the problems to be investigated, and the standards by which research is to be judged. There are, of course, a number of parallels with our conceptualization of an institutional paradigm, a matter which we shall take up in a later article.

3. The paradigm is a "rough" or "fuzzy" rule complex. Levels of knowledge of it vary among participants (Burns & Roszkowska 2004). Also, it is "distributed knowledge" with variations among different individuals and groups.

4. A shared paradigm must be simplified for purposes of communication. At the same time it has definitional power – the power to define, interpret, and prescribe action for dealing with reality.

5. In this respect, it relates to the notion of "master frame" used in the social movements literature (Nylander 2000), or that of "meta-narrative", within which individual issues or policy questions can be contextualized and "framed" (Gottweis 1998: 30–33).

6. This phenomenon is expressed in its more extreme form in the saying "if your only tool is a hammer, then every problem is a nail".

7. Such inconsistencies can be conceptualized as a source of cultural/institutional dissonance, a sociological version of the cognitive dissonance experienced by individuals and described by Leon Festinger's theory (Festinger 1957; Machado 1998; Machado & Burns 1998).

8. Discourses are written or verbal expressions which are shaped and regulated according to particular rule complexes or codes. historical documents, reports, narratives, diaries,

letters, accounts, explanations, etc. Typically, discourses are embedded in particular institutional contexts. For any given institution, there are appropriate forms and contents, for instance, for the giving and asking of accounts, normative assessments and interpretations, and explanations – all of this relating to shaping and regulating conceptions and practices of social reality. At the same time, agents in their interactions restructure the forms and content of discourses. We stress the embeddedness of discourses in institutions and institutional arrangements and the role of human agents in shaping and reshaping discourses in interactional dynamics.

9. In this sense, the introduction and spread of Christianity and Islam (and, undoubtedly, the other Axial Transformations (Eisenstadt 1978) entailed socio-cultural revolutions.

10. For our purposes here we ignore external conflicts.

11. In light of "bounded rationality" or "asymmetrical information," situation A may contribute to a false sense of security – an ill-founded confidence that all is well and good. The potential for complacency is a latent problem here, and there is likely to be a subsequent lack of preparation for possible paradigm failure in the sense that new problems might (invariably will) arise that cannot be understood or analyzed effectively within the existing framework.

12. It is possible to envision a situation in which actors guided by different paradigms compete under conditions of general consensus regarding the failure of the previously established paradigm. This was arguably the case immediately following the Second World War, when a broad consensus about the failures of the system of sovereign states spawned experiments in supranational and international organizations ranging from the United Nations to European Free Trade Area to the European Community.

13. There are discourses that are "stabilizing" and others that are aimed at radical change, i.e. transformative discourses. In the "stabilizing" discourses, actors emphasize how much they know (or can know) and that systemic problems will be solved. Also, that there are no fundamental disagreements among agents. Even in cases of high uncertainty, participants emphasize their consensus and their capability to mobilize and develop the necessary knowledge. Some transformative discourses are of the form that Max Weber indicated: When a charismatic leader breaks with tradition or prevailing legal norms, he states "It is written that... but I say unto you...". This is a prototype for discourses of paradigm shifts. That is, in times of crisis there is the possibility that a "prophet from the wilderness" emerges who promises solution to ignorance, performance failure, and social disorder.

14. Actions freely taken based on the values contained in a given paradigm have their own reinforcing quality. Research in social psychology, indicates that, for instance, when people struggle for something based on their beliefs and values, action tends to reinforce those values and beliefs. The reverse also appears to be true: failing to act in accordance with values tends to undermine them (see Aronson 1976: 131–139).

References

Andersen, Svein & Burns, Tom R. (1992). *Societal Decision-making: Democratic Challenges to State Technocracy*. Aldershot, Hampshire: Dartmouth.

Aronson, Elliot (1976). *The Social Animal* (2nd edition). San Francisco: W. H. Freeman & Co.

Baumgartner, Tom & Burns, Tom R. (Eds.). (1984). *Transitions to Alternative Energy Systems: Entrepreneurs, New Technologies and Social Change*. Boulder, CO: Westview.

Berger, P. L. (Ed.). (1998). *The Limits of Social Cohesion: Conflict and Mediation in Pluralist Societies*. Boulder, CO: Westview Press.

Burns, Tom R. (2001). "Revolution: An Evolutionary Perspective." *International Sociology, 16*(4), 531–555.

Burns, T. R. (2004). "The Sociology Of Complex Systems." *Kybernetes*, in press.

Burns, Tom R., Baumgartner, Tom, & DeVille, Philippe (1985). *Man, Decision and Society*. London: Gordon and Breach.

Burns, Tom R., Baumgartner, Thomas, Dietz, Thomas, & Machado, Nora (2003). "The Theory of Actor-System Dynamics: Human Agency, Rule Systems, and Cultural Evolution." In Francisco Parra-Luna (Ed.), *Encyclopedia of Life Support Systems (EOLSS), Systems Science and Cybernetics, Developed under the Auspices of UNESCO*. Oxford, UK: Eolss Publishers. [http://www.eolss.net]

Burns, Tom R. & Carson, Marcus (2002). "Actors, Paradigms, and Institutional Dynamics: The Theory of Social Rule Systems Applied to Radical Reforms." In J. R. Hollingsworth, K. H. Muller, & E. J. Hollingsworth (Eds.), *Advancing Socio-Economics: An Intuitionalist Perspective* (pp. 109–145). Oxford: Rowman & Littlefield Publishers.

Burns, Tom R., DeVille, Philippe, & Baumgartner, Thomas (2002). "Actor-System Dynamics Theory and its Application to the Analysis of Modern Capitalism." *Canadian Journal of Sociology, 27*(2), 211–243.

Burns, Tom R. & Engdahl, Erik (1998a). "The Social Construction of Consciousness: Collective Consciousness and its Socio-Cultural Foundations." *Journal of Consciousness Studies, 5*, 67–85.

Burns, Tom R. & Engdahl, Erik (1998b). "The Social Construction of Consciousness: Individual Selves, Self-Awareness, and Reflectivity." *Journal of Consciousness Studies, 5*(2), 166–184.

Burns, Tom R. & Flam, Helena (1987). *The Shaping of Social Organization*. London: Sage Publications.

Burns, Tom R. & Gomolinska, Anna (2000). "The Theory of Socially Embedded Games: The Mathematics of Social Relationships, Rule Complexes, and Action Modalities". *Quality and Quantity: International Journal of Methodology, 34*(4), 379–406.

Burns, Tom R. & Gomolinska, Anna (2001). "Socio-cognitive Mechanisms of Belief Change: Applications of Generalized Game Theory to Belief Revision, Social Fabrication, and Self-fulfilling Prophesy". *Cognitive Systems Research, 2*(1), 39–54.

Burns, Tom R. & Roszkowska, Ewa (2004). "Fuzzy Games and Equilibria: The Perspective of the General Theory of Games on Nash and Normative Equilibria." In S. K. Pal, L. Polkowski, & A. Skowron (Eds.), *Rough-Neural Computing: Techniques for Computing with Words* (pp. 435–470). Berlin: Springer-Verlag.

Carson, Marcus (1999). "Competing Discourses in the EU". Discussion paper for research project: "How is EU Policy Made?". Uppsala University, 1999.

Carson, Marcus (2000a). *From Commodity to Public Health Concern: Shifting Policy Paradigms and the Transformation of Food Policy in the European Union*. D-Uppsats, Department of Sociology, Uppsala University 2000.

Carson, Marcus (2000b). *From the Peoples' Home to the Market: Paradigm Shift to System Shift in the Swedish Welfare State*. Research Report 1/01. Gävle: Institute for Housing and Urban Research, Uppsala University.

Carson, Marcus (2004). *From Common Market to Social Europe? Paradigm Shift and Institutional Change in European Union Policy on Food, Asbestos and Chemicals, and Gender Equality*. Stockholm: Almqvist & Wiksell International. Doctoral dissertation in sociology, Stockholm University.

Coleman, William, Skogstad, Grace, & Atkinson, M. (1997). "Paradigm Shifts and Policy Networks: Cumulative Change in Agriculture." *Journal of Public Policy, 16*(3), 273–301.

Dosi, G. (1984). *Technical Change and Industrial transformation – The Theory and An Application to the Semiconductor Industry*. London: MacMillan Press.

Dryzek, John S. (1996). "The Informal Logic of Institutional Design." In R. Goodin (Ed.), *The Theory of Institutional Design* (pp. 103–125). Cambridge: Cambridge University Press.

Eisenstadt, S. N. (1978). *Revolution and the Transformation of Society: A Comparative Study of Civilization*. New York: Free Press.

Festinger, Leon (1957). *A Theory of Cognitive Dissonance*. Stanford: Stanford University Press.

Flam, Helena (Ed.). (1994). *States and Anti-Nuclear Movements*. Edinburgh: Edinburgh University Press.

Gerhards, J. & Rucht, Dieter (1992). "Mesomobilization: Organizing and Framing in Two Protest Campaigns in West Germany." *American Journal of Sociology, 98*(3), 555–595.

Gitahy, Leah (2000). *A New Paradigm of Industrial Organization: The Diffusion of Technological and Managerial Innovations in the Brazilian Industry*. Uppsala: Ph.D. Dissertation in Sociology.

Gottweis, Herbert (1998). *Governing Molecules: The Discursive Politics of Genetic Engineering in Europe and the United States*. Cambridge, MA: MIT Press.

Gubrium, J. F. & Holstein, J. A. (1997). *The New Language of Qualitative Method*. New York: Oxford University Press.

Hall, Peter (1992). "The Movement from Keynesianism to Monetarism: Institutional Analysis and British Economic Policy in the 1970s." In Sven Steinmo, Kathleen Thelen, & Frank Longstreth (Eds.), *Stucturing Politics: Historical Institutionalism in Comparative Analysis* (pp. 90–113). Cambridge: Cambridge University Press.

Hardy, Cynthia & Phillips, N. (1999). "No Joking Matter: Discursive Struggle in the Canadian Refugee System." *Organizational Studies, 20*(1), 1–24.

Kemeny, Jim (1999). *Narratives, Sagas and Social Policy – State and Society in Housing Research*. Working Paper No. 24. Gävle: Institute for Housing and Urban Research, Uppsala University.

Kuhn, Thomas (1970). *The Structure of Scientific Revolutions* (2nd edition). Chicago: University of Chicago Press.

Lakoff, George & Johnson, Mark (1980). *Metaphors We Live By*. Chicago: University of Chicago Press.

Levi, M. (1990). "A Logic of Institutional Change." In K. S. Cook & M. Levi (Eds.), *The Limits of Rationality* (pp. 402–418). Chicago: University of Chicago Press.

Machado, Nora (1998). *Using the Bodies of the Dead: Legal, Ethical, and Organizational Dimensions of Organ Transplantation*. Aldershot: Dartmouth Publishing.

Machado, Nora & Burns, Tom R. (1998). "Complex Social Organization: Multiple Organizing Modes, Structural Incongruence, and Mechanisms of Integration". *Public Administration: An International Quarterly, 76*, 355–386.

Machado, Nora & Burns, Tom R. (2000). "Discretionary Death: Cognitive and Normative Problems Resulting from Boundary Shifts between Life and Death". Paper presented at the *Third International Symposium on Coma and Death*. Havana, Cuba, February 22–25, 2000.

Machado, Nora & Burns, Tom R. (2001). "The New Genetics: A Social Science and Humanities Research Agenda." *Canadian Journal of Sociology, 25*(4), 495–506.

Michels, Robert (1962). *Political Parties: A Sociological Study of the Oligarchical Tedencies of Modern Democracy*. New York: The Free Press.

Nylander, Johan (2000). *The Power of Framing: A New-Institutional Approach to Interest Group Participation in the European Union*. Doctoral Dissertation. Uppsala: Uppsala University.

Perez, C. (1985). "Microelectronics, Long Waves and World Structural Change: New Perspectives for Developing Countries." *World Development, 13*(3), 441–463.

Schelling, T. C. (1963). *The Strategy of Conflict*. Cambridge: Harvard University Press.

Spector, Malcom & Kitsuse, John (1987). *Constructing Social Problems*. New York: Aldine de Gruyter.

Schutz, A. (1970). *On Phenomenology and Social Relations*. Chicago: University of Chicago Press.

Sutton, Carolyn (1998). *Swedish Alcohol Discourse: Construction of a Social Problem*. Uppsala: Acta Universitatis Upsaliensis. Ph.D. dissertation in sociology.

Weber, Max (1951). *The Religion of China*. NY: Macmillan Company.

Weber, Max (1946). *From Max Weber: Essays in Sociology*. H. H. Gerth & C. W. Mills (Eds.). New York: Oxford University Press.

Weiss, Gilbert & Wodak, Ruth (Eds.). (2003). *Critical Discourse Analysis: Theory and Interdisciplinarity*. New York: Palgrave Macmillan.

Wodak, Ruth & van Dijk, Teun (2000). *Racism at the Top*. Klagenfurt, Austria: Drava.

Woodward, W. E., Ellig, J., & Burns, T. R. (1994). *Municipal Entrepreneurship and Energy Policy: A Five Nation Study of Politics, Innovation, and Social Change*. New York: Gordon and Breach.

Biographical notes

Christoph Bärenreuter studied Political Sciences, Sociology and Russian at the Universities of Vienna and Stockholm. He is currently working on his Ph.D. thesis ("The European Public Sphere. Theory of Democracy and Empirical Evidence"). For this project he was granted a DOC-scholarship by the Austrian Academy of Sciences. In 2004 he was Junior Visiting Fellow at the IWM, Vienna (*Institut für die Wissenschaften vom Menschen* / Institute for Human Sciences).

Irène Bellier is a political anthropologist, research director at the National Center for Scientific Research, affiliated to the Laboratory for Anthropology of the Institutions and Social Organizations (LAIOS), in Paris. She is responsible for the research program on "Transnational practices and institutions" at LAIOS, and vice president of GEMDEV, an interdisciplinary network focused on "globalization and development". She is the author of *An Anthropology of the European Union: Building, imagining, experiencing Europe* (2000), with Thomas Wilson (Eds.); *L'ENA comme si vous y étiez* (1993); *El temblor y la luna. Ensayo sobre las relaciones entre las mujeres y los hombres mai huna*, 2 volumes (1991).

Tom R. Burns is Professor Emeritus at the University of Uppsala, Uppsala, Sweden and Norfa Professor, Norwegian University of Life Sciences. He also serves as a Member of the EU Commission's Advisory Group on the Social Sciences and Humanities. Among his engagements, he has been Jean Monnet Professor at the European University Institute (2002), Clarence J. Robinson University Professor at George Mason University (1987–1990), Visiting Scholar, Stanford University (Spring, 2002, 2004, 2005), Fellow at The Swedish Collegium for Advanced Study in the Social Sciences (Spring, 1992, Autumn, 1998), Fellow at the European University Institute (Spring, 1998), Gulbenkian Professor at the University Institute for Business and Social Studies (ISCTE), Lisbon, Portugal (2002–2003); Fellow, Center for Interdisciplinary Research (ZIF), Bielfeld Germany, 2002; and a Visiting Researcher at the Wissenschaftszentrum Berlin (1985). Burns has published more than 10 books and numerous articles in the areas of governance and politics, studies of administration and management, the sociology of technology and environment, and the analysis of capitalism and capitalist development. He has published extensively on social theory and methodology, with a focus on new institutional theory, a social theory of games, and socio-cultural evolutionary theory.

Marcus Carson, Ph.D., is a researcher at the Department of Sociology, Stockholm University, and is engaged in research and teaching at South Stockholm University College. He has authored or co-authored several scholarly articles exploring the role of cognitive frameworks in policymaking and social change. His recently completed dissertation, entitled, "From Common Market to Social Europe?", explores the relationship between cognitive models and institutional change. He is presently collaborating with Tom Burns in research on policymaking and governance processes in the European Union. He was previously involved in policymaking as a policy analyst and organizer with a number of public interest organizations in the US over an eighteen-year period.

Paul Chilton is currently Professor of Linguistics at the University of East Anglia, and has been Professor of Language and Communication at the University of Aston. He is author of *Security Metaphors: Cold War Discourse from containment to Common House* (1996), and of *Analysing Political Discourse: Theory and Practice* (2003), as well as of numerous articles and papers in the field of cognitive linguistics, discourse and international politics. Together with Ruth Wodak he is the editor of the *Journal of Language and Politics* and the book series "Discourse Approaches to Politics, Society and Culture" (John Benjamins). Paul Chilton is also the author of two translations: Jean Piaget's *Mental Imagery in the Child* and a collection of stories, *The Heptameron*, by the 16th century French writer, reformer and stateswoman, Marguerite de Navarre.

Teun A. van Dijk was professor of discourse studies at the University of Amsterdam until 2004, and is at present professor at the Universitat Pompeu Fabra, Barcelona. After earlier work on generative poetics, text grammar, and the psychology of text processing, his work since 1980 takes a more 'critical' perspective and deals with discursive racism, news in the press, ideology, knowledge and context. He is the author of several books in most of these areas, and he edited *The Handbook of Discourse Analysis* (4 vols., 1985) and the recent introduction *Discourse Studies* (2 vols., 1997). He founded 4 international journals, *Poetics, Text, Discourse & Society,* and *Discourse Studies*, of which he still edits the latter two. His last monograph is *Ideology* (1998), and his last edited book *Racism at the Top* (2000, with Ruth Wodak). He is currently working on a new book on the theory of context. Teun van Dijk, who holds two honorary doctorates, has lectured widely in many countries, especially also in Latin America. For a list of publications, recent articles, resources for discourse studies and other information, see his homepage: www.discourse-in-society.org

Norman Fairclough has recently retired from his post of Professor of Language in Social Life at Lancaster University, UK, and is now Emeritus Professorial Fellow in the Institute for Advanced Studies in Management and Social Sciences. He is currently working on aspects of 'transition' in Central and Eastern Europe from a discourse analytical point of view. He has published and lectured widely in the area of critical discourse analysis. His most recent book is *Analysing Discourse: Textual Analysis for Social Research* (2003).

Adam O. Horvath is a Professor at Simon Fraser University (Graduate Program in Counselling Psychology). He has received a BA (Concordia), MSW (McGill), Ed.D (UBC). Prior to his academic career he was in clinical practice as a psychotherapist working with youth and families. His main research interest is the process of psychotherapy: how therapeutic relationships and therapy conversations contribute in changes in the patients? He is past president of the Society for Psychotherapy Research (North American Chapter).

András Kovács, Ph.D., Professor at Central European University, Budapest, Nationalism Studies Program / Jewish Studies Program; Senior researcher at the Institute for Ethnic and Minority Research at the Hungarian Academy of Sciences. Research subjects: Jewish identity and antisemitism in post-war Hungary; memory and identity; socio-economic attitudes and political choice. His most recent publications in foreign language include: *NATO, Neutrality and National Identity: The case of Austria and Hungary* (2003, Ed. with R. Wodak); *New Jewish Identities* (2003, Ed. with Zvi Gitelman, Barry Kosmin); 'Jewish Groups and Identity Strategies in Post-Communist Hungary' (2003, Gitelman, Kosmin and Kovács (Eds.): *New Jewish Identities*).

Michał Krzyżanowski, M.A., is a Research Associate at the Department of Linguistics and English Language, Lancaster University, UK. Since 2002, he has also been a Research Associate at the Department of Applied Linguistics and the Research Centre 'Discourse, Politics, Identity', University of Vienna, Austria. He is currently finishing his Ph.D. in Applied Linguistics (focusing on national and European identities at the times of post-1989 transition in Central- and Eastern-Europe) at the Department of Applied Linguistics, University of Vienna. Michał's main research activities and interests are in discursive formations of EU institutions and European societies (with a particular focus on their impact on constructions of collective memories and social, political and cultural identities), as well as in Critical-Analytic approaches to politics and institutional practices of racial discrimination. His recent publications include: 'Haider: the new symbolic element of the ongoing discourse of the past' (Wodak & Pelinka 2002, *The Haider Phenomenon in Austria*) and 'My European feelings are not only based on the fact that I live in Europe': On the new mechanisms of European identification emerging under the EU Enlargement (*Journal of Language and Politics*, 2003).

Theo van Leeuwen is Professor of Language and Communication at Cardiff University. He has published widely in the areas of critical discourse analysis, social semiotics and multimodality. His most recent books are *Speech Music, Sound* (1999), and *Multimodal Discourse* (2001, with Gunther Kress).

Peter Muntigl is Assistant Professor in the Department of English at the University of Salzburg and is Adjunct Professor in the Faculty of Education at Simon Fraser University (Vancouver, Canada). He has recently published a book on psychotherapy entitled *Narrative Counselling* (2004). His research on psychotherapy is currently being funded by the Social Sciences and Humanities Research Council of Canada.

Florian Oberhuber, Ph.D., is a Research Associate at the Department of Applied Linguistics and the Research Center "Discourse, Politics, Identity", University of Vienna. He studied

Sociology, Political Science, Philosophy and History at the Universities of Salzburg, Bowling Green (Ohio, USA) and Vienna. His main research fields are European Studies, Political Sociology and Political Theory. Since 2000, he is a member of the editorial board of the journal *Sinn-haft. Zeitschrift zwischen Kulturwissenschaften*. In December 2002, he finished a dissertation on "The Problem of the Political in Central Europe".

Ron Scollon is Professor of Linguistics at Georgetown University and is Editor of *Visual Communication*. *Suzie Won Scollon* is Network Coordinator, Associated Sociocultural Research Projects, Georgetown University. Their most recent books are *Discourses in Place: Language in the Material World* (2003), and *Nexus Analysis: Discourse and the Emerging Internet* (2004).

Gilbert Weiss, Ph.D., studied Sociology and Political Science at the University of Vienna. From 1997–2002 he was Vice director of the Research Centre: Discourse, Politics, Identity at the Austrian Academy of Sciences. From 2002 to January 2004 he held the position of research officer at the newly founded Alfried Krupp Wissenschaftskolleg Greifswald (Germany). He is co-founder of the Ludwig Boltzmann Institute for Politics, Religion and Anthropology at the University of Innsbruck (2001) and since February 2004 Assistant Professor at the University of Salzburg. His major research fields are political and social theory, and European Union studies. Gilbert Weiss is the author or editor of several books, including: *Theorie, Relevanz und Wahrheit. Eine Rekonstruktion des Briefwechsels zwischen Eric Voegelin und Alfred Schütz (1938–1959)* (2000); *The Collected Works of Eric Voegelin, Vol. 4, The Authoritarian State. An essay on the problem of the Austrian State* (1999); *Critical Discourse Analysis: Theory and Interdisciplinarity* (2003, edited with Ruth Wodak); *Europas Identitäten. Mythen, Konflikte, Konstruktionen* (2003, edited with Monika Mokre and Rainer Bauböck); *Politische Religion?* (2003, edited with Michael Ley and Heinrich Neisser); *The Collected Works of Eric Voegelin, Vol. 32, The Theory of Governance and other Miscellaneous Papers 1921–1938* (2003, edited with William Petropulos).

Ruth Wodak is Professor of Applied Linguistics at the Department of Linguistics at the University of Vienna. Since September 2004, she is located at Lancaster University where she was offered a personal chair in Discourse Studies. Beside various other prizes, she was awarded the Wittgenstein-Prize for Elite Researchers (1996), the Prize of the City of Vienna for excellent research (2001) and the Verkauf-Verlons Prize for anti-Fascist scholarship (2003). She is Director of the Research Centre "Discourse, Politics, Identity" (http://www.univie.ac.at/discourse-politics-identity) at the University of Vienna. Her publications are mainly in the areas of Discourse and Discrimination, Identity Politics, Gender Studies and Organisational Research. She edits the *Journal of Language and Politics* together with Paul Chilton, as well as the book series Discourse Approaches to Politics, Society and Culture. She co-edits the journal *Critical Discourse Studies* together with Norman Fairclough, Jay Lemke and Phil Graham. Her most recent publications include: *NATO, Neutrality and National Identity* (2003, with András Kovács), *CDA. Theory and Interdisciplinarity* (2003, with Gilbert Weiss), *Re/reading the Past* (2003, with Jim Martin) and *Wie Geschichte gemacht wird* (2003, with Hannes Heer, Alexander Pollak and Walter Manoschek).

Name index

Subject index

In the series *Discourse Approaches to Politics, Society and Culture* the following titles have been published thus far or are scheduled for publication: